First World War

and Army of Occupation

War Diary

France, Belgium and Germany

46 DIVISION
Headquarters, Branches and Services
General Staff
3 September 1916 - 21 March 1919

WO95/2666/1

The Naval & Military Press Ltd
www.nmarchive.com
Published in association with The National Archives

Published by

The Naval & Military Press Ltd

Unit 10 Ridgewood Industrial Park,

Uckfield, East Sussex,

TN22 5QE England

Tel: +44 (0) 1825 749494

www.naval-military-press.com

www.nmarchive.com

Contents

Document type	Place/Title	Date From	Date To
Heading	WO95/2666 46 Div Gen Staff Sept'18-Mar'19		
Heading	46th Division General Staff Sep 1918-Mar 1919		
Heading	Map to be put away with 46th Div: G.S. Diary September 1918. 46th Division. G.S. September 1918.		
Heading	September 1918 Divisional Headquarters situate at Les Charmeux-Gosnay holding Right Section XIII Corps		
War Diary	Les Charmeux Gosnay	01/09/1918	01/09/1918
War Diary	Ref Sheet La SE 36 S.W. 1/20,000.	01/09/1918	02/09/1918
War Diary	Les Charmeux Gosnay	03/09/1916	03/09/1916
War Diary	Vraignes	21/09/1918	28/09/1918
War Diary	R.8.b.5.5 Sheet.	28/09/1918	29/09/1918
War Diary	R.8.b.5.5	28/09/1918	30/09/1918
Map			
Miscellaneous	Advance Enemy Withdrawal in the Lys Salient July/Sept. 18. From 106/50 (inch).		
Miscellaneous	46th Division No. 4/174	03/09/1918	03/09/1918
Operation(al) Order(s)	138th. Infantry Brigade Order No. 244.	03/09/1918	03/09/1918
Miscellaneous	46th Division No. 4/173	03/09/1918	03/09/1918
Operation(al) Order(s)	46th Divisional Artillery Order No. 306.	03/09/1918	03/09/1918
Diagram etc	Sheet 36 S.W 3 1.10000		
Miscellaneous	46th Division No. 4/172	03/09/1918	03/09/1918
Operation(al) Order(s)	139th Infantry Brigade Order No. 201.	03/09/1918	03/09/1918
Miscellaneous	46th. Division No. 4/171	03/09/1918	03/09/1918
Operation(al) Order(s)	138th Infantry Brigade Order No. 243.	03/09/1918	03/09/1918
Miscellaneous	46th Division No. 4/170	03/09/1918	03/09/1918
Miscellaneous	139th Infantry Brigade Order No. 200.	03/09/1918	03/09/1918
Miscellaneous			
Miscellaneous	46th Division No. 4/169.	03/09/1918	03/09/1918
Operation(al) Order(s)	XIII Corps Counter Battery Operation Order No: 33.	03/09/1918	03/09/1918
Miscellaneous	46th Division No. 4/167	03/09/1918	03/09/1918
Miscellaneous	Heavy Artillery XIII Corps Instructions No. 90.	02/09/1918	02/09/1918
Operation(al) Order(s)	XIII Corps Counter Battery Operation Order No: 32.	02/09/1918	02/09/1918
Miscellaneous	46th Division No. 4/165	02/09/1918	02/09/1918
Operation(al) Order(s)	All recipients of 138th. Inf. Bde. Order No. 242.	02/09/1918	02/09/1918
Operation(al) Order(s)	Addendum No. 1 to 138th. Inf. Bde. Order No. 242.	02/09/1918	02/09/1918
Operation(al) Order(s)	138th. Infantry Brigade Order No. 242.	02/09/1918	02/09/1918
Miscellaneous	46th Division No. 4/164.	02/09/1918	02/09/1918
Operation(al) Order(s)	46th Battalion Machine Gun Corps Warning Order No 57.	02/09/1918	02/09/1918
Diagram etc	46th Battn M.G.C. Sept: 2nd 1918.		
Miscellaneous	46th Division No. 4/163.	02/09/1918	02/09/1918
Miscellaneous	All recipients of 139 I. Bde. Order No. 199.	02/09/1918	02/09/1918
Operation(al) Order(s)	139th Infantry Brigade Order No. 199	02/09/1918	02/09/1918
Miscellaneous	46th Division No. 4/162.	02/09/1918	02/09/1918
Operation(al) Order(s)	46th: Divisional Artillery Order No. 305.	02/09/1918	02/09/1918
Miscellaneous	46th Division. No. 4/161.	02/09/1918	02/09/1918
Miscellaneous	Headquarters. 46th: Division.	01/09/1918	01/09/1918
Miscellaneous	46th Division No. 4/160		
Operation(al) Order(s)	46th: Divisional Artillery Order No. 304.	01/09/1918	01/09/1918
Miscellaneous	46th Division No. 106/60.	04/09/1918	04/09/1918

Heading	Enemy Withdrawal.	04/09/1918	04/09/1918
Miscellaneous	Brigade Transport Officers.	04/09/1918	04/09/1918
Miscellaneous	46th Division. No. 106/59.	04/09/1918	04/09/1918
Miscellaneous	Enemy Withdrawal.	04/09/1918	04/09/1918
Miscellaneous	46th Division G.106/58. 4th September, 1918. Enemy Withdrawal.	04/09/1918	04/09/1918
Diagram etc	Reference Sheet 36 S.W. 1/20000 to accompany 46th Div. G.106/58.		
Miscellaneous	46th Division No. 106/57.	02/09/1918	02/09/1918
Operation(al) Order(s)	XIII Corps Order No. 147.	02/09/1918	02/09/1918
Miscellaneous	46th Division. No. 106/57.	03/09/1918	03/09/1918
Miscellaneous	55th Division No. G.S. 1420.	02/09/1918	02/09/1918
Miscellaneous	55th Division No. G.S. 1421.	03/09/1918	03/09/1918
Miscellaneous	46th Division. No. 106/56.	02/09/1918	02/09/1918
Operation(al) Order(s)	19th Division Order No. 236.	02/09/1918	02/09/1918
Map			
Miscellaneous			
Miscellaneous	46th Division G.106/55. 2nd September, 1918.	02/09/1918	02/09/1918
Miscellaneous	46th Division. No. 106/54.	02/09/1918	02/09/1918
Operation(al) Order(s)	XIII Corps Order No. 146.	02/09/1918	02/09/1918
Miscellaneous	C Form. Messages And Signals.		
Miscellaneous	Amendment No. 1 to XIII Corps Order No. 144.	02/09/1918	02/09/1918
Miscellaneous	46th Division. No. 106/52.	02/09/1918	02/09/1918
Miscellaneous	Preliminary instruction as to action in the event of an Enemy Withdrawal.	02/09/1918	02/09/1918
Miscellaneous	46th Division. No. 106/51.	02/09/1918	02/09/1918
Miscellaneous	55th Division.	01/09/1918	01/09/1918
Miscellaneous	46th Division G.106/50. 1st September, 1918.	01/09/1918	01/09/1918
Heading	G.S. 46th Division September 1918.		
Heading	War Diary and Appendices September 1918.		
Operation(al) Order(s)	46th Division Warning Order No. 14.	31/08/1918	31/08/1918
Miscellaneous	46th Division G.56./15. 1st September, 1918.	01/09/1918	01/09/1918
Miscellaneous	C Form. Messages And Signals.		
Miscellaneous	46th Division G.90/12. 1st September, 1918.	01/09/1918	01/09/1918
Miscellaneous	46th Division G.106/50. 1st September, 1918. Appx 1.	01/09/1918	01/09/1918
Miscellaneous	46th Division G.106/55. 2nd September, 1918.	02/09/1918	02/09/1918
Miscellaneous	C Form. Messages And Signals.	02/09/1918	02/09/1918
Miscellaneous	46th Division G.106/50. 1st September, 1918.	01/09/1918	01/09/1918
Miscellaneous	55th Division No. G.S. 1417.	02/09/1918	02/09/1918
Miscellaneous	General Staff, 55th Div.	02/09/1918	02/09/1918
Operation(al) Order(s)	46th Division Order No. 316.	02/09/1918	02/09/1918
Miscellaneous	Issued at 3 pm.-		
Map			
Miscellaneous			
Miscellaneous	46th Division-Daily Disposition Return. Dispositions at 9 a.m., 2nd September, 1918. Appx 2.	02/09/1918	02/09/1918
Map	Vieille Chapelle 3rd Edition.		
Map	Trenches Corrected to 16-6-18.		
Heading	War Diary Appendix I.B.		
Map	To accompany 46th Div. Order No. 316.		
Operation(al) Order(s)	46th Division Order No. 316. Apps 3.	02/09/1918	02/09/1918
Miscellaneous	Issued at 3 pm.-		
Operation(al) Order(s)	Addendum No. 1 to 46th Division Order No. 316. Appx 3.	02/09/1918	02/09/1918
Operation(al) Order(s)	Addendum No. 1 to 46th Division No. 316.	02/09/1918	02/09/1918
Miscellaneous	55th Division No. G.S. 1414.	02/09/1918	02/09/1918

Miscellaneous	C Form. Messages And Signals.	03/09/1918	03/09/1918
Miscellaneous	C Form. Messages And Signals.		
Operation(al) Order(s)	46th Division Order No. 317.	03/09/1918	03/09/1918
Miscellaneous	Issued at 12.15. pm.-		
Operation(al) Order(s)	46th Division Order No. 318.	03/09/1918	03/09/1918
Miscellaneous	Trench Map. France. Sheet 36 S.W. Edition 11.A.		
Operation(al) Order(s)	46th Division Order No. 317. Appx 4.	03/09/1918	03/09/1918
Miscellaneous	Issued at 12.15. pm.-		
Operation(al) Order(s)	46th Division Order No. 318. App 5.	03/09/1918	03/09/1918
Miscellaneous	46th Division-Daily Disposition Return. Disposition at 9 a.m., 4th September, 1918. App 6.	04/09/1918	04/09/1918
Miscellaneous	46th Division G.106/58. 4th September, 1918.	04/09/1918	04/09/1918
Diagram etc	Reference Sheet 36 S.W 1/20000 to accompany 46th Div. G.106/58.		
Miscellaneous	46th Division G.106/58. 4th September, 1918. App 7.	04/09/1918	04/09/1918
Diagram etc	Reference Sheet 36 S.W. 1/20000 to accompany 46th Div. G. 106/58.		
Operation(al) Order(s)	46th Division Order No. 319. App 8.	04/09/1918	04/09/1918
Miscellaneous	Table to accompany 46th Division Order No. 319.		
Miscellaneous	46th Division-Daily Disposition Return. Dispositions at 9 a.m., 5th September, 1918. App 9.	05/09/1918	05/09/1918
Operation(al) Order(s)	Addendum No. 1 to 46th Division Order No. 319. App 10.	05/09/1918	05/09/1918
Miscellaneous	46th Division-Daily Disposition Return. Disposition at 9 a.m., 6th September, 1918. App 11.	06/09/1918	06/09/1918
Miscellaneous	46th Division G.5/15. 5th September, 1918. App 12.	05/09/1918	05/09/1918
Operation(al) Order(s)	Addendum No. 1 to 46th Division Order No. 319.	05/09/1918	05/09/1918
Miscellaneous	Policy to be Followed by Troops of 19th Division.	05/09/1918	05/09/1918
Operation(al) Order(s)	46th Division Order No. 320. App. 13.	11/09/1918	11/09/1918
Operation(al) Order(s)	46th Division Order No. 321. App 13A.	15/09/1918	15/09/1918
Miscellaneous	A Form. Messages And Signals. App 14.		
Miscellaneous	A Form. Messages And Signals. App 15.		
Operation(al) Order(s)	46th Division Order No. 322. App 16.	10/09/1918	10/09/1918
Operation(al) Order(s)	46th Division Order No. 323. App 17.	20/09/1918	20/09/1918
Miscellaneous	46th Division G.113/13. 21st Sept: 1918. App:19.	21/09/1918	21/09/1918
Miscellaneous	46th Division-Daily Disposition Return. Dispositions at 6 a.m., 21st Septr. 1916. App:18.	21/09/1918	21/09/1918
Miscellaneous	46th Division-Daily Disposition Return. Dispositions at 6 a.m., 22nd Septr. 1918. App. 20.	22/09/1918	22/09/1918
Miscellaneous	46th Division-Daily Disposition Return. Dispositions at 6 a.m., 23rd Septr. 1918. App. 23.	23/09/1918	23/09/1918
Miscellaneous	46th Division. Summary of Operations and Intelligence from 4 am 21st to 4 am 22nd September, 1918. App. 21.	22/09/1918	22/09/1918
Miscellaneous	46th Division-Daily Disposition Return. Disposition at 6 a.m., 24th Septr. 1918. App: 26.	24/09/1918	24/09/1918
Miscellaneous	46th Division. Summary of Operations and Intelligence from 4 am 22nd to 4 am 23rd September, 1918. App:24.	23/09/1918	23/09/1918
Operation(al) Order(s)	46th Division Order No. 324. App: 25.	23/09/1918	23/09/1918
Miscellaneous	46th Division Summary of Operations and Intelligence from 4 am, 23rd, to 4 am, 24th September, 18. App : 27.	23/09/1918	23/09/1918
Operation(al) Order(s)	46th Division Order No. 325. App: 28.	25/09/1918	25/09/1918
Miscellaneous	46th Division-Daily Disposition Return. Disposition at 6 a.m., 25th Septr. 1918. App : 29.	24/09/1918	24/09/1918
Operation(al) Order(s)	46th Division Order No. 326. App 44.	25/09/1918	25/09/1918
Miscellaneous	Appendix "A" to accompany 46th Division Order No. 326.		

Miscellaneous	46th Division. Summary of Operations and Intelligence from 4 am 24th to 4 am 25th September, '18. App 32.	25/09/1918	25/09/1918
Operation(al) Order(s)	46th Division Order No. 327. App :30.	25/09/1918	25/09/1918
Miscellaneous	Amendment No. 1 to 46th Division Order No. 327. App 31.	25/09/1918	25/09/1918
Miscellaneous	46th Division-Daily Disposition Return. Dispositions at 6 a.m., 26th Septr. 1918. App :33.	26/09/1918	26/09/1918
Miscellaneous	46th Division-Daily Disposition Return. Dispositions at 6 a.m., 27th Septr. 1918.	27/09/1918	27/09/1918
Miscellaneous	46th Division Instructions-Operation "C". No. 1. App 45.	25/09/1918	25/09/1918
Miscellaneous	Operation "C". 46th Division Instruction No. 2. App 46.	26/09/1918	26/09/1918
Miscellaneous	Operation "C". 46th Division Instruction No. 3. App 47.	26/09/1918	26/09/1918
Miscellaneous	Operation "C". 46th Division Instruction No. 4. App : 48.	26/09/1918	26/09/1918
Miscellaneous	Operation "C". 46th Division Instruction No. 5. App 49.	26/09/1918	26/09/1918
Miscellaneous	46th Division. Summary of Operations and Intelligence from 4 am 25th to 4 am 26th September, '18. App 35.	26/09/1918	26/09/1918
Miscellaneous	Operation "C". 46th Division Instructions No. 6. App 50.	27/09/1918	27/09/1918
Miscellaneous	Operation "C". 46th Division Instructions No. 7. App 51.	27/09/1918	27/09/1918
Miscellaneous	Operation "C". 46th Division Instructions No. 8. App 52.	27/09/1918	27/09/1918
Miscellaneous	Operation "C". 46th Division Instructions No. 9. App 53.	27/09/1918	27/09/1918
Operation(al) Order(s)	46th Division Order No. 328. App:36.	27/09/1918	27/09/1918
Miscellaneous	46th Division-Daily Disposition Return. Dispositions at 6 am, 28th Septr: 1918. App 37.	28/09/1918	28/09/1918
Miscellaneous	46th Division-Daily Disposition Return. Dispositions at 6 a.m., 29th Septr. 1918. App 58.	29/09/1918	29/09/1918
Miscellaneous	Operation "C". 46th Division Instruction No. 10. App 54.	28/09/1918	28/09/1918
Miscellaneous	Operation "C". 46th Division Instruction No. 11. App 55.	28/09/1918	28/09/1918
Miscellaneous	46th Division No. G.85/39. 28/11/1918.	28/11/1918	28/11/1918
Miscellaneous	A Form. Messages And Signals. App 57.		
Miscellaneous	A Form. Messages And Signals. App 67.		
Miscellaneous	A Form. Messages And Signals. App 66.		
Miscellaneous	A Form. Messages And Signals. App 63.		
Miscellaneous	A Form. Messages And Signals. App 64.		
Miscellaneous	A Form. Messages And Signals. App 65.		
Miscellaneous	A Form. Messages And Signals. App 60.		
Miscellaneous	A Form. Messages And Signals. App 59.		
Miscellaneous	46th Division-Daily Disposition Return. Dispositions at 6 am., 30th Septr: 1918. App 58.	29/09/1918	29/09/1918
Miscellaneous	Appendix "A". App 56.		
Map	Omissy		
Map	Map "C".		
Miscellaneous	Appx 42.		
Map	Map "D"		
Miscellaneous	Appx 43.		
Map	Map "A". Enemy Rear Organisation.		
Map	Omissy Map "A". App 40.		
Map	Map "B".		
Diagram etc	46th Division Instructions No. 3		

Diagram etc	To accompany 46th Divn G114/15.		
Map	France.		
Map	France		
Map	Map A, France.		
War Diary	Map A, France.		
Miscellaneous	46th Division-Daily Disposition Return. Dispositions at 6 a.m., 1st October, 1918.	01/10/1918	01/10/1918
Heading	War Diary. G.S. 46th Division. October 1918.		
Heading	G.S. 46 Div. Vol. Month of October 1918. Divisional Headquarters at Vendelles.		
War Diary	R.8.b.5.5. Etaves Sheet 1:40,000.	01/10/1918	02/10/1918
War Diary	R.8.b.5.5	02/10/1918	03/10/1918
War Diary	La Baraque G.29.c.9.3 Etaves.	03/10/1918	06/10/1918
War Diary	R.8.b.5.5.	06/10/1918	07/10/1918
War Diary	Magny La Fosse	08/10/1918	08/10/1918
War Diary	G.30.b.9.5.	08/10/1918	09/10/1918
War Diary	Fresnoy Le Grand I.18 (1:40,000)	10/10/1918	10/10/1918
War Diary	Fresnoy Le Grand I.18.a.7.5	11/10/1918	12/10/1918
War Diary	Fresnoy Le Grand	12/10/1918	26/10/1918
War Diary	Fresnoy	27/10/1918	30/10/1918
War Diary	Bohain	31/10/1918	01/11/1918
Miscellaneous	List of Casualties for period 29th September to 7th October.	29/09/1918	29/09/1918
Operation(al) Order(s)	46th Division Order No. 329. App 1.	01/10/1918	01/10/1918
Miscellaneous	Account of the part taken by the 46th Division in the battle of Bellenglise on the 29th September, 1918.	29/09/1918	29/09/1918
Miscellaneous	Account of the part taken by the 46th Division in the battle of Ramicourt, on the 3rd October, 1918.-	03/10/1918	03/10/1918
Operation(al) Order(s)	46th Division Order No. 330. App 3.	02/10/1918	02/10/1918
Operation(al) Order(s)	46th Division Order No. 332. App 27.	07/10/1918	07/10/1918
Miscellaneous	A Form. Messages And Signals. Appendix 5.		
Miscellaneous	A Form. Messages And Signals. App. 6.		
Miscellaneous	A Form. Messages And Signals. App. 7.		
Miscellaneous	A Form. Messages And Signals. App 8.		
Miscellaneous	A Form. Messages And Signals. App 9.		
Miscellaneous	A Form. Messages And Signals. App 10.		
Miscellaneous	A Form. Messages And Signals. App 11.		
Miscellaneous	A Form. Messages And Signals. App 12.		
Miscellaneous	A Form. Messages And Signals. App 13.		
Miscellaneous	A Form. Messages And Signals. App 14.		
Miscellaneous	A Form. Messages And Signals. App 15.		
Miscellaneous	Copies to:-		
Miscellaneous	A Form. Messages And Signals. App 16.		
Miscellaneous	A Form. Messages And Signals. App 17.		
Miscellaneous	A Form. Messages And Signals. App. 18.		
Miscellaneous	A Form. Messages And Signals. App 19.		
Miscellaneous	A Form. Messages And Signals. App 20.		
Miscellaneous	A Form. Messages And Signals. App 21.		
Miscellaneous	A Form. Messages And Signals. App 22.		
Miscellaneous	Operation "D". 46th Division Instructions No. 1. App 24.	07/10/1918	07/10/1918
Miscellaneous	Account of the part taken by the 46th Division in the battle of Ramicourt, on the 3rd October, 1918.-	03/10/1918	03/10/1918
Miscellaneous	Report on Operations of 3/10/18.	03/10/1918	03/10/1918
Miscellaneous	To H.Q. Pige.		
Miscellaneous	Report on Operations. 'B' Company.	06/10/1918	06/10/1918

Miscellaneous	'C' Company.	06/10/1918	06/10/1918
Miscellaneous	Report on Operations. 'D' Company.		
Miscellaneous	No. G.4.	04/10/1918	04/10/1918
Miscellaneous	137th Bde: C/495.	21/10/1918	21/10/1918
Miscellaneous	Account of the part taken by the 46th Division in the battle of Bellenglise on the 29th September, 1918.	29/09/1918	29/09/1918
Miscellaneous			
Operation(al) Order(s)	46th Division Order No. 353. App 48.	15/10/1918	15/10/1918
Map	Etaves		
Miscellaneous	Report on the Evacuation of the wounded, during the attacks carried out by the 46th Division, on the 29th September, 3rd October, and 17th October, 1918.	29/09/1918	29/09/1918
Miscellaneous	Nature of Wounds.	21/10/1918	21/10/1918
Miscellaneous	To all recipients of 46th Division Order No. 333. App 49.	15/10/1918	15/10/1918
Miscellaneous	To all Recipients of 46th Division Order No. 333. App 50.	16/10/1918	16/10/1918
Miscellaneous	A Form. Messages And Signals. App 44.		
Miscellaneous	A Form. Messages And Signals.		
Miscellaneous	A Form. Messages And Signals. App 45.		
Miscellaneous	A Form. Messages And Signals.		
Miscellaneous	Notes by the Divisional Commander on training during a short rest after active operations. App 66.	20/10/1918	20/10/1918
Miscellaneous	46th Division No. G.115/97. 16th October, 1918. App 51.	16/10/1918	16/10/1918
Miscellaneous	To 138th Inf: Bde. App 67.	19/10/1918	19/10/1918
Miscellaneous	Amendment No. 1 to 46th Division Order No. 334. App 68.	30/10/1918	30/10/1918
Operation(al) Order(s)	46th Division Order No. 334.	29/10/1918	29/10/1918
Miscellaneous	Movement table to accompany 46th Division Order No. 334.		
Operation(al) Order(s)	46th Division Order No. 335. Operation "F". App 69.	30/10/1918	30/10/1918
Miscellaneous	Operation "F". 46th Division Instructions No. 1. Appx 70.	31/10/1918	31/10/1918
Operation(al) Order(s)	46th Division Order No. 331. App 23.	06/10/1918	06/10/1918
Miscellaneous	Report on Operation on October 17th, 1918.	17/10/1918	17/10/1918
Miscellaneous	Attack of 46th Division on Regnicourt-Andigny-Les-Fermes. Oct 17th 1918.	17/10/1918	17/10/1918
Miscellaneous	Action on the 18th October, 1918.	18/10/1918	18/10/1918
Miscellaneous	E.21.a.		
Miscellaneous	137th Bde: C/496.	21/10/1918	21/10/1918
Miscellaneous	Report on Operations on Mericourt, Fresnoy-le-Grand, Riquerval Wood, Regnicourt & Andigny-Les-Fermes.	21/10/1918	21/10/1918
Miscellaneous	Headquarters, 46th: Division.	30/10/1918	30/10/1918
Miscellaneous	Operation "D". 46th Division Instructions No. 2. App 25.	07/10/1918	07/10/1918
Miscellaneous	Operation "D". 46th Division Instructions No. 3. App 26.	07/10/1918	07/10/1918
Miscellaneous	Reference 46th Division Order No. 329.	01/10/1918	01/10/1918
Miscellaneous	A Form. Messages And Signals. App 64.		
Miscellaneous	A Form. Messages And Signals. App 65.		
Heading	D.A.G. 3rd Echelon Base.		
Heading	HQ GS 46 Div Vol 45 November 18.		
Heading	Month of November 1918. Division in Rest with Headquarters at Bohain.		
War Diary	Bohain	01/11/1918	03/11/1918

War Diary	Molain	04/11/1918	04/11/1918
War Diary	L'Abbe de Guise	05/11/1918	05/11/1918
War Diary	Catillon	06/11/1918	06/11/1918
War Diary	Prisches N 17 Sheet 57 A (1:40,000)	10/11/1918	10/11/1918
War Diary	Catillon	07/11/1918	07/11/1918
War Diary	Prisches	08/11/1918	11/11/1918
War Diary	Sains Du Nord (Q. 11 Sheet 57 A 1:40000)	12/11/1918	12/11/1918
Miscellaneous			
War Diary	Sains Du Nord	12/11/1918	14/11/1918
War Diary	Landrecies	14/11/1918	30/11/1918
Miscellaneous	Operation "F". 46th Division Instructions No. 2. App No. 1.	01/11/1918	01/11/1918
Miscellaneous	Operation "F" 46th Division Instructions No. 3. App No. 2.	02/11/1918	02/11/1918
Map	Barzy.		
Miscellaneous	Operation "F". 46th Division Instructions No. 5. App 3.	04/11/1918	04/11/1918
Miscellaneous	A Form. Messages And Signals. App 4.		
Miscellaneous	Messages And Signals.		
Miscellaneous	A Form. Messages And Signals. App 6.		
Miscellaneous	A Form. Messages And Signals. App 7.		
Miscellaneous	A Form. Messages And Signals. App 8.		
Miscellaneous	A Form. Messages And Signals. App 9.		
Miscellaneous	A Form. Messages And Signals. App 10.		
Miscellaneous	A Form. Messages And Signals. App 11.		
Miscellaneous	App 12.		
Miscellaneous	A Form. Messages And Signals. App 13.		
Miscellaneous	A Form. Messages And Signals. App 14.		
Miscellaneous	A Form. Messages And Signals. App 15.		
Miscellaneous	A Form. Messages And Signals. App 16.		
Miscellaneous	A Form. Messages And Signals. App 17.		
Miscellaneous	A Form. Messages And Signals. App 18.		
Operation(al) Order(s)	46th Division Order No. 337. App 19.	10/11/1918	10/11/1918
Operation(al) Order(s)	46th Division Order No. 338. App 20.	10/11/1918	10/11/1918
Miscellaneous	Location of Units.-12th Novr. 1918. Appx 21.	12/11/1918	12/11/1918
Miscellaneous	A Form. Messages And Signals. App 22.		
Operation(al) Order(s)	46th Division Order No. 339. App 13.	12/11/1918	12/11/1918
Miscellaneous	Table "A", to accompany 46th Division Order No. 339.		
Operation(al) Order(s)	46th Division Order No. 340. App 24.	13/11/1918	13/11/1918
Miscellaneous	March Table.		
Miscellaneous	Locations-46th Division-16/11/18.	16/11/1918	16/11/1918
Miscellaneous	46th Division G.17/49. 18th Novr: 1918. App 25 A.	18/11/1918	18/11/1918
Miscellaneous	Clearing of the Battle Fields. 46th Division G. 17/45. 17th November, 1918. App 25 A	17/11/1918	17/11/1918
Miscellaneous	To all recipients of 46th Division G. 17/45. App 26.	18/11/1918	18/11/1918
Heading	D.A.G. G.H.Q. 3rd Echelon, France.		
Heading	46 Division Gen Staff 1918 Dec-1919 Mar		
Heading	H.Q. G.S. 46 D Vol 46. Month of December 1918. Divisional Headquarters at Landrecies.		
War Diary	Landrecies	01/12/1918	29/12/1918
Operation(al) Order(s)	46th Division Order No. 342. App II.	07/12/1918	07/12/1918
Miscellaneous	Movement Table to Accompany 46th Division Order No. 342.		
Operation(al) Order(s)	46th Division Order No. 343. App III	23/12/1918	23/12/1918
Miscellaneous	A Form. Messages And Signals. App IV.		
Miscellaneous	App V		
Miscellaneous	Location-46th Division-2/1/19.	02/01/1919	02/01/1919

Miscellaneous	Location-46th Division-12/12/18.	12/12/1918	12/12/1918
Operation(al) Order(s)	46th Division Order No. 341. App I.	05/12/1918	05/12/1918
Heading	H.Q. G.S. 46 D Vol 47. Month of January 1919. Divisional Headquarters at Landrecies.		
War Diary	Landrecies.	07/01/1919	09/01/1919
War Diary	Lecateau	09/01/1919	31/01/1919
Operation(al) Order(s)	46th Division Order No. 345. App II.	09/01/1919	09/01/1919
Operation(al) Order(s)	46th Division Order No. 344. App I.	07/01/1919	07/01/1919
Miscellaneous	Amendment to 46th Division Order No. 345. App III.	11/01/1919	11/01/1919
Miscellaneous	Location-46th Division-9/1/19.	09/01/1919	09/01/1919
Miscellaneous	Location-46th Division-12/1/19.	12/01/1919	12/01/1919
Heading	G.S. 46 Division Vol 48. Month of February 1919 Divisional Headquarters at Le Cateau.		
War Diary	Le Cateau	03/02/1919	28/02/1919
Miscellaneous	46th Division G.5/38. 27th January, 1919. Inspections by the Divisional Commander. App I.	27/01/1919	27/01/1919
Operation(al) Order(s)	46th Division Warning Order No. 346. App 2.	14/01/1919	14/01/1919
Operation(al) Order(s)	46th Division Order No. 346.A. App 3.	14/01/1919	14/01/1919
Miscellaneous Map	March Table to accompany 46th Division Order No. 346.A.		
Miscellaneous	Amendment to 46th Division Order No. 348.A. App 4.	15/02/1919	15/02/1919
Miscellaneous	Locations-46th Division-21/2/19.	21/02/1919	21/02/1919
Heading	Month of March 1919. Divisional Headquarters at Le Cateau.		
War Diary	Le Cateau	01/03/1919	20/03/1919
War Diary	Le Cateau.	01/03/1919	21/03/1919
War Diary	Le Cateau	21/03/1919	21/03/1919
Diagram etc	Suggested Memorial Bellenglise.		
Miscellaneous	Headquarters, 46th (North Midland) Division. 17th March, 1919.	17/03/1919	17/03/1919

WO 95/2666 (1)

46 Div Gen Staff

Sept '18 – Mar '19

46TH DIVISION

GENERAL STAFF

SEP 1918-MAR 1919

Map to be put away with 46th Div: G.S. Diary. Septbr 1918.

46th Division.

G. S.

September 1918.

Army Form C.

Instructions regarding War Diaries and Intelligence Summaries are contained in F. S. Regs., Part II. and the Staff Manual respectively. Title pages will be prepared in manuscript.

WAR DIARY
or
INTELLIGENCE SUMMARY.
(Erase heading not required.)

Place	Date	Hour	Summary of Events and Information	Remarks and references to Appendices
			September — 1918	
			Divisional Headquarters situated at LES CHARMEUX — GOSNAY holding Right Section XIII Corps	

D. D. & L., Ld. (A8004) Wt. W1771/M23

Instructions regarding War Diaries and Intelligence Summaries are contained in F. S. Regs., Part II. and the Staff Manual respectively. Title pages will be prepared in manuscript.

WAR DIARY
or
INTELLIGENCE SUMMARY.
(*Erase heading not required.*)

Army Form C. 2118.

Place	Date	Hour	Summary of Events and Information	Remarks and references to Appendices
LES CHARMEUX GOSNAY	SEPT. 1st	4pm	The line is unchanged today except that a post has been established at X 6 c 9.5. Enemy artillery shelled [illegible] CORRE and [illegible] SWITCH with 200 rds 5.9 [illegible] [illegible] artillery [illegible] harassing fire. Our own artillery carried out harassing fire on roads [illegible]	Trench maps 36 C S.W. [illegible] [illegible] 1A 1B [illegible]
[illegible]			46 Div G 106/50 dated 1/9/18 dealing with [illegible] Relief at 9am 2/9/18	App. 1 App. 2
			During the night we occupied HUNTER and SCOTT POSTS and [illegible] today we have established posts at [illegible] [illegible] enemy artillery [illegible] harassing fire	
		3pm	Maj. General [illegible] [illegible] 46th Div Order No 316	App. [illegible]

D. D. & L., London, E.C. (A8004) Wt. W1771/M2 31 750,000 5/17 Sch. 52 Forms/C2118/14

Instructions regarding War Diaries and Intelligence Summaries are contained in F. S. Regs., Part II. and the Staff Manual respectively. Title pages will be prepared in manuscript.

WAR DIARY
or
INTELLIGENCE SUMMARY.
(*Erase heading not required.*)

Army Form C. 2118.

Place	Date	Hour	Summary of Events and Information	Remarks and references to Appendices
[illegible] GRENAY	Sept 5	5.30 am	At 5.30 am in co-operation with an attack by the 19th Division on the left the 159 Bde (left side) advanced their line and occupied RAGS POST.	
		5 pm	Further progress was made later and by 5 pm today the left Bde had occupied ORCHARD POST, ALBERT POST, DOGS POST and a portion of S.3.C.7.8. One Prisoner belonging to the 6 R.I.R. 9th Division was taken in these operations.	
			The Right Brigade also made progress and [illegible] had reached S14C54 and S14C37 close to RUM CORNER.	
			During the evening both Brigades advanced their line and dislodged the enemy from HENS and LORETTO POST, RUM CORNER and HAYSTACKS POST. In this operation some resistance was encountered. The 5th [illegible] in taking RUM CORNER, worked round the post on the NORTH side and charged it with the bayonet, approximately one officer and 25 men were holding the post, the officer and about 15 men were bayoneted and 5 men and a light machine gun captured.	
			The 6th [illegible] in advancing their line captured a prisoner, a light machine gun and an Anti-Tank rifle.	
			Hostile shelling was chiefly confined to areas [illegible] Some slight retaliation on our forward posts [illegible] the attack [illegible] Division on our left	
	Sept 5 Cont			

D. D. & L., London, E.C.
(A8004) Wt. W1771/M2 31 750,000 5/17 Sch. 52 Forms/C2118/14

Instructions regarding War Diaries and Intelligence Summaries are contained in F. S. Regs., Part II. and the Staff Manual respectively. Title pages will be prepared in manuscript.

WAR DIARY
or
INTELLIGENCE SUMMARY.
(Erase heading not required.)

Army Form C. 2118.

Place	Date	Hour	Summary of Events and Information	Remarks and references to Appendices
VRAIGNES	21		DHQ closed at CAUVIGNY FARM at noon and opened at VRAIGNES (Q19b7.7 Sheet 62C 1/40000) at the same hour. 138th Inf Bde relieved 4th & 12th Bdes (less 1 Battalion) of 4th Australian Division from a line L23 a0.0 - G24 Central on the North to the left boundary of 139th Inf Bde on the South. The Brigade comes under orders of GOC 4th Australian Division. 138th & 139th Inf Bdes are each holding their front with 2 Battalions in the front line and 1 Battalion in close support. 137th Inf Bde opened their HQ at Q18c0.8 and the Brigade came into Divisional Reserve, the Battalions being disposed in the area L32, L33 & L34.	
			46th Division G113/13 Policy of holding the line and outline of probable future operation	App 19
			Daily Disposition Return for 6 am 22/9/18.	App 20
	22			
			Div G 113/21. Preliminary instructions in connection with a minor operation against the village of [illegible] 23/9/18	App 22
			Daily Disposition Return	App 23

(A8004) Wt. W1771/M2 31 730,000 5/17 D. D. & L., London, E.C. Sch. 52 Forms/C2118/14

Instructions regarding War Diaries and Intelligence Summaries are contained in F. S. Regs., Part II. and the Staff Manual respectively. Title pages will be prepared in manuscript.

WAR DIARY
or
INTELLIGENCE SUMMARY.
(Erase heading not required.)

Army Form C. 2118.

Place	Date	Hour	Summary of Events and Information	Remarks and references to Appendices
VRAIGNES	23		In connection with the attack made by the Germans yesterday evening along GALLICHET ALLEY and the PONTRUET – BERTHAUCOURT Road – an account of which is contained in the Div'l Intelligence Summary – it is interesting to note that the 5th Bn Sherwood Foresters repulsed the attack by small arm fire. The main theme of all offensive and defensive training for the Infantry for some months past in the Division has been that the Rifle is the Infantryman's primary weapon in opposition to the bomb. Instances such as this show that the Infantry are more thoroughly impressed by the doctrine.	
			Intelligence Summary No. 2	App 24
			46th Div. Orders No. 324	App 25
			Daily Disposition Return 6 am 24/9/18	App 26
	24		At [illegible] the [illegible] attack on PONTRUET [illegible] in conjunction with the 5th Sherwood Foresters who [illegible] the [illegible] from [illegible] GALLICHET ALLEY [illegible] GRICOURT [illegible] 1/10,000 [illegible] left flank of an offensive carried out by 46th, 1st & 6th Divisions (N. of [illegible]) [illegible] XXXI French Corps on the [illegible] of the 6th Division. The [illegible] of 46th [illegible] TROUT and FORGANS Trench [illegible] the [illegible] of the 1st & 6th Divisions and the French Corps [illegible] of high ground of tactical importance. The situation [illegible] 6 pm 24th [illegible] Intelligence Summary No. 3. [illegible]	App 27

D. D. & L., London, E.C. (A8004) Wt. W1771/M2 31 750,000 5/17 Sch. 52 Forms/C2118/14

Instructions regarding War Diaries and Intelligence Summaries are contained in F. S. Regs., Part II. and the Staff Manual respectively. Title pages will be prepared in manuscript.

WAR DIARY
or
INTELLIGENCE SUMMARY.
(Erase heading not required.)

Army Form C. 2118.

Place	Date	Hour	Summary of Events and Information	Remarks and references to Appendices
VRAIGNES			came there at one time during the morning our troops were in FORGANS trench at M4C and in the Northern elements of PONTRUET and that both the Cemetery and the Blockhouse were in our hands. The situation was obscure in the village for some time but the enemy bombed his way back up FORGANS trench to M4a 05.30, where he established and maintained a posn. Two of our Stokes Mortars which would have assisted materially in the fighting N of PONTRUET were knocked out almost immediately after zero. The team of one of them killed several of the enemy with their rifles and took 11 prisoners. At 7.45 pm a further attempt was made by the 5th Leicester Regt together with 1 Company of the 5th Sherwood Foresters to enter PONTRUET from the North West but it was unsuccessful owing to the strength in which the enemy were holding the village. This attack was made silently, without Artillery support. It appeared from prisoners statements that the enemy was expecting an attack on PONTRUET and had made very strong preparations to meet it. His probable dispositions were: 3 Companies in PONTRUET & PALADIC Trenches, 1 Battalion in the village, 1 Battalion in FORGANS Trench and 1 Battalion	

Instructions regarding War Diaries and Intelligence Summaries are contained in F. S. Regs., Part II. and the Staff Manual respectively. Title pages will be prepared in manuscript.

WAR DIARY
or
INTELLIGENCE SUMMARY.
(Erase heading not required.)

Army Form C. 2118.

Place	Date	Hour	Summary of Events and Information	Remarks and references to Appendices
VRAIGNES			in Reserve either in the vicinity of FRIGATE WORK (M5c) or E of the ST QUENTIN Canal. Total number of prisoners taken by us during the day amounted to 1 officer & 136 OR. At 1.40 am 25.9.18 orders were issued (Division Order No 325) that the village of PONTRUET was to be evacuated but the posts N. and W. of it were to be held. Our line now runs approx. along the sunken road running N.W. – S.E. through M3 b & d as far as M3d 77 – PRUE Copse – BELX Trench – LEDUC Trench where we join the 2nd Inf. Bde.	App 28
			Disposition Return for 6 am 25/9/18 [illegible]	App 29
	25		The situation remains unchanged. 138th Inf. Bde. handed over to the 139th Bde that part of the 139th Bde area they were occupying after the attack which was made at 7.45 pm yesterday evening. The inter-brigade boundary is now the same as it was previous to the attack on 5th and 24.9.18. [illegible] assumed command of 6th Bn South Staffords [illegible]	
			[illegible] Div Order No 327	App 30
			Amendment No 1 to Div Order No 327	App 31
			Intelligence Summary No 4	App 32
			Disposition Return for 6 am 26/9/18	App 33
			We shelled PONTRUET heavily this morning putting 400 x 4.2" and 1100 x 25 6" into the village	

(A7092). Wt. W12839/M1293. 750,000. 1/17. D. D. & L., Ltd. Forms/C.2118/14.

Instructions regarding War Diaries and Intelligence Summaries are contained in F. S. Regs., Part II. and the Staff Manual respectively. Title pages will be prepared in manuscript.

WAR DIARY
or
INTELLIGENCE SUMMARY.
(Erase heading not required.)

Army Form C. 2118.

Place	Date	Hour	Summary of Events and Information	Remarks and references to Appendices
VRAIGNES	26		The enemy artillery was active on our forward areas and on roads. He is making a good deal of use of his H.V. and Long Range guns. His airmen are active in reconnaissance and on bombing forward and back areas. The 1st Inf. Bde took over that part of our line from the southern boundary to G33b3.3. The northern boundary remains as before. Our southern boundary now runs as follows:- V24 central to M1b3.0, thence up road running NE to G32b10.4 thence to St QUENTIN Canal through G34 central. 138th Inf Bde remained in line to 2 Battalion frontage and 155th Inf Bde was withdrawn from the line to the area R8, 14, 9 & 15.	Sheets 62C NE & 62B NW
	Sept 26/9		Daily Disposition Return for 6 am 27/9/18	App 34
			Intelligence Summary No 5	35
			138th Bde pushed forward posts on their right along BELL Copse G33 to x G34a to G33b95.40, G34a0.4, G27d80.15 & G27d8.2. The left Battalion also attempted to push forward to trenches running through G28A and G22 1.3 round about PIKE Wood but found them strongly held by the enemy and did not achieve their object. A bombardment with HE and gas shell in the proportion of 3 gas shells to 1 HE was carried out on the following areas:- BELLENGLISE and to the North of it from the St QUENTIN Canal Eastwards from G29 central to G35d6.1; G23a and an area in G17d, G18c, G23b and G24a. The bombardment was carried out in 4 periods of 1 hour each, the first	

(A7092). Wt. W12839/M1293. 750,000. 1/17. D. D. & L., Ltd. Forms/C.2118/14.

WAR DIARY
or
INTELLIGENCE SUMMARY.
(Erase heading not required.)

Army Form C. 2118.

Instructions regarding War Diaries and Intelligence Summaries are contained in F. S. Regs., Part II. and the Staff Manual respectively. Title pages will be prepared in manuscript.

Place	Date	Hour	Summary of Events and Information	Remarks and references to Appendices
VRAIGNES			period commencing at 10 pm and the last ending at 5.30 am 27.9.18. The enemy did not reply to the bombardment. Enemy artillery less active.	
	27		In accordance with Division Order No 328 the 138th Inf. Bde. after a preliminary bombardment, attacked the enemy trenches from G28c8.8 to PIKE Wood inclusive, bombing south towards G34b1.7 and NE to about G28b3.8. The 4th Bn Leicestershire Regt carried out this attack which was successful. It resulted in the capture of 2 officers and 146 OR, 8 of whom were wounded, and an advancement to a general line G22c3.4 - G28a4.8 - G34a9.6. At the conclusion of this operation 137th Inf Bde relieved 138th Inf Bde in the line & 138th Inf. Bde went back to the area E of LE VERGUIER and 139th Inf. Bde came up to the area South of them.	App 36 Ref. Sheets 62C NE & 62B NW
	Early morning 28.9.18		Brigades were disposed as follows:- 137th in line, 138th in L21c, L30a & d (1 Battalion) and 2 Battalions N & NE of LE VERGUIER. 139th Bde in L36, G31 and R6a and M1c (1 Battalion) and 2 Battalions in LE VERGUIER and SE of it. (Division Order [illegible] 28.9.18)	App 37

(A7092). Wt. W12839/M1293. 750,000. 1/17. D. D. & L., Ltd. Forms/C.2118/14.

Instructions regarding War Diaries and Intelligence Summaries are contained in F. S. Regs., Part II. and the Staff Manual respectively. Title pages will be prepared in manuscript.

WAR DIARY
or
INTELLIGENCE SUMMARY.
(Erase heading not required.)

Army Form C. 2118.

Place	Date	Hour	Summary of Events and Information	Remarks and references to Appendices
R8b.5.5 Sheet	28		DHQ closed at VRAIGNES at 6 pm and opened at R8b.5.5 (Ref Sheet 62C) at the same time. Headquarters of Infantry Brigades moved forward to positions as stated on Disposition Return for 6 am 29th inst. At [illegible] the enemy [illegible] captured by 138th Bde yesterday. Owing to [illegible] the dispositions of the Infantry Brigades at 5.50 am 29.9.18 are shewn on Map B.	App 38. App 39
	29		At 5.50 am the 46th Division launched an attack against the HINDENBURG LINE E & W of the St QUENTIN CANAL. The objectives of the attack are shewn on Map A. The 137th Inf. Bde were to storm the Canal and push forward to the Brown Line: on reaching this line the 138th & 139th Inf. Bdes were to go through the 137th Inf. Bde and advance to the Green Line: on arriving at this line the 32nd Div. who were following up behind were to pass through the 46th Div and push forward to the Red Line. The story of the attack is issued separately. Maps C & D shew	App 40. App 41. Apps. 42 & 43

(A7092). Wt. W12839/M1293. 750,000. 1/17. D. D. & L., Ltd. Forms/C.2118/14.

Instructions regarding War Diaries and Intelligence Summaries are contained in F. S. Regs., Part II. and the Staff Manual respectively. Title pages will be prepared in manuscript.

WAR DIARY
or
INTELLIGENCE SUMMARY.
(Erase heading not required.)

Army Form C. 2118.

Place	Date	Hour	Summary of Events and Information	Remarks and references to Appendices
28 b 5.5	29		the dispositions of the Brigades before and after Zero. Preliminary Orders and Instructions are attached as follows:–	
			Division Order no 326	App 44
			46th Division Instructions no 1	App 45
			" " " 2	App 46
			" " " 3	App 47
			" " " 4	App 48
			" " " 5	App 49
			" " " 6	App 50
			" " " 7	App 51
			" " " 8	App 52
			" " " 9	App 53
			" " " 10	App 54
			" " " 11	App 55
			Appendix A (giving intervals and pace of barrage)	App 56

(A7092). Wt. W12839/M1293. 750,000. 1/17. D. D. & L., Ltd. Forms/C.2118/14.

Army Form C. 2118.

WAR DIARY
or
INTELLIGENCE SUMMARY.

(Erase heading not required.)

Instructions regarding War Diaries and Intelligence Summaries are contained in F. S. Regs., Part II. and the Staff Manual respectively. Title pages will be prepared in manuscript.

Place	Date	Hour	Summary of Events and Information	Remarks and references to Appendices
R8b5.5.	29		Dispositions for night 29/30	App 57
			Dispositions for 6 am 30th Sept	App 58
	30		G453. Dispositions to be taken up today	App 59
			G468 Dispositions to be taken up by 139th Inf. Brigade etc	App 60
			Daily Disposition Return (6 am 1.10.18)	App 61
			~~Special Order of the Day by G.O.C. IX Corps~~	~~App 62~~
			Ser of 5 photographs showing the ST QUENTIN CANAL	App 62

(A7092). Wt. W12839/M1293. 750,000. 1/17. D. D. & L., Ltd. Forms/C.2118/14.

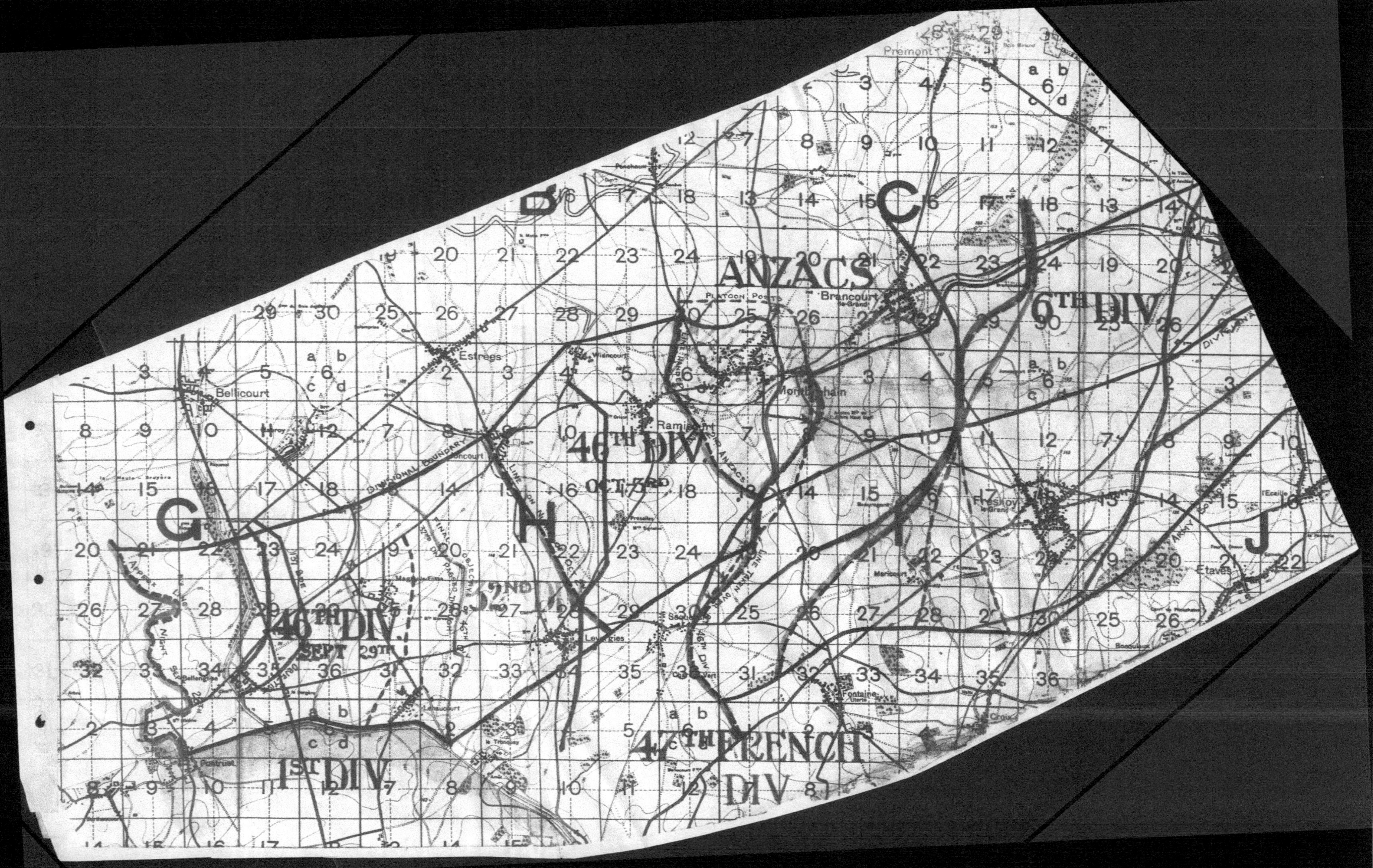

Premont
Bellicourt
Estrees
Joncourt
Wiancourt
Ramicourt
Montbrehain
Brancourt le Grand
Fresnoy le Grand
Levergies
Sequehart
Fontaine Uterte
Etaves
Mericourt
Preselles
Lehaucourt
Pontruet
ANZACS
PLATOON POSTS
6TH DIV
46TH DIV
OCT 3RD
46TH DIV
SEPT 29TH
32ND
1ST DIV
47TH FRENCH DIV
DIVISIONAL BOUNDARY
ARMY BOUNDARY
FINAL OBJECTIVE OF 46TH DIV
32ND DIV PASSED THROUGH
LINE TAKEN OVER
C
D
G
H
J

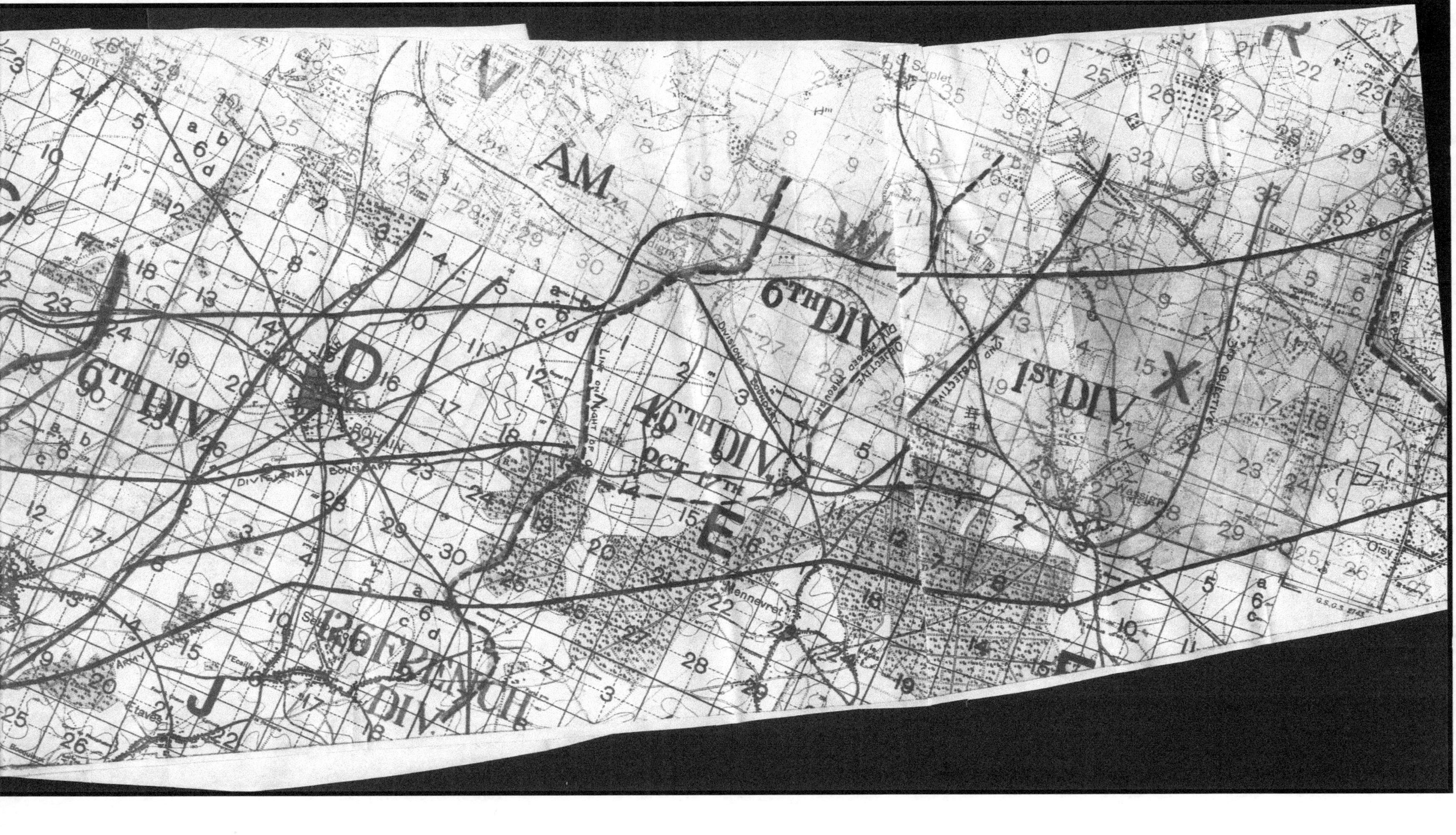

6TH DIV
1ST DIV
46TH DIV
OCT 17TH
126 FRENCH DIV
LINE ON NIGHT OF
DIVISIONAL BOUNDARY
2ND OBJECTIVE
3RD OBJECTIVE
DIV. OBJECTIVE
BOHAIN
Mennevret
Wassigny
Prémont
St Souplet
Etaves
Oisy

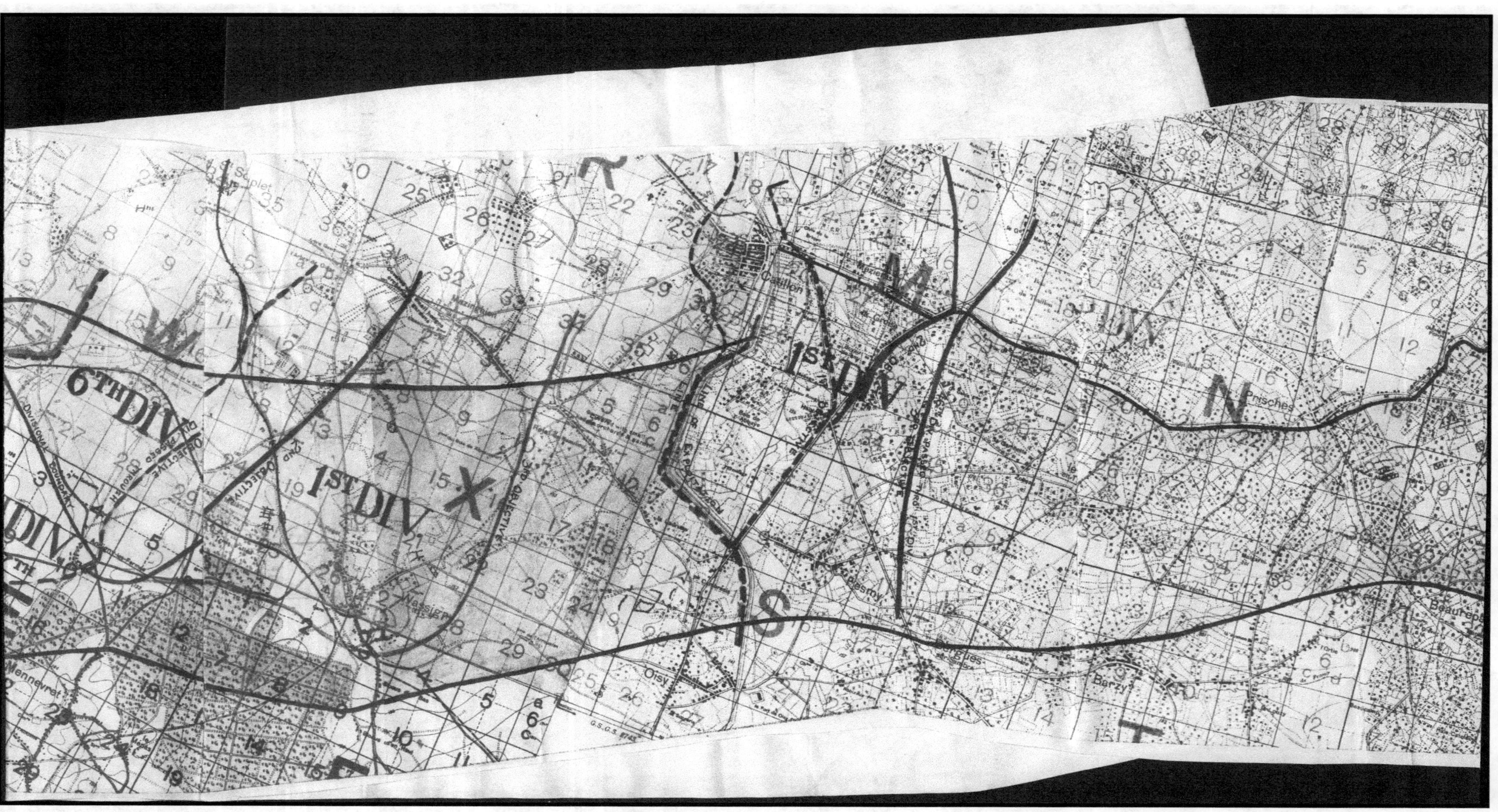

6TH DIV
1ST DIV
1ST DIV
Catillon
Prisches
Wassigny
Oisy
Barzy
Mennevret

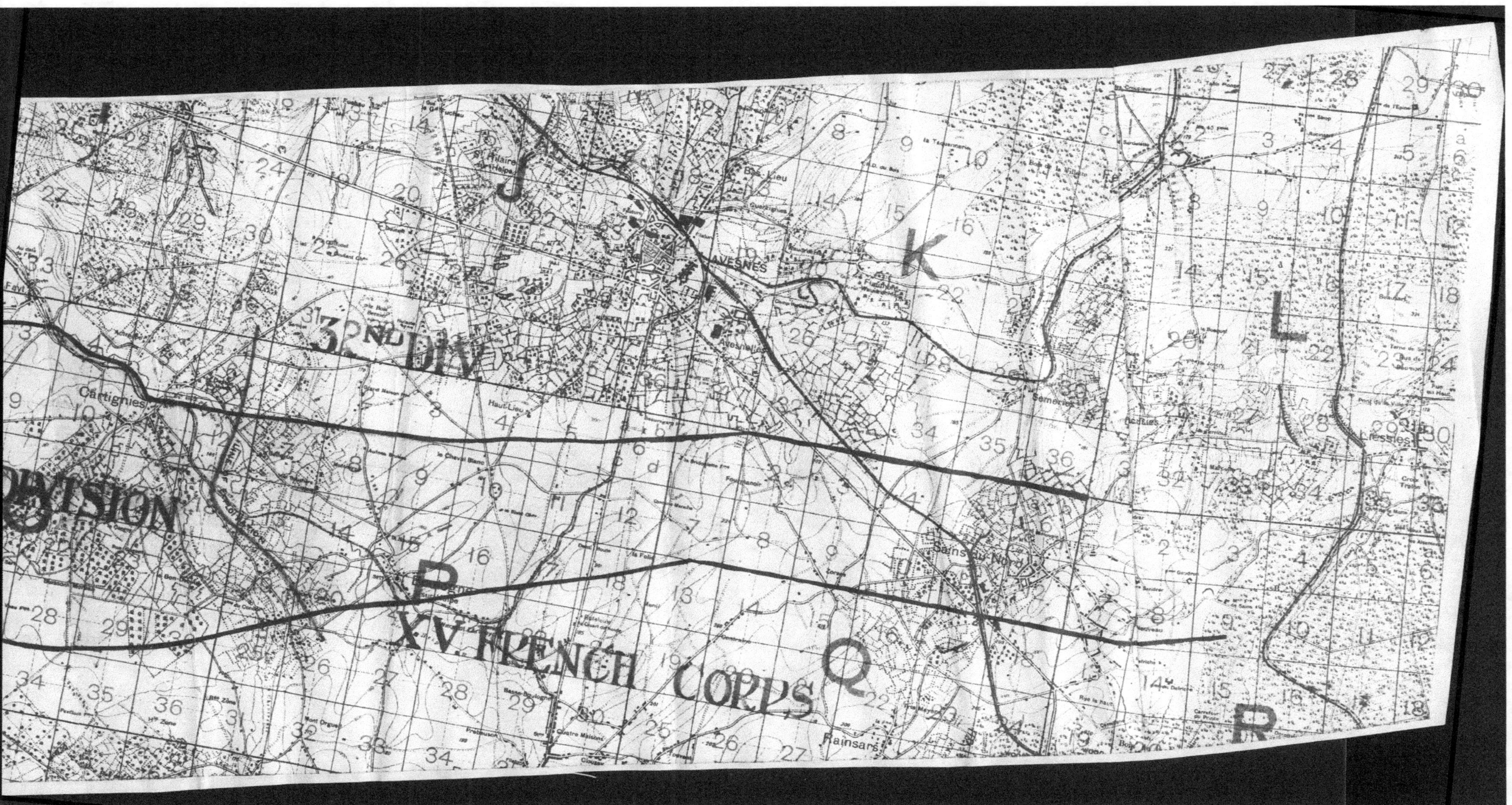
32ND DIV
XV FRENCH CORPS
DIVISION
J
K
L
P
Q
R
AVESNES
Avesnelles
Cartignies
Sains-du-Nord
Rainsars
Liessies
Semeries

28031 W3125/M2250 1000m 6/17 M.R.Co.,Ltd. (1367) Forms W3091.

Army Form W. 3091.

Cover for Documents.

46 DIV

106.

Nature of Enclosures.

46TH DIVISION.
GENERAL STAFF.
No. ....
Date 7.9.18

Advance.

Enemy Withdrawal in the Lys Salient July/Sept: 18.

From 106/50 (incl:)

Notes, or Letters written.

46th DIVISION. No. 4/174

Date 3. 9. 18

G.O.C.

G.S.O. 1

G.S.O. 2

G.S.O. 3

Int. Offr.

Att. Offr.

Q. A.

C.R.A. C.R.E.

A.D.M.S. M.G. Batt.

Signals

RETURN TO "G" OFFICE.

Printed in France by A.P. & S.S. Press B. 2008. 5000. 4-18.

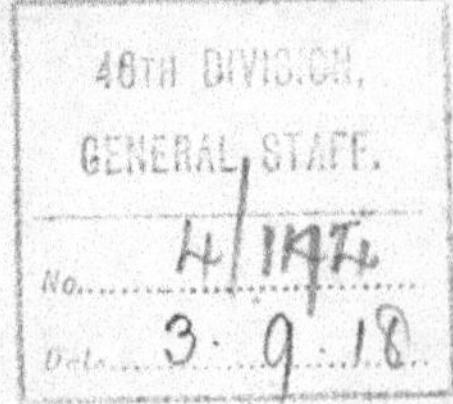

Secret.
****

Copy No. 7
****

138th. Infantry Brigade Order No. 244.
****

Reference maps :-
36.S.W. & 36.A.S.E.
****

Headquarters,
3rd Sept '18.
****

In continuation of 138th. Inf. Bde. Order No. 243. of 3rd September 1918.

1. The Line S.20.c.9.8. - HAYSTACK - PATH - ORCHARD - ALBERT - DOGS - EDWARD and HENS POSTS will be occupied to-day by the 138th. and 139th. Infantry Brigades.

2. Zero Hour will be 5-15 a.m. September 4th. '18.

3. On the objectives being reached, patrols will at once push forward taking every opportunity of the confusion in the enemy lines.
The final objective of these patrols will be our old Front Line in S.16.c. & a. - S.10.c. & b. - S.5.c., where they will be reinforced and this line held as an outpost system.

4. The artillery barrage will be extended 300 yards south of Divisional Boundary to include INDIAN VILLAGE. The last 4 words of para 4. "when it will cease" will be deleted and the following inserted "when it will again move forward at the same rate until it rests on the old German Front Line. It will rest here for a further 10 minutes when it will cease".

5. 468th. Fld Coy R.E. will arrange to attach 2 sappers to each of the 3 leading companies of 5th Leicestershire Regt to search for 'Booby' Traps.

6. Reference para 6 - The 5th Lincolnshire Regt will reorganise after assaulting troops have passed through, and follow up acting as moppers up and supports and keeping close touch with 5th Leicestershire Regt.

7. 1 M.G. Section will follow immediately in rear of the assaulting troops, and take up positions in Old British Front Line. 1 Section will be used as guns of opportunity and to protect the right flank.
2 Sections will be in reserve about S.19.central, and be at the disposal of O.C. 5th Leicestershire Regt. If the latter usesthese guns he will at once notify Brigade H.Qrs.
O.C. M. G. Group will be at Advanced H.Qrs, 5th Leics Regt S.19.b.7.4.

8. 138th. T.M.Battery will arrange for 1 Officer and 2 guns to accompany each flank forward company of 5th Leics Regt and remain at their disposal.

9. Watches will be synchronized at Advd Bde H.Qrs at 12 midnight 3rd/4th Sept 1918.

Acknowledge.

W. C. C. Watson
Captain,
for Brigade Major, 138th. Inf. Bde.

Issued to all recipients of Order No. 243. at 10-15 p.m.

46th DIVISION. No. 4/173

Date 3.9.18

G.O.C.

G.S.O. 1

G.S.O. 2

G.S.O. 3

Int. Offr.

Att. Offr.

Q. A.

C.R.A. C.R.E.

A.D.M.S. M.G. Batt.

Signals

RETURN TO "G" OFFICE.

Printed in France by A.P. & S.S. Press B. 2008. 5000. 4-18.

SECRET 46th: DIVISIONAL ARTILLERY COPY NO. 3.
ORDER NO. 306.

***

3rd: SEPTEMBER, 1918.

REFERENCE - Maps, 1/20,000.
30 . W. and 36 A. S.E.

(1) From the Line S.20.c.9.8. - HAYSTACK - PATH - ORCHARD - ALBERT - DOG'S - EDWARDS - HEM'S - LANSDOWNE POSTS, the 138th: and 139th: Infantry Brigades will attack and gain the Line TUBE STA. POST - PALL MALL (S.15.central) - FACTORY KEEP - FACTORY TRENCH to EDWARDS POST, all inclusive.

The 55th: Division are conforming by occupying the Line S.27.a.2.2. - INDIAN VILLAGE INCLUSIVE.

(2) A Liaison Post with the 55th: Division will be established at TUBE STA. POST.

(3) The 138th: Infantry Brigade must be prepared to throw back a Defensive Flank to protect their RIGHT.

(4) On the objective being reached, patrols will at once push forward taking every opportunity of the confusion in the enemy lines.

The Final Objective of these patrols will be our old front line in S.16.c. and a. - S.10.c. and b. - S.5.c., where they will be reinforced and this line held as an Outpost System.

(5) At ZERO Hour Both Groups will put down an 18 Pdr: Shrapnel Barrage (Map attached *) on a Line 300 yards EAST of the Trench S.20.central to S.14.d.3.3. - HAYSTACK - ORCHARD - ALBERT - DOGS - EDWARD POST, where it will rest four minutes.

(Should Brigades at any time desire any alteration of this line they will inform 46th: Divisional Artillery and D.H.Q. by Priority Wire).

The Barrage will then move forward at the rate of 100 yards in two minutes. As each Battery reaches the PROTECTIVE Barrage Line "A.A." (S.21.b.4.5. - PALL MALL KEEP (S.15.b.8.3.) - JUNCTION ST. - S.10.a.0.0. - Thence a N. and S. Grid to S.4.c.0.0.) it will remain there until the Barrage advances at ZERO plus 30 Minutes.

The Barrage will again move forward at the same rate until it rests on the old German Front Line.

(6) As each Battery reaches the Line "B.B." it will continue for 10 Minutes and thence cease fire.

The Dividing Line between Groups will be a line through ORCHARD POST inclusive to ESSARS GROUP, through FACTORY KEEP inclusive to ESSARS GROUP.

(7) 4.5" Howitzers will Bombard the following points :-

ESSARS GROUP.

ZERO to ZERO Plus 6 Minutes.

FACTORY KEEP and FACTORY CORNER.

ZERO Plus 6 to Plus 40 Minutes.

Cross Roads S.10.b.75.90.

ZERO Plus 40 to ZERO Plus 60 Minutes.

Cross Roads S.11.a.90.60.

GORRE GROUP.

ZERO to ZERO Plus 8 Minutes.

2 Hows: TUBE STA. POST.
2 Hows: S.15.central.

ZERO Plus 8 to ZERO Plus 38 Minutes.

4 Hows: Cross Roads S.17.a.85.60.
2 Hows: will walk up RUE DU CAILLOUX.
200 yards in advance of 18 Pdr: Barrage.

P.T.O.

CONTINUED (2)

(8) RATES OF FIRE.

18 Pdr: BARRAGE.

ZERO to Plus 4 Minutes.	INTENSE.
ZERO Plus 4 Minutes to Line "A.A."	NORMAL.
PROTECTIVE Barrage on Line "A.A."	SLOW.
ZERO plus 30 Minutes to Plus 32 Minutes. then SLOW.	INTENSE.

4.5" HOWITZERS.

ZERO to Plus 4 Minutes. then NORMAL. throughout.	INTENSE.

(9) Watches will be synchronised at Midnight September 3rd:/4th:.

(10) ZERO Hour will be 5.15 a.m. SEPTEMBER 4th:.

(11) Group Commanders will keep in very close touch with Infantry Brigades in order to obtain latest dispositions of Outposts.

(11) ACKNOWLEDGE.

Captain R.A.
A/Brigade Major.
48th: Divisional Artillery.

Headquarters R.A.

ISSUED at 9.30 p.m.

COPIES NO.

*	1	ESSARS GROUP.
*	2	GORRE GROUP.
*	3	46th: Division.)
	4	R.A. XIII Corps.)
*	5	H.A. XIII Corps.
*	6	55th: Div: Arty.
*	7	138th: Infantry Bde:
*	8	139th: Infantry Bde:
	9	137th: Infantry Bde:
	10	52nd: Brigade R.G.A.)
	11	C.B.S.O.)
*	12	19th: Div: Arty:)
	13	21st: Squadron R.A.F)
	14	D.T.M.O.
	15 - 16	War Diary.
	17	File.

* Tracing attached.
(For information.

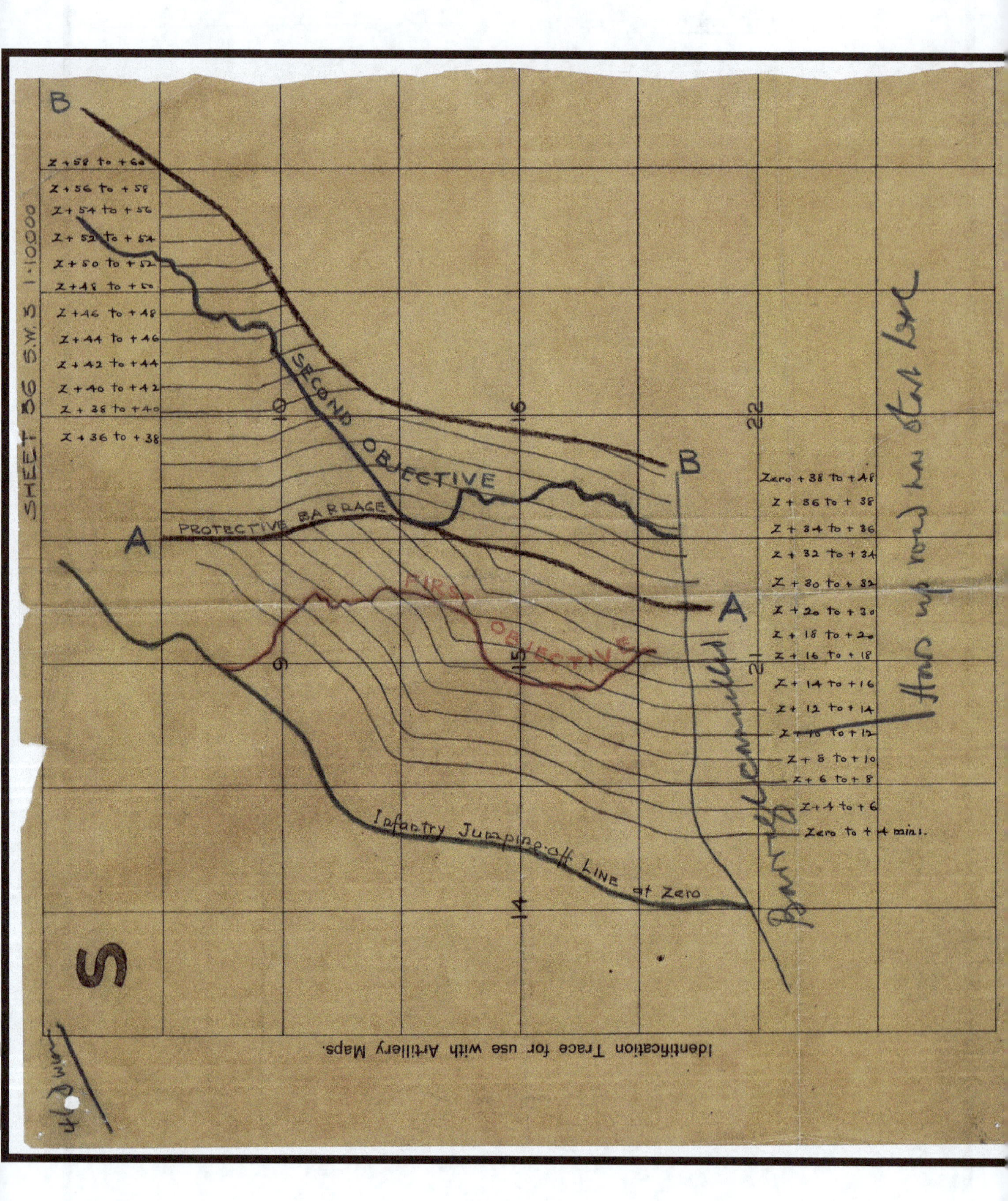

SHEET 36 S.W.3 1:10000
B
Z + 58 to + 60
Z + 56 to + 58
Z + 54 to + 56
Z + 52 to + 54
Z + 50 to + 52
Z + 48 to + 50
Z + 46 to + 48
Z + 44 to + 46
Z + 42 to + 44
Z + 40 to + 42
Z + 38 to + 40
Z + 36 to + 38
SECOND OBJECTIVE
PROTECTIVE BARRAGE
A
B
A
FIRST OBJECTIVE
Zero + 38 to + 48
Z + 36 to + 38
Z + 34 to + 36
Z + 32 to + 34
Z + 30 to + 32
Z + 20 to + 30
Z + 18 to + 20
Z + 16 to + 18
Z + 14 to + 16
Z + 12 to + 14
Z + 10 to + 12
Z + 8 to + 10
Z + 6 to + 8
Z + 4 to + 6
Zero to + 4 mins.
Infantry Jumping-off LINE at Zero
10
16
22
9
15
21
14
S
Identification Trace for use with Artillery Maps.

46th DIVISION. No. 4/172

Date 3 Sept 18

G.O.C.

G.S.O. 1

G.S.O. 2

G.S.O. 3

Int. Offr.

Att. Offr.

Q. A.

C.R.A. C.R.E.

A.D.M.S. M.G. Batt.

Signals

RETURN TO "G" OFFICE.

Printed in France by A.P. & S.S. Press B. 2008. 5000. 4-18.

S E C R E T
* * * * * *

Copy No.

139th INFANTRY BRIGADE ORDER No. 201.

Ref: Maps :- 36.S.W., and
36.a.S.E., 1/20,000.

September 3rd,1918.

In continuation of 139th Inf.Brigade Order 200 of 3rd September.

1. The line ORCHARD - ALBERT - DOGS - EDWARD and HENS POSTS will be occupied today by the 139th Infantry Brigade. As relief is now in progress, the 8th Sherwood Foresters will occupy any of these Posts that are not already in possession of 6th Sherwood Foresters at time of handing over.
The 138th Infantry Brigade are to occupy the line S.20.c.9.8., HAYSTACK and PATH POSTS to-day.

2. O.C. 139 T.M.Battery will get into touch with Officer Commanding 8th Sherwood Foresters and will place 1 section of 3" Stokes Mortars, at his disposal.

3. ZERO HOUR will be 5.15 am., 4th September.

4. On the objective being reached, patrols of 8th Sherwood Foresters will at once push forward taking every oppor--tunity of the confusion in the enemy lines.
The final objective of these patrols will be our old front line in S.16.c., and a - S.10.c. & b - S.5.c., where they will be reinforced and this line held as an Outpost system.
O.C. 5th Sherwood Foresters will dispose two Companies of his Battalion along line CHAVATTES POST - BEND OF STREAM S.8.c.2.3. - SCOTT POST - HUNTER POST - RICHEBOURG POST - these Companies to be in position by ZERO minus 15 mins.
When O.C. 8th Sherwood Foresters reinforces his patrols in the Outpost system, the two Companies of 5th Sherwood Foresters will move up and occupy posts along the original 'jumping off line' i.e. ORCHARD - ALBERT - DOGS - EDWARD and HENS POSTS. The closest liaison must be kept between Os.C. 5th and 8th Sherwood Foresters.

5. As regards para. 3 of 139 Brigade Order 200, the last 4 words "when it will cease" will be deleted and the following substituted "when it will again move forward at the same rate until it rests on the Old German front line. It will rest for a further 10 minutes when it will cease"

6. Prisoners will be sent back to Headquarters 5th Sherwood Foresters X.17.a.8.7., under arrangements to be made by 8th Sherwood Foresters. From this point they will be taken back to Brigade Headquarters under arrangements to be made by O.C. 5th Sherwood Foresters.

7. Watches will be synchronised at 139 Brigade H.Qrs., at 12 midnight, under arrangements to be made by Brigade Signal Officer. A synchronised watch will be sent up to Os.C. 5th and 8th Sherwood Foresters at 1 am., 4th inst.

8. ACKNOWLEDGE.

[signature]
Captain,
Brigade Major, 139th Inf.Brigade.

P.T.O.

Issued at 9 p.m., to :-

Copy No. 1. 57th Infantry Brigade.
2. 138th Infantry Brigade.
3. 46th Division.
4. ESSARS GROUP R.A.
5. No. 2 Group M.G.Corps.
6. 5th Sherwood Foresters
7. 6th Sherwood Foresters
8. 8th Sherwood Foresters
9. 139 T.M.Battery.
10. 465 Field Coy.R.E.
11. Brigade Signal Officer.

46th. DIVISION. No. 4/171

Date 3 Sept 18

G.O.C. [illegible]

G.S.O. 1 [illegible]

G.S.O. 2

G.S.O. 3 [illegible]

Int. Offr. [illegible]

Att. Offr. [illegible]

Q. A.

C.R.A. C.R.E.

A.D.M.S. M.G. Batt.

Signals

RETURN TO "G" OFFICE.

Printed in France by A.P. & S.S. Press B. 2008. 5000. 4-18.

Secret.
****

Copy No. 7
****

138th. Infantry Brigade Order No. 243.
****

Reference maps :-
36.S.W. & 36.A.S.E.
****

Headquarters,
3rd September '18.
****

1. As soon as the line RUM CORNER - HAYSTACK - PATH ORCHARD - ALBERT - DOGS - EDWARDS - HENS and LANSDOWNES POST has been established the 138th. Inf. Bde. and 139th. Inf. Bde. will attack and gain a line TUBE STATION POST - PALL MALL (S.15. central) - FACTORY KEEP - FACTORY TRENCH to EDWARDS POST all inclusive.
The 55th Division are conforming by occupying the line S.27.a.2.2. - INDIAN VILLAGE inclusive.

2. The 138th. Inf. Bde. will establish Liaison Posts with the 139th. Inf. Bde. at the following points :- TEETOTALL CORNER - CATS POST and FACTORY KEEP, and with the 55th Division at TUBE STATION POST.

3. The 5th LEICESTERSHIRE REGT will carry out the attack and will be formed up by 5 p.m. under arrangements already made with O.C. Battalion. They will be prepared to throw back a defensive flank on their right.

4. At Zero the artillery will bring their barrage down on a line 200 yards E. of the trench S.20.central to S.14.d.2.6. - HAYSTACK - ORCHARD - ALBERT - DOGS - EDWARDS POST where it will rest 4 minutes.
The barrage will then move forward at the rate of 100 yards in 2 minutes.
On lifting from the ~~from~~/final objective the barrage will rest on the line S.21.b.4.6. PALL MALL KEEP S.15.b.8.3. - JUNCTION STREET - S.10.a.0.0. thence a N. and S. grid to S.4.c.0.0. for 10 minutes when it will cease.

5. Zero Hour will be notified later. by wire + on - from Spm

6. The 5th Lincolnshire Regt will notify by priority wire the moment they are in possession of RUM CORNER, HAYSTACK and PATH giving exact locations of forward posts.
The 5th Lincolnshire Regt will await orders from Bde H.Qrs before moving after assaulting troops have passed through.
Carrying parties will be found by the 4th LEICS REGT according to arrangements already made.

Acknowledge. Done

[signature]
Captain,
for Brigade Major, 138th. Infantry Bde.

Issued through Sigs at to :-

All recipients of Order No. 242.
****

46th DIVISION. No. 4/170

Date 3. 9. 18

G.O.C. JR

G.S.O. 1

G.S.O. 2

G.S.O. 3

Int. Offr.

Att. Offr.

Q. A.

C.R.A. C.R.E.

A.D.M.S. M.G. Batt.

Signals

RETURN TO "G" OFFICE.

Printed in France by A.P. & S.S. Press B. 2008. 5000. 4-18.

48TH DIVISION,
GENERAL STAFF.
No. 4/170
Date 3.9.18

S E C R E T
* * * * * * *

Copy No. 1

139th INFANTRY BRIGADE ORDER No. 200.

Ref. Maps :- 36.S.W. and
36.a.S.E., 1/20,000.

September 3rd, 1918.

1. As soon as the line RUM CORNER - HAYSTACK - PATH - ORCHARD - ALBERT - DOG'S - EDWARDS - HENS - LANSDOWNE POSTS has been established, the 138th and 139th Infantry Brigade will attack and gain the line TUBE STA. POST - PALL MALL (S.15.central) FACTORY KEEP - FACTORY TRENCH to EDWARDS POST, all inclusive.
The 55th Division are conforming by occupying the line S.27.a.2.2 - INDIAN VILLAGE inclusive.

2. The 8th Battalion Sherwood Foresters will carry out the operation within the 139 Brigade boundaries and will take over the line from the 6th Battalion Sherwood Foresters. The latter Battalion on relief will move back into Brigade Reserve.
The 5th Battalion Sherwood Foresters will move up to Brigade ~~Reserve~~ Support at once.

3. At ZERO HOUR the Artillery will bring their barrage down 200 yards E. of the line - HAYSTACK - ORCHARD - ALBERT - DOGS - EDWARD POST - where it will rest for 4 minutes. The barrage will move forward at the rate of 100 yards in two minutes. On lifting from the final objective, the barrage will rest on the line PALL MALL KEEP (S.15.b.8.3) - JUNCTION STREET - S.10.a.0.0., thence along N and S grid line to S.4.c.0.0., for 10 minutes when it will cease.

4. Liaison Post with 138 Inf.Brigade will be established as the advance progresses at the following points - TEETOTAL CORNER - CATS POST and FACTORY KEEP.

5. ZERO HOUR will be notified later. It is hoped to be able to carry out this operation shortly after 5 p.m., today, by which time troops must be in position.
ZERO HOUR will be notified by wire plus or minus from 5 pm.

6. Map shewing Brigade Boundaries etc., is forwarded to Units Marked *.

Brigade Boundaries are shewn in	GREEN.
Jumping off positions shewn in	RED
Final objective shewn in	VIOLET.

7. Watches will be synchronised under arrangements to be made by O.C. Brigade Signals at 4 pm., at 139 Brigade H.Qrs. A synchronised watch will be sent to O.C. 8th Sherwood Foresters.

8. ACKNOWLEDGE. done MRP

[signature]
Captain.
Brigade Major, 139th Inf.Bde.

Distribution over

Issued at 3.30 p.m, to :-

Copy No. 1. 46th Division.
2. 57th Inf. Brigade. *
3. 138th Infantry Brigade. *
4. ESSARS GROUP R.A.
5. No. 2 Group M.G.Corps.
6. 5th Sherwood Foresters.
7. 6th Sherwood Foresters *
8. 8thSherwood Foresters *
9. 139 T.M.Battery.
10. 465 Field Coy.R.E.
11. Brigade Signal Officer.

46th DIVISION. No. 4/169

Date 3 Sept 18

G.O.C. [initials]

G.S.O. 1 [initials]

G.S.O. 2

G.S.O. 3 [initials]

Int. Offr. [initials]

Att. Offr. [initials]

Q. A.

C.R.A. C.R.E.

A.D.M.S. M.G. Batt.

Signals

RETURN TO "G" OFFICE.

Printed in France by A.P. & S.S. Press B. 2008. 5000. 4-18.

S E C R E T.

Co py No.....4......

XIII CORPS COUNTER BATTERY OPERATION ORDER No: 33.

1. Our Right Division intend to exploit the success of the Division this afternoon 3rd inst.

2. Hostile Batteries will be neutralized as follows -

10 H.A.Brigade.

113 Siege Battery. S.6b. 80.30. 70.50. S.12c. 80.70. S.12c. 95.30.
150 Heavy Battery. T.8a. 60.80. and 1st, 3rd etc N.F. or A.N.F. calls.
159 Heavy Battery. T.7d. 50.40 and 2nd, 4th etc N.F. or A.N.F. calls.

52 H.A.Brigade.

164 Siege Battery. T.7c. 30.20.

498 Siege Battery. T1.d. 80.80. N.32c.80.90 and long range N.F. calls in N.C. square.

11 A.H.A.Brigade.

544 Siege Battery. T.4c. 80.30. T.2b. 80.80 and long range N.F. calls in T.A. square.

3. C.B.S.O. 1st Corps is arranging to engage active batteries which might fire during the operation.

4. RATE OF FIRE.

Zero to Zero plus 5 minutes. RAPID.
Zero plus 5 minutes to Zero plus 30 minutes. NORMAL.
Zero plus 30 minutes to cease fire. VERY SLOW.

5. Zero hour will be communicated by so many minutes from 5.p.m. Thus. 5.15 p.m.= plus fifteen.
Signal for H.A. to open fire will be opening of F.A. Barrage.

6. ACKNOWLEDGE BY WIRE.

Kearmont

Lieut Co lonel R.A.
C.B.S.O. XIII Corps. R.A.

3rd September 1918.

To:-
1 3. XIII Corps R.A.
4. XIII Corps H.A.
5. 21 Squadron. R.A.F.
6. 20 K.B.Coy.
7. 46 Division.
8. 46 Div. Arty.
9 12. 10 H.A.Brigade.
13 15. 52 H.A.Brigade.
16. 11th Army Brigade. R.G.A.
17. 544 Siege Battery.

46th DIVISION. No. 4/167

Date 3. Sept 18

G.O.C.

G.S.O. 1

G.S.O. 2

G.S.O. 3

Int. Offr.

Att. Offr.

Q. A.

C.R.A. C.R.E.

A.D.M.S. M.G. Batt.

Signals

RETURN TO "G" OFFICE.

Printed in France by A.P. & S.S. Press B. 2008. 5000. 4-18.

~~SECRET~~ Copy No. 26

HEAVY ARTILLERY XIII CORPS INSTRUCTIONS No. 90.

Issued in conjunction with Counter Battery Operation Order No. 32

The 19th and 46th Divisions will co-operate A.M. on the 3rd instant with objective running M.26.b.50.90. - M.27.c.2.5. - M.33.c.05.00. - S.2.d.08.00. after which patrols will be pushed forward after Zero plus 49 minutes.

The following targets will be engaged.

Battery	Guns.	Time		Target.
226 Sge.	2	Zero	to Zero plus 3'	M.32.a.36.95.
259 Sge	Le HAMEL	Zero	to Zero plus 3'	M.32.a.28.65.
259 Sge	Rear	Zero	to Zero plus 3'	M.32.c.6.7.
164 Sge		Zero	to Zero plus 3'	M.26.c.67.82.
264 Sge		Zero	to Zero plus 5'	S.2.a.7.9. Stop
226 Sge		Zero plus 3'	to Zero plus 5'	M.26.a.65.60.
259 Sge		Zero plus 3'	to Zero plus 5'	M.26.c. Cross Roads Croix Barbee.
259 Sge	Rear	Zero plus 3'	to Zero plus 7'	M.32.b.3.3. Stop
164 Sge		Zero plus 3'	to Zero plus 10'	M.32.d.7.3.
226 Sge		Zero plus 5'	to Zero plus 10'	M.26.d.65.60.
259 Sge		Zero plus 5'	to Zero plus 12'	M.32.d.95.95.
226 Sge		Zero plus 10'	to Zero plus 16'	M.27.c.0.8.
164 Sge		Zero plus 10'	to Zero plus 35'	M S.33.b.2.6.
259 Sge		Zero plus 12'	to Zero plus 30'	M.33.b.25.50.
226 Sge		Zero plus 16'	to Zero plus 30'	M.33.a.95.60.
164 Sge		Zero plus 35'	to Zero plus 49'	M.34.a.2.9.
259 Sge		Zero plus 30'	to Zero plus 49'	M.34.a.25.15.
226 Sge		Zero plus 30'	to Zero plus 49'	M.34.a.2.9.
159 Hvy	2	Zero	to Zero plus 25'	Rouge Croix Cross Roads M.33.b.0.6. - M.27.d.2.2.
10 Sge	2	Zero	to Zero plus 49'	S.3.d.8.8. LANSDOWN
12" Hows.				
	1	Zero	to Zero plus 25'	M.27.b.1.8. Rouge Croix.
		Zero plus 25'	to Zero plus 49'	M.22.c.3.4.
	1	Zero	to Zero plus 25'	M.33.b.3.5. LORETTO
		Zero plus 25'	to Zero plus 45'	M.34.a.2.9.
	1	Zero	to Zero plus 35'	S.3.d.8.8. LANSDOWN
		Zero plus 35'	to Zero plus 49'	M.34.c.6.5.
544 Sge	Rear 1	Zero	to Zero plus 50'	M.29.c.6.6. ~~Cross~~ Roads FAUQUISSART
	1	Zero	to Zero plus 50'	M.22.c.3.4. - M.22.b.8.5. Road. 1 round per minute.

~~After Zero plus 49'~~

Rate of fire

6" How.	XO Fire	40 seconds.
60 Pdr.	XO Fire	40 seconds.
9.2"	XO Fire	2 minutes.
12" How.		1 round per 3 minutes.

Zero hour in separate cover

P.T.O.

Watches will be synchronized by 10th and 52nd Brigades with 19th Division, 11th Army Brigade with XIII Corps H.A.

Ammunition

Hows. H.E, 106 Fuze.
60 pdr. Shrapnel.

Instructions as to further action will be issued from these Headquarters.

PLEASE ACKNOWLEDGE RECEIPT.

for Major. R.G.A.

2nd Spptember 1918. a/Brigade Major Heavy Arty. XIII Corps.

DISTRIBUTION:-

Copies			
1 to 3	File.
4 to 6	R.A. XIII Corps.
7 to 14	10th Brigade R.G.A.
15 to 22	52nd Brigade R.G.A.
23	C.B.S.O. XIII Corps.
24	19th Division "G"
25	19th Division Arty.
26	46th Division "G"
27	~~46th Division Arty.~~
28	No. 21 Squadron R.A.F.
29	No. 20 K.B.Coy. R.A.F..
30 to 37	11th Army Bde RGA

Copy No....9.....

SECRET.

XIII CORPS COUNTER BATTERY OPERATION ORDER No: 32.

1. In support of an attack by our Left Division and possible exploitation by the Right Division tomorrow 3rd September 1918, Hostile Batteries will be neutralized as follows -

10 H.A.Brigade

113 Siege Battery. S.6b. 68.40(A) T.1a. 28.66 (B) M.36b. 92.60 (C).
150 Heavy Battery. N.31b.65.05 (A) T.2a.50.00 (B). T.2a. 03.67 (C).
159. do. T.7a. 75.67 (A).T.7d.90.10 (B) remaining section to take up "N.F" calls.

52 H.A.Brigade.

164 Siege Battery (Forward). S.6d.30.20.
498 do M. 24a.50.50 (A).N.31d. 70.80 (B).

11 A.H.A.Brigade.

544 Siege Battery. T.2b. 80.80.

2. Rate of fire.
Zero to Zero plus 5 minutes. RAPID.
Zero plus 5 minutes to Zero plus 49 minutes. NORMAL.
Zero plus 49 minutes to further orders. VERY SLOW.

Each new "N.F" will be engaged with a rapid burst of 5 minutes.

3. O.C. 21st Squadron will please detail 2 Artillery patrol machines, one to observe the M.D, N. C. squares and the other S.B, T.A. squares.

113 Siege Btty will answer N.F.& A.N.F. or G.F. calls in M.D.squares.

164 Siege Battery. do do do S.B. do (less S.6b & d)

150 Heavy Battery. do do do N.C.squares.

159 Heavy Battery. do do do T.A. plus S.6.b & d.

498 Siege Battery. calls beyond reach of 60 Pdrs in N.C. squares.

544 Siege Battery. do do T.A. do

Batteries will drop their targets in favour of "N.F" calls in the order C. B. A. and the new target will be engaged.

Continued.

3. (Contd)

C.B.S.O. 1st Corps and Xl Corps are arranging to take up N.F. A.N.F. calls in their areas, which may affect our operations.

4. Zero hour will be communicated to Brigades by Divisions.

5. All Neutralization Fire will take the form of searching and sweeping.

6. ACKNOWLEDGE BY WIRE.

Lieut Colonel. R.A.
C.B.S.O. Xlll Corps. R.A.

2nd September 1918.

To:-

1 3. Xlll Corps R.A.
4. Xlll Corps H.A.
5. 21 Squadron. R.A.F.
6. 20 K.B. Coy.
7. 19 Division.
8. 19 Div Arty.
9. 46 Division.
10. 46 Div Arty.
11 14. 10. H.A.Brigade.
15 17. 52. H.A.Brigade.
18. Xl. Army Brigade. R.G.A. (copy direct to 544 Siege Btty.)
19. 544 Siege Battery.
20. C.B.S.O. 1st Corps.
21. C.B.S.O. Xl Corps.

46th DIVISION. No. 4/165

Date 2 Sept 18

G.O.C. ....

G.S.O. 1 W

G.S.O. 2 ....

G.S.O. 3 [illegible]

Int. Offr. [illegible]

Att. Offr. [illegible]

Q. .... A. ....

C.R.A. .... C.R.E. ....

A.D.M.S. .... M.G. Batt. ....

Signals ....

RETURN TO "G" OFFICE.

Printed in France by A.P. & S.S. Press B. 2008. 5000. 4-18.

Secret.

G.329/207.

All recipients of 138th. Inf. Bde. Order No. 242.

Reference 138th. Infantry Brigade Order No. 242 of 2nd September.

Zero Hour will be 5-30 a.m.

Acknowledge.

46TH DIVISION.
GENERAL STAFF.
No. 4/165
Date 2.9.18

Captain,

for Brigade Major, 138th. Infantry Bde.

2nd September 1918.

Secret.
****

Addendum No. 1 to

138th. Inf. Bde. Order No. 242.

2nd September 1918.

The following notes on the 19th Division arrangements are issued in continuation of 138th. Inf. Bde. Order of the 2nd September.

1. At Zero Hour, the Artillery Barrage will open 200 yards in front of the 19th Division Jumping Off Line and will advance at the rate of 100 yards in 2 minutes. Ten minutes after reaching the Final Objective the Protective barrage will cease.

2. The 19th Division attack will be covered by a number of our aeroplanes flying low and attacking the enemy with M.G. fire.

The following apply equally to the 46th Division. :-

1. A Contact Aeroplane will call for flares at 7-00 a.m. Flares will be lit by troops on the Final Objective and by Forward Patrols.

2. O.C. Signals, 46th Division will synchronize watches with the 19th Division to-day at 7-00 p.m. and 12 midnight, 2nd/3rd September. He will further arrange for the synchronization of watches with the C.R.A., 138th. and 139th. Infantry Bdes 46th Battn: M.G.C., at 8-00 p.m. 2nd September and 1-00 a.m. 3rd September.

Acknowledge.

for. Captain,

for Brigade Major, 138th. Inf. Bde.

Issued at 8 p.m. to :-

All recipients of 138th. Inf. Bde. Order No.242.

Secret.
****

Copy No. 7
****

138th. Infantry Brigade Order No. 242.
****

Reference maps :-
Gorre & Vieille Chapelle.
****

Headquarters,
2nd Sept '18.
****

1. The 19th Division is attacking on the morning of 3rd September 1918, and the 46th Division will conform and be prepared for further advance.

2. The present line of our troops is shewn in Red on attached trace: the first objective of 19th Division being shewn in Blue, and final objective of XIII Corps in Green. (Map issued to those marked *).

3. The 139th. Infantry Brigade are arranging for the capture of the 46th Division objective.

4. Silent batteries will not fire on barrage lines but will be prepared to open fire if necessary for exploiting success or in case of counter-attack.

5. The whole line will be prepared to advance should the enemy shew signs of retiring, patrols being pushed forward towards the line - RUM CORNER - PATH POST - ORCHARD POST - DOGS POST - EDWARD POST - HENS POST.

6. The 5th Lincolnshire Regt will ensure liaison with Battalions on left flank and in case of an advance will establish a liaison post at ORCHARD POST.

7. Zero hour will be notified by wire - minutes minus or plus from 5-00 a.m. e.g. if Zero is 5-30 a.m., order will be plus 30'.

8. Acknowledge.

Captain,

for Brigade Major, 138th. Infantry Brigade.

Issued through Signals at 7 p.m. to :-

Copy No.1. Bde Major for B.G.C.
2. Staff Captain.
3. 5th Lincs Regt. *
4. 4th Leics Regt. *
5. 5th Leics Regt. *
6. 138th. T.M.Bty. *
7. 46th Division. "
8. 139th. Inf. Bde.
9. 165th. Inf. Bde. *
10. Gorre Group R.F.A. *
11. M. G. Group. *
12. Brigade Signals.
13 & 14. War Diary

46th DIVISION. No. 4/164

Date 2 Sept 18

G.O.C. To see Jk

G.S.O. 1

~~G.S.O. 2~~

G.S.O. 3

Int. Offr.

Att. Offr.

Q. A.

C.R.A. C.R.E.

A.D.M.S. M.G. Batt.

Signals

RETURN TO "G" OFFICE.

Printed in France by A.P. & S.S. Press B. 2008. 5000. 4-18.

S E C R E T.

Copy No 10

46th BATTALION MACHINE GUN CORPS WARNING ORDER No 57.

46TH DIVISION, GENERAL STAFF. No. 4/164 Date 2.9.18

Reference Maps 36a.S.E. & 36 S.W.) 1/20,000
GORRE.)

1\. FIRST OBJECTIVE. Orders have been received that, at a very early date, the 46th and 19th Divisions will attack and occupy such portions of the following line as are not already in our possession :-

L'EPINETTE EAST POST (S.19.a.) - River in S.8.a. and C. - RICHEBOURG ST.VAAST - CROIX BARBEE.

2\. SECOND OBJECTIVE. Subsequently an operation will be carried out to establish the General Line ROUGE CROIX - PONT LOGY (M.34.c.) WINDY CORNER (S.9.a.6.9) - S.15.a.3.6 to SOUTHERN DIVISIONAL BOUNDARY, about S.27.a.5.5.

3\. FIRST ATTACK. Group and Company Commanders will at once put in hand all preparations for supporting those attacks as follows :-
For the attack detailed in Para.I. by covering fire from as many guns as can be brought to bear upon the enemy's probable lines of approach to the objective, and, if required by the Brigade Commander concerned, by sending guns forward to assist in consolidation and defence of the objective.

4\. SECOND ATTACK. For the attack detailed in Para.2, 'D' Company will be allotted to the right Brigade and will detail sections as under.
One Section for the immediate defence of the captured objective.
One Section as a mobile battery of opportunity, which will remain on the right flank, and will be always in readiness to protect it against counter attacks.
One Section for the provision of Barrage fire from about the first objective.
One Section as a Reserve.

B.Company will be allotted to the Left Brigade and will detail sections as under :-
One Section for the immediate defence of the captured objective.
One Section as a Battery of opportunity.
One Section for the provision of Barrage Fire from about the first objective.
One Section as a Reserve.

The Reserve Sections will be disposed where they can bring fire to bear over the heads of our own troops when they have reached the objective, and will be allotted areas to barrage.
The Batteries of opportunity will take advantage of every chance of inflicting loss on the enemy and will give close support by direct fire to the infantry during counter attacks. They will also engage low flying hostile aeroplanes and keep in close touch with infantry commander.

C.Company will be disposed as follows for the defence of the Line of Retention.
One Section in Nos.1, 2, 3 & 4 Positions.
One Section in Nos 5, 6, 9 & 10 Positions.
One Section in LOISNE CENTRAL & X.17.c.
One Section in X.17.a. and SLOANE SQUARE.

5\. DETAILS. Orders for the rearrangement of guns in readiness for the attack will be issued later. In the meantime the officers concerned will make all possible reconnaissance of the ground, carefully avoiding unnecessary movement by day, and will make all preparations such as the provision of S.A.A. dumps well forward, the selection of battery positions, assembly areas and Battle Headquarters so that the above arrangements may be put into operation at very short notice.

As/

As far as possible the guns nearest the final positions will be chosen to move forward and ammunition etc should be taken up by pack or limber as far as possible the night before the attack.

6. DIAGRAM. A diagram showing the action of the machine guns and their approximate disposition after the objective has been consolidated is attached. This is not intended in any way to tie down Group and Company Commanders to the positions shown thereon, but is merely to show the general scheme upon which the machine guns will be employed.

7. ACKNOWLEDGE.

Issued at 7-0 pm.

2/9/1918.

Major,
46th Battn.Machine Gun Corps.

Distribution:-

1. A. Coy.
2. B. Coy.
3. C. Coy.
4. D. Coy.
5. No.1 Group
6. No 2 Group
7.) War Diary.
8.)
9. File.
10. 46th Division.
11. 19th Bn.M.G.Corps.
12. 55th Bn.M.G.Corps.
13. 137th Inf:Bde.
14. 138th Inf:Bde.
15. 139th Inf:Bde.

Q
R
W
X
SECRET.
MACHINE GUN DISPOSITIONS AFTER FINAL OBJECTIVE HAS BEEN GAINED.
THIS TRACING TO BE SUPERIMPOSED ON "LE HAMEL" SHEET. SCALE 1/20000.
46TH BATN M.G.C.
SEPT. 2ND 1918.
DIVISIONAL BOUNDARY
R
M
X
S
BRIGADE BOUNDARY
DIVISIONAL BDY

46th DIVISION. **No.** 4/163

Da[te] 2 Sept 18

G.O.C.

G.S.O. 1

G.S.O. 2

G.S.O. 3

Int. Offr.

Att. Offr.

Q. A.

C.R.A. C.R.E.

A.D.M.S. M.G. Batt.

Signals

RETURN TO "G" OFFICE.

Printed in France by A.P. & S.S. Press B. 2008. 5000. 4-18.

48TH DIVISION,
GENERAL STAFF.
No. 4/163
Date 2.9.18

S E C R E T
* * * * * *

No.199/1.

To:-

All recipients of 139 I.Bde. Order No. 199.

1. ZERO HOUR will be 5.30 am., Sept.3rd.

2. ACKNOWLEDGE.

Done

[signature]

Captain.
Brigade Major, 139th Inf.Brigade.

2/9/18.

S E C R E T
* * * * * *

Copy No. 1.

139th INFANTRY BRIGADE ORDER No. 199

Ref :- Map attached, or
36.a.S.E., & 36.S.W., 1/20,000.

September 2nd, 1918.

1. The 19th Division is attacking on the morning of the 3rd September. The 139th Infantry Brigade will conform to their movements and be prepared to exploit success.

2. Attached map (issued to Units marked *) shews :-

   RED - Jumping off line of the 19th Divn.
   GREEN - First objective of the 19th Divn.

   VIOLET - Final objective of the XIII Corps.

   Boundaries are shown in Brown.

3. The 1/6th Sherwood Foresters will capture and consolidate that portion of the XIII Corps final objective within the Brigade boundary.

4. A minor operation by 1/6th Sherwood Foresters is now in progress, for the capture of RICHEBOURG Post; should this prove successful, the 1/6th Sherwood Foresters will give every assistance to the advance of the 57th Infantry Brigade by bringing rifle and Lewis Gun fire to bear on enemy snipers and M.G. firing from South Eastern outskirts of RICHEBOURG and will engage with fire any of the enemy seen running away.

5. Should this minor operation not prove successful, the 1/6th Sherwood Foresters will capture RICHEBOURG POST to-morrow morning, jumping off from present Outpost Line at ZERO plus 15 minutes.
   The 139 T.M.Battery will co-operate with 2 guns, by bombarding RICHEBOURG POST from ZERO to ZERO plus 14'
   At ZERO plus 28' an advance will be made to the XIII Corps final objective and posts established.
   Final liaison post with the 57th Infantry Brigade will be established by 1/6th Sherwood Foresters at RAG POST.
   The closest touch and liaison must be maintained by the 1/6th Sherwood Foresters with the right flank Battalion of the 57th Infantry Brigade.

6. After the capture of the final objective, should the enemy shew signs of retiring, the whole line will be prepared to advance and patrols will be pushed forward towards PATH POST-ORCHARD POST - DOG'S POST - EDWARD POST and HENS POST.
   The 19th Division are arranging that after the capture of the final objective, patrols shall be pushed forward towards LANDSDOWNE POST - LORETTO POST and ROUGE CROIX WEST POST.

7. The 8th Sherwood Foresters will place an additional Company in the Line of Retention by 5 am., 3rd instant.

8. The ESSARS Artillery Group will bombard from ZERO plus 12' to ZERO plus 30', the following points - ORCHARD POST, DOGS POST, WINDY CORNER, EDWARD POST, HENS POST.
   This bombardment will take place irrespective of whether we hold RICHEBOURG POST at ZERO or not.

9.

9. ZERO hour will be notified later - ZERO is the hour at which the 19th Divn leave their 'jumping off line'

10. Watches will be synchronised at 139 Brigade H.Qrs., at 1 am 3rd instant. Brigade Signal Officer will arrange for a synchronised watch to be delivered to 6th Sherwood Foresters by 3 am, 3rd instant.

11. A contact aeroplane will call for flares at 7 am. Flares will be lit by troops on the final objective and by forward patrols.

12. The 8th Sherwood Foresters will relieve the 6th Sherwood Foresters in the OUTPOST LINE on night 3rd/4th September, the latter moving into Brigade RESERVE on relief. The 5th Sherwood Foresters will take over Brigade Support positions from the 8th Sherwood Foresters prior to the latter moving forward to relieve the OUTPOST LINE. All arrangements for relief will be made between Commanding Officers concerned.

13. ACKNOWLEDGE.

Captain.
Brigade Major, 139th Infantry Brigade.

Issued at 8.30 pm., to :-

Copy No. 1. 46th Division.
2. 138th Inf.Brigade.
3. 57th Infantry Brigade.
4. ESSARS GROUP R.A.
5. No. 2 M.G.Group.
6. 465 Field Coy.R.E.
7. 5th Sherwood Foresters *
8. 6th Sherwood Foresters *
9. 8th Sherwood Foresters *
10. 139 T.M.Battery *
11. Brigade Signal Officer.

46th DIVISION. No. 4/162

Date 2. 9. 18

G.O.C. [illegible]

G.S.O. 1 [illegible]

G.S.O. 2

G.S.O. 3 [illegible]

Int. Offr. [illegible]

Att. Offr. [illegible]

Q. A.

C.R.A. C.R.E.

A.D.M.S. M.G. Batt.

Signals

RETURN TO "G" OFFICE.

Printed in France by A.P. & S.S. Press B. 2008. 5000. 4-18.

SECRET 46th: DIVISIONAL ARTILLERY COPY NO...3...

ORDER NO. 305.

****

2nd: SEPTEMBER, 1918.

46th DIVISION GENERAL STAFF. No. 4/162 Date 2.9.18

(1) The 19th: Division will carry out an operation on the morning of September 3rd:, to establish their line East of RICHEBOURG ST VAAST.

(2) Zero will be notified later.

(3) The 46th: Divisional Artillery will co-operate as follows :-

(i) ESSARS GROUP.

ZERO to ZERO Plus 12 Minutes.

6 - 18 Pounders will enfilade Line of Trenches from M.32.a.70.70. to CROIX ROUGE.

ZERO to ZERO Plus 10 Minutes.

One Section 4.5" Hows: will Bombard CROIX BARBEE Cross Roads M.26.d.90.20.

(ii) GORRE GROUP.

ZERO to ZERO Plus 8 Minutes.

6 - 18 Pounders will engage Houses in RICHEBOURG ST VAAST in S.2.a.

ZERO to ZERO Plus 6 Minutes.

One Section 4.5" Hows: Will Bombard Roads and Houses S.2.a.40.00. to S.2.a.80.90.

RATES OF FIRE - INTENSE. 18 Pdrs: 70% Shrapnel.

(4) On completion of above tasks the 18 Pdrs: and Hows: that have been engaged will harass the following Roads and Points at a SLOW Rate of Fire until ZERO Plus 60 Minutes.

ESSARS GROUP.

6 - 18 Pounders. WINDY CORNER (S.9.a.) to LA BASSEE RD.

2 - 4.5" Hows: Bombard LANSDOWN POST S.3.d. and 4.c.

GORRE GROUP.

6 - 18 Pounders. FACTORY CORNER (S.9.d.) to LA BASSEE RD.

2 - 4.5" Hows: Bombard FACTORY CORNER.

(5) All Batteries will Stand To from ZERO, and be prepared to repel a Counter Attack, or to support our own Infantry to exploit any success.

(6) The 19th: Divisional Artillery are keeping their fire North of a Line running East and West through RICHEBOURG Cross Roads S.2.c.1.8.

(7) ACKNOWLEDGE.

[signature]

Captain R.A.
A/Brigade Major.
46th: Divisional Artillery.

Headquarters R.A.
ISSUED AT 6 p.m.

P.T.O.

COPIES NO.

1	ESSARS GROUP.	
2	GORRE GROUP.	
3	46th: Division.	For information.
4	R.A. XIII Corps.	
5	H.A. XIII Corps.	
6	55th: Div: Arty:	
7	19th: Div: Arty:	
8	D.T.M.O.	
9	52nd: Brigade R.G.A.	
10	21st: Squadron R.A.F.	
11	C.B.S.O.	
12	137th: Infantry Bde:	
13	138th: Infantry Bde:	
14	139th: Infantry Bde:	
15	S.C.R.A.	
16-17	War Diary.	
18	File.	

46th DIVISION. No. 4/161

Date 2. 9. 18

G.O.C.

G.S.O. 1

G.S.O. 2

G.S.O. 3

Int. Offr.

Att. Offr.

Q. A.

C.R.A. C.R.E.

A.D.M.S. M.G. Batt.

Signals

RETURN TO "G" OFFICE.

Printed in France by A.P. & S.S. Press B. 2008. 5000. 4-18.

SECRET

HEADQUARTERS.
46th: Division.
R.A. XIII Corps.
H.A. XIII Corps.
C.B.S.O.
21st: Squadron R.A.F.
46th: Bn: M.G. Corps.
O.C.
52nd: Brigade R.G.A.
Divisional Ammunition Column.
R.A. Signals.

In continuation of 46th: Divisional Artillery Order No. 304 of 1st: September :-

Dispositions of Divisional Artillery.

ESSARS GROUP.

A/230 Battery.	6 Guns	X.15.b.35.84.
B/230 Battery.	6 Guns	X.16.d.75.30.
C/230 Battery.	6 Guns	X.10.d.10.20.
A/46 Battery.	6 Guns	X.16.b.20.30.
D/46 Battery.	4 Hows:	X.15.d.95.30.
	2 Hows:	X.16.c.95.30.

GORRE GROUP.

A/231 Battery.	6 Guns	X.21.d.02.20.
B/231 Battery.	6 Guns	F.3.a.80.10.
C/231 Battery.	6 Guns	F.2.b.00.60.
B/46 Battery.	6 Guns	F.9.b.40.30.
C/46 Battery.	6 Guns	X.22.d.80.85.
D/231 Battery.	4 Hows:	F.3.b.10.90.
	2 Hows:	X.29.a.05.70.

R.J. Martin.
Captain R.A.
A/Brigade Major.
46th: Divisional Artillery.

Headquarters R.A.
1/9/18

46th DIVISION. No. 4/160

Date ....

G.O.C. .... Jk

G.S.O. 1 ....

G.S.O. 2 ....

G.S.O. 3 ....

Int. Offr. ....

Att. Offr. ....

Q. .... A. ....

C.R.A. .... C.R.E. ....

A.D.M.S. .... M.G. Batt. ....

Signals ....

RETURN TO "G" OFFICE.

Printed in France by A.P. & S.S. Press B. 2008. 5000. 4-18.

SECRET 46th: DIVISIONAL ARTILLERY COPY NO....4..

ORDER NO. 304.

******

REFERENCE - 36 S.W. & 36 A. S.E. 1/20.000.

1st: September, 1918.

(1) The 138th: Infantry Brigade will relieve the 139th: Infantry Brigade in the Southern Section of the Divisional Sector tonight the 1st:/2nd: September.

(2) The Boundary between Brigades in the line will be as shown on attached tracing (to Groups only).

(3) At 7 p.m. tonight the following will become the Line of RETENTION, for the maintenance of which the whole resources of the Division may be used.

TUNING FORK Switch from Southern Divisional Boundary at Junction with 55th: Division's Line of Retention in F.5.b. - LOISNE Central Post - Breastwork through X.22.b. - X.17.a. - SLOANE SQUARE to Northern Divisional Boundary at X.5.d.8.6.

(4) S.O.S. Barrages will be arranged to protect :-

(i) Outpost Line at the moment.

(ii) Battle Zone - i.e. new Line of RETENTION (Para: 3)

S.O.S. Signals :-

(i) From Outpost Zone RED/RED/RED.

(ii) From Line of RETENTION. GREEN/GREEN/GREEN.

(5) The Outpost Line of Resistance will be the general line L'EPINETTE. E. - L'EPINETTE N. -CHAVATTE'S Post - thence RUE DES CHAVATTES to KING GEORGE'S Road thence along the Road to the line of Retention.

Minor enemy attacks will be held on this line.

In the event of a serious attack which cannot be held here, the Outposts will fall back fighting on to the Line of Retention. (Para: 3).

(6) On completion of above relief, the Divisional Artillery will again be divided into two Groups as before.

(7) The following moves of Batteries will take place and be completed by midnight tonight.

ESSARS GROUP.

A/230 Battery.	6 Guns	to	X.10.c.
B/230 Battery.	6 Guns	to	X.15.c.
C/230 Battery.	6 Guns	to	X.10.d.
A/46 Battery.	6 Guns	to	X.13.b.
D/46 Battery.	6 Guns	to	X.13.c.

GORRE GROUP.

A/231 Battery.	4 Guns	to	(being reconnoitred)
	2 Guns	to	F.17.b.15.80.
B/231 Battery.	6 Guns	to	F.5.a.8.1.
C/231 Battery.	6 Guns	to	X.21.c.02.20.
D/231 Battery.	4 Hows:	to	F.3.b.10.90.
	2 Hows:	to	X.29.a.05.70.
B/46 Battery.	6 Guns	to	F.9.b.4.6.
C/46 Battery.	6 Guns	to	X.22.d.80.85.

Exact Locations will be wired to this office by Groups as soon as possible.

(8) Groups will arrange to do their Harassing Fire with Roving Guns.

(9) AMMUNITION.

Batteries will have 300 rounds a gun up by tonight, and 450 rounds a Gun up by Midnight 2nd:/3rd: September.

Ammunition should be moved forward from positions being vacated, and kept boxed as far as possible.

(10) HEADQUARTERS.

Left Infantry Brigade and ESSARS Group. at ESSARS.

Right Infantry Brigade and GORRE Group. at F.13.central.

P.T.O.

CONTINUED (2)

ACKNOWLEDGE.

Captain R.A.
A/Brigade Major.
46th: Divisional Artillery.

Headquarters. R.A.

ISSUED AT 5 p.m.

COPIES NO.

1 ESSARS GROUP.
2 GORRE GROUP.
3 46th: Brigade R.F.A.
4 46th: Division.
5 R.A. XIII Corps.
6 H.A. XIII Corps.
7 C.B.S.O.
8 137th: Infantry Bde:
9 138th: Infantry Bde:
10 139th: Infantry Bde:
11 21st: Squadron. R.A.F.
12 19th: Div: Arty:
13 55th: Div: Arty:
14 D.A.C.
15 D.T.M.O.
16 46th: Bn- M.G. Corps
17 R.A. Signals.
18 52nd: Brigade R.G.A.
19 S.C.R.A.
20 - 21 War Diary.
22 File.

46th DIVISION. No. 106/60

Date 4 Sept 18

G.O.C.

~~G.S.O. 1~~

~~G.S.O. 2~~

G.S.O. 3

Int. Offr.

Att. Offr.

Q. A.

C.R.A. C.R.E.

A.D.M.S. M.G. Batt.

Signals

RETURN TO "G" OFFICE.

Printed in France by A.P. & S.S. Press B. 2008. 5000. 4-18.

Secret.
****

G.329/211.
****

O.C. 5th Lincs Regt.
4th Leics Regt.
5th Leics Regt.
138th. T.M.Bty.
Brigade Signals.
Staff Captain.
****

O.C. 468th Fld Coy R.E.
Gorre M.G. Group.
Gorre Group R.F.A.
H.Q. 46th Division.
165th. Inf. Bde.
****

Enemy Withdrawal.
****

1. Our troops now occupy the Old British Front Line within the Divisional boundary. The 55th Division are arranging to occupy the same line on our RIGHT and the 19th Division are moving forward on our LEFT.

2. The enemy is located in his Old Front Line opposite the LEFT Brigade front, but opposite this Brigade front his position is not clear.

3. It is not the intention at present to push forward against enemy opposition; patrols will, however be sent out to gain touch with the enemy and occupy any ground which he has evacuated.

4. The Outpost Line of Resistance of the 46th Division will be as shown on the attached trace in BLUE: the Line of RETENTION is shown in RED.

5. In the event of hostile attacks, the first S.O.S. will be sent up by our foremost Posts; second from the Line of RETENTION.

6. The Brigade will be relieved tomorrow, and all preparations will be made to ensure that the area turned over is organized, so far as time permits either for offence or defence.
Roads are to be pushed forward - Forward Dumps will be established - Headquarters selected and Posts organized for defence.

F.L. Perrott
for Captain,

for Brigade Major, 138th. Infantry Brigade.

4th September 1918.
****

No trace enclosed

A R Ottewanders

Secret. G.329/212.
******* **********

O.C. 5th Lincs Regt.
4th Leics Regt.
5th Leics Regt.
138th. T.M.Bty.
H.Q. 139th. Inf. Bde.
165th. Inf. Bde.
H.Q. 46th Division.
Staff Captain.
O.C. 468th. Fld Coy R.E.
Gorre Group R.F.A.
Gorre M.G.Group.
Brigade Transport Officer.

****

1. The following dispositions will be taken up immediately on receipt of these instructions :-

(a) OUTPOST BATTALION - 5th Leicestershire Regt. - 2 Outpost Companies in Old British Front Line: Support Company in B. LINE and Breastworks about Road in S.14.d., and one Company disposed on right flank in S.21.b.
Battalion Headquarters - S.20.b.7.9.

(b) SUPPORT BATTALION - 5th Lincolnshire Regt - 2 Companies in S.14.c.& d. and S.20.a.& b., Support Companies about L'EPINETTE EAST & NORTH POSTS.
Battalion Headquarters - X.23.a.8.2.

(c) RESERVE BATTALION - 4th Leicestershire Regt - 2 Companies in X.23. and 24. between Old British Front Line and RUE du L'EPINETTE both exclusive; 2 Companies in Old British Front Line between LOISNE CENTRAL and Right Divisional Boundary.
Battalion Headquarters - Old Company Headquarters in TUNING FORK SUPPORT.

2. Maps shewing dispositions by platoons, also Company Headquarters, to be forwarded to this office by 6-00 p.m. today without fail.

3. The 4th & 5th LEICESTERSHIRE REGTS will arrange to leave rear parties at the Battalion Headquarters at F.10.a.4.8. and LE QUESNOY respectively.

4. All available water tins in the Brigade area will be collected at the Forward Headquarters of each Battalion.

[signature]
Captain,
for Brigade Major, 138th. Infantry Bde.

4th September 1918.
****

46th DIVISION. No. 106/59

Date 4.9.18

G.O.C.

G.S.O. 1

~~G.S.O. 2~~

G.S.O. 3

Int. Offr.

Att. Offr.

Q. A.

C.R.A. C.R.E.

A.D.M.S. M.G. Batt.

Signals

RETURN TO "G" OFFICE.

Printed in France by A.P. & S.S. Press B. 2008. 5000. 4-18.

S E C R E T.
* * * * * *

No. G.1829/12.

5th Sherwood Foresters.
6th Sherwood Foresters.
8th Sherwood Foresters.
139th T.M.Battery.
No. 2 Group M.G.C.
Staff Captain.

46th Division.
138th Infantry Brigade.
57th Infantry Brigade.
ESSARS Group R.A.
Brigade Signals.

ENEMY WITHDRAWAL.

1. Our troops now occupy the Old British Front Line within the Divisional Boundary. The 55th Division are arranging to occupy the same line on our RIGHT and the 19th Division are moving forward on our LEFT.

2. We have located the enemy in his Old Front Line opposite our LEFT Brigade Front; on the RIGHT, however, the 138th Infantry Brigade report that they are out of touch.

3. It is not the intention at present to push forward against enemy opposition; patrols will, however, be sent out to gain touch with the enemy and occupy any ground which he has evacuated.

4. The Outpost Line of Resistance of the 46th Division will be as shown on the attached Map in VIOLET: the Line of RETENTION is shewn in RED. Maps sent to all Battalions, Trench Mortar Battery and ESSARS Group R.A.

5. In the event of hostile attack, the first S.O.S. will be sent up by our foremost Posts; the second from the Line of RETENTION.

6. The 8th Battalion, Sherwood Foresters will hold the VIOLET line as the outpost line of Resistance with patrols in front in touch with the enemy.

7. The 5th Battalion, Sherwood Foresters will garrison the LINE OF RETENTION (RED LINE) This Battalion will also garrison the line of Posts ORCHARD to HENS both inclusive. (2 Coys on each line of posts.) Battalion Headquarters will move to S.7.d.?.2. Moves of this Battalion to be complete by 8 pm. to-night.

8. O.C. 139 T.M.Battery will place one Section at disposal of O.C. Outpost Battalion, two Sections will be disposed for defence of the LINE OF ~~RESISTANCE~~ (RETENTION) & one Section will be held in Reserve at Battery H.Qrs.

9. It is probable that the Division will be relieved almost immediately, and all preparations will be made to ensure that the area turned over is organized, so far as time permits, either for offence or defence.
Roads will be pushed forward - Forward Dumps established - Headquarters selected and Posts organised for defence.

[signature]
Captain.
Brigade Major, 139th Infantry Brigade.

4.9.18.

File

Secret.

C.R.A.	137th I.B.	46th Bn, MGC.	A.D.M.S.	S.S.O.
C.R.E.	138th :	1st Monmouths.	Div: Train.	D.A.D.V.S.
Signals.	139th :	A.A & Q.M.G.	A.P.M.	D.A.D.O.S.
Div: Depot.	Div: Wing.	D.G.O.	Camp C't.	
19th Div:	55th Div:	XIII Cps H.A.	XIII Corps (2).	

46th Division G.106/58. 4th September, 1918.

Enemy Withdrawal.

****

1. Our troops now occupy the Old British Front Line within the Divisional Boundary. The 55th Division are arranging to occupy the same line on our RIGHT and the 19th Division are moving forward on our LEFT.

2. We have located the enemy in his Old Front Line opposite our LEFT Brigade Front: on the RIGHT, however, the 138th Infantry Brigade report that they are out of touch.

3. It is not the intention at present to push forward against enemy opposition; patrols will, however, be sent out to gain touch with the enemy and occupy any ground which he has evacuated.

4. The Outpost Line of Resistance of the 46th Division will be as shown on the attached Map in BLUE: the Line of RETENTION is shown in RED. (Maps sent to 138th and 139th I.Bdes; traces to 19th and 55th Divs: XIII Corps H.A, XIII Corps, C.R.A and 46th Bn, MGC.)

5. In the event of hostile attack, the first S.O.S will be sent up by our foremost Posts; the second from the Line of RETENTION.

6. It is probable that the Division will be relieved almost immediately, and all preparations will be made to ensure that the area turned over is organized, so far as time permits, either for offence or defence.
Roads will be pushed forward - Forward Dumps established - Headquarters selected and Posts organised for defence.

Lieut-Colonel,
General Staff, 46th Division...

Identification Trace for use with Artillery Maps.

REFERENCE SHEET 36 S.W. 1/20000

TO ACCOMPANY 46TH DIV.

G.106/58.

SECRET
4·9·18

S

1 2 3 4

DIV BDY

7 8 9 10

BDE BDY

13 14 15 16

DIV BDY

19 20 21 22

NOTE.—(1). These traces are intended to facilitate the communication of information as to the position of targets, which have been located on a squared map.

(2). The squares on this trace are 500 yards in length on the 1/10,000 scale, 1,000 yards in length on the 1/20,000 scale, and 2,000 yards in length on the 1/40,000 scale.

(3). The squares on the trace are fitted to the squares of the map showing the targets, which are then drawn on the trace. Sufficient letters and numbers must also be added to enable the recipient to place the trace in the correct position on his own map. A little detail may also be traced, but this is not essential. The name and scale of the map to which the trace refers must be always given. The trace can be used for the 1/10,000, 1/20,000, or 1/40,000 scale.

G.S.G.S. 3023.

Tracing taken from Sheet ....

of the 1: .... *map of* ....

Signature .... *Date* ....

46th DIVISION. No. 106/57

Date 2 Sept 18

G.O.C. To See JK

G.S.O. 1 JK

G.S.O. 2

~~G.S.O. 3~~ [illegible]

Int. Offr. JK

Att. Offr. [illegible]

Q. A.

C.R.A. C.R.E.

A.D.M.S. M.G. Batt.

Signals To See [illegible]

RETURN TO "G" OFFICE.

Printed in France by A.P. & S.S. Press B. 2008. 5000. 4-18.

SECRET.
****

Copy No......4

XIII CORPS ORDER No. 147.
************************** 2nd September, 1918.

1. The distance to which our troops have advanced and the continuance of the enemy's withdrawal necessitates revision of our plans.

2. The policy will be to maintain touch with the enemy by the employment of a minimum force; with this force to act vigorously against enemy rear guards; and to be prepared to take advantage of opportunities created by success elsewhere.

3. To effect this policy a return to conditions as nearly as possible approximate to mobile warfare is necessary, and certain general objectives will be given to Divisions as circumstances require. The objectives will mark for purposes of Defence, the Battle positions, and the main forces will move up to them when the Advanced Guards have made good the ground for some 3000 - 5000 yards in advance.

4. In accordance with the above policy, the initial objective of the Corps is the general line TUNING FORK - LOISNE Central - LA COUTURE - VIEILLE CHAPELLE, and this will automatically become the Battle position as soon as the Advanced Guards are sufficiently in front of it.

The second objective of the Corps will be the general line RICHEBOURG L'AVOUE - ROUGE CROIX which will in turn become the Battle position as the advance progresses.

5. In order that touch may be maintained between Divisions during the present advance, and to ensure mutual co-operation, arrangements will be made for combined posts to operate on the flanks of Divisions.

I and XI Corps are issuing similar instructions to their Left and Right Divisions respectively.

6. As objectives are reached, Divisions will choose Battle positions in case of attack, and organize defences. It is not the intention at present to construct new works. It will, however, be necessary to strengthen localities and to improve and adapt such defences as exist and are suitable. The conversion to our use of existing wire entanglements in the area will save time and labour.

The bivouac positions of the troops will be carefully selected with a view to the defence of the Battle position.

The construction and protection of gun positions will be undertaken.

A system of inter-communication will be effected on a consistent plan.

7. Signal Communications will be run upon the lines laid down in S.S. 191 Chapter III.

A.D.Signals will arrange in conjunction with Divisions a succession of points on the line of advance of each.

These points are to be the most likely positions of Brigade and Divisional Headquarters, and Signals will make all such points Communication-Centres.

/All telephone

7. (Contd)
All telephone lines will be laid to these Communication-Centres only, and very early information as to their positions will be necessary to enable Signals to establish and equip them for Signal traffic as soon as they are needed.

8. A mobile reserve of Artillery at the disposal of the Corps, will be formed from those units which are training out of the line. The Counter Battery organization will be maintained as at present.

Ian Stewart

Brigadier-General,
General Staff.

Issued at 7 p.m.

Copies to -

No. 1 & 2	Fifth Army.
3	19th Division.
4	46th Division.
5 & 6	G.O.C.R.A.
7	Q.
8	C.E.
9	I.G.
10	A.D. Signals.
11	D.D.M.S.
12	A.P.M.
13	21 Squadron R.A.F.
14	I Corps.
15	XI Corps.
16	Diary.
17, 18, 19	File.

46th DIVISION. No. 106/56/57

Date 3 Sept 18

G.O.C. TO Sy [illegible] –

G.S.O. 1 [illegible]

G.S.O. 2

G.S.O. 3 [illegible]

Int. Offr. SR

Att. Offr. [illegible]

Q. A.

C.R.A. C.R.E.

A.D.M.S. M.G. Batt.

Signals

RETURN TO "G" OFFICE.

Printed in France by A.P. & S.S. Press B. 2008. 5000. 4-18.

SECRET.

55th Division No. G.S. 1420

165th Infantry Brigade.

1. The 19th Division attacked this morning and now occupy the line M.32.a.0.0. - M.27.b.7.4. - M.27.d.7.4. - LANSDOWNE POST.

2. To conform with this the Division on our left are advancing to the line RUM CORNER - HAYSTACK - PATH - ORCHARD - ALBERT - DOG'S - EDWARD'S - HEN'S - LANSDOWNE Posts, and have been ordered to carry out an operation about 5 p.m. today with the object of gaining the line TUBE STATION POST - PALL MALL (S.15.central) - FACTORY KEEP - FACTORY TRENCH - EDWARD'S Post (all inclusive).

Zero hour will be notified later in minutes from 5 p.m.

3. The 165th Infantry Brigade will co-operate with the Division on our left by attacking and gaining the line from S.27.a.20.20. to INDIAN VILLAGE (inclusive) and will establish a liaison post with the Division on our left at TUBE STATION Post.

4. The Right Brigade of the Division on our left have orders to be prepared to throw back a defensive flank to protect their Right.

5. Brigadier General Commanding 165th Infantry Brigade will arrange with Left Artillery Group Commander for the Artillery support required for the operation.

* 6. Copy of order of Division on our left is attached.

7. ACKNOWLEDGE.

R. T. Lee
Lieut-Colonel,
General Staff, 55th Division.

55th Division H.Q.,
3rd September, 1918.

Copies to :-
* Div.Artillery.
164th Inf.Bde.
* 48th Division.
* 1 Corps.

* Not attached.

46TH DIVISION GENERAL STAFF. No. 106/57 3·9·18

SECRET. 55th Division No. G.S.1421.

165th Inf. Brigade.

Reference 55th Division No. G.S.1420 of today's date.

1. The operation in question is postponed until the morning of 4th September.
Zero hour will be notified verbally to B.G.C. 165th Infantry Brigade.

2. Reference para. 5 of above letter and para. 6 of the order of the Division on our left attached thereto, the arrangements for artillery support will be made by the representative of C.R.A. 55th Division with B.G.C. 165th Infantry Brigade direct.

3. B.G.C. 165th Infantry Brigade will arrange to synchronize watches with Right Brigade of the Division on our left, and with O.C. our Left Artillery Group.

4. The B.G.C. of the Right Infantry Brigade of the Division on our left will be at Headquarters 165th Infantry Brigade at 6.30 pm today.

5. ACKNOWLEDGE.

Done

R.T. Lee

55th Division H.Q., Lieut-Colonel,

3rd September 1918. General Staff, 55th Division.

Copies to -
Div. Artillery.
164th Inf. Brigade.
46th Division.
I Corps.

46th DIVISION. No. 106/56

Date 2.9.18

G.O.C.

G.S.O. 1

G.S.O. 2

G.S.O. 3

Int. Offr.

Att. Offr.

Q. A.

C.R.A. C.R.E.

A.D.M.S. M.G. Batt.

Signals

RETURN TO "G" OFFICE.

Printed in France by A.P. & S.S. Press B. 2008. 5000. 4-18.

SECRET. Copy No. 14

19th DIVISION ORDER No. 236.

References to attached
1/10,000 Map.

2nd September 1918.

1. The 19th Division will, on the morning of 3rd Sept., advance to the general line RICHEBOURG ST. VAAST - CROIX BARBEE - M.26.b., which is believed to be the present hostile outpost Line of Resistance.

The attack will be carried out by the 57th and 58th Inf. Bdes.

2. Objectives and boundaries will be as shown on the attached map.

The rate of advance of the infantry will be 2 mins. per 100 yds. A pause of 5 mins. will be made on reaching the FETTES Rd. - OXFORD Rd. Line.

3. At Zero hour the artillery barrage will open 200 yds. in front of the Jumping Off Line and the infantry will advance as close up to it as possible before it lifts forward. Ten minutes after reaching the Final Objective the protective barrage will cease. Covering fire for the fighting patrols will be arranged by Brigadiers.

4. On the capture of the final objective, strong fighting patrols will be sent forward to gain ground towards the LA BASSEE Rd. and to try and occupy LANSDOWNE POST, LORETTO POST and ROUGE CROIX WEST POST.

46th Divn. will cover the right flank by occupying RICHEBOURG POST and WINDY CORNER.

59th Divn. will cover the left flank by occupying ETON and HARROW POSTS.

5. D.M.G.C. will arrange, in consultation with C.R.A. and Brigadiers to put down a M.G. Barrage on certain selected localities.

6. The attack will be covered by a number of our aeroplanes flying low and attacking the enemy with M.G. fire.

A contact aeroplane will call for flares at 7 a.m.

Flares will be lit by troops on the final objective and by patrols which have established themselves in localities further forward.

7. Joint Liaison Posts will be established at RAGS POST with 46th Divn. and at M.20.c.9.0. and M.20.d.5.0. with 59th Divn.

8. Watches will be synchronised today, under arrangements to be made by O.C. Divl. Signals, at 6 p.m. and 12 midnight.

-/ 9. P.T.O.

9. One battalion of the Reserve Bde. will be in position about X.2.a. and b. and R.32.c. and d. by 5 a.m. 3rd Sept. and will reconnoitre routes forward with a view to occupying the Line of Resistance along the West bank of the LAWE and LOISNE in case of necessity.

The Dr. Comdr. will have a liaison officer at Hd Qrs. of 58th Inf. Bde. from 5 a.m. onwards to keep him in touch with the situation.

The remainder of Reserve Bde. will be ready to move forward at ½ hour's notice from 5 a.m. onwards.

10. Zero hour will be 5.30 a.m. 3rd Sept.

11. ACKNOWLEDGE. Done

H F Montgomery
Lieutenant-Colonel,
General Staff.

Issued at 3-0 P.M.

to :-
File.
War Diary.
G.O.C.
A & Q.
19th D.A. x
C.R.E. o
Signals.
56th Bde.
57th Bde. x
58th Bde. x
D.M.G.C. x
5th S.W.B. o

46th Divn. x
59th Divn.
XIII Corps.
21st Squadron, R.A.F.

x Map already forwarded

o Map not forwarded

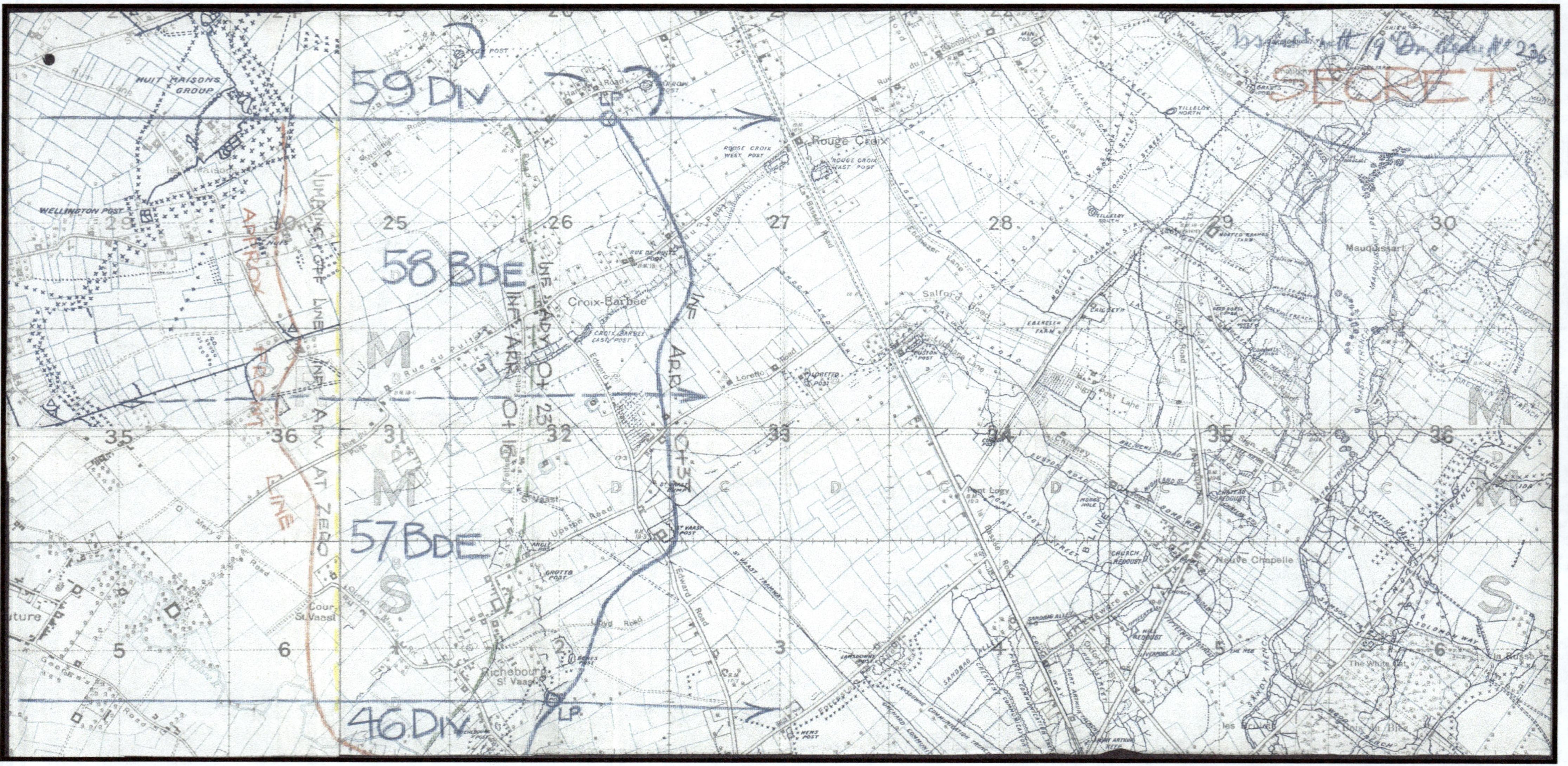

SECRET
59 DIV
58 BDE
57 BDE
46 DIV
INF ADV O+ 25
INF ARR O+ 16
INF ARR O+37
JUMPING OFF LINE INF ADV AT ZERO
APPROX FRONT LINE
LP
Rouge Croix
Croix-Barbée
Neuve Chapelle
Richebourg St Vaast
Cour St Vaast
Mauquissart
Salford Road
Loretto Road
Edward Road
Upstan Road
Sign Post Lane
Rue du Bois
Rue de Pulle
La Bassée Road
Huit Maisons Group
Wellington Post
The White City

Hangar	Shed, Hangar.
Hôpital	Hospital.
Hôtel-de-Ville	Town hall.
Houillère	Colliery.
Huilerie	Oil factory.
Imprimerie, Impr[ie]	Printing works.
Jetée	Pier.
Laminerie	Rolling mills.
Ligne / Laisse } de haute marée	High water mark.
„ de basse marée	Low „ „
Maison Forestière / M[on]. F[re].	Forester's house.
Malterie	Malt-house.
Marbrerie	Marble works.
Marais	Marsh.
Marais salant	Saltern, Salt marsh.
Marché	Market.
Mare	Pool.
Meule	Rick.
Minière	Mine.
Monastère	Monastery.
Moulin, M[in]	Mill.
„ à vapeur	Steam mill.
Mur	Wall.
„ crénelé	Loop-holed wall.

Peuplier	Poplar tree.
Phare	Light-house.
Pilier, Pil[r]	Post.
Plaine d'exercice	Drill ground.
Pompe	Pump.
Ponceau	Culvert.
Pont	Bridge.
„ levis	Drawbridge.
Poste / Station } de garde-côte	Coast-guard station.
Poteau P[au]	Post.
Poterie	Pottery.
Poudrière, Poud[re] / Magasin à poudre	Powder magazine.
Prise d'eau	Water supply.
Puits	Pit-head, Shaft, Well.
„ artésien	Artesian well.
„ d'aérage / „ ventilateur	Ventilating shaft.
„ de sondage	Boring.
Quai	Quay, Platform.
„ aux bestiaux	Cattle platform.
„ aux / „ des } marchandises	Goods platform.
Raccordement	Junction.
Raffinerie	Refinery.
„ de sucre	Sugar refinery
Râperie	Beet-root factory.

Scierie, Sc[ie]	Saw-mill.
Sondage	Boring.
Source	Spring.
Sucrerie, Suc[ie]	Sugar factory.
Tannerie	Tannery.
Tir à la cible	Rifle range.
Tissage	Weaving mill.
Tôlerie	Rolling mill
Tombeau	Tomb.
Tour	Tower.
Tourbière	Peat-bog, Peat-bed.
Tourelle	Small tower.
Tuilerie	Tile works.
Usine à gaz	Gas works.
„ électrique / „ d'électricité	Electricity works.
„ métallurgique	Metal works.
„ à agglomérés	Briquette factory.
Verrerie, Verr[ie]	Glass works.
Viaduc	Viaduct
Vivier	Fish Pond.
Voie de chargement / „ „ déchargement / „ „ d'évitement / „ „ formation / „ „ manœuvre	Siding.
Zinguerie	Zinc works.

given by the first figure. Thus the point Z would be [illegible] divisions East and 3 divisions North from origin.

3. When more accurate definition is wanted (on the 1 : 20,000 or 1 : 10,000 scales) use exactly the same method, but divide sides into 100 parts and use four figures instead of two. Thus 9847 denotes 98 parts East and 47 parts North of origin (see point X). Point Y is 6503.

4. Use 0 but not 10; use either two or four figures; do not use fractions (8½, 4½, etc.).

On squared maps all bearings should be given with reference to the vertical grid lines, which are parallel to the East and West edges of the sheet. Bearings should always be reckoned clockwise from 0° to 360°.

Grid bearings are less than compass bearings, the difference being called the deviation of the compass. To find out what this deviation is, take a compass bearing to a distant point, and measure on the map the grid bearing to that point. The difference between the two bearings is the deviation of that compass from Grid North. To obtain the grid bearing of any point this deviation must be subtracted from the compass bearing (adding 360° to the latter if necessary).

On this sheet the mean deviation of a normal compass is 11° 41', but to obtain accurate results the exact deviation of each compass should be tested as described above, and this test should be repeated in each locality.

TABLE FOR CONVERTING METRES TO FEET.

Mtrs.	0	1	2	3	4	5	6	7	8	9
0	0	3·3	6·6	9·8	13·1	16·4	19·7	23·0	26·2	29·5
10	32·8	36·1	39·4	42·6	45·9	49·2	52·5	55·8	59·0	62·3
20	65·6	68·9	72·2	75·4	78·7	82·0	85·3	88·6	91·8	95·1
30	98·4	101·7	105·0	108·2	111·5	114·8	118·1	121·4	124·6	127·9
40	131·2	134·5	137·8	141·0	144·3	147·6	150·9	154·1	157·4	160·7
50	164·0	167·3	170·6	173·8	177·1	180·4	183·7	187·0	190·2	193·5
60	196·8	200·1	203·4	206·6	209·9	213·2	216·5	219·8	223·0	226·3
70	229·6	232·9	236·2	239·4	242·7	246·0	249·3	252·6	255·8	259·1
80	262·4	265·7	269·0	272·2	275·5	278·8	282·1	285·4	288·6	291·9
90	295·2	298·5	301·8	305·0	308·3	311·6	314·9	318·1	321·4	324·7
100	328·0	331·3	334·6	337·8	341·1	344·4	347·7	351·0	354·3	357·5

INDEX TO ADJOINING SHEETS.

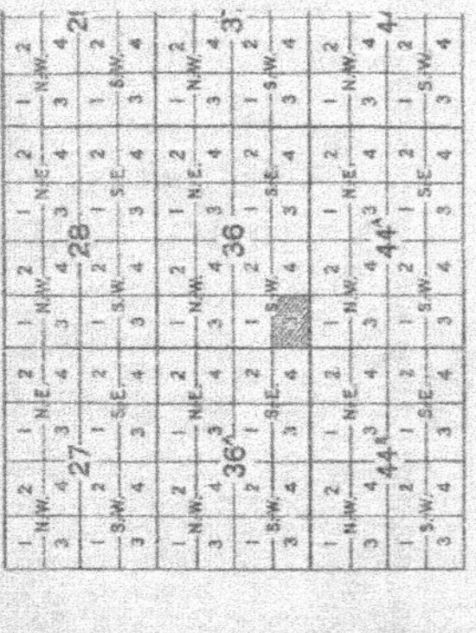

SECRET.

138th Infantry Brigade.
139th Infantry Brigade.
58th Division.

46th Division G.106/55. 2nd September, 1918.

Reference Map attached to 46th Divisional Order 316 -

The following should have been written against the first objective of 19th Division (GREEN LINE).

"Inf. arrive 0 + 18'
Inf. Advance 0 + 23'

[signature]

Lieut-Colonel,

General Staff, 46th Division.

46th DIVISION. No. 106/54

Date 2.9.18.

G.O.C. [illegible]

G.S.O. 1 [illegible]

~~G.S.O. 2~~

G.S.O. 3 [illegible]

Int. Offr. [illegible]

Att. Offr. [illegible]

Q. A.

C.R.A. C.R.E.

A.D.M.S. M.G. Batt.

Signals

RETURN TO "G" OFFICE.

Printed in France by A.P. & S.S. Press B. 2008. 5000. 4-18.

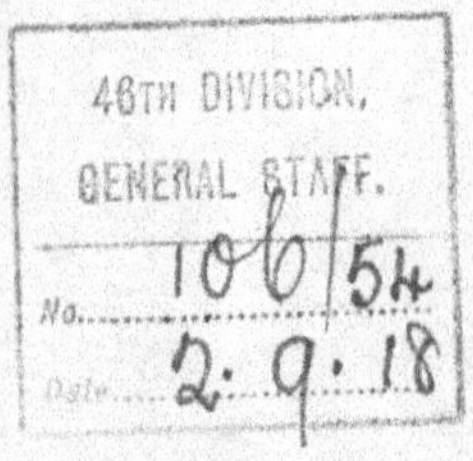

SECRET.
****

Copy No. 4

XIII CORPS ORDER No. 146.
****

2nd September, 1918.

1. The operation ordered in para. 1 of XIII Corps Order No. 145 will be carried out early to-morrow morning.

2. XI Corps are issuing orders to 59th Division to co-operate on the left flank of 19th Division and establish a line East of HARROW and CHARTER HOUSE POSTS (R.20).

3. Zero hour will be arranged by 19th Division in consultation with 59th and 46th Divisions and notified to Corps H.Q.

4. ACKNOWLEDGE.

[signature] Major for
Brigadier-General,
General Staff.

Issued at 12-30 p.m.

Copies to -

No. 1 & 2 Fifth Army.
3 19th Division.
4 46th Division.
5 & 6 G.O.C.R.A.
7 Q.
8 C.E.
9 I.G.
10 A.D. Signals.
11 D.D.M.S.
12 A.P.M.
13 21 Squadron R.A.F.
14 I Corps.
15 XI Corps.
16 Diary.
17)
18) File.
19)

"C" Form.

MESSAGES AND SIGNALS.

Army Form C. 2123.
(In books of 100.)

No. of Message

Prefix ... Code ... Words ... 28

£ s. d.

Charges to Collect

Service Instructions. nco.

Received. From nco By [illegible]

Sent, or sent out. At ... m. To ... By ...

Office Stamp

Handed in at ... Office ... m. Received 4.16 p.m.

TO 46 Divn.

*Sender's Number.	Day of Month.	In reply to Number.	AAA
G670	2		

Refce	amendt	no	1
to	13th	Corps	order
no	144	for	para
3	wherever	it	occurs
read	para	6	

FROM 13th Corps.

TIME & PLACE 3.45 pm.

*This line should be erased if not required.

100,000.—John Mason Ltd.—2/13.—3141. Forms C2123.

S E C R E T.
****

Ref: para 6 (?)

Copy No. ....4.

Amendment No. 1 to XIII Corps Order No. 144.

2nd September, 1918.

1. Para. 6 (a), Line 3, after "bridges" add "other than temporary and floating bridges erected under Divisional arrangements".

2. Para. 6 (b), after word "above" add "and in addition such temporary and floating bridges West of the line given in para. 3 (a) above as may be required".

3. ACKNOWLEDGE.

[signature] Major for
Brigadier-General,
General Staff.

Copies to -

No. 1 & 2	Fifth Army.
3	19th Division.
4	48th Division.
5 & 6	G.O.C.R.A.
7	Q.
8	C.E.
9	I.G.
10	A.D. Signals.
11	D.D.M.S.
12	A.P.M.
13	21 Squadron R.A.F.
14	13th Cyclist Battalion.
15	'C' Sqdn. K.E.H.
16	I Corps.
17	XI Corps.
18	Diary.
19) 20) 21)	File.

Please amend orders accordingly

[initials]

46th DIVISION. No. 106/52

Date 2 Sept 18

G.O.C.

G.S.O. 1

G.S.O. 2

G.S.O. 3

Int. Offr.

Att. Offr.

Q. A.

C.R.A. C.R.E.

A.D.M.S. M.G. Batt.

Signals

RETURN TO "G" OFFICE.

Printed in France by A.P. & S.S. Press B. 2008. 5000. 4-18.

S E C R E T.

55th Division No. G.S. 1410

Div.Artillery. 55th Bn.M.G.C.
Div.Engineers. Div.Signals.
164th Inf.Bde. 46th Divn. (no map).
165th Inf.Bde. 16th Divn. (no map).
166th Inf.Bde.

PRELIMINARY INSTRUCTIONS AS TO ACTION IN THE EVENT OF AN ENEMY WITHDRAWAL.

1. As is it possible that the enemy's withdrawal on the front of the Division on our left may be extended so as to involve the whole Corps front, it is necessary that certain preliminary arrangements should be made, so that he can be followed up with the least possible delay.

2. It may be expected that some indications will be forthcoming as to the extent of the enemy's withdrawal, and the lines upon which he is likely to stand, but it is unlikely that any notice will be received as to the time selected for the withdrawal.

3. The rapid obtaining of information as to the enemy's withdrawal is dependent upon good and bold patrolling; our ability to follow up quickly is dependent on good plans having been previously prepared by commanders of all units.

4. Brigadier Generals Commanding Infantry Brigades, and Battalion Commanders in formulating their plans will be guided by the following principles :-

(a) The advance will be by bounds; the first of which will be to the enemy's old front line system, and the second to a line BOIS DE DIX HUIT - HULLUCH - CITE ST ELIE - FOSSE 8 - AUCHY - CANTELEUX - S.28.central - S.22.central (all inclusive). The attached map shows the boundaries of the Division and Brigades for an advance.

(b) The method of advance will be to obtain information of the enemy's intentions by means of the fewest number of men possible, and to follow up those with platoons acting boldly and with initiative.
It must be impressed upon all ranks that it is not necessary to advance in any definite line, but that each body of troops must push forward as far as it can up to the limits which may have been set by superior authority, without waiting for neighbouring bodies which have been temporarily held up.

(c) Enemy posts which hold out must be dealt with by bold out flanking movements and full use made of Artillery, Stokes Mortars and Machine Guns.

5. Artillery will cover the advance of the Infantry by pushing forward in successive bounds to positions from which counter attacks can be dealt with, the enemy's lines of retreat engaged, and counter battery work carried on.

Forward positions should be reconnoitred and the approaches thereto thoroughly known to all officers and Nos. 1. Means of communication must be thought out and positions for likely O.Ps. considered. The object to be attained is that there should always be an organised line of Artillery and Infantry defence during each successive advance.

6. O.C., Divisional Signal Company will be prepared with schemes for carrying forward to our new positions all means of communication including Visual Signalling, and Brigade and Battalion Headquarters in moving forward will select sites which are on the buried cable.

7. The C.R.E. will be responsible for making the following roads fit for horse transport :-

ESTAMINET CORNER - RATION CORNER - FESTUBERT - QUINQUE RUE.
WESTMINSTER BRIDGE - LONE FARM - WINDY CORNER - GIVENCHY.

8. Machine Guns will be allotted to Brigades on the basis of one Company to an Infantry Brigade. The guns, however, should not be pushed forward too rapidly - half of them should be used for covering fire from back positions, and those which are sent forward should be used to help to consolidate new positions after they have been taken by the Infantry.

O.C., Machine Gun Battalion will arrange for any reconnaissances which are possible, to be carried out with the above object.

9. Brigadier Generals Commanding Infantry Brigades will arrange for :-

(i) Pack Trains to be reorganised and practised.
(ii) Forward dumps of Ammunition, Stores, Tools and Rations.

10. It must be clearly understood that although the advance is not timed to take place at any particular time yet pressure must be constantly applied with a view to forcing a withdrawal and that touch must be kept, at all costs, with flank divisions should they move forward; and although our advance is not a set attack, yet, if the Division on our ~~Right~~ left makes a definite attack, it will be for Infantry Brigades in the Line not only to do everything possible to assist, but also to take advantage of the situation brought about, to push on on their own account.

Acknowledge. Done

R T Lee

55th Division H.Q.,
1st September, 1918.

Lieut-Colonel,
General Staff, 55th Division.

46th DIVISION. No. 106/51

Date 2.9.18

To see

G.O.C. [illegible]

G.S.O. 1 W

G.S.O. 2

G.S.O. 3 [illegible]

Int. Offr. [illegible]

Att. Offr. [illegible]

Q. A.

C.R.A. C.R.E.

A.D.M.S. M.G. Batt.

Signals

RETURN TO "G" OFFICE.

Printed in France by A.P. & S.S. Press B. 2008. 5000. 4-18.

S E C R E T.

55th Division.

No. 560 (G.O.) 1st September, 1918.

In conjunction with any advance made by the 46th Division, the Corps Commander wishes the 55th Division to push forward and establish posts in the O.B.L. but to make no change at present in the existing main line of resistance.

O Davies Major
for Brigadier General,
General Staff, I Corps.

Copy to:- XIII Corps.
46th Division.

File

Secret.

C.R.A.	137th I.Bde.	1st Monmouths.	A.D.M.S.
C.R.E.	138th :	46th Bn, MGC.	19th Division.
Signals.	139th :	A.A & Q.M.G.	55th :
			XIII Corps.

46th Division G.106/50. 1st September, 1918.

Enemy Withdrawal.
****

1. The future policy of the Division will be towards a more rapid and offensive policy in following up the retreating enemy.

2. Close touch will be maintained with the enemy and patrols will push forward wherever possible.
On enemy posts being located, arrangements will be made to surround or to assault them.

3. Such minor operations will be carried out by Brigadiers concerned, who will arrange direct for any Artillery support they may require.

4. Should considerable opposition be met, entailing the use of more than about one company of Infantry, reference will be made to Divisional Headquarters before any operation is carried out.
Divisional Sanction for the operation will then be given or the attack will be carried out under Divisional arrangements.

Lieut-Colonel,
General Staff, 46th Division....

G. S. 46th Division

September 1918

Nov 19

2 P
97 sheets

On His Majesty's Service.

War Diary

and

appendices

September 1918

Secret.

Copy No. 13

9 am 1/9/18 MM

46th DIVISION WARNING ORDER No. 14.
****

Ref: Maps :- 1/20,000,
36A.S.E and 36 S.W. & GORRE.

31st August, 1918.

1. Orders have been received that, at a very early date, the 46th and 19th Divisions will attack and occupy such portions of the following line as are not already in our possession.-
L'EPINETTE EAST POST (S 19 a) - River in S 8 a and c -
RICHEBOURG ST VAAST - CROIX BARBEE.

2. Subsequently an operation will be carried out to establish the General Line -
ROUGE CROIX - PONT LOGY (M 34 c) - WINDY CORNER (S 9 a 6.9) -
S 15 a 3.6 to SOUTHERN Divisional Boundary about S ~~27~~ 21 a 5.5.

3. The necessary preliminary arrangements for both these operations as regards disposal of artillery and machine guns; provision of R.E, ammunition and ration dumps, roads, bridges, etc, will be put in hand forthwith.

4. The C.R.E will, after consulting with the Brigadiers concerned, arrange for the supply of such Light Bridges as they may require.
Preparations will be made to throw a horse transport bridge across the LOISNE RIVER at S 7 a 9.8 as soon as it has been captured by us.

5. The C.R.A will arrange to place his artillery in such positions as will enable him, without further moves, to give the most efficient support to both the above operations; and, further, to cover the Infantry up to and including our old Front System in S 16 and 10, should they be ordered to push forward up to this Line..

6. The Boundary between Brigades will be as shown on Map attached to 46th Division Order No. 315.

7. Battle Headquarters will be established as follows :-

RIGHT Brigade at LOISNE.
LEFT : : LE HAMEL Village.

8. ACKNOWLEDGE.

Ack

[signature]

Lieut-Colonel,
General Staff, 46th Division.

Issued at 10. pm.

Copy No. 1 to C.R.A. -
2 C.R.E. -
3 Signals. -
4 137th I.B.
5 138th :
6 139th :
7 46th Bn, MGC. -
8 1st Monmouths.
9 A.A & Q.M.G. -
10 A.D.M.S. -
11 A.P.M. -
12 19th Division.
13 55th :
14 XIII Corps H.A.
15/16 XIII Corps.
17/18 File.
19/20 War Diary.

paras 1, 2 and 7 to 165 Inf Bde
RSL

9am
2/9/18

19th Division.
55th :

****

46th Division G.56/15. 1st September, 1918.

Will you please inform me as to the position of the Headquarters of the Brigade on my / RIGHT and also of their Battle Headquarters should they not correspond.

for

Major-General,
Commanding 46th Division......

Army Form C. 2123.
(In books of 100.)

"C" FORM.

MESSAGES AND SIGNALS.

No. of Message

Prefix SM Code 11 Words 21

Received from ACO By Jan

Service Instructions

Sent, or sent out. Office Stamp.

At ... m.

To

By

ARMY TELEGRAPHS YEE 1 IX.18

Handed in at YDF Office 9.45 m. Received 9.59 m.

TO 55 Div

*Sender's Number.	Day of Month.	In reply to Number.	AAA
G 934	1		

Re MEG1 warning order 14 para 2 last coordinate should read S21A5.5

9.81 10 am

FROM 48 Div

PLACE & TIME 9.45 am

* This line, except **AAA**, should be erased, if not required.

(3287) Wt.W54/P738. 691,000 Pads. 3/18. A.P.Ltd. (E3013)

9am 2/9/18 [illegible]

137th Infantry Brigade.
138th " "
139th " "
========================

40th Division G.90/12. 1st September, 1918.

Until further orders, Brigade Headquarters and Headquarters of Outpost Battalions, will send a Liaison Officer to communicate with similar formations on their RIGHT and LEFT flanks, at least twice daily.

[illegible signature]

Lieut-Colonel,
General Staff, 46th Division...

Copies to :-

19th Division.
55th "

Copy to 165
166

War Diary

Appx 1

Secret.

C.R.A.	137th I.Bde.	1st Monmouths.	A.D.M.S.
C.R.E.	138th :	46th Bn, MGC.	19th Division.
Signals.	139th :	A.A & Q.M.G.	55th :
			XIII Corps.

46th Division G.106/50. 1st September, 1918.

Enemy Withdrawal.

****

1. The future policy of the Division will be towards a more rapid and offensive policy in following up the retreating enemy.

2. Close touch will be maintained with the enemy and patrols will push forward wherever possible.
On enemy posts being located, arrangements will be made to surround or to assault them.

3. Such minor operations will be carried out by Brigadiers concerned, who will arrange direct for any Artillery support they may require.

4. Should considerable opposition be met, entailing the use of more than about one company of Infantry, reference will be made to Divisional Headquarters before any operation is carried out.
Divisional Sanction for the operation will then be given or the attack will be carried out under Divisional arrangements.

[signature]

Lieut-Colonel,
General Staff, 46th Division...

SECRET.

138th Infantry Brigade.
139th Infantry Brigade.
55th Division.

46th Division G.106/55. 2nd September, 1918.

Reference Map attached to 46th Divisional Order 316 -

The following should have been written against the first objective of 19th Division (GREEN LINE).

"Inf. arrive 0 + 18'
Inf. Advance 0 + 23'

Lieut-Colonel,

General Staff, 46th Division.

"C" FORM.
MESSAGES AND SIGNALS.

Army Form C. 2123
(In books of 100.)

No. of Message ....

Prefix SM Code ACX Words 17

Received from ACon By Lan

Service Instructions

Sent, or sent out.
At .... m.
To ....
By ....

Office Stamp.

Handed in at YDF Office 6.19 m. Received 6.30 m.

TO 55 Divn

* Sender's Number.	Day of Month.	In reply to Number.	AAA
G977	2		
Ref	DO 316	of	2/9/18
plus	thirty	aaa	
acknowledge			

Notified Arty 164 165

Kn

44 6.50 JC

FROM 46 Div

PLACE & TIME 6 10 pm

* This line, except **A A A**, should be erased, if not required.

(3287) Wt. W34/P738. 691,000 Pads. 3/18. A.P.Ltd. (E3013)

Encl
5.40/F
1.9.18

Secret.

C.R.A.	137th I.Bde.	1st Monmouths.	A.D.M.S.
C.R.E.	138th :	46th Bn, MGC.	19th Division.
Signals.	139th :	A.A & Q.M.G.	55th :
			XIII Corps.

46th Division G.106/50. 1st September, 1918.

Enemy Withdrawal.
****

1. The future policy of the Division will be towards a more rapid and offensive policy in following up the retreating enemy.

2. Close touch will be maintained with the enemy and patrols will push forward wherever possible.
On enemy posts being located, arrangements will be made to surround or to assault them.

3. Such minor operations will be carried out by Brigadiers concerned, who will arrange direct for any Artillery support they may require.

4. Should considerable opposition be met, entailing the use of more than about one company of Infantry, reference will be made to Divisional Headquarters before any operation is carried out.
Divisional Sanction for the operation will then be given or the attack will be carried out under Divisional arrangements.

[signature]

Lieut-Colonel,
General Staff, 46th Division....

SECRET.

55th Division No. G.S. 1247

165th Inf.Bde.
164th Inf.Bde.
Div.Artillery.

The following extracts from 46th Division Order No. 318 dated 2nd September, 1918, are forwarded for your information :-

"1. The 19th Division is attacking on the morning of the 3rd Sept. The 46th Division will conform to their movements and be prepared to exploit success.

2. The present line our troops occupy,
Jumping off line of the 19th Division,
First Objective of the 19th Division,
Final Objective of the XIII Corps,
are shown on the attached map.

6. The whole line will be prepared to advance should the enemy show signs of retiring and patrols will be pushed forward towards :-

RUM CORNER - PATH Post - ORCHARD Post - DOG'S Post - EDWARD Post and HEN'S Post.

The 19th Division are arranging that, after the capture of the final objective, patrols shall be pushed forward towards LANSDOWNE Post - LORETTO Post and ROUGE CROIX WEST Post.

8. Zero hour will be notified later by wire in minutes plus or minus from 5 a.m. Thus, if Zero hour is at 5.30 a.m. the order will read "Plus 30".
Zero is the hour at which the 19th Division leave their "jumping off line"."

Notified PLUS THIRTY

ACKNOWLEDGE.

55th Division H.Q.,
2nd September, 1918.

Lieut-Colonel,
General Staff, 55th Division.

GENERAL STAFF, 55th DIV.

No. 137 G.S.

Date. 2/9/18

Subject 19 Divn attacking – 46 Divn to be prepared to conform

G.O.C.
G.
G.A.
G.I.
A.A.&.Q.M.G.
R.A.
R.E.
FILE.......

ack

Copies 183 164 CRA

Recd 5.30 pm 29.8.

Secret.

Copy No. 11

46th DIVISION ORDER No. 316.

Ref: attached Map, or
36A.S.E and 36 S.W, 1/20,000.

2nd September, 1918.

1. The 19th Division is attacking on the morning of the 3rd Sept. The 46th Division will conform to their movements and be prepared to exploit success.

2. The Present Line our troops occupy,
Jumping off line of the 19th Division,
First Objective of the 19th Division,
Final Objective of the XIII Corps,
are shown on the attached Map (issued to those marked *).

3. The arrangements for the capture of the 46th Division objective are left to the G.O.C, 139th Infantry Brigade.

4. The C.R.A will arrange to place such available artillery as is not required by the G.O.C, LEFT Brigade, at the disposal of the 19th Division.
Silent batteries will not open on Barrage Lines but must be prepared to open on request of Infantry Brigade Commanders should they require artillery assistance in exploiting success, or in the event of an enemy counter-attack.

5. The O.C, 46th Bn, M.G Corps, will arrange with the Infantry Brigade Commanders to give such assistance as they may require: and will also arrange, in consultation with the RIGHT Brigade of the 19th Division, for enfilade fire to be brought to bear along the line RAG, BONE and ST VAAST Posts. SUCH FIRE MUST BE WITH DIRECT OBSERVATION.

6. The whole line will be prepared to advance should the enemy show signs of retiring and patrols will be pushed forward towards :-

RUM CORNER - PATH Post - ORCHARD Post - DOG'S Post - EDWARD Post and HEN'S POST.

The 19th Division are arranging that, after the capture of the final objective, patrols shall be pushed forward towards LANSDOWNE Post - LORETTO Post and ROUGE CROIX WEST Post.

7. The closest liaison must be maintained between the G.O.C, 139th and G.O.C, 57th Infantry Brigades, as in the event of the capture of RICHEBOURG Post by us prior to Zero hour, very great assistance can be given to the 19th Division: and between the G.O.C, 139th Infantry Brigade and the C.R.A, 46th Division, to ensure that the barrage is so arranged as to clear our LEFT Post.

8. Zero hour will be notified later by wire in minutes plus or minus from 5.00 am. Thus, if Zero hour is at 5.30 am, the order will read "Plus 30".
Zero is the hour at which the 19th Division leave their "jumping off Line".

9. ACKNOWLEDGE.

ackd

[signature]

Lieut-Colonel,
General Staff, 46th Division.....

Distribution over.-

Issued at 3 pm.-

Copy No. 1 to C.R.A.*
2 C.R.E.
3 Signals.*
4 137th I.B.*
5 138th : *
6 139th : *
7 46th Bn, M.G Corps.*
8 A.A & Q.M.G.
9 A.D.M.S.*
10 19th Division.*
11 55th : *
12 21st Sqdn, R.A.F.*
13 XIII Corps.*
14 do.
15 XIII Corps H.A.
16 XIII Corps CBSO.
17/18 File.
19 G.S.O I.
20/21 War Diary.

INF. ARR. 0+37
INF. ADV. 0+23
HALT 5 MINS
59TH DIV
58TH BDE
57TH BDE
19TH DIV. JUMPING OFF LINE
APPROX FRONT LINE

Magnetic
Grid North

Bac -	Ferry.
„ à traille - -	„
Bains - -	Baths.
Place aux bains -	Bathing place.
Balise - -	Boom, Beacon.
Banc de sable -	Sand-bank.
„ „ vase -	Mud-bank.
Baraque -	Hut.
Barrage - -	Dam.
Barrière -	Gate, Stile.
(Machine à) Bascule	Weigh-bridge.
Bassin - -	Dock, Pond.
„ d'échouage -	Tidal dock.

	Dock yard.
Chantier de construction	Slip-way.
Chapelle, Ch^lle -	Chapel.
Charbonnage -	Colliery.
Château d'eau -	Water tower.
Chaussée - -	Causeway. Highway.
Chemin de fer -	Railway.
Cheminée, Ch^née -	Chimney.
Chêne - -	Oak tree.
Cimetière, Cim^re -	Cemetery.
Clocher - -	Belfry.
Clouterie - -	Nail factory.
Colombier -	Dove-cot.

„ chimiques -	Chemical works.
Fab^e de faïence / Faïencerie	Pottery.
Ferme, F^me -	Farm.
Filature, Fil^re -	Spinning mill.
Fonderie, Fond^ie	Foundry.
Fontaine, Font^ne -	Spring, fountain.
Forêt -	Forest
Forme de radoub -	Dry dock.
Forge - -	Smithy.
Fosse - -	Mine, Pit.
Fossé - -	Moat, Ditch.
Four - - -	Kiln.
„ à chaux -	Lime-kiln.

Malterie - -	Malt-house.
Marbrerie -	Marble works.
Marais - -	Marsh.
Marais salant -	Saltern, Salt marsh.
Marché - -	Market.
Mare - - -	Pool.
Meule - -	Rick.
Minière - -	Mine.
Monastère - -	Monastery.
Moulin, M^in -	Mill.
„ à vapeur -	Steam mill.
Mur - -	Wall.
„ crénelé - -	Loop-holed wall.

„ artésien -	Artesian well.
„ d'aérage / „ ventilateur	Ventilating shaft.
„ de sondage -	Boring.
Quai - -	Quay, Platform.
„ aux bestiaux -	Cattle platform.
„ aux / des marchandises	Goods platform.
Raccordement -	Junction.
Raffinerie - -	Refinery.
„ de sucre	Sugar refinery
Râperie - -	Beet-root factory.

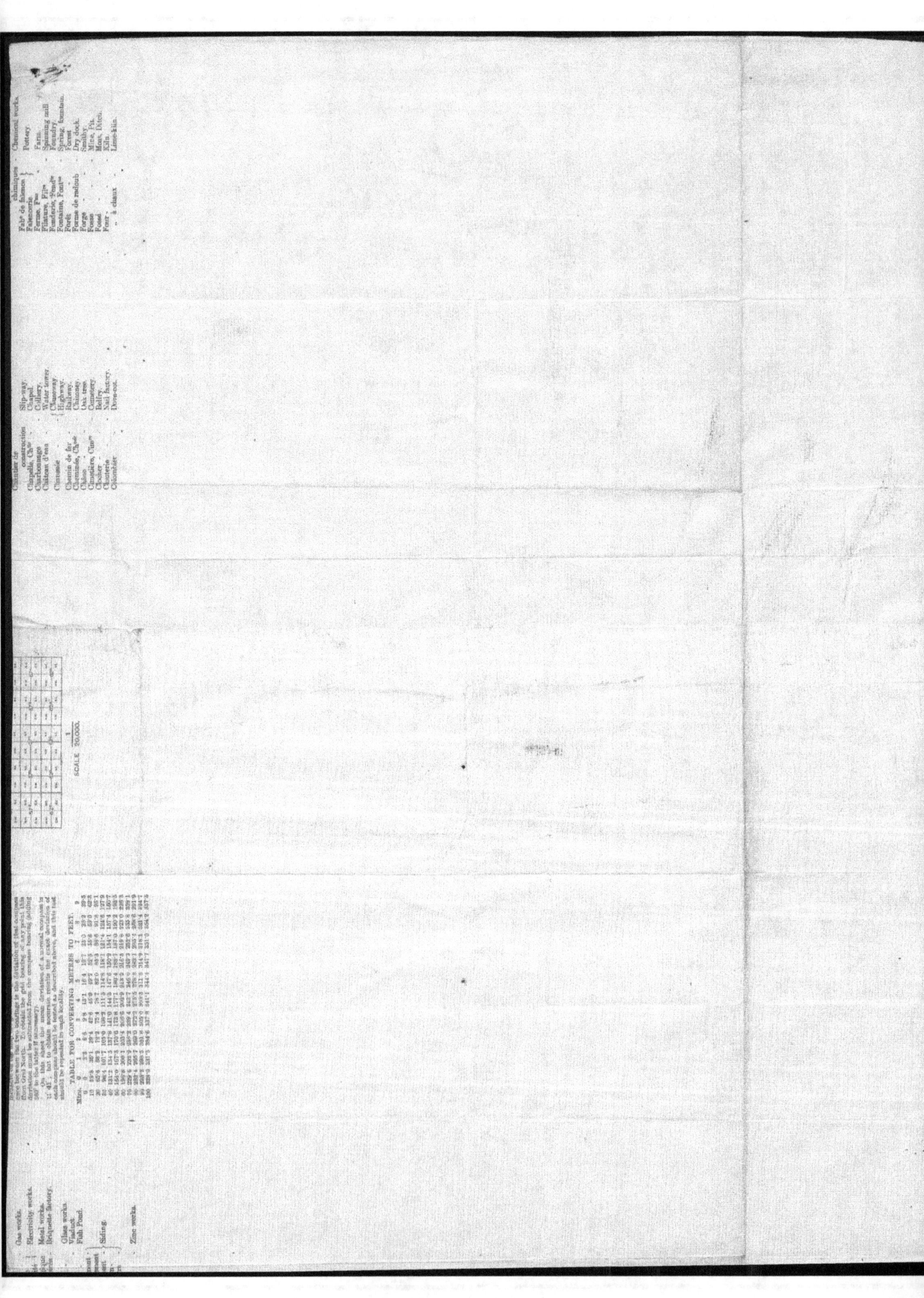

TABLE FOR CONVERTING METRES TO FEET.

Mtrs.	0	1	2	3	4	5	6	7	8	9
0	0	3·3	6·6	9·8	13·1	16·4	19·7	23·0	26·2	29·5
10	32·8	36·1	39·4	42·6	45·9	49·2	52·5	55·8	59·0	62·3
20	65·6	68·9	72·2	75·4	78·7	82·0	85·3	88·6	91·8	95·1
30	98·4	101·7	105·0	108·3	111·5	114·8	118·1	121·4	124·6	127·9
40	131·2	134·5	137·8	141·0	144·3	147·6	150·9	154·1	157·4	160·7
50	164·0	167·3	170·6	173·8	177·1	180·4	183·7	187·0	190·2	193·5
60	196·8	200·1	203·4	206·6	209·9	213·2	216·5	219·8	223·0	226·3
70	229·6	232·9	236·2	239·4	242·7	246·0	249·3	252·6	255·8	259·1
80	262·4	265·7	269·0	272·2	275·5	278·8	282·1	285·4	288·6	291·9
90	295·2	298·5	301·8	305·0	308·3	311·6	314·9	318·1	321·4	324·7
100	328·0	331·3	334·6	337·8	341·1	344·4	347·7	351·0	354·2	357·5

Appx 2

Secret.

46th Division - Daily Disposition Return.

Dispositions at 9 a.m., 2nd September, 1918.

Unit	Location.	Headquarters.
46th Div. H.Q.	Gosnay.	
46th Div. Art'y H.Q.	Gosnay.	
137th Inf. Bde. H.Q.	Vorquin.	E.29.c.5.4.
Div'l Reserve.		
5th South Staffs.	Vorquin.	
6th ,,	Vaudricourt Wood.	
6th North Staffs.	Fouquieres.	
138th Inf. Bde. H.Q.	Ottawa House.	F.13.central.
Right Section.		
5th Lincolns.	Outpost Line.	X.23.a.8.0.
4th Leicesters.	Support.	Loisne Chateau.
5th ,,	Reserve.	F.10.a.4.8.
139th Inf. Bde. H.Q.	Essars.	X.25.a.7.2.
Left Section.		
5th Sherwoods.	Reserve.	X.19.b.9.4.
6th ,,	Outpost Line.	(Tuning Fork (Breastwork, X.11.c.
8th ,,	Support.	X.20.d.8.4.
46th Bn. M.G.Corps.	Hesdigneul.	E.25.d.5.7.
C.R.E.	Gosnay.	
465th Field Coy.	Bethune.	E.10.b.95.95.
466th ,,	Fouquieres.	E.20.b.2.5.
468th ,,	Chicory Factory.	F.7.a.3.6.
1st Monmouths.	Bethune.	E.10.d.3.9.

137th Inf. Bde. H.Q. probable location at 6 pm. 4/9/18. - E.29.c.5.4.
138th : : : : : : : : - F.13.central.
139th : : : : : : : : - X.25.a.7.2.

R. Ch. Thomas Capt
for Lieut-Colonel,
General Staff, 46th Division.

1st September, 1918.

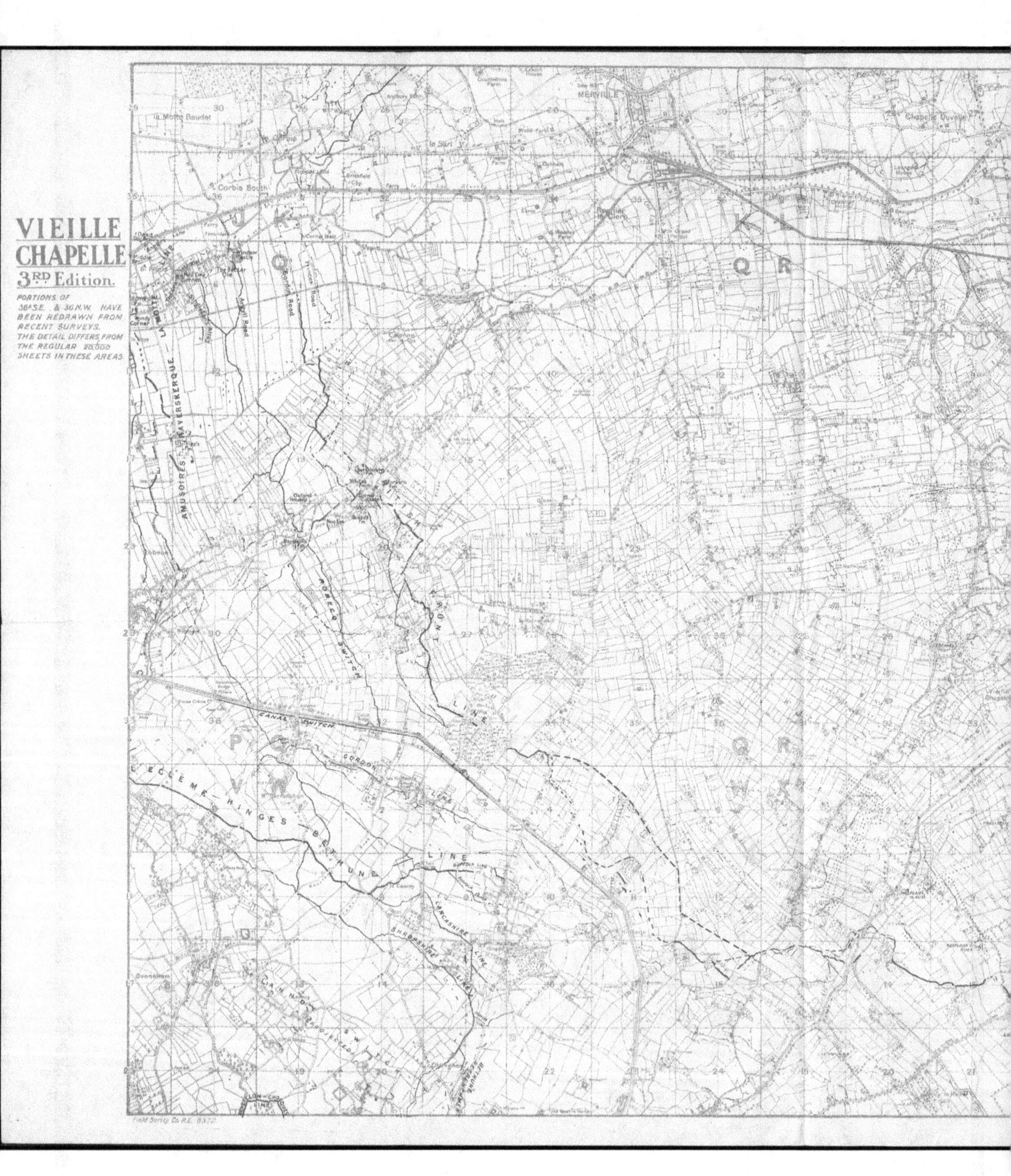
VIEILLE
CHAPELLE
3RD Edition.
PORTIONS OF
36A S.E. & 36 N.W. HAVE
BEEN REDRAWN FROM
RECENT SURVEYS.
THE DETAIL DIFFERS FROM
THE REGULAR 20,000
SHEETS IN THESE AREAS.
MERVILLE
la Motte Baudet
Chapelle Duvelle
Corbie South
AMUSOIRES
HAVERSKERQUE
ROBECQ SWITCH
FRONT LINE
CANAL SWITCH
GORDON LINE
LECLEME HINGES BETHUNE LINE
LANCASHIRE LINE
SHROPSHIRE LINE
Field Survey Co. R.E. 8372.

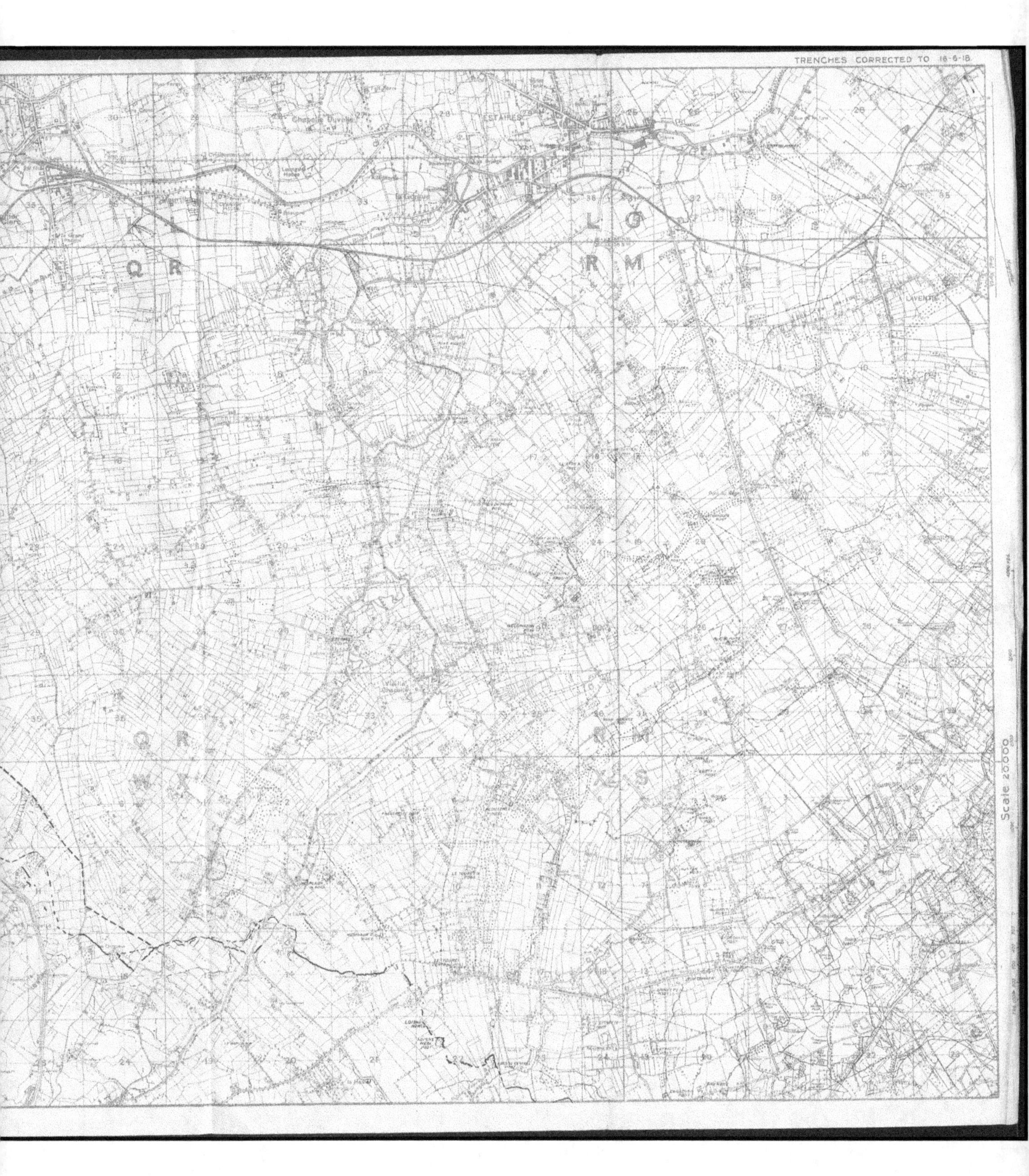
TRENCHES CORRECTED TO 18-6-18
ESTAIRES
LAVENTIE
Scale 20000

War Diary

Appendix 1. B.

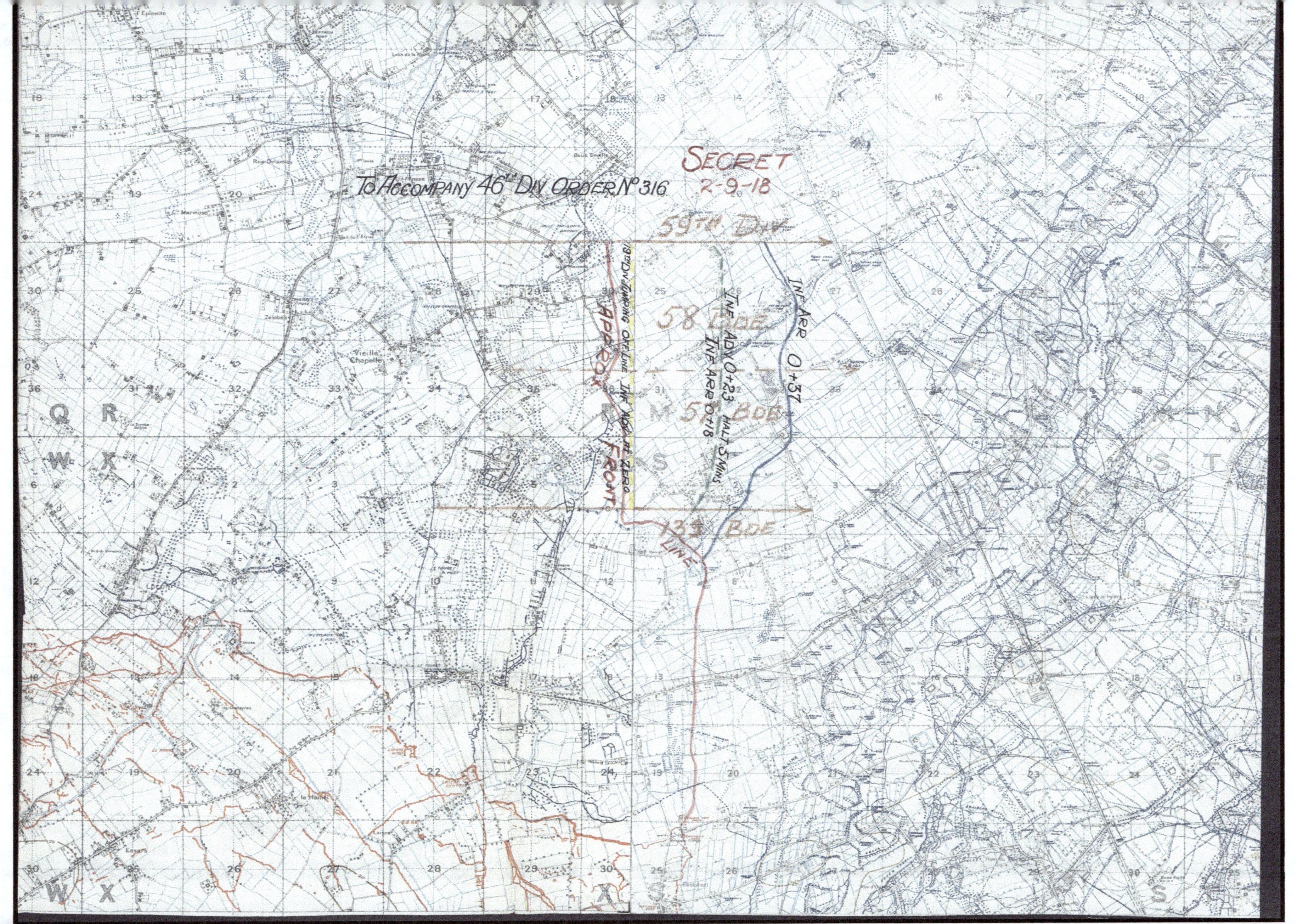
To Accompany 46th Div Order No 316
SECRET
2-9-18
59th Div
58 Bde
57 Bde
133 Bde
Inf Arr 0+37
Inf Adv 0+23 Halt 5 Mins
Inf Arr 0+18
19th Div Jumping Off Line Inf Adv at Zero
Approx Front Line
Vieille Chapelle

War Diary App 3

Secret. Copy No. 20

46th DIVISION ORDER No. 316.

Ref: attached Map, or
36A.S.E and 36 S.W, 1/20,000. 2nd September, 1918.

1. The 19th Division is attacking on the morning of the 3rd Sept. The 46th Division will conform to their movements and be prepared to exploit success.

2. The Present Line our troops occupy,
Jumping off line of the 19th Division,
First Objective of the 19th Division,
Final Objective of the XIII Corps,
are shown on the attached Map (issued to those marked *).

3. The arrangements for the capture of the 46th Division objective are left to the G.O.C, 139th Infantry Brigade.

4. The C.R.A will arrange to place such available artillery as is not required by the G.O.C, LEFT Brigade, at the disposal of the 19th Division.
Silent batteries will not open on Barrage Lines but must be prepared to open on request of Infantry Brigade Commanders should they require artillery assistance in exploiting success, or in the event of an enemy counter-attack.

5. The O.C, 46th Bn, M.G Corps, will arrange with the Infantry Brigade Commanders to give such assistance as they may require: and will also arrange, in consultation with the RIGHT Brigade of the 19th Division, for enfilade fire to be brought to bear along the line RAG, BONE and ST VAAST Posts. SUCH FIRE MUST BE WITH DIRECT OBSERVATION.

6. The whole line will be prepared to advance should the enemy show signs of retiring and patrols will be pushed forward towards :-

RUM CORNER - PATH Post - ORCHARD Post - DOG'S Post - EDWARD Post and HEN'S POST.

The 19th Division are arranging that, after the capture of the final objective, patrols shall be pushed forward towards LANSDOWNE Post - LORETTO Post and ROUGE CROIX WEST Post.

7. The closest liaison must be maintained between the G.O.C, 139th and G.O.C, 57th Infantry Brigades, as in the event of the capture of RICHEBOURG Post by us prior to Zero hour, very great assistance can be given to the 19th Division: and between the G.O.C, 139th Infantry Brigade and the C.R.A, 46th Division, to ensure that the barrage is so arranged as to clear our LEFT Post.

8. Zero hour will be notified later by wire in minutes plus or minus from 5.00 am. Thus, if Zero hour is at 5.30 am, the order will read "Plus 30".
Zero is the hour at which the 19th Division leave their "jumping off Line".

9. ACKNOWLEDGE.

[signature]

Lieut-Colonel,
General Staff, 46th Division....

Distribution over.-

Issued at 3 pm.-

Copy No. 1 to C.R.A.*
2 C.R.E.
3 Signals.*
4 137th I.B.*
5 138th : *
6 139th : *
7 46th Bn, M.G Corps.*
8 A.A & Q.M.G.
9 A.D.M.S.*
10 19th Division.*
11 55th : *
12 21st Sqdn, R.A.F.*
13 XIII Corps.*
14 do.
15 XIII Corps H.A.
16 XIII Corps CBSO.
17/18 File.
19 G.S.O I.
20/21 War Diary.

App x 3

Secret.

Addendum No. 1 to

46th DIVISION ORDER No. 316.
****

2nd September, 1918.

The following notes on the 19th Division arrangements are issued in continuation of 46th Division Order of the 2nd Septr.

1. At Zero Hour, the Artillery Barrage will open 200 yards in front of the 19th Division Jumping Off Line and will advance at the rate of 100 yards in 2 minutes.
   Ten minutes after reaching the final objective the protective Barrage will cease.

2. The 19th Division attack will be covered by a number of our aeroplanes flying low and attacking the enemy with M.G fire.

The following apply equally to the 46th Division :-

1. A Contact Aeroplane will call for flares at 7.00 am. Flares will be lit by troops on the final objective and by forward patrols.

2. A joint Liaison Post with the 19th Division will be established at RAGS POST.

3. O.C, Signals, 46th Division, will synchronise watches with the 19th Division to-day at 7.00 pm and 12.00 midnight, 2nd/3rd Septr.
   He will further arrange for the synchronisation of watches with the C.R.A, 138th and 139th Infantry Brigades, 46th Bn, M.G.C, at 8.00 pm, 2nd September, and 1.00 am, 3rd September.

ACKNOWLEDGE.

[signature]

Lieut-Colonel,
General Staff, 46th Division...

Issued at 6.30 pm.-

To all recipients of 46th Division Order No. 316.

9 Ahe 2/9/18

Secret.

Addendum No. 1 to

46th DIVISION ORDER No. 316.
****

2nd September, 1918.

The following notes on the 19th Division arrangements are issued in continuation of 46th Division Order of the 2nd Septr.

1. At Zero Hour, the Artillery Barrage will open 200 yards in front of the 19th Division Jumping Off Line and will advance at the rate of 100 yards in 2 minutes.
Ten minutes after reaching the final objective the protective Barrage will cease.

2. The 19th Division attack will be covered by a number of our aeroplanes flying low and attacking the enemy with M.G fire.

The following apply equally to the 46th Division :-

1. A Contact Aeroplane will call for flares at 7.00 am. Flares will be lit by troops on the final objective and by forward patrols.

2. A joint Liaison Post with the 19th Division will be established at RAGS POST.

3. O.C, Signals, 46th Division, will synchronise watches with the 19th Division to-day at 7.00 pm and 12.00 midnight, 2nd/3rd Septr.
He will further arrange for the synchronisation of watches with the C.R.A, 138th and 139th Infantry Brigades, 46th Bn, M.G.C, at 8.00 pm, 2nd September, and 1.00 am, 3rd September.

ACKNOWLEDGE.

Ack

Lieut-Colonel,
General Staff, 46th Division...

Issued at 6.30 pm.-

To all recipients of 46th Division Order No. 316.

S E C R E T.

55th Division No. G.S. 1414

46th Division.

The Headquarters of our Left Infantry Brigade are at BEUVRY MILL, F.20.d.10.35.

The position of the Battle Headquarters of this Brigade will be notified to you if and when they are established.

R T Lee Lt Col

55th Division H.Q., 2nd September, 1918.

for Brigadier-General, Commanding 55th Division.

"C" FORM.
MESSAGES AND SIGNALS.

Army Form C. 2123
(In books of 100.)

No. of Message

Prefix Mn	Code KKW	Words 50	Sent, or sent out.	Office Stamp.
Received from ACO	By Bailey		At m.	
Service Instructions			To	
			By	

Handed in at YDG Office 1052 m. Received 1144 m.

TO	55 DIV

*Sender's Number	Day of Month.	In reply to Number.	AAA
G 29	3		

Ref Conversation barrage will not now be put down South of DEAD COW WATERS KEEP aaa 55 DIV have reached TUBE STA POST and are arranging not to go beyond this tonight aaa Addsd CRA repeated 55 DIV aaa 138 Bde informed verbally

RR

FROM	46 DIV
PLACE & TIME	

* This line, except AAA, should be erased, if not required.

(3287) Wt. W54/P738. 691,000 Pads. 3/18. A.P.Ltd. (E3013)

Army Form C. 2123.
(In books of 100.)

"C" FORM.
MESSAGES AND SIGNALS. No. of Message..........

Prefix SB Code SP Words 19

Received from aco By Skene

Service Instructions Priority

Sent, or sent out. At ....m. To .... By ....

Office Stamp.

Handed in at YDF Office 5-30 pm. Received 5-54 pm.

TO 55 Div

* Sender's Number.	Day of Month.	In reply to Number.	AAA
G 16	3rd	–	
Ref	D.	O.	317
Para	8	aaa	Plus
735	acknowledge		

Ackd

6 pm RR

FROM 46 Div
PLACE & TIME 5.30 pm

* This line, except AAA, should be erased, if not required.

(3267) Wt. W34/P738. 691,000 Pads. 3/18. A.P.Ltd. (E3013)

Secret. Copy No. 11

46th DIVISION ORDER No. 317.

****

Ref: Maps, 1/20,000
36 S.W and 36A. S.E.

3rd September, 1918.

1. As soon as the Line RUM CORNER - HAYSTACK - PATH - ORCHARD - ALBERT - DOG'S - EDWARDS - KEN'S - LANSDOWNE POSTS has been established the 138th and 139th Infantry Brigades will attack and gain the line TUBE STA. POST - FALL MALL (S 15 central) - FACTORY KEEP - FACTORY TRENCH to EDWARDS POST, all inclusive.
   The 55th Division are conforming by occupying the Line S 27 a 2.2 - INDIAN VILLAGE inclusive.

2. A Liaison Post with the 55th Division will be established at TUBE STA. POST.

3. The 138th Infantry Brigade must be prepared to throw back a Defensive Flank to protect their RIGHT.

4. Brigades will inform Divisional Headquarters by Priority wire immediately they are on the line RUM CORNER - LANSDOWNE POST.

5. In order that there may be no delay, owing to the difficulty of getting orders through to present Front Line Troops, immediate steps will be taken to bring forward fresh troops for this attack, close in rear of the present advanced companies.

6. At Zero Hour the artillery will bring their Barrage down on a line 200 yards EAST of the Trench S 20 central to S 14 d 3.6 - HAYSTACK - ORCHARD - ALBERT - DOGS - EDWARD POST, where it will rest four minutes,.
   (Should Brigades at any time desire any alteration of this line they will inform 46th Divisional Artillery and D.H.Q by Priority Wire).
   The Barrage will then move forward at the rate of 100 yards in two minutes.
   On Lifting from the Final Objective the Barrage will rest on the line ~~S 24 b 4.5~~ S.21 b.4.6 - FALL MALL KEEP (S 15 b 8.3) - JUNCTION ST. - S 10 a 0.0 - Thence a N. and S. Grid to S 4 c 0.0, for ten minutes, when it will cease.

7. The C.R.A, 46th Division, will make the necessary counter battery arrangements and also arrange for a special bombardment of the areas about TUBE STA. POST - S 15 central - FACTORY KEEP and CORNER.

8. Zero hour will be notified later; it is hoped to be able to carry out this operation at 5 pm to-day; by which time troops must be in position. Zero will be notified by wire plus or minus from 5.00 pm.

9. Watches will be synchronized under arrangements to be made by O.C, Signals, at 2.00 pm.

10. ACKNOWLEDGE.

Lieut-Colonel,
General Staff, 46th Division.

Distribution over.-

Issued at 12.15 pm.-

Copy No.	to
1	C.R.A.
2	C.R.E.
3	Signals.
4	137th I.Bde.
5	138th :
6	139th :
7	46th Bn, M.G Corps.
8	A.A & Q.M.G.
9	A.D.M.S.
10	19th Division.
11	55th :
12	XIII Corps H.A.
13/14	XIII Corps.
15	G.S.O I.
16/17	File.
18/19	War Diary.
20	21st Squadron, R.A.F.

6.5 pm
3/9/18
[illegible]

Copy No. 11

Secret.

46th DIVISION Order No. 318.

****

Ref: Maps, 1/20,000,.
36A. S.E and 36 S.W.

3rd September, 1918.

In continuation of 46th Division Order No. 317 of 3rd Septr.

1. The Line S 20 c 9.8 - HAYSTACK - PATH - ORCHARD - ALBERT - DOGS - EDWARD and HENS POSTS will be occupied to-day by the 138th and 139th Infantry Brigades.

2. Zero hour will be 5.15 am, 4th September.

3. On the objective being reached, patrols will at once push forward taking every opportunity of the confusion in the enemy lines.
The final objective of these patrols will be our old Front Line in S 16 c and a - S 10 c and b - S 5 c, where they will be reinforced and this line held as an outpost system.

4. As regards para. 6, the C.R.A, 46th Division, will arrange to extend the barrage 300 yards south of the Divisional Boundary to include INDIAN VILLAGE. The last four words of para. 6, "when it will cease" will be deleted and the following inserted "when it will again move forward at the same rate until it rests on the old German Front Line. It will rest here for a further ten minutes when it will cease."

5. Watches will be synchronised under arrangements to be made by O.C, Signals, as follows :- With 55th Division Signals at 11.00 pm to-night, 3rd September: with all concerned at 12.00 midnight 3rd/4th September.

6 Acknowledge.

Ackd.

[signature]
Lieut-Colonel,
General Staff, 46th Division..

Issued at 5.40 pm.-

Copy No. 1 to ✝C.R.A.
2 C.R.E.
3 Signals.
4 137th I.B.
5 ✕ 138th :
6 ✕ 139th :
7 ✝ 46th Bn, MGC.
8 A.A & Q.M.G.
9 A.D.M.S.
10 ✝ 19th Division.
11 ✝ 55th :
12 XIII Corps H.A.
13 21st Sqdn, R.A.F.
14/15 XIII Corps.
16 G.S.O I.
17/18 File.
19/20 War Diary.

✕ Map attached

TRENCH MAP.

FRANCE.

SHEET 36 S.W.

EDITION 11. A

INDEX TO ADJOINING SHEETS.

SCALE $\frac{1}{20,000}$.

DIAGRAM

INSTRUCTIONS AS TO THE USE OF THE SQUARES.

1. The large rectangles on the map, lettered M.N.S. etc., are divided into squares of 1,000 yards side, which are numbered 1, 2, 3, etc. Each of these squares is sub-divided into four minor squares of 500 yards side. These minor squares are considered as lettered a, b, c, d. (See Square No. 6 in each rectangle.)

A point may thus be described as lying within Square B.6, M.5.b, etc.

2. To locate a point within a small square, consider the sides divided into tenths, and define the point by taking so many tenths from W. to E. along Southern side, and so many from S. to N. along Western side; the S.W. corner always being taken as origin, and the distance along the Southern side being always given by the first figure. Thus the point Z would be 63, *i.e.*, 6 divisions East and 3 divisions North from origin.

3. When more accurate definition is wanted (on the 1 : 20,000 or 1 : 10,000 scales) use exactly the same method, but divide sides into 100 parts and use four figures instead of two. Thus 0847 denotes 08 parts East and 47 parts North of origin (see point X). Point Y is 6503.

4. Use 0 but not 10; use either two or four figures; do not use fractions (8½, 4¼, etc.).

On squared maps all bearings should be given with reference to the vertical grid lines, which are parallel to the East and West edges of the sheet. Bearings should always be reckoned clockwise from 0° to 360°.

Grid bearings are less than compass bearings, the difference being called the deviation of the compass. To find out what this deviation is, take a compass bearing to a distant point, and measure on the map the grid bearing to that point. The difference between the two bearings is the deviation of that compass from Grid North. To obtain the grid bearing of any point this deviation must be subtracted from the compass bearing (adding 360° to the latter if necessary).

On this sheet the mean deviation of a normal compass is 11° 41′; but to obtain accurate results the exact deviation of each compass should be tested as described above, and this test should be repeated in each locality.

TABLE FOR CONVERTING METRES TO FEET.

Mtrs.	0	1	2	3	4	5	6	7	8	9
0	0	3·3	6·6	9·8	13·1	16·4	19·7	23·0	26·2	29·5
10	32·8	36·1	39·4	42·6	45·9	49·2	52·5	55·8	59·0	62·3
20	65·6	68·9	72·2	75·4	78·7	82·0	85·3	88·6	91·8	95·1
30	98·4	101·7	105·0	108·2	111·5	114·8	118·1	121·4	124·6	127·9
40	131·2	134·5	137·8	141·0	144·3	147·6	150·9	154·1	157·4	160·7
50	164·0	167·3	170·6	173·8	177·1	180·4	183·7	187·0	190·2	193·5
60	196·8	200·1	203·4	206·6	209·9	213·2	216·5	219·8	223·0	226·3
70	229·6	232·9	236·2	239·4	242·7	246·0	249·3	252·6	255·8	259·1
80	262·4	265·7	269·0	272·2	275·5	278·8	282·1	285·4	288·6	291·9
90	295·2	298·5	301·8	305·0	308·3	311·6	314·9	318·1	321·4	324·7
100	328·0	331·3	334·6	337·8	341·1	344·4	347·7	351·0	354·2	357·5

Remblai	Embankment.
Remise {des / aux} Machines	Engine-shed.
Réservoir, Résr	Reservoir.
Route cavalière	Bridle road.
Rubanerie	Ribbon Factory.
Ruine / Ruines / En ruine / Ruiné - e	Ruin.
Sablière	Sand-pit.
Sablonnière, Sablonre	„
Sapin	Fir tree.
Saule	Willow tree.
Saunerie	Salt-works.
Scierie, Scie	Saw-mill.
Sondage	Boring.
Source	Spring.
Sucrerie, Sucie	Sugar factory.
Tannerie	Tannery.
Tir à la cible	Rifle range.
Tissage	Weaving mill.
Tôlerie	Rolling mill
Tombeau	Tomb.
Tour	Tower.
Tourbière	Peat-bog, Peat-bed.
Tourelle	Small tower.
Tuilerie	Tile works.
Usine à gaz	Gas works.
„ électrique / „ d'électricité	Electricity works.
„ métallurgique	Metal works.
„ à agglomérés	Briquette factory.
Verrerie, Verrie	Glass works.
Viaduc	Viaduct.
Vivier	Fish Pond.
Voie de chargement / „ „ déchargement / „ „ d'évitement / „ „ formation / „ „ manœuvre	Siding.
Zinguerie	Zinc works.

116,000 m.W.

G.S.G.S. 2742

REFERENCE.

Enemy Trenches { Any trench apparently organised for fire / Other Trenches / (Important ones are shown by thick line. Old or disused by dotted line.)

British Trenches

Wire Entanglement or Other Obstacle

Enemy's Tracks

Buried Pipeline or Cable

Airline

Supply Dumps

Ammunition „

Earthworks

Dug-outs

Huts

Works reinforced by concrete

Gun Emplacements

Machine Gun „

Trench Mortar „

A-A. Gun „

Observation Posts

Listening Posts

Mine Craters

„ Fortified

Organised Shell Holes

Hedge, Fence or Dit

Ditch with Permanen

Conspicuous Points (Position of point shows that point is

Houses

War Diary Appx 4

Secret. Copy No. 19

46th DIVISION ORDER No. 317.

****

Ref: Maps, 1/20,000
36 S.W and 36A. S.E.

3rd September, 1918.

1. As soon as the Line RUM CORNER - HAYSTACK - PATH - ORCHARD - ALBERT - DOG'S - EDWARDS - KEN'S - LANSDOWNE POSTS has been established the 138th and 139th Infantry Brigades will attack and gain the line TUBE STA. POST - PALL MALL (S 15 central) - FACTORY KEEP - FACTORY TRENCH to EDWARDS POST, all inclusive.
The 55th Division are conforming by occupying the Line S 27 a 2.2 - INDIAN VILLAGE inclusive.

2. A Liaison Post with the 55th Division will be established at TUBE STA. POST.

3. The 138th Infantry Brigade must be prepared to throw back a Defensive Flank to protect their RIGHT.

4. Brigades will inform Divisional Headquarters by Priority wire immediately they are on the line RUM CORNER - LANSDOWNE POST.

5. In order that there may be no delay, owing to the difficulty of getting orders through to present Front Line Troops, immediate steps will be taken to bring forward fresh troops for this attack, close in rear of the present advanced companies.

6. At Zero Hour the artillery will bring their Barrage down on a line 200 yards EAST of the Trench S 20 central to S 14 d 3.6 - HAYSTACK - ORCHARD - ALBERT - DOGS - EDWARD POST, where it will rest four minutes,.
(Should Brigades at any time desire any alteration of this line they will inform 46th Divisional Artillery and D.H.Q by Priority Wire).
The Barrage will then move forward at the rate of 100 yards in two minutes.
On Lifting from the Final Objective the Barrage will rest on the line ~~S 24 b 4.5~~ S 21 b 6.6 - PALL MALL KEEP (S 15 b 8.3) - JUNCTION ST. - S 10 a 0.0 - Thence a N. and S. Grid to S 4 c 0.0, for ten minutes, when it will cease.

7. The C.R.A, 46th Division, will make the necessary counter battery arrangements and also arrange for a special bombardment of the areas about TUBE STA. POST - S 15 central - FACTORY KEEP and CORNER.

8. Zero hour will be notified later; it is hoped to be able to carry out this operation at 5 pm to-day; by which time troops must be in position. Zero will be notified by wire plus or minus from 5.00 pm.

9. Watches will be synchronized under arrangements to be made by O.C, Signals, at 2.00 pm.

10. ACKNOWLEDGE.

[signature]

Lieut-Colonel,
General Staff, 46th Division.

Distribution over.-

Issued at 12.15 pm.-

Copy No.	to
1	C.R.A.
2	C.R.E.
3	Signals.
4	137th I.Bde.
5	138th :
6	139th :
7	46th Bn, M.G Corps.
8	A.A & Q.M.G.
9	A.D.M.S.
10	19th Division.
11	55th :
12	XIII Corps H.A.
13/14	XIII Corps.
15	G.S.O I.
16/17	File.
18/19	War Diary.
20	21st Squadron, R.A.F.

War Diary

App 5

Secret.

Copy No. 19

46th DIVISION Order No. 318.

****

Ref: Maps, 1/20,000,
36A, S.E and 36 S.W.

3rd September, 1918.

In continuation of 46th Division Order No. 317 of 3rd Septr.

1. The Line S 20 c 9.8 - HAYSTACK - PATH - ORCHARD - ALBERT - DOGS - EDWARD and HENS POSTS will be occupied to-day by the 138th and 139th Infantry Brigades.

2. Zero hour will be 5.15 am, 4th September.

3. On the objective being reached, patrols will at once push forward taking every opportunity of the confusion in the enemy lines.
   The final objective of these patrols will be our old Front Line in S 16 c and a - S 10 c and b - S 5 c, where they will be reinforced and this line held as an outpost system.

4. As regards para. 6, the C.R.A, 46th Division, will arrange to extend the barrage 300 yards south of the Divisional Boundary to include INDIAN VILLAGE. The last four words of para. 6, "when it will cease" will be deleted and the following inserted "when it will again move forward at the same rate until it rests on the old German Front Line. It will rest here for a further ten minutes when it will cease."

5. Watches will be synchronised under arrangements to be made by O.C, Signals, as follows :- With 55th Division Signals at 11.00 pm to-night, 3rd September: with all concerned at 12.00 midnight 3rd/4th September.

[signature]
Lieut-Colonel,
General Staff, 46th Division..

Issued at 5.40 pm.-

Copy No. 1 to+ C.R.A.
2 C.R.E.
3 Signals.
4 137th I.B.
5 x 138th :
6 x 139th :
7 + 46th Bn, MGC.
8 A.A & Q.M.G.
9 A.D.M.S.
10 + 19th Division.
11 + 55th :
12 XIII Corps H.A.
13 21st Sqdn, R.A.F.
14/15 XIII Corps.
16 G.S.O I.
17/18 File.
19/20 War Diary.

x Map attached

War Diary

App 6

Secret.

46th Division - Daily Disposition Return.

Dispositions at 9 a.m., 4th September, 1918.

Unit.	Location.	Headquarters.
46th Div. H.Q.	Gosnay.	
46th Div. Art'y H.Q.	Gosnay.	
137th Inf. Bde. H.Q.	Verquin.	E.29.c.5.4.
Div'l Reserve.		
5th South Staffs.	Verquin.	
6th ,,	Vaudricourt Wood.	
6th North Staffs.	Fouquieres.	
138th Inf. Bde. H.Q.	Loisne Chateau.	X.28.a.3.6.
Right Section.		
5th Lincolns.	Outpost Line.	X.23.a.90.20.
4th Leicesters.	Support.	F.10.a.4.8.
5th ,,	Reserve.	F.2.d.2.1.
139th Inf. Bde. H.Q.	Essars.	X.25.a.7.2.
Left Section.		
6th ~~5th~~ Sherwoods.	Reserve.	X.19.c.95 95 ~~b.9.4.~~
8th ~~6th~~ ,,	Outpost Line.	S.7.d.35.25.
5th ~~8th~~ ,,	Support.	X.20.d.8.4.
46th Bn. M.G.Corps.	Hesdigneul.	E.25.d.5.7.
C.R.E.	Gosnay.	
465th Field Coy.	Bethune.	E.10.b.95.95.
466th ,,	Fouquieres.	E.20.b.2.5.
468th ,,	Chicory Factory.	F.7.a.3.6.
1st Monmouths.	Bethune.	E.10.d.3.9.

137th Inf. Bde. H.Q. probable location at 6 pm. 5/9/18 - E.29.c.5.4.
138th : : : : : : : : - X.28.a.3.6.
139th : : : : : : : : - X.25.c.59 59 ~~a.7.2.~~

[signature] Capt
for Lieut-Colonel,
General Staff, 46th Division.

3rd September, 1918.

Cd 5/- 4.9.18

Secret.

C.R.A.	137th I.B.	46th Bn. MGC.	A.D.M.S.	S.S.O.
C.R.E.	138th :	1st Monmouths.	Div: Train.	D.A.D.V.S.
Signals.	139th :	A.A & Q.M.G.	A.P.M.	D.A.D.O.S.
Div: Depot.	Div: Wing.	D.G.O.	Camp C't.	
19th Div:	55th Div:√	XIII Cps H.A.	XIII Corps (2).	

46th Division G.106/58. 4th September, 1918.

Enemy Withdrawal.
****

1. Our troops now occupy the Old British Front Line within the Divisional Boundary. The 55th Division are arranging to occupy the same line on our RIGHT and the 19th Division are moving forward on our LEFT.

2. We have located the enemy in his Old Front Line opposite our LEFT Brigade Front: on the RIGHT, however, the 138th Infantry Brigade report that they are out of touch.

3. It is not the intention at present to push forward against enemy opposition; patrols will, however, be sent out to gain touch with the enemy and occupy any ground which he has evacuated.

4. The Outpost Line of Resistance of the 46th Division will be as shown on the attached Map in BLUE: the Line of RETENTION is shown in RED. (Maps sent to 138th and 139th I.Bdes; traces to 19th and 55th Divs: XIII Corps H.A, XIII Corps, C.R.A and 46th Bn, MGC.)

5. In the event of hostile attack, the first S.O.S will be sent up by our foremost Posts; the second from the Line of RETENTION.

6. It is probable that the Division will be relieved almost immediately, and all preparations will be made to ensure that the area turned over is organized, so far as time permits, either for offence or defence.
Roads will be pushed forward - Forward Dumps established - Headquarters selected and Posts organised for defence.

[signature]

Lieut-Colonel,
General Staff, 46th Division...

Identification Trace for use with Artillery Maps.

REFERENCE SHEET 36 S.W. 1/20000

SECRET.
4-9-18

TO ACCOMPANY 46TH DIV.
G.106/58

S
1 2 DIV. BDY

BDE BDY

DIV. BDY

30.S

NOTE.—(1). These traces are intended to facilitate the communication of information as to the position of targets, which have been located on a squared map.

(2). The squares on this trace are 500 yards in length on the 1/10,000 scale, 1,000 yards in length on the 1/20,000 scale, and 2,000 yards in length on the 1/40,000 scale.

(3). The squares on the trace are fitted to the squares of the map showing the targets, which are then drawn on the trace. Sufficient letters and numbers must also be added to enable the recipient to place the trace in the correct position on his own map. A little detail may also be traced, but this is not essential. The name and scale of the map to which the trace refers must be always given. The trace can be used for the 1/10,000, 1/20,000, or 1/40,000 scale.

G.S.G.S. 3023.

Tracing taken from Sheet............................

of the 1:..................*map of*............................

Signature..................................*Date*..................

War Diary

App. 7

Secret.

C.R.A.	137th I.B.	46th Bn, MGC.	A.D.M.S.	S.S.O.
C.R.E.	138th :	1st Monmouths.	Div: Train.	D.A.D.V.S.
Signals.	139th :	A.A & Q.M.G.	A.P.M.	D.A.D.O.S.
Div: Depot.	Div: Wing.	D.G.O.	Camp C't.	
19th Div:	55th Div:	XIII Cps H.A.	XIII Corps (2).	

46th Division G.106/58. 4th September, 1918.

Enemy Withdrawal.
****

1. Our troops now occupy the Old British Front Line within the Divisional Boundary. The 55th Division are arranging to occupy the same line on our RIGHT and the 19th Division are moving forward on our LEFT.

2. We have located the enemy in his Old Front Line opposite our LEFT Brigade Front: on the RIGHT, however, the 138th Infantry Brigade report that they are out of touch.

3. It is not the intention at present to push forward against enemy opposition; patrols will, however, be sent out to gain touch with the enemy and occupy any ground which he has evacuated.

4. The Outpost Line of Resistance of the 46th Division will be as shown on the attached Map in BLUE: the Line of RETENTION is shown in RED. (Maps sent to 138th and 139th I.Bdes; traces to 19th and 55th Divs: XIII Corps H.A, XIII Corps, C.R.A and 46th Bn, MGC.)

5. In the event of hostile attack, the first S.O.S will be sent up by our foremost Posts; the second from the Line of RETENTION.

6. It is probable that the Division will be relieved almost immediately, and all preparations will be made to ensure that the area turned over is organized, so far as time permits, either for offence or defence.
Roads will be pushed forward - Forward Dumps established - Headquarters selected and Posts organised for defence.

[signature]

Lieut-Colonel,
General Staff, 46th Division...

Identification Trace for use with Artillery Maps.

REFERENCE SHEET 36 S.W 1/20000

TO ACCOMPANY 46TH DIV.

G.106/58.

SECRET

4·9·18

S

1 2 3 4

DIV BDY

7 8 9 10

BDE BDY

13 14 15 16

DIV BDY

19 20 21 22

NOTE.—(1). These traces are intended to facilitate the communication of information as to the position of targets, which have been located on a squared map.

(2). The squares on this trace are 500 yards in length on the 1/10,000 scale, 1,000 yards in length on the 1/20,000 scale, and 2,000 yards in length on the 1/40,000 scale.

(3). The squares on the trace are fitted to the squares of the map showing the targets, which are then drawn on the trace. Sufficient letters and numbers must also be added to enable the recipient to place the trace in the correct position on his own map. A little detail may also be traced, but this is not essential. The name and scale of the map to which the trace refers must be always given. The trace can be used for the 1/10,000, 1/20,000, or 1/40,000 scale.

G.S.G.S. 5023.

Tracing taken from Sheet ....

of the 1:.............. *map of*..................

Signature .... *Date*..............

Secret. War Diary Copy No. 29

app I

46th DIVISION ORDER No. 319.

****

Ref: Maps, 1/20,000. 36.A.S.E. & 36 S.W.
1/40,000. 36.A. & 44.B.

4th September, 1918.

1. The 46th Division will be relieved in the RIGHT SECTION of the XIII Corps Front by the 19th Division, commencing on the 5th September, 1918.

2. The 138th and 139th Infantry Brigades will be relieved on the night of the 5th/6th September by the 56th Infantry Brigade.
All arrangements being made between Brigadiers concerned.
On completion of relief of both Brigades, the G.O.C. 56th Infantry Brigade becomes responsible for the front.

3. The C.R.E., 46th Division will arrange direct with the C.R.E., 19th Division for the taking over of all R.E. and Pioneer Work, including that being undertaken by the Field Company and Infantry Battalion of the Portuguese Corps. Reliefs to be completed by 6 am, 6th September, at which hour the Portuguese troops will be transferred to the 19th Division.

4. The A.D.M.S. and A.P.M. will make all necessary arrangements with the A.D.M.S. and A.P.M., 19th Division; personnel of the 46th Division being relieved by 6 am, 6th September.

5. Battle Details rejoin their Brigades; present billets being clear by 2 pm, 5th September.

6. The 46th Battalion, Machine Gun Corps will be relieved by the 19th Battalion, Machine Gun Corps, on the 5th September, under arrangements to be made between Battalions.

7. Artillery reliefs will be notified later.

8. Divisional Headquarters remain at GOSNAY.

9. Moves of units are shown on the attached table.

10. Acknowledge.

[signature]

Lieut-Colonel,
General Staff, 46th Division.

Issued at 11.15 pm.

Copy No. 1 to C.R.A.
2 C.R.E.
3 Signals.
4 137th Inf: Bde:
5 138th : :
6 139th : :
7 1st Monmouths.
8 46th Bn: M.G.C.
9 A.A. & Q.M.G.
10 A.D.M.S.
11 Div'l: Train.
12 S.S.O.
13 A.P.M.
14 D.A.D.V.S.
15 D.A.D.O.S.

Copy No. 16 to D.G.O.
17 Div: Depot.
18 Div: Wing.
19 55th Div:
20 19th Div:
21 XIII Corps H.A.
22 XIII Corps C.B.S.O.
23/24 XIII Corps.
25 British Offr: attchd: 24th Portuguese Inf: Bn:
26 British Mission with 2nd Portuguese Brigade.
27/28 File.
29/30 War Diary.

Table to accompany 46th Division Order No. 319.

Date.	Unit.	Moves from	To	Remarks.
September. 5th.	137th I.Bde:	FOUQUIERES Area.	ALLOUAGNE Area.	ALLOUAGNE - LOZINGHEM - BURBURE. Bde: Headquarters, ALLOUAGNE.
5th.	466th Fd. Co. R.E.	FOUQUIERES.	ALLOUAGNE Area.	Joins 137th Bde: Group by whom billeted.
5th.	46th Bn: M.G.C.	Line.	HESDIGNEUL.	Billets at present occupied by Battle Details will be clear at 2 pm.
5th.	Battle Details.	HESDIGNEUL.	Brigade Billeting Areas.	To clear HESDIGNEUL by 2 pm. Rejoin Bdes: on arrival. 139th Bde: Details direct to MARLES Areas
Night 5th/6th.	138th Inf: Bde:	Line.	FOUQUIERES Area.	FOUQUIERES - VERQUIN - VAUDRICOURT WOOD. Bde: H.Qrs. to present rear Headquarters.
Night 5th/6th.	139th Inf: Bde:	Line.	BETHUNE Area.	2 Bns: BETHUNE - 1 Bn: BEUVRY. Bde: H.Qrs. to present rear Headquarters.
6th.	468th Fd. Co. R.E.	Line.	FOUQUIERES Area.	Joins 138th Bde: Group by whom billeted.
6th.	465th Fd. Co. R.E.	Line.	MARLES-les-MINES area.	Billets from 139th Inf: Bde: - join Bde: Group on arrival of Inf: Bde:
6th.	1 Fld. Amb:	BRUAY.	ALLOUAGNE Area.	Joins 137th Bde: Group by whom billeted.
7th.	139th Inf: Bde:	BETHUNE Area.	MARLES les MINES Area.	MARLES - LAPUGNOY - AUCHEL. Bde: H.Rs: MARLES.
	1 Fd. Amb:			Remain in HESDIGNEUL: joins 138th Bde: Group.
	1 Fd. Amb:			Remain in BRUAY: joins 139th Bde: Group.

War Diary

App 9.

Secret.

46th Division - Daily Disposition Return.

Dispositions at 9 a.m., 5th September, 1918.

Unit.	Location.	Headquarters.
46th Div: H.Q.	Gosnay.	
46th Div: Art'y: H.Q.	Gosnay.	
137th Inf: Bde: H.Q.	Verquin.	E.29.c.5.4.
Div'l: Reserve.		
5th South Staffs.	Verquin.	
6th : :	Vaudricourt Wood.	
6th North Staffs.	Fouquieres.	
138th Inf: Bde: H.Q.	Loisne Chateau.	X.28.a.3.6.
Right Section.		
5th Lincolns.	Support.	X.23.a.90.20.
4th Leicesters.	Reserve.	F.10.a.4.8.
5th :	Outpost Line.	S.19.b.7.4.
139th Inf: Bde: H.Q.	Essars.	X.25.c.95.95.
Left Section.		
5th Sherwoods.	Support.	X.17.a.8.7.
6th :	Reserve.	X.19.b.9.4.
8th :	Outpost Line.	S.7.d.35.25.
46th Bn: M.G.C.	Hesdigneul.	E.25.d.5.7.
C.R.E.	Gosnay.	
465th Field Co: R.E.	Essars.	X.25.a.95.70.
466th : : :	Fouquieres.	E.20.b.2.5.
468th : : :	Chicory Factory.	F.7.a.3.6.
1st Monmouths.	Bethune.	E.10.d.3.9.

137th Inf: Bde: H.Q. probable location at 6 pm, 7/9/18 - E.29.c.5.4.
138th : : : : : : : : - X.28.a.3.6.
139th : : : : : : : : - X.25.c.95.95.

R C Thomas Capt
for Lieut-Colonel,
General Staff, 46th Division........

4th September, 1918.

War Diary App 10

SECRET.

Copy No. 29

Addendum No. 1 to 46th Division Order No. 319.
****

5th September, 1918.

1. In continuation of 46th Division Order No. 319 of 4th September.

1. The 46th Divisional Artillery will be withdrawn from action on the night of the 6th/7th September, under arrangements to be made between C.R.As., 46th and 19th Divisions.

2. The 46th Brigade, R.F.A., will come under the orders of the 19th Division.

3. On completion of relief, the 46th Divisional Artillery will return to their wagon lines.

4. Tactical command of the artillery covering 46th Division front will pass to 19th Div: Art'y at 12 midnight, 5th/6th September, 1918.

[signature]
Lieut-Colonel,
General Staff, 46th Division.

Issued at 10.40 a.m.

To all recipients of 46th Div: Order No. 319.
Copies as before.

War Diary

App. 11

Secret.

46th Division - Daily Disposition Return.

Dispositions at 9 a.m., 6th September, 1918.

Unit.	Location at 9 am 6/9/18.	Probable moves before 6.30 pm 6/9/18.
46th Div. H.Q.	Gosnay.	
46th Div. Art'y H.Q.	Gosnay.	
137th Inf. Bde. H.Q.	ALLOUAGNE.	
5th South Staffs.	LOZINGHEM.	
6th " "	ALLOUAGNE.	
6th North Staffs.	BURBURE.	
138th Inf. Bde. H.Q.	Chateau, FOUQUIERES.	
5th Lincolns.	VERQUIN.	
4th Leicesters.	FOUQUIERES.	
5th "	VAUDRICOURT.	
139th Inf. Bde. H.Q.	PRIEURE ST PRY, FOUQUIERES.	
5th Sherwoods.	BETHUNE.	
6th "	BETHUNE.	
8th "	BEUVRY.	
46th Bn. M.G.C.	HESDIGNEUL.	
C.R.E.	GOSNAY.	
465th Field Co, R.E.	BETHUNE.	MARLES-LES-MINES. Area.
466th " " "	BURBURE.	
468th " " "	FOUQUIERES.	
1st Bn. Monmouthshire Rt.	BETHUNE.	

137th I.B. H.Q. probable location at 6 pm, 8/9/18.	ALLOUAGNE.
138th " " " " " " "	FOUQUIERES.
139th " " " " " " "	MARLES-LES-MINES.

for Lieut-Colonel,
General Staff, 46th Division.

5th September, 1918.

War Diary

App. 12.

C.R.A.
C.R.E.
137th Infantry Brigade.
138th " "
139th " "
1/1st Bn, Monmouthshire Regt.
46th Bn, M.G Corps.

46th Division G.5/15. 5th September, 1918.

TRAINING.
****

1. The Training Areas allotted to Infantry Brigades are shown on the attached map (to Infantry Brigades and C.R.A only).
The Rifle Range at D 23 b is allotted to the 1/1st Bn, Monmouthshire Regt and 46th Bn, M.G Corps, who will arrange mutually for its use.
R.A and R.E will use the Training Areas by arrangement with Brigades concerned.
The use for a special purpose of the Training Area or facilities of another Brigade will be arranged between Brigades.

2. It is not known how long the Division will be out of the line; from the experience of other Divisions it will not be long.

3. It is not proposed to issue an elaborate programme from this office; and it will be left to Brigadiers to decide what form of training is most required by their respective units.
The following general instructions, however, will be carried out :-

(i) Concentrate first on Platoon and Company Training. The automatic assistance given by one section of a Platoon to another and by one platoon of a Company to another.
Perfect organisation is essential to this.

(ii) A certain amount of Trench to Trench attack in waves should be done; closing into Artillery Formations after passing the First Objective.

(iii) Exercises with Flagmen representing Tanks.

(iv) Steady Drill and Marches in Full Marching Order.

(v) Tactical Exercises for Officers, without troops. Artillery and Machine Gun Officers should be included in these in their proper capacity as Battery or Forward Section Commanders, Liaison Officers, etc.

(vi) When the Companies are considered fit, a Battalion and Brigade exercise will be carried out. These Exercises should be those which have previously been carried out without troops and which have been thoroughly explained to all officers

4. The following notes on the recent operations of this Division should be carefully considered during the training and, where necessary, should be rectified.-

P.T.O.

(i) Orders. Written orders in all branches were sometimes badly put together, and were often a mere repetition of those of higher formations. Orders should be cut down to what is essential for those concerned to know; that is, generally speaking, the action required of them and the action of units on their immediate flanks. It is of no use and is often inadvisable in an order to tell a Company, for instance, what is going on at the opposite flank of the Corps; such information having filtered down through Corps, Divisional, Brigade and Battalion Orders.

(ii) Messages. The passing back of messages was generally bad. It must be impressed on all ranks that it is essential to the success of any operation for the higher formations to know how the attack or advance is progressing. The more the information passed back, the greater will be the assistance given to the attacking troops.

(iii) Several successful minor enterprises were carried out by platoons working round the flanks of posts which were holding up the advance. The almost invariable result of such action was that the whole line was enabled to advance.

(iv) Liaison. Liaison generally left a good deal to be desired. The closest liaison must be kept by every unit with those on its flanks. On one occasion our Flank was left some 2,000 yards in rear of the Flank of a neighbouring Division until the news of the advance had filtered back from his advanced troops to Divisional H.Q across to these H.Q and so back to the advanced infantry. This could not have happened had the Battalion Commanders been in close touch with each other.

(v) Stokes and Rifle Grenades. Rifle Grenades were freely used by some units with excellent results and posts captured under their covering fire.
It is thought that a great deal more use might have been made of Stokes Mortars. The whole Battery could well have been in action as arrangements for ammunition supply could very easily have been made.

(vi) Generally speaking, the Patrol work and initiative of units of the Division were excellent and it merely requires attention to the above few points to make them perfect.

5. In order that the Divisional Staff may keep in touch with the training; Brigades, C.R.A, C.R.E and O.C, 1/1st Bn, Monmouthshire Regt, will send in daily by 6.00 pm the outlines of the work their units are doing on the morrow.
In the case of a Tactical exercise, the principles to be brought out and place and time of commencement, and, in the case of Route Marches, the starting point, time and route will be forwarded.

[signature]

Copy to XIII Corps.

Lieut-Colonel,
General Staff, 46th Division..

SECRET. Copy No. 19

Addendum No. 1 to 46th Division Order No. 319.
****

5th September, 1918.

1. In continuation of 46th Division Order No. 319 of 4th September.

1. The 46th Divisional Artillery will be withdrawn from action on the night of the 6th/7th September, under arrangements to be made between C.R.As., 46th and 19th Divisions.

2. The 46th Brigade, R.F.A., will come under the orders of the 19th Division.

3. On completion of relief, the 46th Divisional Artillery will return to their wagon lines.

4. Tactical command of the artillery covering 46th Division front will pass to 19th Div: Art'y at 12 midnight, 5th/6th September, 1918.

[signature]
Lieut-Colonel,
General Staff, 46th Division.

Issued at 10.40 am.

To all recipients of 46th Div: Order No. 319.
Copies as before.

7.35
5.9.18.

19th Division
GA 381/48

56th Bde. (4)
57th Bde. (4)
58th Bde. (4)
C.R.A. (5)
D.M.G.O. (1)
O.C. Signals. (1)

POLICY TO BE FOLLOWED BY TROOPS OF 19th DIVISION.

1. Whilst the present advance continues the following general policy will be adopted.

The next objective for the Division will be given to the Brigades in the line.

The latter will then send forward patrols to reconnoitre the ground and obtain information regarding the enemy's strength and location.

All ground gained by these patrols will be held. If some opposition is encountered, strong fighting patrols covered by artillery fire will advance and establish themselves at selected points on or near the objective, and will then work their way outwards towards the flanks so as to cut off any pockets of Germans still remaining.

This artillery covering fire will be arranged direct between Brigadiers and their respective Artillery Group Commanders.

2. Unless it is considered that the enemy are in some strength, each Brigade in the line will carry out the above policy independently, the object being deliberately to establish ourselves in Salients at certain points in the German outpost screen, and thus compel him to fall back from the remainder of the line if he is to avoid being cut off. Such tactics were very successfully employed against us by the enemy in his recent offensives in March and April of this year.

3. Each Inf. Bde. and Battn. concerned will detail a special unit, such as a Company or a Platoon, to protect each flank of the Salient thus formed and to keep in touch by means of patrolling with the units of our own troops on either flank.

4. If the enemy is considered to be in some strength, Divl. Hd Qrs. will be informed and a combined operation will be arranged as soon as practicable.

5. It must be impressed on all ranks that at present the hostile troops opposite this portion of the front comprise second rate troops or units which have been recently exhausted in the main battles in the South. It is also known that the rearguard screen have orders to fall back if seriously attacked. A vigorous policy will therefore be followed by Brigadiers combined with enterprise and initiative on the part of junior officers.

/ 6. P.T.O.

6. To carry out the above policy it is essential that Battn. Hd Qrs. should be well forward (not more than 1,000 to 2,000 yards from the Picquot Line) and that Hd Qrs. of Bdes. in the line should be as close as possible to one another and not more than about 4,000 to 5,000 yards from the Picquet Line.

7. What is the ultimate line of resistance on which the enemy intends to stand firm is at present uncertain, but it may possibly be as far back as the HAUTE DEULE CANAL which runs through DON.

8. Liaison between Bdes. and Battns. and the corresponding units on each flank is all important and can only be ensured by the personal visits of Liaison Officers at least twice daily. If necessary, officers from the Reserve Battns. must be employed on these duties.

9. With constant changes of Hd Qrs., lateral communication by wire is impracticable and every effort will be made to establish visual signal communication laterally between adjoining Bdes. and Battns.

Arrangements are being made to supply Hd Qrs. of Battns. holding the line with Aldis lamps whereby messages can be sent back direct via the Balloon of No. 4 Balloon Section which is working in rear of the Divl. front. Such visual signals have been read up to distances of 10,000x under favourable conditions.

B L Montgomery

Lieutenant-Colonel,
General Staff.

19th Division,
5th September 1918.

Copy to 55th Division.

59th Division.

XIII Corps.

War Diary

App 13

Copy No. 29

Secret.

46th DIVISION ORDER No. 320.
****

Ref: Map - HAZEBROUCK,
5.A, - 1/100,000.

11th September, 1918.

46th Divisional Headquarters will close at GOSNAY at midnight 11th/12th September.

[signature]

Lieut-Colonel,
General Staff, 46th Division.

Issued at 11.30 am.

Copy No. 1 to C.R.A.
2 C.R.E.
3 Signals.
4 137th I.B.
5 138th :
6 139th :
7 1st Monmouths.
8 46th Bn, MGC.
9 A.A & Q.M.G.
10 Div'l Train.
11 S.S.O.
12 A.D.M.S.
13 D.A.D.V.S.
14 D.A.D.O.S.
15 D.A.P.M.
16 D.G.O.
17 Div'l Depot.
18 Camp Comm't.
19 G.S.O I.
20/21 XIII Corps.
22/23 III Corps.
24 19th Div'n.
25 47th :
26 55th :
27/28 File.
29/30 War Diary.

War Diary

App^x 13A

Secret.

Copy No. 25

46th DIVISION ORDER No. 321.

Ref: Map FRANCE 62.C, 1/40,000.

15th September, 1918.

1. 46th Divisional Artillery, less S.A.A Section of the D.A.C, will move to the area H 1 and H 2, NORTH of HEM, on the morning of the 16th September, reporting to the Area Commandant, SUZANNE, for Billets.

2. It is expected that orders as to their disposal will be awaiting their arrival.

3. There are no restrictions as to routes.

4. 46th Divisional Artillery to acknowledge.

[signature]

Lieut-Colonel,
General Staff, 46th Division.

Issued at 8.45 pm.-

Copy No.		Copy No.	
1	to C.R.A.	15	to D.G.O.
2	C.R.E.	16	D.A.P.M.
3	Signals.	17	Camp Commandant.
4	137th I.Bde.	18	Div'l Depot.
5	138th :	19/20	III Corps.
6	139th :	21	G.S.O I.
7	1st Monmouths.	22/23	File.
8	46th Bn, M.G.C.	24/25	War Diary.
9	A.A & Q.M.G.		
10	Div'l Train.		
11	S.S.O.		
12	A.D.M.S.		
13	D.A.D.V.S.		
14	D.A.D.O.S.		

"A" Form
MESSAGES AND SIGNALS.

Army Form C. 2121
(In pads of 100)

No. of Message..............

Prefix.......... Code..........m | Words | Charge | This message is on a/c of: | Recd. at..........m.
Office of Origin and Service Instructions | Sent At..........m. To.......... By.......... | ....Service. Signature of "Franking Officer." | Date.......... From.......... By..........

TO Div'l Train. Q

App 14

Sender's Number.	Day of Month.	In reply to Number.	AAA
* G.153	18th		

IX Corps wire begins AAA Transport of 46th Division (less artillery) will move forthwith from present area by march route to BAYONVILLERS - LA MOTTE - FRAMERVILLE - RAINECOURT Area AAA Accommodation from Area Commandant FRAMERVILLE route CORBIE - VILLERS BRETTONNEUX - LA MOTTE - BAYONVILLERS AAA Officers in command of transport to establish his H.Q near and be in touch with Area Commandant FRAMERVILLE AAA ends Further wire from IX Corps begins AAA Transport to include S.A.A Section of D.A.C AAA ends.

3 + men 162 ~~196~~ 200 Com

From 46th Div:
Place
Time

The above may be forwarded as now corrected. (Z)

Censor. Signature of Addressor or person authorised to telegraph in his name.

[signature] for G.S.

* This line should be erased if not required.

(4715) Wt. W3253/P511 1,113,336 Shts. 2/18 C. & Co. (E634)

"A" Form
MESSAGES AND SIGNALS.

Army Form C. 2121
(In pads of 100.)

No. of Message............

Prefix..............Code..............m.	Words	Charge.	This message is on a/c of:	Recd. at......m.
Office of Origin and Service Instructions	Sent		..............Service.	Date..............
	At ....m.			From ....
	To			
	By		(Signature of "Franking Officer")	By..........

TO War Diary

Sender's Number.	Day of Month.	In reply to Number.	AAA
G. 155	10		

Transport of Division (less Artillery) will move as under AAA, Ref. map AMIENS sheet 17 AAA WUGU Group to FRAMERVILLE starting 7.45 pm AAA WUWO Group to BAYONVILLERS starting 8.45 pm AAA WUFA Group RAINECOURT starting 9.45 pm AAA DHQ PIGE and HULU in above order of march to LA MOTTE starting point for DHQ Group road junction FRANVILLERS - BONNAY Road with PONT NOYELLES-ALBERT Road AAA Head of DHQ transport to pass S.P at 10.45 pm AAA S.A.A Section DAC to move with WUFA Group and proceed to LA MOTTE AAA Route from present billets to new areas for all above via CORBIE-VILLERS BRETONNEUX - LA MOTTE AAA Bde transport officers will be in charge of Bde Groups and Camp Commandant of DHQ Group AAA Acknowledge.

App: 15

From
Place VANA
Time

The above may be forwarded as now corrected. (Z)

(sgd) S.Hay, Major.

Censor. Signature of Addressor or person authorised to telegraph in his name

* This line should be erased if not required.

Order No 1625 Wt. W3253/ P 511. 27/2 H. & K., Ltd. (E. 263/

War Diary

App: 16

Secret.

Copy No. 27

46th Division Order No. 322.

Ref: Maps, 1/20,000,-
62.B. SW., 62.B. NW., 62.C. SE.

19th September, 1918.

1. The 46th Division is taking over a portion of the 1st Division and 4th Australian Division fronts.

2. The 138th Infantry Brigade will probably relieve the Right Brigade of the 4th Australian Division on the night of the 21st/22nd September.
The 139th Infantry Brigade will relieve the Left Brigade (2nd Infantry Brigade) of the 1st Division on the night of the 20th/21st September.

3. A Conference will be held at the 2nd Infantry Brigade H.Q at 10.00 am, on the 20th September, at which all details will be arranged. The following officers of 46th Division will attend the Conference :-
G.O.C, 139th Infantry Brigade.
Battalion Commanders, do.
O.C, 46th Battn, Machine Gun Corps.
C.R.E.

4. On completion of relief, the 139th Infantry Brigade will come temporarily under orders of the 1st Division.

5. The O.C, 46th Bn, M.G Corps, will arrange to take over the 2nd Infantry Brigade front with one Company.

6. The C.R.E, 46th Division, will arrange to take over the work in progress on the 2nd Infantry Brigade front.

7. Administrative arrangements for the 139th Infantry Brigade Group will be made by 46th Division.

8. ACKNOWLEDGE.

NOTES.-
1. 2nd Infantry Brigade H.Q are at MAISSEMY, R 23 b central.
Cars should be left in sunken road about R 23 a 5.9.
Route - Past Crucifix in R 25 d - Cross roads R 32 a 2.8. VERMAND - Over River to 27 c central - MAISSEMY.

2. The Brigade front will probably be held by one Battalion in the front line.

3. A certain amount of bomb fighting in trenches is taking place and will probably continue.

4. The front line of the 2nd Infantry Brigade is from about :- M 9 c 5.2 to M 9 d 0.8 thence to M 3 a 8.8 where it joins the 4th Australian Division.

[signature]
Lieut-Colonel,
General Staff, 46th Division.

Distribution over.-

Issued at 10.00 pm.

Copy No. 1 to C.R.A.
2 C.R.E.
3 Signals.
4 137th I.Bde.
5 138th :
6 139th :
7 1st Monmouths.
8 46th Bn, M.G.C.
9 "Q".
10 Div'l Train.
11 S.S.O.
12 A.D.M.S.
13 D.A.D.V.S.
14 D.A.D.O.S.
15 D.A.P.M.
16 D.G.O.
17 Camp Commandant
18 Div'l Depot
19 G.S.O I.
20 1st Division.
21 2nd Infantry Brigade.
22 4th Australian Division.
23/24 IX Corps.
25/26 File.
27/28 War Diary.

War Diary

App: 57

Secret.

Copy No. 27

46th DIVISION ORDER No. 323.

Ref: Sheets, 1/20,000,
62.B.SW; 62.B.NW; 62.C.SE; 62.C.NE.

20th September, 1918.

1. The 138th Infantry Brigade will night of the relieve the 4th and 12th Australian Infantry Brigades on the 21st/22nd September; details being arranged between Brigadiers concerned.

2. Boundaries are shown on the attached trace (issued to those marked #).
The 139th Infantry Brigade will be on their RIGHT.
The 1st Australian Division on their LEFT.

3. The 137th Infantry Brigade will move on the 21st September into the Reserve Brigade Area with two Battalions disposed about squares R 4, L 34, L 28 and one battalion about R 8 and R 2. Battalions of this Brigade to be E. of the VENDELLES Railway Line by Noon.

4. The O.C, 46th Bn, M.G Corps, will arrange to relieve with three companies the Machine Guns of the 4th Australian Division forward of a line L 36 c 0.0 - L 24 c 0.0 on the night of the 22nd/23rd September. Forward parties will be sent up on the 22nd September, under arrangements to be made between M.G. Battalions.

5. The C.R.E will arrange to take over from the C.R.E, 4th Australian Division the more important of the R.E and Pioneer work now in progress.

6. The A.D.M.S will arrange for R.A.M.C reliefs, in consultation with the A.D.M.S, 4th Australian Division.

7. At 10.00 am, 22nd September, the command of the front held by the 139th and 138th Infantry Brigades will be taken over by the G.O.C, 46th Division.

8. At 10.00 am, 22nd September, the 46th Division will be disposed as follows :-

Divisional H.Q.-	VRAIGNES.
RIGHT (139th) Bde .	MAISSEMY.
LEFT (138th) I.B .	VENDELLES (R 2 c 4.2).
Reserve (137th) I.B .	do.-

9. As soon as possible after taking over the line, the G.O's.C, 138th and 139th Infantry Brigade, will in consultation with the O.C, 46th Div'l Signal Co, R.E, select a combined headquarters close to the inter-brigade boundary about DEAN TRENCH; to which they will move as soon as it can be prepared.

10. The role of the 46th Division will be to maintain the line already won, to improve the observation over the BELLENGLISE Salient and to conform with any advance made by the 1st Division on our right.
The Line of RETENTION, for the maintenance of which all the resources of the Division may be used, will be the EASTERN edge of BERTHAUCOURT and the ridge from G 34 c 3.2 along the old German Support Line to the NORTHERN Divisional Boundary.

P.T.O.

11. Artillery arrangements will be notified later.

12. ACKNOWLEDGE.

Lieut-Colonel,
General Staff, 46th Division.

Issued at 5·30 pm.

Copy No. 1*to C.R.A.
2* C.R.E.
3* O.C, Signals.
4* 137th I.Bde.
5* 138th "
6* 139th "
7 1st Monmouths.
8* 46th Bn, M.G Corps.
9* "Q".
10 Div'l Train.
11 S.S.O.
12* A.D.M.S.
13 D.A.D.V.S.
14 D.A.D.O.S.
15 D.A.P.M.
16 D.G.O.
17 Camp Commandant.
18 Div'l Depot.
19* G.S.O I.
20 1st Division.
21* 4th Australian Division.
22 1st Australian Division.
23/24 IX Corps.
25/26* File.
27/28 War Diary.

War Diary

App: 19

Secret.

C.R.A.	1st Bn, Monmouthshire Regt.
C.R.E.	46th Bn, M.G Corps.
137th Inf: Bde.	"Q".
138th : :	IX Corps.
139th : :	1st Division. 1st Aus: Div:

46th Division G.113/13. 21st Sept: 1918.

Ref: Maps: 1/20,000 Sheets.

46th Division Instructions for the Defence of the LEFT (S. HELENE) Sector of the IX Corps Front.

1. The line will be held as thinly as possible consistent with safety, and full use will be made of Vickers and Lewis Guns to economise men.

2. The Valley between BERTHAUCOURT and HELENE Ridge will be wired as soon as possible by the 139th Inf: Bde; the C.R.E making special arrangements to assist.

3. The defence of this Valley will be carried out primarily by patrolling and by machine guns; and the wire should be arranged with this in view.

4. That portion of the HINDENBERG Line which is in our possession will be wired, the Old GERMAN Front Line being wired first.

5. The retention of the HELENE Ridge is of vital importance and especially the ground which has been gained at the SOUTHERN end. In order to strengthen this position and facilitate the capture of PONTRUET the 138th Inf: Bde will clear the enemy out of any trenches he occupies in the N.W corner of M 4 a as soon as possible and will establish a post about M 4 a 0.4.

6. The 139th Inf: Bde will drive the enemy back down BEUX Trench and GALLICHET Alley and prepare a plan for the capture of PONTRUET Village, FORGANS Trench EAST of that Place and the Spur in M 10 b.
This operation will probably be undertaken in conjunction with an attack by the 1st Division in three days time.
It is suggested that the attack should be made from the NORTH and if this is done it is important to ascertain the condition of the ground shown as flooded on the map.

7. Any suggestions for bombardments should be forwarded as early as possible and will be carried out if circumstances permit.

8. Stokes Mortars should prove invaluable to assist in the above minor operation and also to assist in the holding of Trench Bomb Stops.

[signature]

Lieut-Colonel,
General Staff, 46th Division.....

War Diary App: 18

Secret.

46th Division - Daily Disposition Return.

Dispositions at 6 a.m., 21st Septr. 1918.

46th Div. H.Q.	GAUVIGNY FME., Q.32.d.9.1.
137th Inf. Bde. H.Q.	Q.28.d.1.4.
138th " " "	TERTRY, W.2.c.1.6.
139th " " "	MAISSEMY.

for Lieut-Colonel,
General Staff, 46th Division.

20/9/18.

Secret.

War Diary

46th Division - Daily Disposition Return.

Dispositions at 6 a.m., 22nd Septr. 1918.

App: 20

46th Div. H.Q.	VRAIGNES, Q.19.b.7.7.
137th Inf. Bde. H.Q.	VENDELLES.
138th " " "	VENDELLES.
139th " " "	MAISSEMY.

[signature] for

Lieut-Colonel,
General Staff, 46th Division.

21/9/18.

War Diary App. 23

Secret.

46th Division - Daily Disposition Return.

Dispositions at 6 a.m., 23rd Septr. 1918.

46th Div. H.Q.	VRAIGNES, Q.10.b.7.7.
137th Inf. Bde. H.Q.	Q.18.c.0.8.
138th " " "	R.8.b.4.6.
139th " " "	~~R.[illegible]~~ R9b6.6.

CAR[illegible] for

Lieut-Colonel,
General Staff, 46th Division.

23/9/18.

War Diary App: 21

Confidential. To be destroyed when finished with. No. 1.

46th DIVISION.
Summary of OPERATIONS and INTELLIGENCE from
4 am 21st to 4 am 22nd September, 1918.

OPERATIONS. At midnight, one of our patrols fired on and dispersed an enemy patrol of 18 men at M 3 d 50.52. ST HELENE was found to be occupied by hostile L.M.G posts. Other patrols examined wood about M 9 a 7.8 and trench running S.E from M 3 b 40.95 to M 3 b 80.55, both being found clear of enemy. Shots came from M 3 b 95.45, where there is a possible enemy post.

Our Stokes Mortars fired 100 rounds on trench junction M 9 c 9.7.

ENEMY OPERATIONS. Yesterday afternoon and evening hostile artillery shelled woods and low ground in MAISSEMY Area, apparently searching for Battery positions. BERTHAUCOURT received 200 rds H.E during the 24 hours. There was also some Blue X Gas Shelling of area G 32, guns apparently firing from G 35 a 80.75.

Trench mortar fire consisted chiefly of occasional rounds on front line of our left brigade section.

At night enemy aircraft dropped bombs around G 32 central.

INTELLIGENCE. Individual movement (totalling 50 men in all) in Easterly direction from PONT RUET during the afternoon indicated a local relief, men being in full marching order.

Documents identifying 58 I.R, 119 Div, and dated 18th inst, were found in G 27 b in dug-outs vacated by enemy apparently on 19th inst.

Photographs of PONT RUET Area taken yesterday show what appears to be new work (dug-outs, machine gun positions and trenches), in M4 c and M10 a.

A Map of these features has already been issued to those concerned.

Read
for

Lieut-Colonel,
General Staff, 46th Division...

22/9/18.

War Diary

App: 26

Secret.

46th Division - Daily Disposition Return.

Dispositions at 6 a.m., 24th Septr. 1918.

46th Div. H.Q.	VRAIGNES, Q.19.b.7.7.
137th Inf. Bde. H.Q.	Q.18.c.0.8.
138th " " "	R.8.b.5.5.
139th " " "	R.9.b.6.8.

[signature]

25/9/18.

Lieut-Colonel,
General Staff, 46th Division.

War Diary

App: 24

Confidential. To be destroyed when finished with. No: 2.

46th DIVISION.
Summary of OPERATIONS and INTELLIGENCE from
4 am 22nd to 4 am 23rd September, 1918.

OPERATIONS. At 7 pm, the enemy put down a heavy artillery and T.M. barrage of all calibres on BERTHAUCOURT and followed it up at 7.15 pm by an infantry attack along the line of GALLICHET ALLEY and the PONTRUET-BERTHAUCOURT Road. The attackers, estimated at 150 men, came over the open on both sides of the road and also bombed down the trench. Parties advancing over the open were repulsed by small arm fire. Bombing parties, after reaching sunken road at M 9 c 3.3 were ejected by an immediate counter-attack. One dead German, identified as 13th Jager Battalion, was left in our lines. The remainder of the period under review was fairly quiet.

At 5 pm, one of our small patrols killed one and probably wounded several others of an enemy party encountered in BEUX TRENCH.

ENEMY OPERATIONS. Apart from barrage preceding infantry attack, enemy's artillery activity was of a desultory harassing character, including shelling of battery areas, roads, and high ground about TUMULUS. A 7.7 cm battery firing from near BELLENGLISE shelled M 2 d. during the evening.

Trench mortars and machine guns showed no special activity.

INTELLIGENCE. Individual movement was again noticeable E. of PONTRUET, the direction of movement being away from the front line and the number of men counted (about 30 in all) being about the same as yesterday.

S Read Lt
for

Lieut-Colonel.
General Staff, 46th Division.

23/9/18.

War Diary

App: 25

Secret.

Copy No. 17

46th DIVISION ORDER No. 324.

Ref: Maps:- 1/20,000,
62.B.SW; 62.B.NW; 62.C.SE; 62.C.NE.

23rd September, 1918.

1. In conjunction with an attack by the 1st Division, the 46th Division will attack and capture PONTRUET, on the plan laid down in 46th Division G.113/21 of the 22nd September.

2. The LEFT Attacking Brigade of the 1st Division is the 2nd Inf: Bde, with Headquarters at ~~R 30 a 4.2.~~ R29 d 9.6.

3. On reaching the S.E- point of their objective (M 10 b 5.4) the 138th Inf: Bde will send up the Success Signal (White over White over White) repeating it after five minutes.

4. Watches will be synchronised by O.C, 46th Div: Sig: Co, R.E, with A.D, Signals, IX Corps, at noon and 6.00 pm on the 23rd September.

O.C, Signals will arrange to synchronize with
Infantry Brigade.
C.R.A.
M.G Bn.
"G" Office.
at 1.00 pm and 7.00 pm, 23rd September.

5. Artillery Barrage Tables will be sent separately to those concerned.

6. Zero Hour will be notified by wire in minutes Plus or Minus from 5.00 am.

Thus a zero of 5.20 am would be "Plus 20".

7. ACKNOWLEDGE.

S. Hay Mai
for Lieut-Colonel,
General Staff, 46th Division..

Issued at 10.00 am.

Copy No. 1 to C.R.A.
2 C.R.E.
3 Signals.
4 137th Inf: Bde.
5 138th : :
6 139th : :
7 46th Bn, M.G Corps.
8 1st Monmouths.
9 "Q".
10 A.D.M.S.
11 D.A.P.M.
12 1st Australian Division.
13 1st Division.
14/15 IX Corps.
16 G.S.O I.
17/18 War Diary.
19/20 File.

War Diary

App: 27

Confidential. To be destroyed when finished with. No. 3.

46th DIVISION
Summary of OPERATIONS AND INTELLIGENCE from 4 am, 23rd, to 4 am, 24th September, 18.

OPERATIONS. At 5 am, 24th inst, we attacked enemy positions in PONTRUET Area in co-operation with attacks by the divisions on our right. Our attacking troops occupied BEUX Trench and LEDUC Trench in M 9 c and d, part of PONTRUET N. of road in M 9 b, FOURMI Trench in M 3 a, b and d, and FORGANS Trench N. of BELLENGLISE - S.HELENE Road.

Up to 6 pm, 24th inst, enemy were holding out in PONTRUET Trench, PALARIC Trench, Southern portion of PONTRUET and FORGANS Trench S. of BELLENGLISE - S.HELENE Road. About 130 prisoners, exact number not yet ascertained, and six machine guns were captured in this operation.

Identifications are given below.

INTELLIGENCE. Prisoners captured this morning comprised approximately 100 men of 262 R.I.R. (79 R.D.), 6 of 44 I.R. (2 Div.), 11 of 15th Jager Bn. (197 Div.), 2 of 2 Gren. Rgt., the last are probably attached to 4 Gren. Rgt. (2 Div.) The 2 Div., previously in line S. of ST QUENTIN, is stated to have reinforced the front in PONTRUET Sector between the 18th and 21st inst. The order of battle in this sector has been somewhat confused owing to numerous recent reliefs. The 44 I.R. appear to have held FORGANS Trench, N. of PONTRUET; the 262 R.I.R. holding PONTRUET and part of FORGANS Trench in M 4 c. and M 10 a.

Some of the prisoners stated that a British attack was expected on the 24th inst. or 25th inst., and that special orders had been issued to meet it. There was also stated to be a general expectation that the Germans would attack very soon with the object of regaining high ground overlooking their present positions.

for S Readle
Lieut-Colonel.
General Staff, 46th Division.

24/9/18.

War Diary

App. 28

Secret. Copy No. 12

46th DIVISION ORDER No. 325.

Ref: Maps - Sheets, 1/20,000.
62.B.SW; 62.B.NW; 62.C.SE; 62.C.NE. 25th September, 1918.

1. The Battalion of the 138th Inf: Bde which carried out the attack on PONTRUET will be withdrawn to-night into Reserve.

2. All Posts NORTH and WEST of the Village now held by us will continue to be held but the village itself will be evacuated.

3. The Battalion of the 137th Inf: Bde now in support to 138th Inf: Bde will remain in its present position pending further orders.

4. The C.R.A will arrange S.O.S. Lines not to come SOUTH of an E. and W. Line through M 10 c 0.3, and will keep FORGANS Trench, the Communication Trench in M 4 d, PALARIC and PONTRUET trenches under fire during the night.
On the 25th September, the PALARIC, PONTRUET Quadrilateral, the BLOCKHOUSE and selected points in PONTRUET will be heavily bombarded under arrangements to be made by the C.R.A.
During this bombardment, the G.O.C, 139th Inf: Bde will arrange to thin out his front lines.

6. The 139th Inf: Bde will make the necessary preparations to attack the QUADRILATERAL and BLOCKHOUSE from the S.W, in case the Division is instructed to take these trenches.

5. The 139th Inf: Bde is responsible for holding the line held by it prior to the attack, and, in addition, all ground outside the Village captured by it to-day.
The 138th Inf: Bde is responsible for withdrawing the Company of 139th Inf: Bde now attached to it and returning it to its Battalion.
This Company is now occupying the trench running S.W. and N.E. just S. of PONTRUET Church.

7. ACKNOWLEDGE.

P. Hayman
for Lieut-Colonel,
General Staff, 46th Division...

Issued at 1.40 am.

Copy No. 1 to C.R.A.
2 137th Inf: Bde.
3 138th : :
4 139th : :
5 46th Bn, M.G Corps.
6 1st Division.
7/8 IX Corps.
9 G.S.O I.
10/11 File.
12/13 War Diary.

War Diary

App: 29

Secret.

46th Division - Daily Disposition Return.

Dispositions at 6 a.m., 25th Septr. 1918.

46th Div. H.Q.	VRAIGNES, Q.19.b.7.7.
137th Inf. Bde. H.Q.	Q.18.c.0.8.
138th " " "	R.6.a.7.5. (In line).
139th " " "	R.9.b.6.6. (In line).

[signature]

Lieut-Colonel,
General Staff, 46th Division.

24/9/18.

War Diary

App 44

Secret.

Copy No. 17

40th DIVISION ORDER No. 326.

Ref: Map :- OMISSY, 1/20,000.

25th September, 1918.

OPERATION "C".

1. At an hour and date to be notified later, the 46th Division, as part of a major operation, will cross the S.QUENTIN CANAL between G 34 d 6.5 and G 22 b 6.0, capture the HINDENBURG LINE and advance to a position shown on the attached Map "A" (GREEN LINE).

2. The 30th American Division is operating with its RIGHT some 1,000^{x} to the NORTH and, on crossing the CANAL, turns SOUTH and occupies a position on the DOTTED GREEN LINE.

3. The 137th Inf: Bde will capture the First and Second Objectives "BROWN LINE"; after which the 139th Inf: Bde on the RIGHT and 138th Inf: Bde on the LEFT will pass through to the final objective, joining hands with the 30th American Division.

4. On completion of the capture of the GREEN LINE, the 32nd Division passes through to the RED LINE.

5. Objectives and approximate times are shown on Map "A" and Appendix "A".

6. One Battalion of Tanks is being allotted to the Division and will operate half each with the 138th and 139th Inf: Bdes, passing through the gap made by the American Division and joining the 46th Division before the advance to the YELLOW LINE.

7. Further detailed instructions will follow, and these, together with Minutes of Conferences held from time to time will be acted upon as orders.

8. ACKNOWLEDGE.

[signature]

Lieut-Colonel,
General Staff, 46th Division....

Issued at 9.00 am

Copy No. 1 to C.R.A.
2 C.R.E.
3 Signals.
4 137th Inf: Bde.
5 138th : :
6 139th : :
7 46th Bn, M.G Corps.
8 A.A. & Q.M.G.
9 A.D.M.S.
10 1st Division.
11 30th American Division.
12/13 IX Corps.
14 G.S.O I.
15/16 File.
17/18 War Diary.
19 32nd Division.

Appendix "A" on back.

APPENDIX "A" to accompany 46th DIVISION ORDER No. 326.

Objective.	Barrage lifts off.	Pause.	Infantry again advance.	Pace of Barrage per 100^{x}.
BLUE.	0 plus 1 hour 40 minutes.	30 minutes.	0 plus 2 hours 10 minutes.	2 mins.
BROWN.	0 plus 2 hours 30 minutes.	3 hours.	0 plus 5 hours 30 minutes.	4 mins.
YELLOW.	0 plus 6 hours 10 minutes.	30 minutes.	0 plus 6 hours 40 minutes.	4 mins.
DOTTED BLUE.	0 plus 7 hours 20 minutes.	30 minutes.	0 plus 7 hours 50 minutes.	4 mins.
GREEN.	0 plus 8 hours 40 minutes.	-	-	4 mins.

War Diary

App 32

Confidential. To be destroyed when finished with. No. 4.

46th DIVISION
Summary of OPERATIONS and INTELLIGENCE from 4 am 24th to 4 am 25th September, '18.

OPERATIONS. Fighting continued in PONTRUET and FORGANS Trench during the day. During enemy counter attack, we captured 1 Officer and 8 O.R's., of the 51 I.R., 11 Div. Eventually, in view of the number of enemy reinforcements, who arrived from FLUTE Trench and from EASTERN side of ST QUENTIN CANAL, we withdrew from the NORTHERN position of PONTRUET to our original front line.

We continued to hold posts E. of ST HELENE and E. of SUNKEN Road in M.3.b.

The total number of prisoners taken in this operation and passed through Divisional Cage up to 6 pm to-day was 1 Officer and 119 O.R's. In addition to this, a number estimated at 40 to 50 wounded prisoners were cleared through Dressing Stations.

INTELLIGENCE. In addition to the identifications already reported, prisoners of the following units, were captured yesterday in PONTRUET Area :- 51 I.R. (11 Div:), 273 I.R. (197 Div:), 601 Telephone Detachment (79 R.D.), 263 R.I.R. (79 R.D.). Three companies of the last named regiment were brought up from reserve positions in FLUTE Trench during the afternoon, and took up positions in PONTRUET and PALARIC Trenches towards dusk.

Photos taken 24th inst., show following new features :- 9 AE. A 164 - Bank in G.28.d is occupied. Strong tracks leading to it from Canal Bridge in G.29.

9.AE. A 164, 6, 7, 8) Show following differences from BELLICOURT WEST, 1/10,000 map in regard to bridges and dams over ST QUENTIN Canal.

New bridges at G.34.b.60 (light railway bridge), G.29.c.25.38 (foot bridge).

Bridge removed G.34.b.80.45, bridge at G.34.d.80.53 damaged.

Dam removed from G.29.c.37.90; probable dam at G.29.c.37.58. Water level south of this dam lower than north.

Platforms prepared at G.34.d.50.63.

Very little water in canal south of dam at G.34.b.9.3.

9 AE. A 162, 24th Sept: New trench extending 200 yards south west from FORGANS Trench, M.10.a.95.85.

J Read Lt
for
Lieut-Colonel,
General Staff, 46th Division...

25th September, 1918.

War Diary

app: 30

Secret.

Copy No. 15

46th DIVISION ORDER No. 327.

****

Ref: Maps:- Sheets, 1/20,000,
62.B.SW; 62.B.NW; 62.C.SE; 62.C.NE.

25th September, 1918.

1. The 1st Division will relieve the 139th Infantry Brigade and that portion of the 138th Infantry Brigade SOUTH of G 33 b 4.4 on the night of the 26th/27th September.

2. The 139th Infantry Brigade will take over that part of the 138th Infantry Brigade front SOUTH of G 27 b 2.1.

3. On completion of relief, each Brigade will be on a one battalion front.

4. On completion of relief, the SOUTHERN Boundary of the Division will run :- G 33 b 4.4 - G 33 a 0.5 thence along road running S.W. to present boundary (inclusive to 46th Division).

5. Further details, M.G relief, Artillery arrangements, etc, will be notified later.

6. ACKNOWLEDGE.

[signature]

Lieut-Colonel,
General Staff, 46th Division.

Issued at 8.15 pm.

Copy No. 1 to C.R.A.
2 C.R.E.
3 Signals.
4 137th Inf: Bde.
5 138th : :
6 139th : :
7 1st Monmouths.
8 46th Bn, M.G.C.
9 A.A. & Q.M.G.
10 A.D.M.S.
11 O.C, Div'l Observers.
12 G.S.O I.
13/14 File.
15/16 War Diary.
17. 1st Divn
18/19 IX Corps.

War Diary

App 31

SECRET.

Amendment No. 1 to 46th Division Order No. 327.
****

25th September, 1918.

1. Para 2 will be amended to read as follows :-

The 139th Infantry Brigade will be withdrawn into Reserve in the area R.8, 9, 14 and 15.

2. Delete para 3.

S. Haywai
for Lieut-Colonel,
General Staff, 46th Division....

Issued to all recipients
of 46th Division Order No. 327.

War Diary

App: 33

S e c r e t.

46th Division - Daily Disposition Return.

Dispositions at 6 a.m., 26th Septr. 1918.

46th Div. H.Q.	VRAIGNES, Q.19.b.7.7.
137th Inf. Bde. H.Q.	Q.18.c.0.8.
138th : : :	R.8.b.5.5.
139th : : :	R.9.b.6.6.

[signature]

Lieut-Colonel,
General Staff, 46th Division.

25/9/18.

S e c r e t.

War Diary

App. 34

46th Division - Daily Disposition Return.

Dispositions at 6 a.m., 27th Septr. 1918.

46th Div. H.Q.	VRAIGNES, Q.19.b.7.7.
137th Inf. Bde. H.Q.	Q.18.c.0.8.
138th " " "	R.8.b.5.5.
139th " " "	R.9.b.6.6.

[signature]
for Lieut-Colonel,
General Staff, 46th Division.

26/9/18.

War Diary App 45

Secret. Copy No. 21

46th DIVISION INSTRUCTIONS - OPERATION "C". No. 1.

46th Division G.114/2. 25th September, 18.

S E C R E C Y.

1. The necessity for secrecy will be impressed on all ranks. Attention is drawn to Fourth Army Leaflet "Keep your mouth shut", and Commanders are responsible for ensuring that a copy of this leaflet is pasted in A.B. 439 of every officer and A.B. 64 of every N.C.O and man. Demands for any copies required will be forwarded to General Staff, 46th Division, by telephone or wire.

2. Commanders will take all possible steps to prevent the scope or date of the operation becoming known except to those taking part. Any officer, N.C.O or man, discussing the operation in public or communicating details regarding it to any person, either soldier or civilian, not immediately concerned, will be severely dealt with.

3. All movement of troops and transport in an easterly direction after receipt of this order will take place by night, whether in the forward or back areas of the IX Corps, except where absolutely necessary to move by day.

4. No orders will be given or reference made, to the operations on the telephone within 3,000 yards of the front line, and every effort will be made to avoid any telephonic conversations on this subject forward of Divisional Headquarters.

5. Commanders will ensure that the number of officers reconnoitring the enemy's positions is limited to those for whom such reconnaissance is essential.
Nothing attracts attention to an offensive more than a large number of officers with maps looking over the parapet and visiting O.P's, as has again been proved by information received from German prisoners with reference to our attack on the 13th September, which was given away by this means.
Commanding Officers of Units holding the front line should report at once to higher authority any disregard of these orders.

[signature]
Lieut-Colonel,
General Staff, 46th Division...

Issued at 2.00 pm.

Copy No. 1 to	C.R.A.	Copy No. 7 to	46th Bn MGC.
2	C.R.E.	8	A.A & Q.M.G.
3	Signals.	9	A.D.M.S.
4	137th I.Bde.	10	30th American Div'n.
5	138th :	11	G.S.O I.
6	139th :	12/13	File.

Copies Nos. 14/15 War Diary.

War Diary App 46

VERY SECRET. Copy No. 18

OPERATION "C".
46th DIVISION INSTRUCTIONS No. 2

(Based on Notes of a Conference held at Divisional Headquarters, 25th Sept: 1918).

46th Division G.114/4. 26th September, 18.

1. Forming up :- On Y/Z night, the ~~139th and 138th~~ 137th Inf: Bdes, ~~each on a one battalion front~~, will be in the line, with ~~137th~~ 138 & 139 Inf: Bdes in rear, each on a one Bn Front.
The necessary reconnaissances will be carried out by Brigades concerned.
~~During Y/Z night, the 137th Inf: Bde, on a three battalion front, will move through the Brigades in the Line and will form up on its jumping off Line in time to follow the barrage.~~
Engineers and Pioneers will form up in rear of the units for the assistance of which they are detailed to work.

2. Headquarters :- Advanced Divisional Headquarters will be at R 8 b 6.3, S.E. of VERMELLES.
All three Brigade Headquarters will be together, if suitable accommodation can be found.

3. Advance. The 137th Inf: Bde will advance at Zero hour under a barrage. The 138th and 139th Inf: Bdes will not advance until ordered by Divisional Headquarters.

4. Crossing of the CANAL. A General description of the CANAL and a Section at the SOUTHERN end of the Divisional Front has been issued to all concerned.
Water where it exists is probably up to between 7 and 8 feet deep.
The Storming Brigade (137th) will be equipped as lightly as possible.
Each Officer and man will wear a Lifebelt and a large number will carry a light 8 fathom heaving line.
Light 9 foot scaling ladders will be carried at the rate of 6 per Company.
As many collapsible boats, light rafts and mats as possible will be provided.
The positions of existing bridges and dams are probably the most suitable places to cross.
A tot of rum per man will be got across as soon as possible for the Storming Infantry.
Immediately in rear of the Storming Infantry, the 46th Division and 32nd Division Engineers and Pioneers working in conjunction will prepare foot and artillery bridges for the passage of the remaining two Infantry Brigades and for the 32nd Division.

5. Advance from BROWN LINE. Before the 138th and 139th Inf: Bdes advance from the BROWN LINE, it is probable that the Hill in G 23 b, 18 c, which up till then has been neutralised by artillery fire, will have been taken by the Americans.
Thenceforward our LEFT Flank should be secure.
The Tanks should join the Division on this Line, and although impossible to arrange any definite plan of action working with the Infantry, they should prove of the greatest value working on their own initiative for the Infantry.
The Infantry will be instructed to assist them forward by every means in their power and smoke grenades will be carried for this purpose.

P.T.O.

As regards the 139th Inf: Bde, it is intended that a proportion of Tanks should be detailed to advance along the trenches immediately NORTH of the CANAL, where considerable opposition may be expected.

6. Consolidation. After the 138th and 139th Inf: Bdes have passed through, the G.O.C, 137th Inf: Bde will devote the whole of his attention to the maintenance of the Bridgehead he has formed.

7. Preliminary Operations. The capture of the enemy trenches in G 34, 28, 22 c and 21 d on X day or X/Y night, is a possible operation which must be considered.

Further it is quite possible that the preliminary bombardment may induce the enemy to withdraw his troops to the EAST of the CANAL.

Brigades in the Line will therefore actively patrol towards the enemy lines and will occupy any ground vacated by him.

8. Preliminary Reliefs. Prior to Y day the Division will be relieved as far NORTH as its attacking SOUTHERN Boundary (Map "A").

Should time permit, it is intended to relieve the 138th and 139th Inf: Bdes by the 137th Inf: Bde for a period of from 24 to 48 hours.

9. Artillery Arrangements. The assault will be preceded by an intense bombardment by all natures of artillery with a view to breaking up the CANAL and defences and destroying the enemy's moral.

Prior to this bombardment, heavy concentrations of mustard gas shell will be fired into selected areas.

The Field Artillery allotted to the Division allows of one gun per 25 yards and considerable depth of barrage during the earlier stages.

Later, owing to the move forward of certain artillery, this barrage becomes less intense.

It will not be necessary, once the battle has opened, to move forward any artillery in order to cover the GREEN LINE, this Line being covered from the first positions.

A considerable amount of smoke will be used on selected targets and, in the barrage, one round of smoke per gun will be fired just ~~before~~ each lift and in the protective barrages.
after

10. Machine Gun Arrangements. The broad principle of the employment of the machine guns will be as follows :-

The 6th and 100th Machine Gun Battalions will be utilised under Corps arrangements for barrage work against the CANAL Bank.

The 46th Bn, M.G Corps, will closely support the infantry, working in two Groups, and moving from one fire position to another, so that at least one Group is always in action supporting the Infantry advance.

On reaching the Final Objective, the equivalent of one Company will be well forward in close support of the Infantry; the remaining Companies disposed in depth as far back as the KNOBKERRY RIDGE.

A more detailed plan will be issued later.

Preparations must be made to establish ammunition dumps right forward and in the fire positions, so that the mobile ammunition to be carried forward will not be drawn upon until necessary.

Dumps will be formed E. of the CANAL at the earliest possible moment.

Ammunition limbers will follow as closely as possible.

11. Preliminary Arrangements.

(a) Photography. Commencing on W day daily, photographs of the CANAL on the divisional front will be asked for, taken at a low altitude, in order that the amount of destruction and alteration may be noted.

(b) Barges on the CANAL. In consultation with the Intelligence Officer, the C.R.E will note down the position of any barges on the CANAL which may assist the crossing and will keep a map of these for the General Staff.

(c) Bridges, ladders. Bridges, ladders, mats, etc, will be prepared by the C.R.E as rapidly as possible.

(d) Roads. Roads and tracks will be prepared for traffic and a map of these prepared by the C.R.E, showing trench crossings, bridges, etc, existing and proposed, as far forward as the CANAL.

(e) Artillery. Forward routes (to bring his guns to a bridge to be constructed about G 29 c 3.3) will be reconnoitred by the C.R.A, who will inform the C.R.E where he requires trench bridges placed.
Inf: Bde Commanders will notify Divisional Headquarters as to any enemy work they wish destroyed.

(f) Forming up positions - will be reconnoitred by Inf: Bdes and preparations made to have lines taped.

(g) Guides. 138th and 139th Inf: Bdes should detail guides to proceed in rear of 137th Inf: Bde and be prepared to direct their own Brigades to the CANAL crossings.
Guides will also be required to meet the Tanks about the BROWN LINE. These should be detailed at once, so as to study the country; they need not be informed as to the true reason of their employment.

(h) Special Party. The G.O.C, 137th Inf: Bde, will detail a Special Party to look for and guard the exits from the BELLENGLISE TUNNEL. The officers of this party must be given every facility for studying the area.

12. Divisional Observers. Will make a study of the ground EAST of the CANAL within the Divisional area.
During the operation they will work forward in two parties; one party observing and keeping touch with the Division, whilst the other moves forward to the next observation point.

13. Horses. Horses will be kept as far forward as possible and will be moved across the CANAL at the earliest opportunity. Mounted orderlies should prove of great value and officers must use their horses wherever possible.

14. Transport. Pack Transport must be organised and limber transport got forward as soon as possible, but not before 32nd Dn has passed through, or on receipt of orders from D.H.Q.

15. Headquarter Flags. Divisional and Brigade Headquarters will always be marked with their flags.
It is advisable for Battalion Headquarters also to be so marked. A light jointed pole can easily be carried.

P.T.O.

16. Medical Arrangements. The A.D.M.S will work in close touch with the A.D.M.S, 32nd Division. A.D.S in the first instance will be as close to the CANAL as possible.

17. Signal Communications.

The O.C, Signal Company, R.E, will work out the Signal arrangements in consultation with Brigade Commanders.

18. Administrative. Administrative Instructions will be issued by A & Q, 46th Division.

19. ACKNOWLEDGE.

[signature]

Lieut-Colonel,
General Staff, 46th Division..

Issued at 7.00 am.

Copy No. 1 to C.R.A.
2 C.R.E.
3 Signals.
4 137th Inf: Bde.
5 138th : :
6 139th : :
7 46th Bn, M.G Corps.
8 A.A & Q.M.G.
9 A.D.M.S.
10 1st Division.
11 32nd Division.
12 30th American Division.
13/14 IX Corps.
15 G.S.O I.
16/17 File.
18/19 War Diary.

War Diary

App 47

Secret.

Copy No. 19

OPERATION "C".
46th Division Instructions No. 3.

46th Division G.114/5. 26th September, 1918.-

GAS BOMBARDMENT.
****

1. With reference to 46th Division Instructions No. 2, para. 9, the Mustard Gas Bombardment will commence at 10 pm to-day, wind permitting.

2. The areas to be bombarded are shown on the attached tracing.

3. The Bombardment will cease about 6 am, 27th September.

4. Should the wind be in a quarter dangerous to our own troops, the bombardment will be cancelled and units will be notified by the Code Word "OFF" sent direct by C.R.A to Infantry Brigades, 46th Bn, M.G Corps, 1st Division and 30th American Division and 46th Division "G".

5. The D.G.O will arrange for forward wind observations both before and during the Bombardment, and will inform the C.R.A at once should the wind shift to a dangerous quarter.

6. Units in the Line will take every precaution by increasing the number of gas sentries, etc.

7. ACKNOWLEDGE.

[signature]

Lieut-Colonel,
General Staff, 46th Division...

Issued at 11.45 am.

Copy No. 1 to C.R.A.
2 C.R.E.*
3 Signals.*
4 137th Inf: Bde.*
5 138th : :
6 139th : :
7 46th Bn, M.G Corps.
8 A.A & Q.M.G.*
9 A.DM.S.*
10 D.G.O.
11 1st Division.
12 32nd Division.*
13 30th American Division.
14/15 IX Corps.*
16 G.S.O I.
17/18 File.
19/20 War Diary.

* No tracing attached.

Very Secret

War Diary

App: 48

20

OPERATION "C".
46th Division Instructions No. 4.

46th Division G.114/C. 26th September, 1918.

1. Z day. Z day is not known yet but all preparations must be made assuming that the attack commences early on the morning of the 29th September.

2. Zero hour. Will be notified to all concerned on the afternoon of Y day.

3. Watches. Watches will be synchronised by O.C, Signal Co, with Corps Headquarters by telephone between 6 and 7 pm on Y Day; and with C.R.A, C.R.E, three Infantry Brigades, Machine Gun Battalion, 1st Monmouths, O.C, Divisional Observers and "G" Office between 9 and 10 pm on the same day.

4. Bridges. The IX Corps are undertaking the repair of the Bridges at M 5 b 8.0, G 34 d 5.5 and G 22 b 8.0.
The C.R.E, 46th Division, will arrange to construct a road bridge at about G 29 c 3.3.

5. Communications. (a) All possible arrangements will be made so that once the advance has commenced, communications may be maintained by Visual Signalling, Mounted Messengers, etc.

(b) Red Flares, Discs and rifles placed three in a row and parallel to each other, muzzles towards the enemy, will be employed to indicate the position of the troops to aircraft.
It is to be again impressed on all ranks how essential it is to use these means of communication when called for.

(c) The following light signals will be employed :-

(i) Success Signal - "We have reached objective".	32 Grenade,- White over White over White.
(ii) S.O.S.	32 Grenade,- Red over Red over Red.
(iii) Cavalry Signal - "Advanced troops of Cavalry are here".	White star turning to red in a Parachute. (Used by Cavalry only).

6. Pioneers. 1st Monmouthshire Regt will work under the C.R.E, who will give them all necessary instructions.

7. Plans and Maps. The following will forward their detailed plans, with Maps where necessary, to "G", 46th Division, by 8 am, 27th September.

C.R.A.- Barrage Map and action of Heavy Artillery; Artillery bridges across trenches.
C.R.E.- Roads, tracks and proposed foot and road bridges over the CANAL.
Signals.- Map showing Visual Arrangements.
AA & QMG- Map showing Dumps and proposed Forward Dumps.
M.G Bn.- Dispositions of Guns and Barrage Lines.
ADMS.- Medical Arrangements.
DAPM.- Arrangements for collecting prisoners.
(To be sent through the AA & QMG).

P Acknowledge

[signature]
Lieut-Colonel,
GS 46th Division...

(2)

Issued at.- 2 pm.

Copy No. 1 to C.R.A.
2 C.R.E.
3 Signals.
4 137th Inf: Bde.
5 138th " "
6 139th " "
7 46th Bn, MGC.
8 AA & QMG.
9 ADMS.
10 1st Division.
11 32nd Division.
12 CRE, 32nd Division.
13 30th American Division.
14/15 IX Corps.
16 IX Corps HA.
17 GSO I.
18/19 File.
20/21 War Diary.

Very Secret

War Diary

Copy No. 20

App 49

OPERATION "C".
46th Division Instructions No. 5.

46th Division G.114/7. 26th September, 1918.

1. On the night of the 27th/28th September, the 137th Inf: Bde will relieve the 138th Inf: Bde with all three battalions in the Line.

2. By the morning of the 28th September, the Division will be disposed as on attached Map "B", clearing a line R 10 central, L 33 central, L 21 central by 8 pm. 27th September.

3. Advanced Divisional and Brigade Headquarters will be established by 10 pm, 28th September.

4. On Y/Z night, the Division will have moved into positions shown on Map "C" by Zero - 30 minutes.

5. At Zero plus 10 minutes the Division will be disposed as in Map "D"; from these positions, the 138th and 139th Infantry Brigades will not move pending orders from Divisional Headquarters.

6. ACKNOWLEDGE.

[signature]

Lieut-Colonel,
General Staff, 46th Division.

Issued at 3.40 pm.

Copy No. 1 to C.R.A.
2 C.R.E.
3 Signals.
4 137th Inf: Bde.
5 138th : :
6 139th : :
7 46th Bn, M.G.C.
8 AA & QMG.
9 ADMS.
10 1st Division.
11 32nd Division.
12 CRE, 32nd Division.
13 30th American Division.
14/15 IX Corps.
16 IX Corps HA.
17 GSO I.
18/19 File.
20/21 War Diary.

Note.- Maps follow.

War Diary

App 35

Confidential. To be destroyed when finished with. No. 5.

46th DIVISION.
Summary of OPERATIONS and INTELLIGENCE from
4 am 25th to 4 am 26th September, '18.

OPERATIONS. Patrols during the night approached PIKE WOOD, PEG COPSE, and enemy trench in G.28. Hostile M.G's fired from all these localities and bombs were thrown from a forward post near G.34.central. No enemy patrols were encountered.

Our Artillery engaged M.G. nests in PONTRUET with 4.5" hows.

ENEMY OPERATIONS. Hostile artillery was less active than during the previous 24 hours. There was, however, persistent shelling of ASCENSION VALLEY with various calibres and intermittent shelling of our supports. Registration was suspected on LE VERGUIER.

Hostile trench mortars, apparently situated in FORGANS Trench in M.10.b. and M.11.a., were active at night on our forward posts in M.3.b.

INTELLIGENCE. Individual movement and motor and ambulance traffic was seen at various times of the day on roads between NAUROY, JONCOURT and MAGNY. The amount of movement was not excessive. A convoy of 12 wagons moved along BELLICOURT - NAUROY Road towards BELLICOURT at 8.25 pm. Men apparently searching for wounded were seen in PONTRUET, and a party of 20 men in full marching order were seen to run from PONTRUET to FORGANS Trench at 10.30 am.

An enemy post occupied by 7 men was seen at G.23.c.02.60.

Enemy aeroplanes were active. Two red planes flew over our lines between 2 pm and 3 pm.

Read Lt
for
Lieut-Colonel,
General Staff, 46th Division.

26/9/18.

War Diary

App 50

VERY SECRET. Copy No. 20

OPERATION "C".
48th Division Instructions No. 6.

48th Division G.114/10. 27th September, 1918.

1. Immediate Support to Storming Brigade. The Forward Battalion of each of the 138th and 139th Inf: Bdes must keep in closest liaison with the G.O.C, 137th Inf: Bde and have their Headquarters or Observers so placed that they can obtain immediate information (by direct observation, if possible) of the state of affairs EAST of the CANAL.

Should it appear at any time that the 137th Inf: Bde, having crossed the CANAL, are being outfought through lack of support, these battalions will, on their own initiative and without waiting for orders, advance across the CANAL to reinforce; information as to their action being sent to their own and 137th Inf: Bde Headquarters.

A great deal is left to the discretion of these two Battalion Commanders. On their grasp of the situation may depend the success of the operation, whilst at the same time they must remember that it is useless for them to hurl their battalion into an action which has already failed on the WEST side of the CANAL.

In the event of these two Battalions being used, the 138th and 139th Inf: Bdes will at once close up their other two battalions to occupy the line vacated.

2. Success Signals. The 137th Inf: Bde will fire success signals from each Company :-

(a) On gaining the EASTERN Bank of the CANAL.

(b) On reaching the BLUE Line.

(c) On reaching the BROWN Line.

The 138th and 139th Inf: Bdes, on reaching each objective.

3. Supply Tanks. It is hoped that a Supply Tank will be available to follow the Fighting Tanks, in which event it will bring a supply of S.A.A (bundle packed), S.A.A (charger packed) and 36 Grenades; and form a Dump at LA BARAQUE (G 35 a 9.9).

In addition, each Tank will carry as much S.A.A, both bundle and charger packed, as possible.

4. Tank Signals. As a reminder, the 5 Tank Signals are issued herewith for distribution to Platoon Commanders.

5. Advance of Infantry. The two rear Infantry Brigades will necessarily pass through the gun lines. Officers should therefore reconnoitre the best routes through this area.

6. Advanced Headquarters.

Advanced H.Q of 137th Inf: Bde will be at G 31 c 15.35.
: : : 138th : : : : : G 31 d 7.8.
: : : 139th : : : : : G 25 d 4.5.

P.T.O.

After the initial move forward, the 138th and 139th Inf: Bde Headquarters will remain as nearly as possible together and near the Inter-Brigade Boundary.

7. Communications. All Units will remember that, being on their RIGHT, it is necessary for this Division to keep Signal touch with Units of the 30th American Division.
Other than regular Signal Communications, it is the duty of all units to gain touch on both flanks, forwards, and backwards.
The O.C, Signal Co, will arrange that from 8 am, 27th, touch is maintained by D.R to the 30th American Division without passing through the respective Corps.

8. Wire Gaps. The O.C, 46th Bn, M.G Corps, will obtain from the C.R.A a Map showing the positions where it is proposed to cut gaps in the wire- and will arrange to keep such gaps as possible under intermittent fire during the night.

9. ACKNOWLEDGE.

[signature]

Lieut-Colonel,
General Staff, 46th Division...

Issued at 7 am.

Copy No. 1 to C.R.A.
2 C.R.E.
3 Signals.
4 137th Inf: Bde.
5 138th : :
6 139th : :
7 46th Bn, M.G Corps.
8 A.A & Q.M.G.
9 A.D.M.S.
10 1st Division.
11 32nd Division.
12 CRE, 32nd Division.
13 30th American Division.
14 IX Corps HA.
15/16 IX Corps.
17 GSO I.
18/19 File.
20/21 War Diary.

The above notes are from the minutes of Conferences held at 138 Bde H.Qs on the 26 Sept

War Diary app 51

VERY SECRET. Copy No. 20

OPERATION "C".
46th Division Instructions No. 7.

46th Division No. 114/11. 27th September, 18.

Machine Gun Arrangements.

1. The 2nd Life Guards and 100th Machine Gun Battalion are placed at the disposal of the 46th Division for Barrage work.

2. Location -

2nd Life Guards.- DEVISE area V 8 a and c.
100th M.G Bn.- BERNES area Q 10 a and b.

3. On completion of their barrage work, these two Units revert to Corps Reserve.

4. Lt-Col: MATHEW-LANNOWE, DSO, Commanding 46th Bn, M.G Corps, will act as Divisional Machine Gun Commander, with an Officer from the IX Corps as his Staff Officer.
The whole of the machine gun arrangements, etc, will be settled by him in consultation with the General Staff.
Orders will be issued by him direct to all three Battalions.

[signature]

Lieut-Colonel,
General Staff, 46th Division...

Issued at 9.45 am

Copy No. 1 to C.R.A.
2 C.R.E.
3 Signals.
4 137th Inf: Bde.
5 138th : :
6 139th : :
7 46th Bn, MGC.
8 AA & QMG.
9 ADMS.
10 1st Division.
11 32nd Division.
12 CRE, 32nd Division.
13 30th American Division.
14 IX Corps HA.
15/16 IX Corps.
17 GSO I.
18/19 File.
20/21 War Diary.
22 2nd Life Guards.
23 100th Bn, M.GC.

War Diary

App 52

VERY SECRET. Copy No. 20

OPERATION "C".
46th Division Instructions No. 8.

46th Division G.114/13. 27th September, 1918.

1. Action of the 1st Division. (a) A Detachment of the 1st Division is advancing at Zero in touch with 46th Division RIGHT and forming a defensive flank from the RIGHT of the original starting point to the CANAL at about G 34 b 5.0.

(b) During the advance of the 46th Division the 1st Division is maintaining a steady pressure against the enemy with a view to detracting his attention.

2. Machine Gun Arrangements. (General). The 2nd Life Guards and 100th Bn, M.G Corps, have now been placed at the disposal of the 46th Division for an indefinite period.
They will therefore be prepared to move forward under instructions to be issued by the Divisional M.G Commander and assist to cover the consolidation of the Division.

3. Contact Aeroplanes. Contact aeroplanes will be marked with a black rectangular board hanging from the rear edge of the plane.
Flares will be called for at -

Zero plus 3 hours.
Zero plus 5 hours.
Zero plus 7 hours 30 minutes.
Zero plus 9 hours.

4. Tanks. The Tanks working with the 46th Division will be two Companies of the 9th Battalion.-
One Company with each of the 138th and 139th Inf: Bdes.
It is hoped that they will arrive in time to move forward with the Infantry from the BROWN LINE.
Those working with the 139th Inf; Bde will pay special attention to the trenches immediately NORTH of the CANAL.
On the Final Objective being secured, the Tanks will withdraw under cover and be prepared to assist in repelling Counter Attacks.
Other Tanks will be passing through the 46th Division objective with the 32nd Division.
Markings.- Tanks will carry the usual Red and White markings and in addition, those working with the IX Corps will carry a RED "IX" painted on the side immediately abaft the Forward Mark.
Those working with the 46th Division will carry a 46th Division Flag "RED over GREEN".
Troops are to be reminded that great assistance can be given to Tanks by firing smoke grenades to blind Anti-Tank Guns and Strong Points from which they are being engaged.

5. Medical Arrangements. At Zero, the A.D.S will be at R 11 a 9.7, with a Bearer Relay Post at M 2 d 6.8.
Cars will be pushed forward as far as possible.

P.T.O.

When the situation permits, the A.D.S will be advanced to about M 2 d 6.8.

After the BROWN LINE has been taken a suitable place will be looked for near the CANAL Bank.

Bearers :- 16 R.A.M.C Bearers will be attached to each R.M.O of the 137th Inf: Bde and 8 to each R.M.O of the 138th and 139th Inf: Bdes. These will be augmented if found necessary.

Prior to Zero 50 Bearers will be at the A.D.S and 50 at VADENCOURT ready to move.

Reserve Bearers will be kept at VENDELLES.

Directing Boards.- Each party of bearers will carry Directing Sign Boards and the routes to A.D.S and for walking wounded will be clearly marked.

8. ACKNOWLEDGE.

Lieut-Colonel,
General Staff, 46th Division.

Issued at 1.00 pm

Copy No. 1 to C.R.A.
2 C.R.E.
3 Signals.
4 137th Inf: Bde.
5 138th : :
6 139th : :
7 46th Bn, MGC.
8 AA & QMG.
9 ADMS.
10 1st Division.
11 32nd Division.
12 CRE, 32nd Division.
13 30th American Division.
14 IX Corps HA.
15/16 IX Corps.
17 GSO I.
18/19 File.
20/21 War Diary.
22 2nd Life Guards.
23 100th M.G Bn.
24 9th Tank Battalion.
25 9th Sqdn, RAF.

War Diary

VERY SECRET. Copy No. 20

App. WD 53

OPERATION "C".
46th Division Instructions No. 9.

46th Division G.114/15. 27th September, 1918.

R.E. ARRANGEMENTS.

1. General. (a) The 46th Division R.E will construct light foot (Pack if possible) bridges over the CANAL.

(b) The 32nd Division R.E construct a heavy trestle bridge for M.T about G 34 d 5.5 and other Field Artillery Bridges.

(c) The 216th A.T Co, R.E, and 254th Tunnelling Co, R.E, construct a heavy bridge at G 34 d 5.5.

(d) The 574th A.T Co, R.E, and 180th Tunnelling Co, R.E, construct a M.T bridge at H 5 b 8.0.

(e) The 567th A.T Co, R.E and 256th Tunnelling Co, R.E, construct a bridge at G 22 b 8.0.

(f) All the above units send a Liaison Officer to C.R.E, 46th Division, at Zero Hour.
C.R.E, in consultation with the General Staff, will inform them as to the time when they can commence work.

(g) The 1st and 46th Divisional Pioneers commence work when the situation permits on existing roads leading to the above bridges.
Later in the day, these will be relieved by Corps Troops and will be available to work EAST of the CANAL.

2. Artillery Trench Crossings.- will be made at :-

G 33 b.
WATLING ST. in G 27.
G 21 c.
G 20 d.

3. Tracks and Bridges. Proposed Tracks and Bridges are shown on the attached Tracing.

4. Special Arrangements for 46th Division R.E.

(a) 466th Fd Co.- Three Sections are placed at the disposal of the 137th Inf: Bde for assistance in the use of material in crossing the CANAL by the Storming Troops, examining dug-outs, etc.- One Section, Reconnaissance of captured area up to BLUE LINE.

(b) 465th Fd Co.- Two Sections; Cork Pier Bridges and repair of existing Bridges.- Two Sections Reconnaissance in 139th Inf: Bde area.

(c) 468th Fd Co.- As for 465th Fd Co, but in 138th Inf: Bde area.

(d) 1/1st Bn, Monmouthshire Regt. Carrying parties for Cork Pier Bridges - 200 men. Remainder on tracks to these bridges.

P.T.O.

<u>Note</u>.- The Reconnaissance Sections may be diverted by order of their Field Company Commander to bridging work, should more men be required.
These sections will carry demolition charges.

(e) R.E Sections with the 137th Inf: Bde will form up and move as arranged by the Field Company Commander with the 137th Inf: Bde.

(f) The R.E and Pioneers dealing with Cork Piers will form up in front of the 139th and 138th Inf: Bdes and will follow close behind the 137th Inf: Bde and commence their work at the earliest possible moment.

(g) The Pioneers working on forward roads will commence their work immediately the CANAL has been crossed by the 137th Inf: Bde.

(h) Sections for Reconnaissance will form up in rear of the leading Battalions of the Brigades with which they are working and will advance with them.

5. ACKNOWLEDGE.

Lieut-Colonel,
General Staff, 46th Division...

Issued at 3.45 pm.

Copy No. 1 to C.R.A.
2 C.R.E.
3 Signals.
4 137th Inf: Bde.
5 138th : :
6 139th : :
7 46th Bn, MGC.
8 AA & QMG.
9 ADMS.
10 1st Division.
11 32nd Division.
12 CRE, 32nd Division.
13 30th American Division.
14 IX Corps HA.
15/16 IX Corps.
17 GSO I.
18/19 File.
20/21 War Diary.
22 2nd Life Guards.
23 100th Bn, MGC.

War Diary App: 36

Secret. Copy No. 13

46th DIVISION ORDER No. 328.

Ref: Maps :- Sheets,
62.C.NE; 62.C.SE; 62.B.NW; 62.B.SW. 27th September, 1918.

1. The 138th Infantry Brigade will capture the enemy trenches to-night from G 28 c 8.8 to PIKE WOOD inclusive, bombing SOUTH towards G 34 b 1.7 and N.E. to about G 28 b 3.3.

2. The C.R.A will arrange for a bombardment of these trenches and M.G. Posts by Artillery and Trench Mortars to commence at 4 pm; details being arranged in conjunction with the G.O.C, 138th Inf: Bde.
This bombardment will be extended as far SOUTH as G 34 b 1.7.

3. The Field Artillery barrage and all further details will be arranged between the G.O.C, 138th Inf: Bde and C.R.A.

4. Stokes Mortars will be employed in all Bombing work.

5. ACKNOWLEDGE BY WIRE.

[signature]

Lieut-Colonel,
General Staff, 46th Division..

Issued at 2.00 pm.

Copy No. 1 to C.R.A.
2 137th Inf: Bde.*
3 138th : :
4 139th : : *
5 46th Bn, M.G Corps.
6 1st Division.*
7 30th American Division.*
8/9 IX Corps.*
10 GSO I.
11/12 File.
13/14 War Diary.

* For information.

War Diary   App 37

SECRET.

46th Division - Daily Disposition Return.

Dispositions at 6 am, 28th Septr: 1918.

No change since last return.

sd/ M. Burns Lindow.
Capt: G.S.
for Lieut-Colonel,
General Staff, 46th Division.

27th Septr: 1918.

War Diary

App 58

Secret.

46th Division - Daily Disposition Return.

Dispositions at 6 a.m., 29th Septr. 1918.

46th Div. H.Q.	R.3.b.5.5.
137th Inf. Bde. H.Q.	G.21.c.10.65.
138th " " "	G.25.d.4.5.
139th " " "	G.31.d.7.7.

[illegible]

Lieut-Colonel,

29th Septr. 1918. General Staff, 46th Division.

War Diary App 54 46th

VERY SECRET.

Copy No. 25

OPERATION "C".

46th Division Instructions No. 10.

46th Division G.114/20. 28th September, 1918.

1. The 137th Inf: Bde will cut and prepare for crossing all wire between our old front line and present line occupied during the night; and will withdraw to our original line after dark to-night, leaving a few Platoon Posts which will be withdrawn an hour before Zero on Y/Z night.

2. On Y/Z night, the 137th Inf: Bde will form up on their original jumping off line and attack at Zero as previously arranged.

3. The 137th Inf: Bde will arrange to cover their LEFT Flank with Stokes Mortars along the Trench NORTH of PIKE WOOD and round PEG COPSE from Zero to Zero plus 20 minutes.

6" Mortars will shell the trenches NORTH of this as far as G 21 b 3.8 up to Zero plus 15'.

4. The C.R.A will arrange shrapnel harassing fire on the line of the CANAL and its crossing throughout the night.

5. ACKNOWLEDGE.

[signature]

Lieut-Colonel,
General Staff, 46th Division..

Issued at 1045 am.

Copy No. 1 to C.R.A.
2 C.R.E.
3 Signals.
4 137th Inf: Bde.
5 138th " "
6 139th " "
7 46th Bn, MGC.
8 AA & QMG.
9 ADMS.
10 1st Division.
11 32nd Division.
12 CRE, 32nd Division.
13 30th American Division.
14 IX Corps HA.
15/16 IX Corps.
17 GSO I.
18/19 File.
20/21 War Diary.
22 2nd Life Guards.
23 100th Bn, MGC.
24 9th Squadron, RAF.

War Diary App 55

VERY SECRET. Copy No. 20

OPERATION "C".
46th Division Instructions No. 11.

46th Division G.114/21. 28th September, 1918.

1. Mopping up Party for 137th Inf: Bde. The 138th and 139th Inf: Bdes will each detail one Company to follow the 137th Inf: Bde as far as the WESTERN Bank of the CANAL to deal with any enemy that are holding out in this area and collect Prisoners.
   They will rejoin their Battalions as early as possible after completion of this special task.

2. M.G. Danger Areas. The attached Map "E" shows the areas in which no troops, other than those in trenches, must be between Zero and Zero plus 15 minutes.
   At Zero plus 15 minutes the machine guns cease to fire and the area becomes safe.
   The Forward Companies of the 138th and 139th Inf: Bdes will therefore form up with the 137th Inf: Bde.
   The remainder of the leading battalions will form up in rear of the RED LINE marked on Map "E" and will not move forward of this until Zero plus 15 minutes.
   Troops of the 1st Division will be safe in FOURMI Trench provided they keep down in their trench.

3. ACKNOWLEDGE.

H. Hennam.
Lieut-Colonel,
General Staff, 46th Division.

Issued at 12 30 pm.

Copy No. 1 to C.R.A.
2 C.R.E.
3 Signals.
4 137th Inf: Bde.
5 138th : :
6 139th : :
7 46th Bn, MGC.
8 AA & QMG.*
9 ADMS.
10 1st Division.
11 32nd Division.
12 CRE, 32nd Division.*
13 30th American Division.
14 IX Corps.HA.
15/16 IX Corps.
17 GSO I.
18/19 File.
20/21 War Diary.
22 2nd Life Guards.
23 100th Bn, MGC.

* Map not attached.

Appx G.S. vol 48
Sept vol 48

Secret.

D.A.G.

Base.

****

46th Division No. G.85/39. 28/11/1918.

Will you please have attached copies of wires (Nos. G.410, 412, 416, 437, 439) sent out in connection with this Division's operations at BELLE-ENGLISE on 29th September, 1918, placed with the 46th Division General Staff War Diary for September, 1918 as Appendices Nos. 63 to 67 inclusive.

Please acknowledge receipt.

[signature] Capt

for Major-General,

Commanding 46th Division.

"A" Form. Army Form C. 2121.

MESSAGES AND SIGNALS. No. of Message

Prefix ..... Code ..... m.	Words	Charge	This message is on a/c of: ..... Service.	Recd. at ..... m.
Office of Origin and Service Instructions.	Sent At ..... m. To ..... By		(Signature of "Franking Officer.")	Date ..... From ..... By .....

War Diary

App 59

TO

Sender's Number.	Day of Month	In reply to Number	AAA
* G 435	29		

Dispositions for night ~~29/30~~ 29/30 AAA 139 on right 138 on left holding GREEN LINE in depth and CANAL BANK from GREEN to YELLOW AAA 137 holding BROWN LINE and CANAL BANK between BROWN and YELLOW AAA M.G Bn in depth from GREEN to BROWN inclusive AAA especially watching area S. of CANAL AAA 2nd Life Guards and 100th M.G Bn W. of CANAL on high ground round old front lines AAA 137 Bde may stand down keeping a few sentry groups AAA Troops holding N. Bank of CANAL to remain alert AAA 138 and 139 Bdes to stand down with outposts placed AAA Bdes to be prepared to hold GREEN LINE in case of enemy counter attack AAA All Bdes to report definite location of flanks with whom in touch and where AAA Added 3 Bdes M.G Bn CRA CRE reptd Corps.

From 46 Div.

Place

Time 7.10 pm.

The above may be forwarded as now corrected. (Z)

Censor. Signature of Addressor or person authorised to telegraph in his name.

(sgd.) .....

* This line should be erased if not required.

(6188) Wt. W14042 M44 300000 Pads. 12/15. Sir J. C. & S

"A" Form.
MESSAGES AND SIGNALS.

Army Form C. 2121.
(In pads of 100.)

No. of Message............

Prefix........ Code.......... m. | Words. | Charge.

Office of Origin and Service Instructions.

~~Operations~~
Priority
to 138 &
137 MG Bn.

Sent
At..........m.
To..........
By..........

This message is on a/c of:
..........Service.
(Signature of "Franking Officer.")

Recd. at...... m.
Date..........
From..........
By..........

TO 137 138 139 MG Bn. Corps Am. Div.

Sender's Number.	Day of Month.	In reply to Number.	AAA
* G.439	29		

The situation towards JONCOURT is not satisfactory AAA Australian troops are reported at H 19 central AAA 138 Bde will push out towards ETRICOURT to ensure touch in that direction AAA 137 Bde will be prepared to support 138 Bde with one Bn if called upon to do so AAA Reserve MG Co will be placed in position before dawn on general line H 20 central – ETRIGOURT in order to cover approaches from JONCOURT AAA General Line held by Australian Corps appears to be H 19 central – G 12 central AAA Make every effort to reorganise and be prepared to move at short notice AAA Transport must be split up and animals kept as far as possible in SUNKEN ROADS or banks AAA Addsd as above.

From 46 Div.
Place
Time 8.50 pm.

The above may be forwarded as now corrected.
(Z)
..........*Censor.*

(sgd) CF.J. Lt-Col.
Signature of Addressor or person authorised to telegraph in his name.

*This line, except **AAA**, should be erased if not required.

Wt. W 3253/P511. 500,000 Pads. 1/18. B. & S. Ltd. (E2389.)

"A" Form.
MESSAGES AND SIGNALS.

Army Form C. 2121.
(In pads of 100.)
No. of Message........

Prefix........Code........m. Words. Charge.
Office of Origin and Service Instructions.

Operations
Priority.

Sent
At........m.
To........
By........

This message is on a/c of: .... Service.
(Signature of "Franking Officer.")

Recd. at........m.
Date........
From........
By........

TO: 138 Bde.
32 Divn.

Sender's Number.	Day of Month.	In reply to Number.	AAA
* G. 437.	29		

138 Bde will be prepared to move a Bn to support of 32 Divn LEFT in event of enemy attack from N.E and if called upon to do so AAA There appear to be still some enemy about JONCOURT and H 7 and 8 AAA Addsd 138 Bde reptd 32 Div.

From
Place: 46 Div.
Time: 7.32 pm.

The above may be forwarded as now corrected. (Z)
.... Censor.
Signature of Addressor or person authorised to telegraph in his name.
(sgd) G. F. Jarram
Lt.Col.

*This line, except A A A, should be erased if not required.
Wt. W 3253/P511. 500,000 Pads. 1/18. B. & S. Ltd. (E2389.)

Army Form C. 2121
(In pads of 100.)

"A" Form
MESSAGES AND SIGNALS.

No. of Message..........

Prefix............Code..............m. | Words | Charge. | This message is on a/c of: | Recd. at......m.

Office of Origin and Service Instructions

138
139
Priority.

Sent
At ....m.
To ....
By ....

.....................Service.
(Signature of "Franking Officer")

Date..........
From..........
By..........

TO 137 138 139 Inf:Bdes.

Sender's Number.	Day of Month.	In reply to Number.	AAA
* G.410.	29		

Be in immediate readiness to move keep close touch with front by runner posts AAA Leading Battalion Commanders should push out to keep touch as already ordered AAA Addsd WUQU WUWB reptd WUFA

From
Place 46 Div.
Time 7.35 am.

The above may be forwarded as now corrected.
(Z)
(sgd) CF.Jerram, Lt Col.

Censor.
Signature of Addressor or person authorised to telegraph in his name

* This line should be erased if not required.

Order No. 1625. Wt. W3253/ P 511 27/2 H. & K., Ltd. (E. 2634).

Army Form C. 2121
(In pads of 100.)

"A" Form
MESSAGES AND SIGNALS.

No. of Message............

Prefix..............Code..............m. Office of Origin and Service Instructions	Words	Charge.	This message is on a/c of:	Recd. at......m.
	Sent At ....m. To .... By		................Service. (Signature of "Franking Officer.")	Date............ From .... By............

Appx 64

TO 138 139 Bde.

Sender's Number.	Day of Month.	In reply to Number.	AAA
G.412.	29		

Ref. my G.411 Div'l Comdr relies on you not to leave WUFA unsupported if they are across CANAL AAA Addsd WUQU WUWO

From 46 Div.
Place
Time 8.15 am.

The above may be forwarded as now corrected. (Z) (sgd) CE. Jerram. Lt-Col.

Censor. Signature of Addressor or person authorised to telegraph in his name

* This line should be erased if not required.

Order No. 1625. Wt. W2252/ P 511 27/2 H. & K., Ltd. (E. 2634).

"A" Form

Army Form C. 2121
(In pads of 100.)

MESSAGES AND SIGNALS.

No. of Message............

Prefix..............Code..............m.	Words	Charge.	This message is on a/c of:	Recd. at......m.
Office of Origin and Service Instructions	Sent		............Service.	Date..............
Urgent	At ....m.		Appx 65	From ....
Operations Priority.	To			By..............
	By		(Signature of "Franking Officer")	

TO 137 138 139 Bdes, 1st Div. 32nd Div.
30th Amer. Div. CRA. CRE. MG Bn.
IX Corps.

Sender's Number.	Day of Month.	In reply to Number.	AAA
G.416.	29		

BELLICOURT and NAUROY taken by Americans AAA Push straight through up to barrage on your objectives AAA Tanks should be arriving now AAA Enemy surrendering freely AAA Staffords reported in touch with Americans on the LEFT AAA Addsd as above.

From 46 Div.
Place
Time 9.50 am.

The above may be forwarded as now corrected.

(Z)

(sgd) S.Hay, Maj.

Censor. Signature of Addressor or person authorised to telegraph in his name

* This line should be erased if not required.

Order No. 1625. Wt. W8253/ P 511 27/2. H. & K., Ltd. (E. 2634).

"A" Form.

Army Form C. 2121.
(In pads of 100.)

MESSAGES AND SIGNALS.

No. of Message..............

Prefix............ Code............m | Words. | Charge.

Office of Origin and Service Instructions.

WAR
DIARY.

Sent
At..............m.
To..............
By..............

This message is on a/c of:
.... Service.
(Signature of "Franking Officer.")

Recd. at.........m.
Date..............
From..............
By..............

TO — Operations priority to 32 Div
139 Bde
CRA MG Bn.

Sender's Number.	Day of Month.	In reply to Number.	AAA
* G.468	30		

In accordance with Corps wire G.856 the 139 Inf Bde disposed in squares G 36 b c; M 6 a b; H 31 c d; H 32 c; N 1 a b; N 2 a with H.Q at G 29 a 3.7 is placed at disposal of GOC 32 Div as a reserve only to be used in case of emergency for 32 Div attack on the BEAUREVOIR-FONSOMME LINE between SEQUEHART and H 16 a AAA The 139 Bde will be in readiness to move at short notice from 3 pm 1st Oct: AAA L.T.M. Battery will be made up with amtn and will be used boldly if the Bde is called upon AAA GOC 32 Div is requested to keep 46 Div acquainted with any move of 139 Bde AAA 46 Divl Art and attached HA is placed at disposal of 32 Div from the receipt of this order AAA O.C 46 Div MG Bn will place one Company under orders of GOC 139 Bde AAA O.C Company to get in touch with GOC Bde in the morning AAA Addsd 139 Bde 32 Div CRA reptd 137 138 Bdes MG Bn 1st Div.

From 46 Div.
Place
Time 11 pm.

The above may be forwarded as now corrected. (Z) (sgd) C.F.Jerram, L-C.

Censor. Signature of Addressor or person authorised to telegraph in his name.

* This line should be erased if not required.

(3198.) Wt. W 12952/M1294. 375,000 Pads. 1/17. H. W. & V., Ld. (E. 818.)

"A" Form.
Army Form C. 2121.
(In pads of 100.)

MESSAGES AND SIGNALS.

No. of Message..............

Prefix............Code.............. m | Words. | Charge.
Office of Origin and Service Instructions.
This message is on a/c of: ....Service.
(Signature of "Franking Officer.")
Sent At..........m. To.......... By..........
Recd. at ....m. Date.......... From .... By..........

TO { War Diary

App 59

Sender's Number.	Day of Month.	In reply to Number.	AAA
* G. 453	30		

Following dispositions will be taken up today AAA 137 one Bn Square G 23 c and d 29 a and b one Bn Square G 29 c and d and G 35 one Bn Square G 27, 28 AAA 139 Bde two Bns in line M 5 b 5.0 - N 2 a 8.4 - H 32 b 5.4 line to be held thinly with supporting troops handy AAA 138 Bde two Bns in line H 32 b 5.4 - H 20 a 5.8 - to junction with Australians about H 19 central AAA One Bn 139 in billets about G 36 H 31 AAA One Bn 138 Bde in billets G 30 H 25 AAA 46 M.G Bn to pull back one Coy into reserve in Square G 29 flanks to be securely held but men except sentries to stand down Coy sent last night to H 19 area to remain watching LEFT Flank AAA 100 M.G Bn Square G 28 a and b G 22 c and d Pioneer Bn and RE to be collected and organised by CRE AAA 100 M.G Bn will clear battlefield in ~~this~~ their area AAA Brigades to organise and clear their areas without delay AAA Addsd 137 138 139 Bdes M.G Bn CRE reptd CRA Corps flank divs and Q

From 46 Div Adv.
Place
Time 8.50 am.

The above may be forwarded as now corrected. (Z) (sgd) CFJ.
Censor. Signature of Addressor or person authorised to telegraph in his name.

* This line should be erased if not required.

(3198.) Wt. W 12952/M1294. 375,000 Pads. 1/17. H. W. & V., Ld. (E. 818.)

War Diary

App 58

Secret.

46th Division - Daily Disposition Return.

Dispositions at 6 am., 30th Septr: 1918.

46th Div: H.Q.	R.8.b.5.5.
137th Inf: Bden H.Q.	G.21.c.10.65.
138th : : :) 139th : : :)	G.29.c.4.8.

[signature] for
Lieut-Colonel,
General Staff, 46th Division.

29th September, 1918.

War Diary

App 56

APPENDIX "A".

Objective.	Barrage lifts off.	Pause.	Infantry again advance.	Pace of Barrage per 100^{x}.
BLUE.	0 plus 1 hour 40 minutes.	30 minutes.	0 plus 2 hours 10 minutes.	2 mins.
BROWN.	0 plus 2 hours 30 minutes.	3 hours.	0 plus 5 hours 30 minutes.	4 mins.
YELLOW.	0 plus 6 hours 10 minutes.	30 minutes.	0 plus 6 hours 40 minutes.	4 mins.
DOTTED BLUE	0 plus 7 hours 20 minutes.	30 minutes.	0 plus 7 hours 50 minutes.	4 mins.
GREEN.	0 plus 8 hours 40 minutes.	-	-	4 mins.

1:20,000
NOTE CHANGE OF COLOUR.
Enemy Trenches in Blue.
OMISSY
PARTS OF
Bellenglise
Lehaucourt
Levergies
Pontruet
MAP "E"
TO ACCOMPANY
46TH DIVISION
G 114/21 of 28-9-18
M.G. DANGER AREA
DANGER AREA
UNLESS IN
TRENCHES

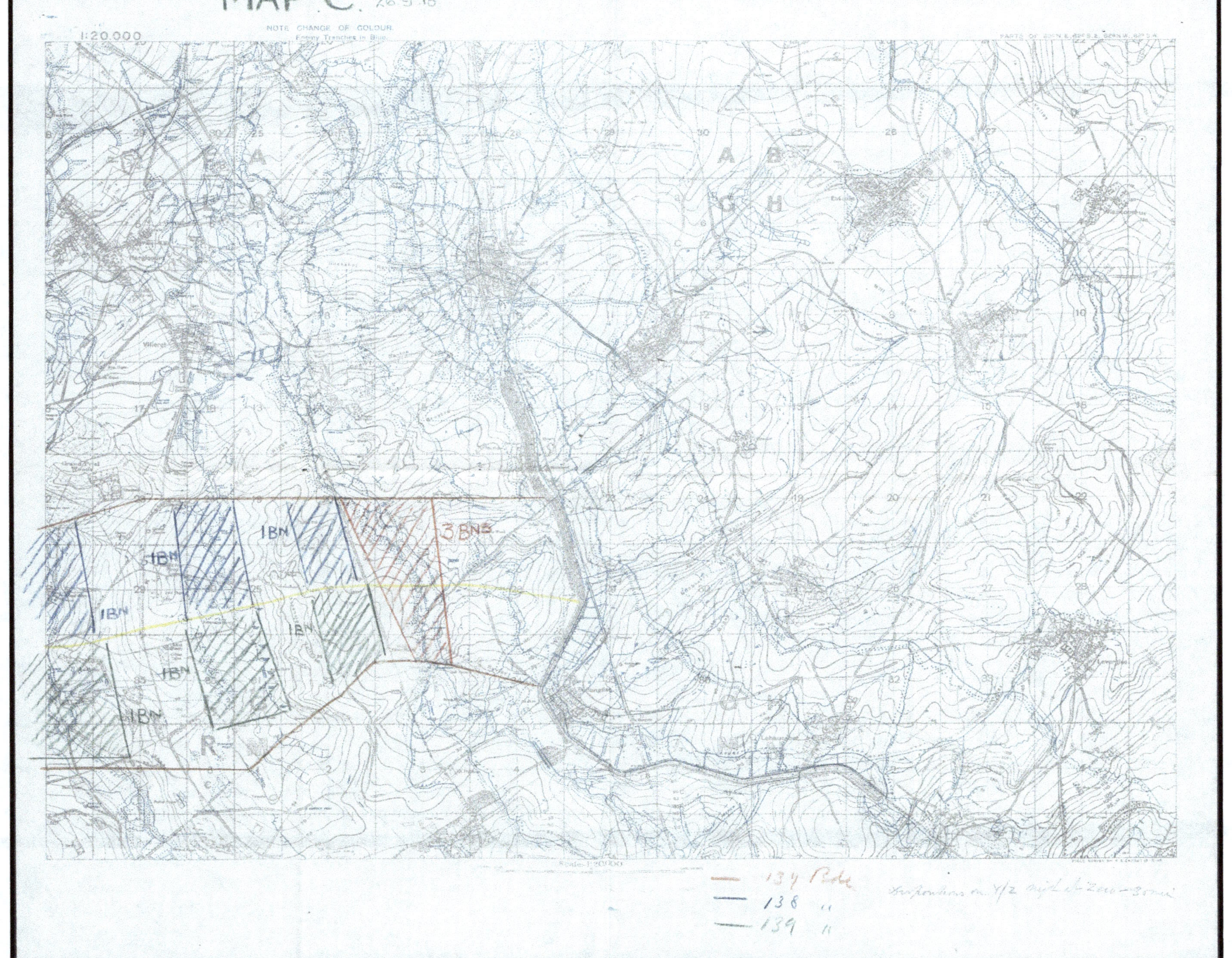

MAP C. 26.9.15
1:20,000
NOTE CHANGE OF COLOUR.
Enemy Trenches in Blue.
3 BNS
1 BN
1 BN
1 BN
1 BN
1 BN
1 BN
1 BN
134 Bde
138 "
139 "

MAP D

26-9-18

1:20,000

NOTE CHANGE OF COLOUR.
Enemy Trenches in Blue.

1 BN

1 BN

1 BN

1 BN

3 BNS

1 BN

1 BN

1 BN

— 137 Bde

— 138 "

— 139 "

appx 43

MAP 'A'

ENEMY REAR ORGANISATION.

EDITION 1.a

SHEET 57[B]

1:40,000

Note :- Additional fences and hedges shown thus

Note :- Shaded Area has not been revised from photographs.

Detail and Organisation revised from information rec

137 BDE

138 BDE

139 BDE

A B C E F G H I K L M N O Q R

LE CATEAU

1:20,000
NOTE CHANGE OF COLOUR.
Enemy Trenches in Blue.
OMISSY
Map 'A' App. 40.
Scale 1:20,000
App x 40

MAP "B" 26-9-18.
1:20,000
NOTE CHANGE OF COLOUR.
Enemy Trenches in Blue.
2 BNS
1 BN
3 BNS
1 BN
2 BNS
Scale 1:20,000
— 137 Bde
— 138
— 139

REFERENCE
OMISSY SHEET
1/20,000

TO ACCOMPANY 46TH DIVISION INSTRUCTIONS
No 3 26-9-18

16 17 18

22 23 24

28 29 30

34 35 36

G

M

4 5 6

To Accompany 46th Divn G114/15. 27·9·18.

Overlay Trace.

Reference.

Thorigny Sheet

1/20,000

26

H.T.

M.T.

M.T.

33

L G
R M

Reference

Tracks to be made passable before Zero

H.T. Bridge (Put in by 32nd Divn) :-

M.T. " " " " ") :-

Approximate sites for Foot Bridges :-

Tracks & Roads to be worked on by Pioneers of 46th Division & 32nd Division after Zero

Division of work to be decided between C.R.E's.

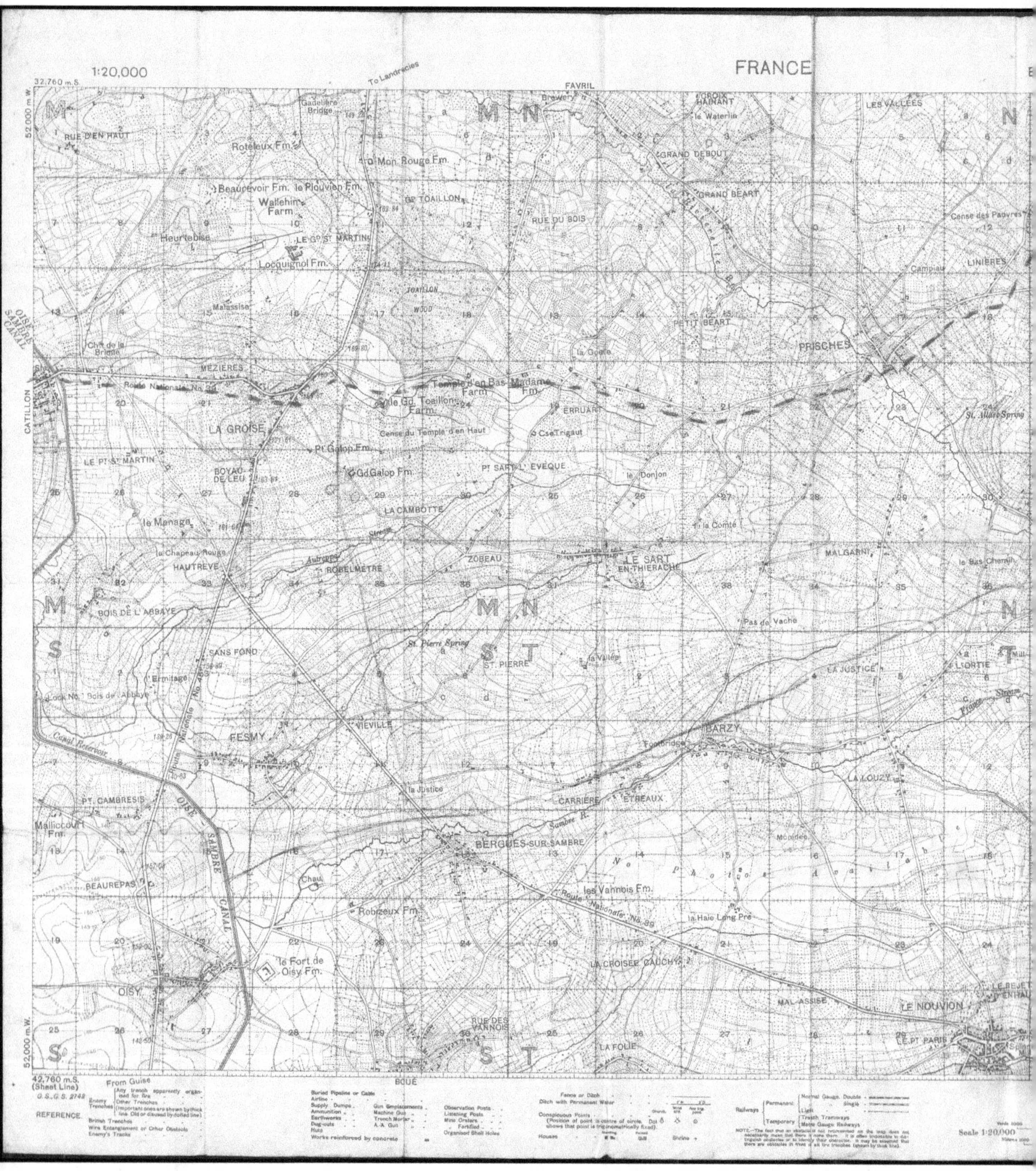

1:20,000
FRANCE
To Landrecies
FAVRIL
PRISCHES
LA GROISE
MEZIERES
CATILLON
OISE SAMBRE CANAL
LE SART EN THIERACHE
FESMY
BARZY
BERGUES-SUR-SAMBRE
OISY
LE NOUVION
ETREAUX
HAUTREVE
BOIS DE L'ABBAYE
ST. PIERRE
LA JUSTICE
Route Nationale No. 39
Sambre R.
BOUE
From Guise
REFERENCE
Scale 1:20,000

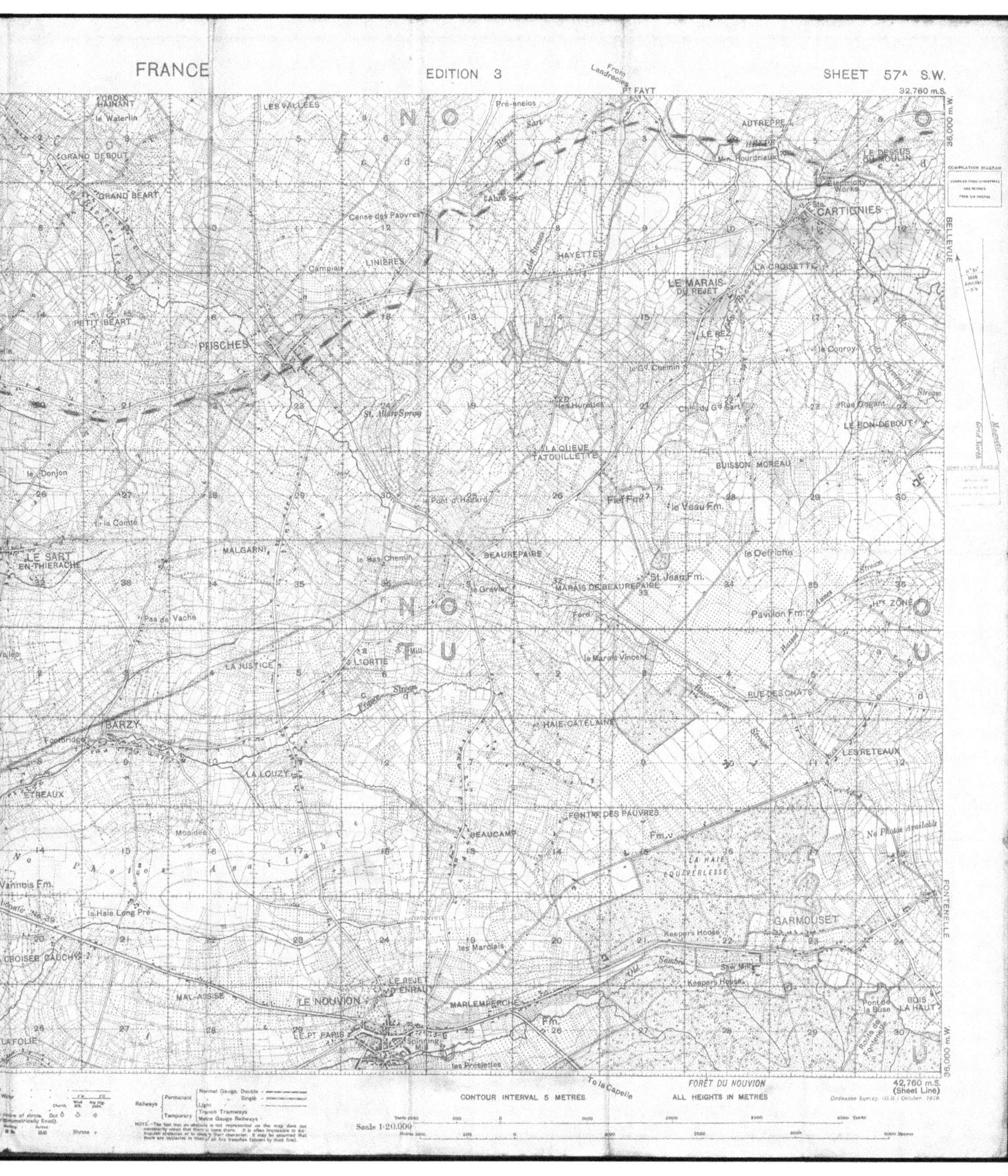

FRANCE
EDITION 3
SHEET 57A S.W.
32,760 m.S.
36,000 m.W.
From Landrecies
Pt FAYT
LES VALLÉES
Pré-enclos
AUTREPPE
le Waterlin
GRAND DEBOUT
LE DESSUS DU MOULIN
Electricity Works
GRAND BEART
Cense des Pauvres
CARTIGNIES
LINIÈRES
HAYETTES
LA CROISETTE
LE MARAIS DU REJET
PETIT BEART
PRISCHES
LE REZ
le Conroy
le Gd Chemin
les Hurettes
St Allard Spring
Chin du Gd Sart
Rue Gogant
LE BON DEBOUT
LA QUEUE TATOUILLETTE
BUISSON MOREAU
le Donjon
le Pont d'Hazard
Fief Fm.
le Veau Fm.
la Comté
LE SART EN-THIERACHE
MALGARNI
BEAUREPAIRE
le Bas Chemin
le Défriche
le Gravier
MARAIS DE BEAUREPAIRE
St Jean Fm.
Pas de Vache
Pavillon Fm.
Ford
LA JUSTICE
L'ORTIE
Mill
le Marais Vincent
RUE DES CHATS
BARZY
Footbridge
HAIE-CATELAINE
LES RETEAUX
LA LOUZY
ETREAUX
FONTNE DES PAUVRES
BEAUCAMP
No Photos Available
LA HAIE EQUIVERLESSE
Vannois Fm.
la Haie Long Pré
GARMOUSET
Keeper's House
les Mardais
CROISEE CAUCHY
Saw Mill
Keeper's House
LE REJET D'ENHAUT
MAL-ASSISE
LE NOUVION
MARLEMPERCHE
Pont de la Buse
BOIS LA HAUT
LE PT PARIS
Spinning Mill
les Preslettes
LA FOLIE
BELLEVUE
FONTENELLE
FORÊT DU NOUVION
To la Capelle
42,760 m.S. (Sheet Line)
CONTOUR INTERVAL 5 METRES.
ALL HEIGHTS IN METRES
Ordnance Survey, (O.B.) October, 1918.
Scale 1:20,000

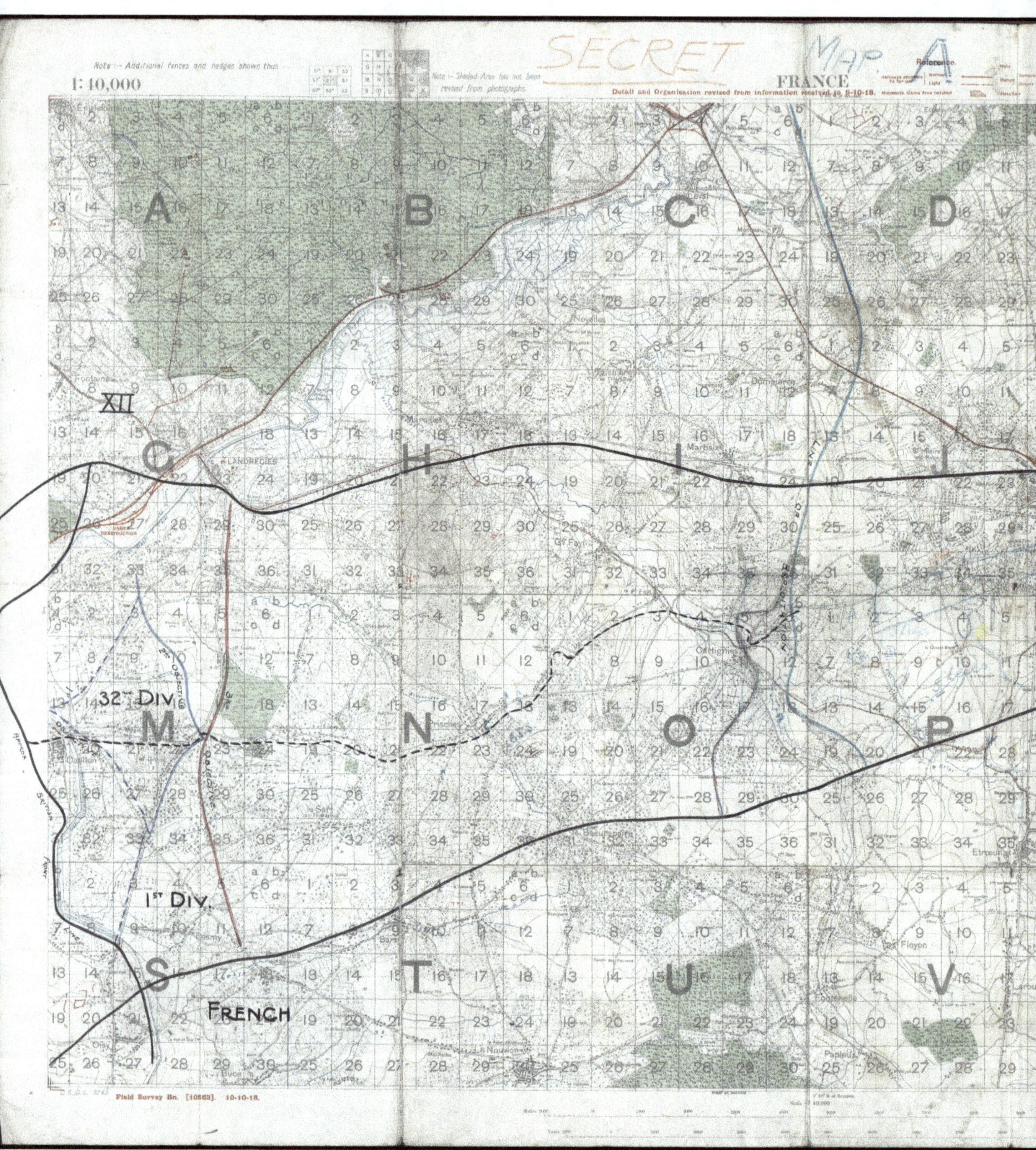

Note :- Additional fences and hedges shown thus
1:40,000
Note :- Shaded Area has not been revised from photographs.
SECRET
Map. A
FRANCE
Detail and Organization revised from information received to 8-10-18.
Reference
A
B
C
D
XII
G
H
I
J
LANDRECIES
Maroilles
Noyelles
Marbaix
Cartignies
32nd DIV.
M
N
O
P
1st DIV.
S
T
U
V
FRENCH
Floyon
Etroeungt
Le Nouvion
Papleux
Field Survey Bn. [10563]. 10-10-18.

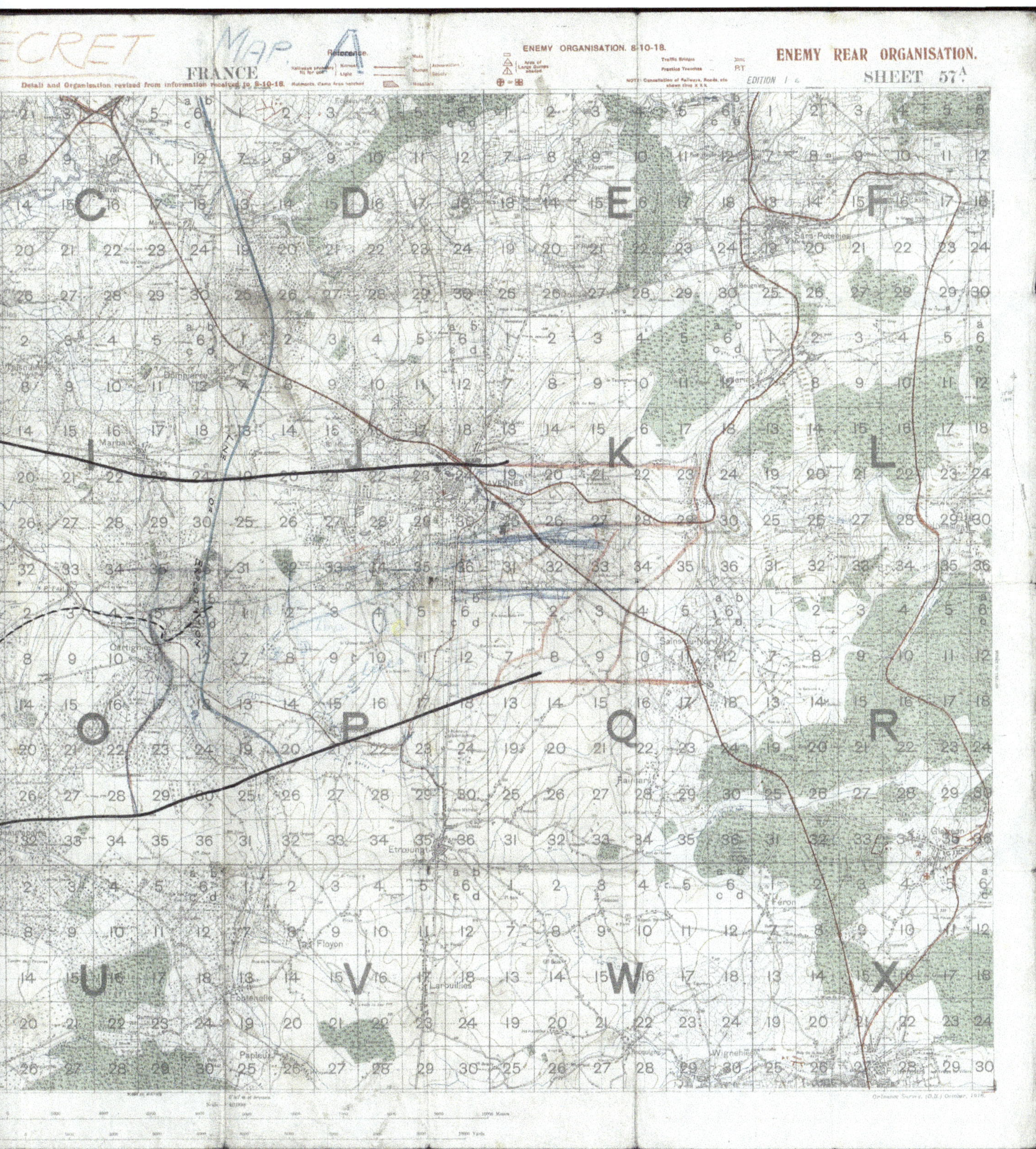
ECRET
MAP A
FRANCE
Detail and Organisation revised from information received to 8-10-18.
Reference
ENEMY ORGANISATION. 8-10-18.
Traffic Bridges
Practice Trenches
ENEMY REAR ORGANISATION.
EDITION 1
SHEET 57A.
C
D
E
F
I
J
K
L
O
P
Q
R
U
V
W
X
Sars-Poteries
Marbaix
Avesnes
Sains-du-Nord
Cartignies
Etroeungt
Floyon
Larouillies
Féron
Glageon
Fontenelle
Papleux
Wignehies

War Diary

Secret.

46th Division - Daily Disposition Return.

Dispositions at 6 a.m., 1st October, 1918.

46th Div. H.Q.	R.8.b.5.5.
137th Inf. Bde. H.Q.	BELLENGLISE TUNNEL.
138th : : :)	G.29.c.4.8.
139th : : :)	

Burn Lindsay Capt
for Lieut-Colonel,
General Staff, 46th Division.

30/9/18.

War Diary.

G.S.

46th Division.

October 1918

Instructions regarding War Diaries and Intelligence Summaries are contained in F. S. Regs., Part II. and the Staff Manual respectively. Title pages will be prepared in manuscript.

WAR DIARY
or
INTELLIGENCE SUMMARY.
(Erase heading not required.)

G.S. 46 Div

Vol

Army Form C. 2118.

Place	Date	Hour	Summary of Events and Information	Remarks and references to Appendices
			Month of October 1918.	
			Divisional Headquarters at VENDELLES.	

D. & L., Ltd. Forms/C.2118/14.

Instructions regarding War Diaries and Intelligence Summaries are contained in F. S. Regs., Part II. and the Staff Manual respectively. Title pages will be prepared in manuscript.

WAR DIARY
or
INTELLIGENCE SUMMARY.

(Erase heading not required.)

Army Form C. 2118.

Place	Date	Hour	Summary of Events and Information	Remarks and references to Appendices
R36 c 5.5. ETAVES Sheet 1.40,000	Oct. 1st 1918		The story of the operations in which the 46th Div. were engaged E of the St QUENTIN CANAL during the period 1st–6th October 1918 are contained in ~~App~~ App. 46th Div. Order No 329 lays down the order of march to be adopted by the Division in the event of the attack by 32nd Div. against the BEAUREVOIR – FONSOMME line meeting with success. The attack however did not meet with sufficient success to make an opening for the Cavalry as it was intended it should do.	App 1
			Daily Disposition Return (for 6 am 2.10.18). CAAA	App 2
	2nd		At a Conference held by G.O.C. IX Corps at 46th Div HQ on the afternoon of the 2nd Oct. 46th Div. were ordered to launch an attack on the 3rd inst against MONTBREHAIN, RAMICOURT and MANNEQUIN HILL. The attack was to be carried out in conjunction with the 2nd Australian Division on our left and the 32nd Div. on our right who had orders to take the village of SEQUEHART. Orders for the attack were issued in 46th Division Order No. 330 CAAA	App 3

(A7092). Wt. W12839/M1293. 750,000. 1/17. D. D. & L., Ltd. Forms/C.2118/14.

Instructions regarding War Diaries and Intelligence Summaries are contained in F. S. Regs., Part II. and the Staff Manual respectively. Title pages will be prepared in manuscript.

WAR DIARY
or
INTELLIGENCE SUMMARY.
(Erase heading not required.)

Army Form C. 2118.

Place	Date	Hour	Summary of Events and Information	Remarks and references to Appendices
R8b55	2		Gives the Disposition of Bri[gades] and Bde HQ for the 3rd Div. A map shewing the objectives of 46th & 96th Division is attached	App 4
	3		Advanced DHQ opened at LA BARAQUE (G29c9.3 Sheet ETAVES 1.40,000) at 6.0 am. At 6.5 am the attack ordered in the above quoted Div order 330 was launched, 137th Inf. Bde being on the Right, 139th Inf. Bde on the Left and 138th Inf. Bde together with the 1/1st Bn Monmouthshire Regt (Pioneers) being in Divisional Reserve. Attention is again called to App 1 of Sept. - the narrative of our engagements. Orders regarding operations and dispositions issued during the day are attached in the following appendices:-	
			G49 — App 5	
			G42 — App 6	
			G5 — App 7	
			G18 — App 8	
			G22 — App 9	
			G27 — App 10	

(A7092). Wt. W12839/M1293. 750,000. 1/17. D. D. & L., Ltd. Forms/C.2118/14.

Army Form C. 2118.

WAR DIARY
or
INTELLIGENCE SUMMARY.
(Erase heading not required.)

Instructions regarding War Diaries and Intelligence Summaries are contained in F. S. Regs., Part II. and the Staff Manual respectively. Title pages will be prepared in manuscript.

Place	Date	Hour	Summary of Events and Information	Remarks and references to Appendices
LA BARAQUE G29 C9.3 ETAVES.	3		G32 App 11 G36 App 12 G38 App 13 G41 App 14	
			[signature]	
	4		During the operations under review the 3rd Inf. Bde (1st Div.), the 5th Cav. Bde and IX Corps Cyclists were all for a time under the Command of G.O.C. 46th Div. Orders to these formations as well as to our own, and dispositions, are contained in the following Divisional orders: G78 App 15 G81 App 16	
	5		App 17 G109 App 18 G110 G111 App 19 G114 App 20	

Army Form C. 2118.

Instructions regarding War Diaries and Intelligence Summaries are contained in F. S. Regs., Part II. and the Staff Manual respectively. Title pages will be prepared in manuscript.

WAR DIARY
or
INTELLIGENCE SUMMARY.

(Erase heading not required.)

Place	Date	Hour	Summary of Events and Information	Remarks and references to Appendices
LA BARAQUE G29C9.3 ETAVES	5		G122 App 21 G125 (Location Return) App 22	[initials]
R8b5.5	6		Command of the sector passed from GOC 46th Div. to GOC 6th Div at 9.30 am. At this hour 46th Div. Advanced Report Centre closed at LA BARAQUE and opened at R8b5.5 (ETAVES Sheet 1.40,000). Order no. 331 App 23	
	7		Operation D. 46th Instruction no. 1. App 24 " D. " " 2 App 25 " Brigades generally situated as follows: 137th in Ascension Valley (E. of St QUENTIN CANAL). 138th between Ascension Valley and St QUENTIN CANAL 139th in line (SEQUEHART sector) under the command of GOC 6th Div.	[initials]

(A7092). Wt. W12839/M1293. 750,000. 1/17. D. D. & L., Ltd. Forms/C.2118/14.

Army Form C. 2118.

WAR DIARY
or
INTELLIGENCE SUMMARY.
(Erase heading not required.)

Instructions regarding War Diaries and Intelligence Summaries are contained in F. S. Regs., Part II. and the Staff Manual respectively. Title pages will be prepared in manuscript.

Place	Date	Hour	Summary of Events and Information	Remarks and references to Appendices
R8b5.5	7		Operation D 46th Div. Instructions no. 3	App 26
			46th Div. Order no. 332	App 27
			Dispositions for 6 am 8.10.18	App 28
			G146 - issued on 6th October [initials]	App 29
MAGNY LA FOSSE G30b9.5	8		Advanced Report Centre opened at 9 am at G30b9.5 (MAGNY LA FOSSE) Orders for relief, dispositions etc as follows: G164	App 30
			G157	App 31
			GA6	App 32
	8		Headquarters of Brigades today as follows. 137th in BELLENGLISE Tunnel, 138th in G21c3.8, 139th in MAGNY LA FOSSE (H25a1.1). [initials]	
	9		G191	App 33
			G208	App 34
			G219 [initials]	App 35

(A7092). Wt. W12839/M1293. 750,000. 1/17. D. D. & L., Ltd. Forms/C.2118/14.

Instructions regarding War Diaries and Intelligence Summaries are contained in F. S. Regs., Part II. and the Staff Manual respectively. Title pages will be prepared in manuscript.

WAR DIARY
or
INTELLIGENCE SUMMARY.
(Erase heading not required.)

Army Form C. 2118.

Place	Date	Hour	Summary of Events and Information	Remarks and references to Appendices
FRESNOY LE GRAND J18 (1:40 000)	10		At 18 hours DHQ closed down at MAGNY LA FOSSE and opened at FRESNOY LE GRAND. 138th Inf. Brigade as the Divisional advanced guard, received orders to push leading troops through RIQUERVAL WOOD. The 6th British Division on our left and 126th French Division on our right are assuming a similar policy. Orders to formations within the Division are contained in the following appendices - G 236	App 36
			G 244	App 37
			G 249	App 38
			G 256. This order also contains the objectives to be reached by 6th British Div and 30th American Division. It also lays down the duties of the 46th Division.	App 39
				[illegible signature]

(A7092). Wt. W12839/M1293. 750,000. 1/17. D. D. & L., Ltd. Forms/C.2118/14.

Army Form C. 2118.

Instructions regarding War Diaries and Intelligence Summaries are contained in F. S. Regs., Part II. and the Staff Manual respectively. Title pages will be prepared in manuscript.

WAR DIARY
or
INTELLIGENCE SUMMARY.
(Erase heading not required.)

Place	Date	Hour	Summary of Events and Information	Remarks and references to Appendices
FRESNOY LE GRAND & 1927?	11		137th Bde relieved 138th Bde in the line in accordance with G262. Owing to the uncertainty as to the definite location of the two right Companies of the 5th Bn Leicestershire Regt, who were the leading Battalion of the 138th Bde, the relief in front was a little difficult & it was completed late in the evening and 138th Bde spent the night 11th/12th in the FRESNOY LE GRAND area with Bde HQ in the village itself. 139th Bde were in the area round MERICOURT with Bde HQ in FRESNOY LE GRAND. 137th Bde HQ at 120 85, with 1 Battalion in the line and 2 in Reserve. Defensive arrangements are as ordered in G277. Owing to BOIS DE RIQUERVAL, BETHEUIL FARM and the South of these places being strongly held by the enemy it was decided by the Divisional Commander to withdraw troops from the wood and bombard it heavily. Orders for the withdrawal and subsequent bombardment were issued under G280	App 40 App 41 App 42
	12		At 12 noon the 126th French Division on our right launched an attack, the ultimate objective of which was MENNEVRET. 137th Inf. Bde cooperated at the same time with orders to	

(A7092). Wt. W12839/M1293. 750,000. 1/17. D. D. & L., Ltd. Forms/C.2118/14.

Instructions regarding War Diaries and Intelligence Summaries are contained in F. S. Regs., Part II. and the Staff Manual respectively. Title pages will be prepared in manuscript.

WAR DIARY
or
INTELLIGENCE SUMMARY.

(Erase heading not required.)

Army Form C. 2118.

Place	Date	Hour	Summary of Events and Information	Remarks and references to Appendices
FRESNOY LE GRAND	12		a line within the Divisional Boundaries – running generally along Eastern Edge of BOIS DE RIQUERVAL and western Edge of FORÊT DOMANIALE D'ANDIGNY. Orders for this attack were issued under G286 and G290. The attack was however unsuccessful owing to intense Enemy M.G. fire which completely stopped the advance of the French. Orders were therefore issued under G299 for 137th Bde to consolidate in depth on their original line: this line runs approximately down Central N.S grid line of E13 to E13d02 – D24c8.2 – D30a6.5 – D30d00 (point of junction with French). a 1:40,000 map showing the Divisional Boundaries is attached.	Apps. 43 & 44 App 45 App 46
	13.		Situation and disposition remained unchanged. A quiet day with comparatively little hostile artillery activity. The Enemy is still holding his position opposite us and has brought up fresh Division from LAON. The G.O.C. attended a Corps Conference which was convened to discuss operations which are to be carried out at an early date.	
	14		Situation unchanged. Hostile artillery and aerial activity	

(A7092). Wt. W12839/M1293. 750,000. 1/17. D. D. & L., Ltd. Forms/C.2118/14.

Instructions regarding War Diaries and Intelligence Summaries are contained in F. S. Regs., Part II. and the Staff Manual respectively. Title pages will be prepared in manuscript.

WAR DIARY
or
INTELLIGENCE SUMMARY.
(Erase heading not required.)

Army Form C. 2118.

Place	Date	Hour	Summary of Events and Information	Remarks and references to Appendices
FRESNOY LE GRAND	14		a good deal more marked than they were yesterday. There are the strongest indications that the enemy is about to continue his retirement; he is blowing up ammunition dumps and bridges for many miles behind his present line and the French Corps on our right report that prisoners just captured state that their main body has been withdrawn to 3000 yards back leaving only outposts on present advanced line.	
			Orders were issued to the CRA to arrange a bombardment by Heavy Artillery tomorrow (G327) This will be in conjunction with an operation to be carried out by the French.	App 47
			In the evening three Alsatians and one Silesian voluntarily surrendered and came into our lines in E25C. They belong to 267 Res Regt (normal). Stated that all troops and guns had gone back from MENNEVRET and that civilians had already been evacuated from that place. Information willingly given but scanty.	
			[initials]	

(A7092). Wt. W12839/M1293. 750,000. 1/17. D. D. & L., Ltd. Forms/C.2118/14.

Instructions regarding War Diaries and Intelligence Summaries are contained in F. S. Regs., Part II. and the Staff Manual respectively. Title pages will be prepared in manuscript.

WAR DIARY
or
INTELLIGENCE SUMMARY.
(Erase heading not required.)

Army Form C. 2118.

Place	Date	Hour	Summary of Events and Information	Remarks and references to Appendices
FRESNOY-LE-GRANDE	15		Situation all day generally quiet, the enemy's artillery was not active.	
			This division at an early date has been ordered to attack, as part of a major operation, with an objective on the ANDIGNY-LES-FERMES - REGNICOURT Road (46th Div Order No 333)	App 48
			Further instructions regarding this attack are given in 46th Div G 115/77.	App 49
	16		The enemy all today has been very quiet and his artillery has been very inactive.	
			Additional instructions re the attack to be made are contained in G 115/89 and	App 50
			G 115/97	App 51

(A7092). Wt. W12839/M1293. 750,000. 1/17. D. D. & L., Ltd. Forms/C.2118/14.

Instructions regarding War Diaries and Intelligence Summaries are contained in F. S. Regs., Part II. and the Staff Manual respectively. Title pages will be prepared in manuscript.

WAR DIARY
or
INTELLIGENCE SUMMARY.
(Erase heading not required.)

Army Form C. 2118.

Place	Date	Hour	Summary of Events and Information	Remarks and references to Appendices
FRESNOY-le-GRAND.	Octr: 17th		At 5.20 am, the Division as part of a major operation, carried out an attack as in 46th Division Order No. 333.	App: 48.
			The objective being the road from E.13.b.5.0 - E.11.a.3.6 including the villages of REGNICOURT and ANDIGNY-les-FERMES.	Reference Sheet 62.B. 1/40,000
			The attack was carried out by the 2nd American Corps on the LEFT and the XV French Corps on the RIGHT of the IX Corps.	App: 48a.
			The 6th Division attacked on the LEFT and the 126th French Division on the RIGHT of the 46th Division, which attacked on a 2 Brigade front.	
			The dispositions of the Division at Zero hour were as follows :-	
			The G.O.C., 137th Infantry Brigade was responsible for holding the RIGHT pivot of the attack, having at his disposal 1 Battalion (1/6th Battalion, North Staffordshire Regiment), one Machine Gun Company and one Light Trench Mortar Battery. The Infantry holding the line from this battalion were withdrawn from RIQUERVAL FARM to a line of safety from our barrage before the latter opened.	
			The 2 remaining Battalions of the Brigade (1/5h Battalion, South Staffordshire Regiment and 1/6th Battalion, South Staffordshire Regiment) being in Divisional Reserve along the SEBONCOURT - BOHAIN Road and in the SOUTHERN part of BOHAIN respectively.	
			The 138th Infantry Brigade attacked on the LEFT of the Divisional front, the 1/5th Battalion Lincolnshire Regiment on the LEFT and the 1/4th Battalion Leicestershire Regiment on the RIGHT, with the 1/5th Battalion Leicestershire Regiment in Brigade Reserve.	
			The 139th Infantry Brigade attacked on the RIGHT of the Divisional front with a one battalion front (1/8th Battalion, Sherwood Foresters). This battalion had 3 companies in the front line of attack with the remaining company in Battalion Reserve. 2 Companies of the 1/5th Battalion Sherwood Foresters were detailed to follow in rear of the 1/8th Battalion Sherwood Foresters.	

(A7092). Wt. W12839/M1293. 750,000. 1/17. D. D. & L., Ltd. Forms/C.2118/14.

Army Form C. 2118.

WAR DIARY
or
INTELLIGENCE SUMMARY.
(Erase heading not required.)

Instructions regarding War Diaries and Intelligence Summaries are contained in F. S. Regs., Part II. and the Staff Manual respectively. Title pages will be prepared in manuscript.

Place	Date	Hour	Summary of Events and Information	Remarks and references to Appendices
			The remaining 2 companies of the 1/5th Battalion Sherwood Foresters were in Brigade Support and the 1/6th Battalion Sherwood Foresters in Brigade Reserve.	
			At Zero hour a very thick mist was on, which only lifted slightly all day. While this acted as an additional screen for the Infantry, it caused the leading wave of the 138th Infantry Brigade to lose direction.	
			At 1035 a report was received from 139th Infantry Brigade that the whole of their final objective had been captured, and at 1220 the 138th Infantry Brigade reported capture of ANDIGNY-les-FERMES, which completed capture of their objective.	
			The situation developed during the day as the French XV Corps on the RIGHT, pushed forward.	
			The orders detailing and dealing with the situation are given in the following appendices :-	
			G.410.	App: 52
			G.418.	: 53
			G.420.	: 54
			G.424.	: 55
			G.425.	: 56
			G.439.	: 57
			G.442.	: 58
			G.443.	: 59
			The Headquarters of formations for this operation were as follows :-	
			Divisional Headquarters, FRESNOY-le-GRAND, I.18.b.5.5.	
			137th Infantry Brigade. BOHAIN.	
			138th : : D.11.b.5.0.	
			139th : : D.11.b.5.0.	

(A7092) Wt. W12839/M1293. 750,000. 1/17. D. D. & L., Ltd. Forms/C.2118/14.

Army Form C. 2118.

Instructions regarding War Diaries and Intelligence Summaries are contained in F. S. Regs., Part II. and the Staff Manual respectively. Title pages will be prepared in manuscript.

WAR DIARY
or
INTELLIGENCE SUMMARY.
(Erase heading not required.)

Place	Date	Hour	Summary of Events and Information	Remarks and references to Appendices
			At 2140 orders were sent for 137th Infantry Brigade to move to take over line tomorrow from 138th and 139th Infantry Brigades (G.446) and for the 138th Infantry Brigade to take over by dawn line held by the 1st Brigade from ANDIGNY to E.5.a.9.2. (G.449).	App: 60 App: 61
	18th		The above arrangements were subsequently altered (in G.452) owing to the French making a further advance on the RIGHT and capturing MENNEVRET, the line taken over by the 137th Infantry Brigade was E.17.b.2.5 - E.11.c.0.8 - E.5.c.7.3 - E.5.a.7.3. The 138th Infantry Brigade on relief were withdrawn to an area about E.1, 2 and 3, and the 139th Infantry Brigade to an area about D.12 and 18 and E.7 and 13.	App: 62
			The 137th Infantry Brigade was ordered to keep touch with the 1st Division on the LEFT and the 126th French Division on the RIGHT (G.457).	App: 63
			About midday the 138th Infantry Brigade was ordered to assemble in FRESNOY in billets and the 139th Infantry Brigade was also ordered to commence assembling in the same place at 1600.	
			At 1830 the two battalions of the 137th Infantry Brigade in BOHAIN and REGNICOURT were instructed to return to FRESNOY at once (G.465), and at 2125 the 1st Division and 126th French Division having joined hands at WASSIGNY, the mission of the 46th Division ceased and orders were sent to the 137th Infantry Brigade to withdraw the battalion remaining in the line to billets in BOHAIN (G.465).	App: 64 App: 65

(A7092). Wt. W12839/M1293. 750,000. 1/17. D. D. & L., Ltd. Forms/C.2118/14.

Instructions regarding War Diaries and Intelligence Summaries are contained in F. S. Regs., Part II. and the Staff Manual respectively. Title pages will be prepared in manuscript.

WAR DIARY
or
INTELLIGENCE SUMMARY.
(Erase heading not required.)

Army Form C. 2118.

Place	Date	Hour	Summary of Events and Information	Remarks and references to Appendices
	18th		The fighting of yesterday and to-day was very stiff, the enemy resisting very stoutly. The following enemy troops were engaged on the Divisional front, 5 Reserve Division, 1 Regiment (267 Regiment) of the 81 Reserve Division, and 2 Regiments (62 and 69 Regiments) of the 15 Reserve Division. From prisoners statements, the enemy intended to hold all the captured ground, and this was borne out by the very steady resistance and determination displayed by the enemy throughout the whole of the operation. The captures in the two days fighting amounted to about 15 Officers 500 Other Ranks 2 Field Guns 100 Machine Guns and several trench Mortars.	

(A7092). Wt. W12839/M1293. 750,000. 1/17. D. D. & L., Ltd. Forms/C.2118/14.

Army Form C. 2118.

WAR DIARY
or
INTELLIGENCE SUMMARY.
(*Erase heading not required.*)

Instructions regarding War Diaries and Intelligence Summaries are contained in F. S. Regs., Part II. and the Staff Manual respectively. Title pages will be prepared in manuscript.

Place	Date	Hour	Summary of Events and Information	Remarks and references to Appendices
	1918			
FRESNOY le Grand	Oct 19		The Division again being out of the line, the whole day was devoted by all units to general cleaning up. Inspections etc. RLS	
	Oct 20		Division Rested. A Divisional Church Parade was held at 10am at FRESNOY when ~~[illegible]~~ detachments from all arms of the Division were present, about 3000 all ranks being on parade, the parade afterwards marched past G.O.C. in columns of route.	
			Notes on Training by Divisional Commander	App 66 ~~61~~
			Letter to G.O.C. 1st Div from G.O.C. 46th Div stating his appreciation of help rendered to 138th Bde by 1st Loyal North Lancs. RLS	App 67 ~~63~~
	Oct 21		General Training carried out by all arms of the Division. RLS	
	Oct 22		General Training RLS	
	23		General Training RLS	
	24		General Training RLS	
	25		General Training RLS	
	26		General Training RLS	

(A7092). Wt. W12839/M1293. 750,000. 1/17. D. D. & L., Ltd. Forms/C.2118/14.

Army Form C. 2118.

Instructions regarding War Diaries and Intelligence Summaries are contained in F. S. Regs., Part II. and the Staff Manual respectively. Title pages will be prepared in manuscript.

WAR DIARY
or
INTELLIGENCE SUMMARY.
(Erase heading not required.)

Place	Date	Hour	Summary of Events and Information	Remarks and references to Appendices
FRESNOY	1918 Oct 27		General Training	RCHS
	28		General Training	RCHS
	29		General Training Order arranging move of 46th Div. (less Artillery) to BOHAIN area on 30 & 31st inst and 1st prox (Appendix ~~54~~ 68 46th Div Order 334)	App ~~54~~ 68
	30		139th Bde moved from FRESNOY to BOHAIN	RCHS
			46th Div Order No 335 (Appendix 69) giving details of projected attack by IX Corps at an early date on the SAMBRE-OISE Canal in conjunction with the XV Corps (French) on the right and the XIII British Corps on the left	RCHS App ~~55~~ 69.
BOHAIN	31		137th ~~139th~~ Bde moved to BOHAIN 138th Bde moved to BUSIGNY 46 Div HQ opened at BOHAIN at 1100 hrs 46th Div Instruction NOT Operation F (Appendix 70) showing dispositions of Division at zero hour to be read in conjunction with Divisional order NO 335	App 70
~~B~~	~~Nov~~			
BOHAIN	Nov 1			

(A7092). Wt. W12839/M1293. 750,000. 1/17. D. D. & L., Ltd. Forms/C.2118/14.

List of Casualties for period

29th September to 7th October.

Officers.	Other Ranks.
110.	2,500.

War Diary App 1.

SECRET. Copy No. 18

46th DIVISION ORDER No. 329.
****

Ref: Sheet 62.B,
1/40,000.

1st October, 1918.

1. Should the operations of to-day against the BEAUREVOIR LINE be successful, the cavalry will be pushing through between LEVERGIES and JONCOURT.

2. The 46th Division will be prepared to follow up this advance.

Advance Guard.
H.Q.- 139th Inf: Bde.
1 Bde, RFA.
1 Fd. Co. RE.
139th Inf: Bde.
1 Coy, 46th Bn, MGC.
1 Coy, 1st Monmouthshire R.
Detachment, Field Amb'ce.
Detachment, IX Corps Cyclists.
Div'l Mounted Troops.

3. Should this operation take place, the Division will march as shown in the margin.
The Advanced Guard will be commanded by the G.O.C, 139th Inf: Bde.

Main Body.
Remainder of Artillery.
Remainder of RE.
137th Inf: Bde.
138th Inf: Bde.
Remainder of 46th Bn, MGC.
Field Ambulances.

137th Bde Group.
"A" Bn, 137th Inf: Bde.
1 Fd. Co. RE.
1 Coy, 46th Bn, MGC.
"B" Bn, 137th Inf: Bde.
Remainder RFA. less DAC
1 Section, 6" How.) If
RGA: 1 Section, 60) avail-
pdr. guns, RGA.) able.
"C" Bn, 137th Inf: Bde.
"B" Field Ambulance.
"A" Coy Div'l Train

4. The Order of March of the Main Body will be as shown in the margin.

138th Bde Group.
"A" Bn, 138th Inf: Bde.
1 Fd. Coy, RE.
1 Coy, 46th Bn, MGC.
"B" Bn, 138th Inf: Bde.
"C" Bn, 138th Inf: Bde.
Remainder HA.
Remaindor 1st Monmouthshire R.
1 Coy, 46th Bn, MGC.
"C" Field Ambulance.
Remainder of "A" Field Amb'ce.
DAC
"B" "C" "D" Coys Div'l Train

5. The general direction of the march will probably be, in the first instance, N.E. towards MONT BREHAIN. The BELLENGLISE - JONCOURT & BELLENGLISE - LEVERGIES Roads should be reconnoitred.

P.T.O.

3. Company Transport will be re-organised and Light Trench Mortar Batteries made up to two Limbered G.S. Wagons per Battery to-day.

[signature]

Lieut-Colonel,
General Staff, 46th Division.

Issued at 1400

Copy No. 1 to CRA.
2 CRE.
3 Signals.
4 137th Inf: Bde.
5 138th : :
6 139th : :
7 1st Monmouths.
8 46th Bn, MGC.
9 AA & QMG.
10 ADMS.
11 Div'l Train.
12 SSO.
13 C.O. Div'l Observers.
14 GSO I.
15/16 File.
17/18 War Diary.
19/20 IX Corps.
21 32nd Division.

Secret.

ACCOUNT OF THE PART TAKEN BY THE 46TH DIVISION IN THE BATTLE OF BELLENGLISE ON THE 29TH SEPTEMBER, 1918.

****

46th Division G.114/24. 7th October, 1918.

1. General Idea of the Operations. The General Idea of these operations was the breaking of the main HINDENBURG LINE NORTH of ST QUENTIN. The Special Role of the 46th Division being to storm the ST QUENTIN CANAL between BELLENGLISE and RIQUEVAL, and take the villages of BELLENGLISE, LEHAUCOURT and MAGNY LA FOSSE.

On the RIGHT of the Division, the 1st Division was to exploit any success gained, by working to the EAST, SOUTH of the CANAL, and occupying the high ground about THORIGNY, should the enemy retire from these positions.

On our LEFT, the American Corps were to storm the BELLICOURT defences and then, turning SOUTH, were to join the 46th Division in the neighbourhood of ETRICOURT.

The 32nd Division and 2nd Australian Division were to move through the 46th Division and 30th American Division respectively, after the capture of their final objectives, and seize the general line LE TRONQUOY - LEVERGIES and to the NORTH.

2. General Description of the Ground on the 46th Division Front.

The defences in front of the 46th Division were of a very formidable nature, consisting of strong lines WEST of the CANAL, the CANAL itself; with the main HINDENBURG LINE, a strong supporting line and four strongly defended Villages to the EAST of it. The CANAL may be divided into two parts, the SOUTHERN half running practically along the ground level contained little water; but, on the other hand, the defences were far stronger than in the NORTHERN part. The NORTHERN half, where the water was from seven to ten feet deep, ran through a deep cutting with almost perpendicular sides, thirty to fifty feet high. The lower ten feet of the CANAL throughout formed a perpendicular obstacle, faced with brick; and both inner and outer banks were strongly wired.

In BELLENGLISE, were the entrances to the famous tunnel which ran from the direction of MAGNY LA FOSSE into this Village, and was known to be capable of holding some 2/3,000 men. The whole area was known to be exceptionally strong in concrete machine gun defences and was believed by the enemy to be impregnable.

3. Preliminary Arrangements.: The first order for the attack was 46th Division Order 326, issued on the 25th September, and prior to the attack many preliminary arrangements had to be made. The main difficulty lay in crossing the CANAL and for this purpose some 3,000 lifebelts were obtained and issued to the storming troops. On the day prior to the attack, these lifebelts together with light portable rafts, ladders, collapsible boats and heaving lines, were tested on the banks of the SOMME, and it was found that the ordinary lifebelt would easily support a man in fighting order, provided that the weight he was carrying was kept low on his body.

A preliminary operation with the object of ensuring that there would be little opposition WEST of the CANAL was undertaken by the 138th Infantry Brigade on the 27th September against the trenches in G 28. These trenches were occupied under a barrage, but on the 28th September, severe fighting ensued here, and it was decided that on Y/Z night, our troops should be withdrawn and formed up WEST, and well clear of any possible enemy opposition.

4. General dispositions of the 46th Division. The area to be occupied by the 46th Division was divided into two main objectives - the BROWN Objective and the GREEN Objectives. These were further sub-divided,- a BLUE Objective included the CANAL and the defences immediately EAST of it, whilst the YELLOW and DOTTED BLUE objectives were inserted between the BROWN and the GREEN on the main tactical features, in order to allow of Inter-Brigade "Leap-frog".

Coldstream Guards

To the 137th Infantry Brigade (Brigadier-General J.V.CAMPBELL, VC, CMG, DSO) was entrusted the storming of the CANAL, the Village of BELLENGLISE and the capture of the BROWN Objective. On this, an halt was made for three hours, in order to allow of the complete mopping up of th area and give time for the 139th Infantry Brigade (Brigadier-General J.HARINGTON, DSO) on the RIGHT, and 138th Infantry Brigade (Brigadier-General F.G.M. ROWLEY, CMG, DSO) on the LEFT, to pass through to capture the final objective.

To the storming infantry were allotted a few sections of Engineers, whilst the remainder of the Royal Engineers and 1/1st Monmouthshire Regt (Pioneers) followed close in rear with the necessary bridging material.

The artillery allotted to the Division consisted of one Brigade, RHA, and eight Brigades of Field Artillery, whilst a very powerful concentration of Heavy Artillery was arranged by the IX Corps, to deal with the enemy defences and engage his batteries.

Two additional machine gun battalions, that of the 2nd Life Guards and "100th Machine Gun Battalion, were also allotted to the Division, and took part in the initial barrage.

Two Companies Mark V Tanks, were to cross over the BELLICOURT Tunnel immediately the Americans had captured their first objective, and moving SOUTH were to join the Division prior to its advance from the BROWN LINE. One Company was allotted to each of the 139th and 138th Infantry Brigades.

5. Forming Up. Forming up was successfully carried out on the night 28th/29th September. 137th Infantry Brigade formed up on a three battalion front, whilst 139th and 138th Infantry Brigades formed up some distance in rear on a one battalion front, with orders that their leading battalion should occupy the trench system on our "jumping off" line, as soon as the 137th Infantry Brigade had left These battalions detailed one company each to follow the 137th Infantry Brigade in order to mop up the area WEST of the CANAL, and the Battalion Commanders were instructed to keep in close touch with the situation, and to so handle their battalions, as to ensure that the 137th Infantry Brigade, having crossed the CANAL, should not be out-fought in the trench system beyond it. The remainder of the 139th and 138th Infantry Brigades were instructed not to move forward pending orders from Divisional Headquarters.

Zero Hour was fixed for 5.50 am.

6. The attack. The attack was launched at Zero in a thick mist which rapidly increased to a dense fog as the smoke which had been placed in the barrage and on the flanks began to make itself felt. Under cover of this fog the 137th Infantry Brigade, having stormed the first line trenches and killed most of the garrison, who put up a tough resistance, reached the CANAL well up to time. At the same time, the 1st Division formed a defensive RIGHT flank from our original trenches along the Spur towards BELLENGLISE. The RIGHT Battalion, (6th Bn, South Staffordshire Regt) found little water in the CANAL, and only in few places were they forced to swim. The enemy here at first put up considerable resistance, but, after a number of our men had crossed, surrendered freely, and the battalion was able to proceed to the BLUE Line and occupy the tunnel entrances in BELLENGLISE, when some hundreds of prisoners were taken

before they were able to put up any organised resistance. The centre (5th South Staffordshire Regt) and the LEFT (6th North Staffordshire Regt) found a considerable depth of water, in the CANAL. The officers swimming over first with were soon joined by the leading lines of their men, and, assisted by bridges, rafts and boats, the whole force was soon across and dealing with the enemy in the strongly held trenches on the EASTERN Bank. At RIQUEVAL, the bridge was found to be intact. The Royal Engineers with some of the storming troops bayonetted the enemy pioneers who were about to light the fuzes, and withdrew the charges. The saving of this bridge, due entirely to the rapidity and gallantry of the advance was of inestimable value, and by it, and the pontoon bridges which were later made by the 46th and 32nd Divisional Engineers and Pioneers, the whole of these two Divisions with their artillery, were later enabled to pass over.

The Infantry rapidly clearing the trenches up to the BLUE Objective, advanced on the BROWN LINE which they reached in scheduled time, capturing on their way a battery of four guns, the gun teams of which were all either killed or captured together with their horses. Owing to the density of the fog, little use could be made of the Divisional Observers' Section. The Divisional Mounted Troop, consisting of men from the DAC and Field Ambulances were, however, sent forward to reconnoitre, and by questioning prisoners and wounded men, were able to send back most valuable information, showing that our infantry had successfully crossed the CANAL. On this information, orders were issued for 139th and 138th Infantry Brigades *

[* to push straight across the Canal up to the barrage and move directly on the objectives assigned to them]

The leading battalion of these two brigades had already pushed forward after the 137th Infantry Brigade and crossed the CANAL close on their heels. The two brigades reached the BROWN LINE in excellent time, where they were joined by the two Companies of Tanks, and in spite of the dense fog, the whole were enabled to move forward towards their objective as the barrage lifted.

After passing the YELLOW Objective, the fog, having cleared considerably, much inconvenience was caused to the RIGHT Battalion by the enemy occupying the high ground SOUTH of the CANAL. Machine guns from this direction swept our RIGHT Flank continuously and enemy field guns firing at point blank range quickly put out of action all six tanks allotted to 139th Infantry Brigade. This battery was in its turn put out of action by a party of 139th Infantry Brigade, who, with great gallantry crossed the CANAL and shot or bayonetted the gunners. Little infantry trouble was experienced from SOUTH of the CANAL; several feeble attempts to counter attack on this flank were made, and one mounted German officer made three gallant attempts to rally his men; on the third attempt, however, both he and his horse were killed, whereupon the enemy immediately retired.

On our LEFT, 138th Infantry Brigade were successfully carrying forward their advance, and at 12.30 pm, we advanced from the YELLOW Line on to MAGNY LA FOSSE. At this time it was definitely ascertained that the troops on our left, who, until now, had been thought to occupy the high ground about NAUROY, had been hung up on their first objective: both flanks of the 46th Division were therefore in the air, and steps were taken to form a left defensive flank and to hold the bridgeheads along the CANAL on the right flank. The advance from the YELLOW Line was slightly delayed by this operation, and the barrage was some distance ahead of the advancing infantry. In spite of this, our infantry advanced and soon caught up the barrage, most ably assisted on our LEFT by the Tanks attached to the 138th Infantry Brigade.

By three pm, the whole of our objectives had been taken, and the 32nd Division, pressing forward, passed through our lines to occupy the RED LINE. During the later stages of our advance, a number of guns were encountered, giving opportunities for many acts of gallantry on the part of both officers and men. One battery was seen to be limbering up EAST of our final defensive barrage, and an attempt was made to pass through our barrage and prevent the withdrawal of these guns. Horses and drivers were shot down, and immediately our barrage began to thin, this battery was captured. Several bayonet charges against the enemy's artillery were made, the crews being killed and the guns captured. The German artillery men fought with the greatest valour and continued to fire their guns at point blank range up to the last.

During the following night, the Division was continuously in action owing to both flanks being open to the enemy. On the morning of the 30th, the 1st Division, on our RIGHT eased the situation by the capture of THORIGNY and TALANA HILL, whilst on the LEFT, the 2nd Australian Division, pushing forward, joined up with our LEFT Flank during the day.

7. Work of the Artillery. The preparatory work of the Heavy Artillery cannot be too highly praised, and, it was owing in a great measure to their excellent shooting that the storming of the CANAL with its concrete defences was made possible. The Field Artillery, in spite of the fact that the majority of the guns were in silent positions up to Zero Hour, and unable to register, put down one of the finest barrages that the troops have ever advanced under. During the action, the majority of the Field Artillery was moved forward to new positions already selected. These movements were so expeditiously carried out as to make little appreciable difference in the intensity of the barrage.

8. The work of the Royal Engineers, Machine Gunners, Pioneers and RAMC, was beyond all praise. The first named, besides saving the RIQUEVAL Bridge, were able to assist the infantry in many ways outside their ordinary scope, and incidents of individual gallantry in attacking machine gun nests, etc, were of common occurrence.

9. Infantry. As for the infantry, in addition to the magnificent behaviour of every officer and man, the leadership shown by regimental officers and NCO's was of a very high nature. The faultless leading of their men across some 5,000 yards of enemy territory in a thick fog, during which some 4,200 prisoners and seventy guns were taken, is worthy of the highest traditions of the Service. Their success, and the lightness of their casualties, some eight hundred in all, is due to this power of leadership and to the fact that not the slightest hesitation was shown throughout the whole engagement.

All ranks were determined to push through to the final objective regardless of the flanks, and right well they carried it out, not only on this occasion but subsequently on the 3rd October.

--- 888 ---

Secret.

ACCOUNT OF THE PART TAKEN BY THE
46TH DIVISION
IN THE BATTLE OF RAMICOURT, ON
THE 3RD OCTOBER, 1918.-

1. At 4.30 pm on the 2nd October, orders were received at a Corps Conference that the 46th Division was to attack and capture the line SEQUEHART (exclusive) - MONTBREHAIN, joining with the 2nd Australian Division, NORTH-WEST of the latter place. At the same time, 32nd Division was to attack and capture SEQUEHART.

The area of attack consisted of the BEAUREVOIR-FONSOMME Line, the last defensive position of the enemy in this neighbourhood, and the villages of RAMICOURT and MONTBREHAIN; whilst on our RIGHT Flank was MANNEQUIN HILL, running in a N.E. direction from SEQUEHART. Little was known about the area to be attacked or about the position of our own troops. For the latter reason, a forming up line was arranged sufficiently far back to ensure that there would be no enemy opposition to our troops forming up for the attack. The 32nd Division, which was holding the line, was asked to withdraw all their troops behind this line.

At 5.5 am, 3rd October, the Division attacked with 137th Inf: Bde: on the RIGHT, 139th Inf: Bde: on the LEFT, and 138th Infantry Brigade to whom was attached the 1/1st Bn, Monmouthshire Regt (Pioneers) in Divisional Reserve.

3 Brigades of Artillery had to be moved up during the night to positions which it was impossible previously to reconnoitre, but in spite of this fact, the barrage opened well to time, and though slightly more short shooting was reported than usual, it was otherwise every thing that could be desired.

Considerable opposition was encountered in the BEAUREVOIR-FONSOMME LINE, where the enemy fought to the last, some few hundreds being killed in the Left Brigade Sector alone.

On our RIGHT, the 32nd Division quickly occupied SEQUEHART, but the troops attacking on our LEFT were unable to break through the very strong defences opposed to them.

The 137th Infantry Brigade was able to report that it had captured all its objectives up to time. The 139th Infantry Brigade, pushing forward to RAMICOURT found its LEFT Flank exposed: two Companies were promptly detailed to move through WIANCOURT and form here a defensive flank. After the capture of RAMICOURT, the defence rapidly weakened, and this Brigade captured over one thousand prisoners in MONTBREHAIN alone. In both RAMICOURT and MONTBREHAIN, French civilians were found and some seventy of them brought back to our lines. In the latter village, a battery of field guns was also captured.

Two companies of Tanks operating with this attack did excellent work, especially in clearing the outskirts of RAMICOURT. Immediately SOUTH of MONTBREHAIN, one of these Tanks attacked a machine gun nest consisting of sixteen guns and killed the whole of the crews before it was in its turn disabled.

By 1030 a severe defeat had been inflicted on the enemy and the whole of the objectives of the 46th Division obtained.

The 5th Cavalry Brigade was thereupon directed to move forward and keep in close touch with 46th Division to exploit their success. Unfortunately, this Brigade was a considerable distance to the rear and by the time they arrived in the forward area, the opportunity for using them had passed.

By 1500 the Division with both flanks exposed and having suffered very severe casualties, was attacked from an EASTERLY direction. At this angle our line was overlooked by the high ground round DOON and MANNEQUIN HILLS, on which the enemy quickly established himself, and by the point blank fire of field guns and machine guns, soon made a gap in our defence immediately SOUTH of MONTBREHAIN. in spite of heavy and continued artillery fire from our guns.

Our troops in this neighbourhood, were slowly pressed back SOUTH WEST of the Village, and a heavy attack commencing shortly afterwards from the NORTH of the Village, our troops were withdrawn to a General Line E. of WIANCOURT - RAMICOURT and the Spur in I 13. In the meantime, 138th Infantry Brigade had been moved forward to occupy the BEAUREVOIR-FONSOMME Line and placed at the disposal of the Brigades in the line. the Australians on our LEFT were enabled to advance, occupying WIANCOURT and gaining touch with our LEFT NORTH-EAST of that place.

During the afternoon, the enemy developed a very strong counter-attack against our RIGHT Brigade and succeeded in forcing us off the slopes of MANNEQUIN HILL.

5th Cavalry Brigade and the IX Corps Cyclists, some 150 strong, were ordered to occupy the BEAUREVOIR-FONSOMME Line and placed under the orders of the GOC, 137th Infantry Brigade. A counter attack restored the situation, and the NORTH-WESTERN Slopes were again occupied by us. We were, however, unable to retain the summit of the HILL which was continuously swept by machine gun fire.

During the night 3rd/4th, 139th Infantry Brigade was relieved by the 138th Infantry Brigade plus 1st Monmouthshire Regt, and the former was withdrawn into divisional reserve. During the whole of the 4th October, the Division retained this line under continuous pressure from the enemy.

On the night 4th/5th October, 2nd Australian Division took over the LEFT Brigade Sector and 3rd Brigade, 1st Division, was placed at the disposal of the GOC, 46th Division, and was used to relieve the 137th Infantry Brigade in the RIGHT Sector.

This completed the action so far as troops of the 46th Division were concerned.

The fighting in this action was of the heaviest nature, and our casualties, especially in officers, were heavy, including the loss of battalion commanders, one hundred other officers.

The captures amounted to some 2,000 prisoners and a battery of guns.

--- *** ---

Between the 29th of September and the 6th of October the 46th Division has fought two general engagements and, with the exception of a small piece of open country to the SOUTH of JONCOURT, has captured a fortified area between its own front line, WEST of the CANAL, and RAMICOURT, on a front of never less than 4,000 yards.

During these operations, inspite of the fact that both its flanks were continuously in the air, it has captured and maintained all objectives with the exception of the Village of MONTBREHAIN, taking six thousand prisoners, over seventy guns, and machine guns too numerous to count, at a loss to the Division of some two thousand, five hundred.

A List of Casualties for the period 29th September to 7th October, is attached.

--- *** ---

War Diary App 3

Secret. Copy No. 23

46th DIVISION ORDER No. 330.

Ref Map - 62.B.NW,
1/20,000.

2nd October, 1918.

1. The 46th Division will attack and capture the enemy trench system from H 24 c 5.3 to H 4 c 7.3, MANNEQUIN HILL and the Villages of RAMICOURT and MONTBREHAIN.

2. The 32nd Division is attacking SEQUEHART on our RIGHT. The 2nd Australian Division is attacking on our LEFT.

3. The objectives and boundaries are shown on the attached Map "A".

4. The 137th Infantry Brigade will attack on the RIGHT, making a defensive flank as shown on Map "A" and pushing Platoon Posts to the Summit of the High Ground to the S.E. and E. and joining up with the 32nd Division.
The 139th Infantry Brigade will attack on the LEFT and on reaching the objective will push out Platoon Posts to cover their front and will join up with the 2nd Australian Division at B 30 a 5.3.
The 138th Inf: Bde and 1/1st Bn, Monmouthshire Regt (Pioneers) will be in Divisional Reserve about MAGNY-LA-FOSSE (1/1st Monmouth Regt in SPRINGBOOK Valley).

5. The 46th Bn, M.G Corps, will in the first instance put down a barrage conforming with the artillery barrage. As soon as possible two companies will be pushed forward to support the Infantry, paying special attention to the flanks.
The other two companies will move forward later with a view to consolidation in depth; special attention being paid to our RIGHT Flank where it joins the 32nd Division.

6. Two Companies of Tanks will co-operate; one Company being allotted to each Inf: Bde.

7. Four Supply Tanks will rendezvous about MAGNY-LA-FOSSE and will get in touch with the GOC, 138th Inf: Bde.

8. The Australian Division are arranging to place a Smoke Barrage on B 30 b and a - 23 d from Zero to Zero plus 90'. (d) (90)

9. Assaulting troops will form up on the Forming Up Line at Zero - 1 hour with posts placed out in front. The Barrage will open at Zero and rest on the opening line for 6 minutes, when it will advance at the rate of 100x in 4 minutes, up to the RED LINE, where it rests for 20 minutes; advancing again at 100x in 6 minutes to the final objective.
Protective barrage lifts to 300x beyond the Dotted Blue Line and remains for 30 minutes. (300)
Mopping up parties will be left in all Trench Systems and Villages.

10. Brigades will report that they are formed up by the word "BULGARIA".

11. Guides for Brigades will be found by the 32nd Division at the rate of six per Battalion.
For RIGHT Brigade :- at WESTERN entrance of LEVERGIES (H 33 b 7.8).
For LEFT Brigade :- SOUTH-WESTERN entrance to JONCOURT. (H 15 b 2.3).

P.T.O.

12. Headquarters in the first instance will be as follows :-

Advanced Divisional Headquarters at LA BARAQUE, G 35 a 9.9.
137th Inf: Bde } as at present. BELLENGLISE TUNNEL
138th " " } G 29 c 4.8
139th Inf: Bde. MAGNY-LA-FOSSE, H 25 a 1.1.-

13. The Day of attack is the 3rd October.
Zero Hour is at 0605 (6.5 am).

14. Aeroplanes will call for flares at Zero plus 3 hours 30 minutes.

15. ACKNOWLEDGE BY WIRE.

Lieut-Colonel,
General Staff, 46th Division.

Issued at 2050

Copy No. 1 to CRA. *%
2 CRE.
3 Signals. *
4 137th Inf: Bde. *%
5 138th " " *%
6 139th " " *%
7 1st Monmouths. *
8 46th Bn, MGC. *%
9 AA & QMG.
10 ADMS.
11 DAPM.
12 O.C, Div: Observers. *
13 GSO I. *
14 32nd Division. *
15 2nd Australian Division. *
16/17 IX Corps. * (1 only).
18 IX Corps HA. *
19 IX Corps CBSO.
20 9th Sqdn, RAF. *
21/22 File. *
23/24 War Diary. *
25. 5th Bn, Tank Corps. *
26. 3rd Bde, Tank Corps.
* Map.
% Map already sent.

War Diary

App 27

Copy No. 22

Secret.

46th DIVISION ORDER No. 332.

7th October, 1918.

1. The Division will be prepared to move forward at short notice from 0800, 8th October, 1918.

2. ACKNOWLEDGE.

[signature]

Lieut-Colonel,
General Staff, 46th Division.

Issued at 2000.

Copy No. 1 to CRA.
2 CRE.
3 Signals.
4 137th Bde.
5 138th "
6 139th "
7 1st Monmouths.
8 46th Bn, MGC.
9 AA & QMG.
10 ADMS.
11 DADVS.
12 DADOS.
13 DAPM.
14 DGO.
15 C.O, Div'l Observers.
16 Div'l Train.
17 SSO.
18 Div'l Depot.
19 Camp Commandant.
20/21 File.
22/23 War Diary.

"A" Form. Army Form C. 2121.
(In pads of 100.)

MESSAGES AND SIGNALS.

No. of Message...............

Prefix.......... Code.............. m | Words. | Charge.

Office of Origin and Service Instructions.

War Diary

Sent At.........m. To......... By.........

This message is on a/c of: Appendix 5 Service.

(Signature of "Franking Officer.")

Recd. at ....m. Date......... From......... By.........

TO 137th Bde.
138th Bde.

Sender's Number	Day of Month.	In reply to Number.	
* G.49	3		AAA

MONTBREHAIN will be bombarded on morning of 4th up to 0630 AAAAs soon as bombardment permits strong patrols will be pushed through village with view to occupying EASTERN outskirts AAA At same time cavalry patrols will be pushing out towards DOON HILL AAA All arrangements to be made for making accurate and immediate report of progress AAA Addsd 138 and 137 Bdes.

From 46th Div.
Place
Time 2359

The above may be forwarded as now corrected. (Z) (sd) C.F.Jerram, Lt-Col.,
G.S.

Censor. Signature of Addressor or person authorised to telegraph in his name.

* This line should be erased if not required.

(3796.) Wt. W 492/M1647. 650,000 Pads. 5/17. H.W. & V., Ld. (E. 1187.)

"A" Form

Army Form C. 2121
(In pads of 100.)

MESSAGES AND SIGNALS.

No. of Message............

Prefix......Code......m. Office of Origin and Service Instructions	Words	Charge.	This message is on a/c of:	Recd. at......m.
War Diary	Sent At ......m. To ...... By		App. 6 ......Service. (Signature of "Franking Officer")	Date...... From ...... By......

TO 137 Bde.

Sender's Number.	Day of Month.	In reply to Number.	AAA
G.42	3		

3rd Cav Bde. available for relieving your troops on MANNEQUIN HILL if required AAA Troops holding this hill should push forward strong patrols to occupy summit and beyond AAA Most important that we hold this hill by morning

From 46th Div.
Place
Time 2125

The above may be forwarded as now corrected

(Z) (sd) C.F.Jerram Lt-Col., G.S.

Censor. Signature of Addressor or person authorised to telegraph in his name

* This line should be erased if not required.

Order No. 1625. Wt. W3253/ P 511. 27/2 H. & K., Ltd. (E. 2634).

"A" Form.

Army Form C. 2121.
(In pads of 100.)

MESSAGES AND SIGNALS.

No. of Message..............

Prefix.......... Code.......... m | Words. | Charge.

Office of Origin and Service Instructions.

Priority to Corps

Sent At..........m. To.......... By..........

This message is on a/c of: War Diary Service.

App. 7

(Signature of "Franking Officer.")

Recd. at ....m. Date.......... From.......... By..........

TO	138 Bde	32 Div.
		2 Aust. Div.
		9th Corps

Sender's Number.	Day of Month.	In reply to Number.	
* G.5	3		AAA

Move both supporting Bns at once to old German Front Line AAA Move third Bn. to Railway Cutting in H.16.a., b. and d AAA Acknowledge AAA Addsd 138 Bde rptd 32 Div. 2nd Aus. Div. and 9th Corps

From 46 Div.
Place
Time 0727

The above may be forwarded as now corrected.

(Z) (sd) C.F.Jerram Lt-Col. G.S.

Censor. Signature of Addressor or person authorised to telegraph in his name.

* This line should be erased if not required.

(3796.) Wt. W 492/M1647. 650,000 Pads. 5/17. H.W.& V., Ld. (E. 1187.)

"A" Form.
Army Form C. 2121.
(In pads of 100.)

MESSAGES AND SIGNALS.

No. of Message..............

Prefix........... Code............. m | Words. | Charge.

Office of Origin and Service Instructions.

Sent
At.................m.
To.................
By.................

This message is on a/c of:
War Diary
Service.
app. 8

(Signature of "Franking Officer.")

Recd. at .... m.
Date..............
From..............
By................

TO			
137 Bde.	9th Corps	R.A.	
138 :	32 Div	M.G.Bn.	
139 :	2 Aus Div.		

Sender's Number.	Day of Month.	In reply to Number.	
* G.18	3		AAA

6-inch Hows will cease fire on DOON COPSE
Ridge at 11 a.m. AAA Be prepared to occupy
Hill at that hour AAA 2 Coys of leading
Bn 138 Bde are at your disposal and remainder
of Bn if necessary but do not use without
ref to D.H.Q. AAA Addsd 137 Bde rptd 138
139 Bdes CRA M.G.Bn. Corps Flank Divs

From 46 Div.
Place
Time 0957

The above may be forwarded as now corrected. (Z)

Censor.

(sd) C.F.Jerram Lt-Col.,
G.S.

Signature of Addressor or person authorised to telegraph in his name.

* This line should be erased if not required.

(3796.) Wt. W 492/M1647. 650,000 Pads. 5/17. H.W.&V., Ld. (E. 1187.)

"A" Form.
Army Form C. 2121.
(In pads of 100.)

MESSAGES AND SIGNALS.

No. of Message..........

Prefix.......... Code.......... m | Words. | Charge. | This message is on a/c of: | Recd. at .... m.

Office of Origin and Service Instructions.

Priority

Sent
At.......... m.
To..........
By..........

War Diary Service.
app 9
(Signature of "Franking Officer.")

Date..........
From..........
By..........

TO
1/Monmouths
138 Inf. Bde.
139 : :

Sender's Number.	Day of Month.	In reply to Number.	AAA
* G.22	3		

LEFT Bn of 138 is placed at disposal of 139 to be used as directed verbally by GOC 139 AAA Support Bn 138 to move to enemy old front lines and get in close touch with Australian Div AAA 1/Monmouths to move to railway about H.16.central and come under orders of GOC 138 AAA Addsd Monmouths 138 139 AAA Acknowledge

Monmouths by hand
138 139 - Priority wire

From 46 Div.
Place
Time 1145

The above may be forwarded as now corrected. (Z)
Censor.

(sd) C.F.Jerram Lt Col.
G.S.
Signature of Addressor or person authorised to telegraph in his name.

* This line should be erased if not required.

(3796.) Wt. W 492/M1647. 650,000 Pads. 5/17. H.W.&V., Ld. (E. 1187.)

"A" Form.
MESSAGES AND SIGNALS.

Army Form C. 2121.
(In pads of 100.)
No. of Message..........

Prefix......Code......m	Words.	Charge.	This message is on a/c of:	Recd. at ......m.
Office of Origin and Service Instructions.	Sent		War Diary Service.	Date
Priority	At......m.		App 10	From
	To			
	By		(Signature of "Franking Officer.")	By

TO 138 Bde
139 :

Sender's Number.	Day of Month.	In reply to Number.	
* G.27	3		AAA

1/Monmouth Rgt. placed at disposal of
139, for purpose of holding MONTBREHAIN
AAA 139 Bde troops now holding village
to be withdrawn to WEST outskirts and
re-organized AAA Monmouths to hold a
line well outside village and push
patrols NORTH AAA Addsd 138 139

From 46 Div.
Place
Time 1410

The above may be forwarded as now corrected. (Z) (sd) C.F.Jerram Lt-Col.
G.S.

Censor. Signature of Addressor or person authorised to telegraph in his name.

* This line should be erased if not required.

(3796.) Wt. W 492/M1647. 650,000 Pads. 5/17. H.W.&V., Ld. (E. 1187.)

"A" Form.

Army Form C. 2121.
(In pads of 100.)

MESSAGES AND SIGNALS.

No. of Message.............

Prefix......Code......m	Words.	Charge.	This message is on a/c of:	Recd. at.......m.
Office of Origin and Service Instructions.	Sent		War Diary Service.	Date
Operations	At.......m.		App 11	From
Priotity	To			
	By		(Signature of "Franking Officer.")	By

TO 137 Bde
138 :
139 :

Sender's Number.	Day of Month.	In reply to Number.	AAA
*G.32	3		

Enemy appear to have broken in SOUTH of MONTBREHAIN AAA 1/Monmouths will be utilized to deal with this supported by 2 Coys of LEFT Bn 138 Bde AAA Cavalry are rounding up all enemy between our EAST flank and FRESNOY Addsd 137 138 139

From 46 Div.

Place

Time 1520

The above may be forwarded as now corrected.

(Z)(sd) C.F.Jerram Lt-Col. G.S.

Censor. Signature of Addressor or person authorised to telegraph in his name.

* This line should be erased if not required.

(3796.) Wt. W 492/M1647. 650,000 Pads. 5/17. H.W.&V., Ld. (E. 1187.)

"A" Form.

Army Form C. 2121.
(In pads of 100.)

MESSAGES AND SIGNALS.

No. of Message..............

Prefix.......... Code.......... m	Words.	Charge.	This message is on a/c of:	Recd. at .... m.
Office of Origin and Service Instructions.	Sent		War Diary Service.	Date..............
Priority to Bdes	At..............m.		App 12	From ....
	To................		(Signature of "Franking Officer.")	By..............
	By................			

TO		
	137 Bde.	9th Corps
	138 :	32 Div.
	139 :	2 Aus Div

Sender's Number.	Day of Month.	In reply to Number.	AAA
* G.36	3		

137 consolidate in BLUE Line from RIGHT boundary to junction with RED Line AAA RED line to junction with 139 AAA 139 consolidate from this point E. of RAMICOURT and WIANCOURT to junction with Australians AAA G.O.C. 138 to take command of LEFT Sector and in consultation with GOC 139 to withdraw such troops of 139 Bde as they consider advisable to re-organize in BEAUREVOIR FONSOMME Line AAA Addsd 3 Bdes rptd 9th Corps 32 Div. 2 Aus Div.

From 46 Div.

Place

Time 1747

The above may be forwarded as now corrected. (Z) (sd) C.F.Jerram Lt-Col. G.S.

Censor. Signature of Addressor or person authorised to telegraph in his name.

* This line should be erased if not required.

(3796.) Wt. W 492/M1647. 650,000 Pads. 5/17. H.W. & V., Ld. (E. 1187.)

"A" Form.

Army Form C. 2121.
(In pads of 100.)

MESSAGES AND SIGNALS.

No. of Message..............

Prefix............Code..............m | Words. | Charge.

Office of Origin and Service Instructions.
Operations Priority
to 1 Divn
5 Cav Bde
137 & 139

Sent
At..............m.
To..............
By..............

This message is on a/c of:
War Diary
A pp. 13
Service.
(Signature of "Franking Officer.")

Recd. at ....m.
Date..............
From..............
By..............

TO			
1 Div.	138 Bde	32 Div	
5 Cav Bde	139 "	2 Aus. Div.	
137 Bde.	9th Corps		

Sender's Number.	Day of Month.	In reply to Number.	
* G.38	3		AAA

5 Cav Bde will at once occupy BEAUREVOIR FONSOMME Line from H.24.b.9.4. to H.17. central and come under orders of GOC 137 Inf. Bde AAA Fighting patrols to push boldly forward towards MONTBREHAIN and gain touch in front and on flanks AAA The 2 Coys 138 Bde now in above line come under orders of GOC 137 Bde AAA 3rd Bde 1 Div on arrival to occupy above line from H.17. central to H.4.c.8.5. obtain touch with Australians and push fighting patrols to gain touch with advanced troops AAA This Bde will be under G.O.C. 138 Bde AAA H.Q. 137 at ~~XXXXX~~. H.26.d.3.7. H.Q. 138 H.25.a.2.3. AAA Every effort will be made by 46 Div to consolidate line as in my G.36 AAA It is of utmost importance that ground gained should be held AAA Addsd all concerned

From 46 Div.
Place
Time 1830

The above may be forwarded as now corrected. (Z) (sd) C.F.Jerram Lt-Col G.S.

Censor. Signature of Addressor or person authorised to telegraph in his name.

* This line should be erased if not required.

(3796.) Wt. W 492/M1647. 650,000 Pads. 5/17. H.W.&V., Ld. (E. 1187.)

"A" Form
Army Form C. 2121
(In pads of 100.)

MESSAGES AND SIGNALS.

No. of Message...........

Prefix.......Code.......m. Office of Origin and Service Instructions	Words	Charge.	This message is on a/c of:	Recd. at......m.
Priority		Sent	War Diary	Date............
1st Div.	At ....m.		..........Service.	From ....
~~138th Bde.~~	To		App. 14	By..............
	By		(Signature of "Franking Officer")	

TO 1 Divn.
138 Bde.
137 Bde.

Sender's Number.	Day of Month.	In reply to Number.	AAA
G.41	3		

3rd Bde of 1 Divn will not now go into BEAUREVOIR FONSOMME Line AAA They will bivouac in neighbourhood of CHATAIGNIERS Wood H.23 aaa Bde H.Q. to 137 Bde H.Q. H.26.d.3.7. AAA Bde to be in Divl. Reserve AAA Addsd 1 Divn 138 Bde rptd 137 Bde

From 46th Div.
Place
Time 2037

The above may be forwarded as now corrected (Z) (sd) C.F.Jerram, Lt-Col.
G.S.

Censor. Signature of Addressor or person authorised to telegraph in his name

* This line should be erased if not required.

Order No. 1625. Wt. W3253/ P 511. 27/2 H. & K., Ltd. (E. 2634).

"A" Form.

MESSAGES AND SIGNALS.

Army Form C. 2121.
(In pads of 100.)

No. of Message...............

Prefix......Code.........m. Office of Origin and Service Instructions.	Words.	Charge.	This message is on a/c of:	Recd. at ....m.
Wire to 138	Sent		..........Service.	Date........
139	At.........m.			From........
32 Div	To.........			
D.R. to rest	By.........		(Signature of "Franking Officer.")	By..........

TO War Diary

Sender's Number.	Day of Month.	In reply to Number.	
* G.78	4		AAA

Night of 5/6 138 Inf: Bde: with 1/Monmouths and 46 M.G. Bn attached will relieve 3rd Bde under G.O.C., 137th Bde from N. Divl: Boundary to a line H.24.d.9.5 H.24.central H.28.central AAA 139 Bde with 2/Life Guards M.G. Bn and 9 Corps Cyclist Bn will relieve 14 and 97 Bdes of 32 Divn from above line to a line I.32.a.0.0 N.4.a.0.0 AAA 137 Bde will be in reserve in MAGNY Area AAA Arrangements to be made between Bdes concerned in consultation with 46 M.G.C. AAA All reliefs to be complete by 0600 6th Oct AAA Time of passing of Divl Comd notified later AAA Line to be taken over runs H.36.c.5.2 where in touch with French Sunken Road to H.36.a.5.5 H.30.d.0.5 Sunken Road to H.19.c.0.0 AAA 14 Bde H.Q. H.31.a.7.7 97 Bde H.25.d.4.8 139 Bde MAGNY LA FOSSE AAA On relief 3rd 14th and 97 Bdes will move under orders of their divns

App 15

From 46 Div
Place
Time 1810

The above may be forwarded as now corrected.

.... Censor.

(Sgd/ C.F. Jerram. Lt-Col:
Signature of Addressor or person authorised to telegraph in his name.

* This line should be erased if not required.

(3796) Wt. W 492/M1647. 650,000 Pads. 5/17. H.W.&V., Ld. (E. 1187.)

Copies to :-

C.R.A.
C.R.E.
Signals.
137th Inf: Bde:
138th : :
139th : :
46th Bn: M.G.C.
1st Monmouths.
A.D.M.S.
A.A. & Q.M.G.
Div'l: Train & S.S.O.
D.A.P.M.
D.A.D.O.S.
D.A.D.V.S.
Div: Observers.
Div: Depot.
Camp Commdt:
46th Div: Rear.
1st Division.
2nd Aus: Div:
32nd Div:
2nd Life Guards.
9th Squadron, R.A.F.
IX Corps.
IX Corps Cyclists.
Liaison Offr: attd: 47th French Div:
War Diary.
File.

"A" Form.

MESSAGES AND SIGNALS.

Army Form C. 2121.
(In pads of 100.)

No. of Message..............

Prefix.......... Code.............. m. | Words. | Charge.

Office of Origin and Service Instructions.

War
Diary

Sent
At..............m.
To..............
By..............

This message is on a/c of:
..................*Service.*
(Signature of "Franking Officer.")

Recd. at.........m.
Date..............
From..............
By..............

TO { 137 Bde 138 Bde 139 Bde 1 Div:
2 Aus: Div: IX Corps 46 M.G.Bn

Sender's Number.	Day of Month.	In reply to Number.	AAA
G.81	4		

2 Australian Div is attacking MONTBREHAIN at 0605 5th Oct under a creeping barrage and supported by tanks AAA Their barrage opens on the line I.7.c.0.6 to H.6.b.8.7 and advances 100 yards in 4 minutes AAA 46 Div will continue thisbarrage to S.E. to cover high ground in I.14.a barrage will advance with Aus barrage AAA 46 Div will also bombard with H.A. high ground in I.8 and 9 a AAA 3rd Bde will push forward patrols during night with view to occupying line MANNEQUIN HILL to I.13.c and spur in I.13 should they meet with no opposition AAA At zero hour patrols will again be pushed out to test opposition AAA If none is found the line MANNEQUIN HILL - DOON HILL - I.2.central will be occupied AAA Should opposition be found 3rd Bde will remain holding present line

App 16

From
Place 46 Div
Time 1950

The above may be forwarded as now corrected. (Z)

Censor. sd/ G.M. Jarrow. Signature of Addressor or person authorised to telegraph in his name.

Lt-Col

* This line should be erased if not required.

(3796.) Wt. W 492/M1647. 650,000 Pads. 5/17. H. W. & V., Ld. (E. 1187.)

"A" Form.

Army Form C. 2121.
(In pads of 100.)

MESSAGES AND SIGNALS.

No. of Message..............

Prefix........ Code.......... m.	Words.	Charge.	This message is on a/c of:	Recd. at ....m.
Office of Origin and Service Instructions.	Sent		..................Service.	Date..............
	At...........m.			From..............
	To............			
	By............		(Signature of "Franking Officer.")	By..............

TO War Diary — 137 CRE, 138 ADMS, 139 DADM Q

* Sender's Number.	Day of Month.	In reply to Number.	AAA
G 109	5		

WUFA Bde Group less BDE HQ will move as early as possible today to area G22 C and d G28 AAA Addsd WUFA repts all concerned

[initials]

From H Dn

Place

Time 1100

The above may be forwarded as now corrected. .... Censor.

(Z) [signature]

Signature of Addressor or person authorised to telegraph in his name.

* This line should be erased if not required.

(3796.) Wt. W 492/M1647. 650,000 Pads. 5/17. H.W.&V., Ld. (E. 1187.)

"A" Form.

Army Form C. 2121.
(In pads of 100.)

MESSAGES AND SIGNALS.

No. of Message............

Prefix........Code..........m. | Words. | Charge. | This message is on a/c of: | Recd. at........m.

Office of Origin and Service Instructions.

Priority to
139, 97, 14 Bdes
1 Div, 138 Bde

Sent At........m. To........ By........

War Diary ....Service.

(Signature of "Franking Officer.")

Date........ From........ By........

TO
139 Bde 97, 14 Bde. 32, 1, 6 Divs, C.R.A.
137 : C.R.E. M.G.Bn, A.D.M.S. 'Q',
138 : 1st Monmouths 9 Corps 2/Life Guards

* Sender's Number.	Day of Month.	In reply to Number.	AAA
G.110	5		

139 Bde plus 2/Life Guards will take over SEQUEHART Sector to-night from 97 and 14 Bdes as already arranged AAA 138 Bde plus 46 M.G. Bn and Pioneers will be prepared to take over from 137 Bde AAA 137 Bde H.Q. with 3rd Bde if not relieved by 138 Bde will be relieved by 6th Div AAA On relief 3rd Bde will concentrate on MAGNY LA FOSSE and move as directed by 1 Div AAA Cyclists on relief will come under orders of G.O.C., 139 Bde and be moved into Bde reserve AAA 137 Bde H.Q. will join own Bde on command passing AAA All reliefs to be reported

App. 18

From 46 Div
Place
Time 1135

The above may be forwarded as now corrected. (Z)
Censor.

sd/ C.F. Jerram Lt-Col
Signature of Addressor or person authorised to telegraph in his name.

* This line should be erased if not required.

(3796.) Wt. W492/M1647. 650,000 Pads. 5/17. H. W. & V., Ld. (E. 1187.)

"A" Form

MESSAGES AND SIGNALS.

No. of Message...........

Prefix.......Code.......m.	Words	Charge.	This message is on a/c of:	Recd. at......m.
Office of Origin and Service Instructions				Date..........
War Diary	Sent At ....m. To .... By		........Service. (Signature of "Franking Officer")	From .... By........

TO	137 138 Bde 139	a adms Da&m	CRE

Sender's Number.	Day of Month.	In reply to Number.	AAA
G 111	5		

Ref G109 for area G22 c and d and G28 read in and WEST of ASCENSION VALLEY AAA added WUFA repeated all concerned

app 19

From 46 Div

Place

Time 1147

The above may be forwarded as now corrected. (Z)

Censor. (sgd) S Hay Maj

Signature of Addressor or person authorised to telegraph in his name

* This line should be erased if not required

Order No 1625 Wt. W3253/ P 511 27/2 H. & K., Ltd. (E. 263

"A" Form

MESSAGES AND SIGNALS.

No. of Message..........

Prefix..........Code..........m. Words Charge.

Office of Origin and Service Instructions

War Diary

This message is on a/c of: ....Service.

Sent At ....m. To .... By ....

(Signature of "Franking Officer")

Recd. at......m. Date.......... From .... By..........

TO { 137 138 MG Bn

Sender's Number.	Day of Month.	In reply to Number.	AAA
G 114	5		

A Bde of 6th Div and NOT the 138 Bde will now be relieving 3rd Bde and HQ 137 Bde tonight AAA Orders later AAA 138 and MG Bn to be prepared to withdraw to area W of CANAL and E of ASCENSION VALLEY AAA Addsd 138 137 MG Bn

From HQ Div

Place

Time 1317

The above may be forwarded as now corrected (Z) Capt [illegible]

Censor. Signature of Addressor or person authorised to telegraph in his name

* This line should be erased if not required.

Order No. 1625. Wt. W3253/ P 511. 27/2. H. & K., Ltd. (E. 2634).

"A" Fo[illegible]

MESSAGES AND SIGNALS.

Army Form C.2121
(In pads of 100).
No. of Message

Prefix .... Code .... m. | Words | Charge

Office of Origin and Service Instructions.
S.D.R except
to 1st Div.
2 Aus.Div.
9 Corps.

Sent
At .... m.
To
By

This message is on a/c of: War Diary Service.

(Signature of "Franking Officer.")

Recd. at .... m.
Date
From
By

TO
137 Bde. 3 Bde. 2 Aus.Div. CRE 2 Life Gds.
138 : 1 Div. IX Corps. ADMS. M.G Bn.
139 : 6 Div. CRA. 5 Cav.Bde. AA & QMG.

Sender's Number.	Day of Month.	In reply to Number.	
* G.122	5		AAA

16 Bde of 6 Divn will relieve H.Q 137 Bde with 3rd Bde tonight under arrangements to be made between G.O.C's concerned AAA On relief HQ 137 will withdraw to join their Bde AAA 3rd Bde moves as ~~already~~ ordered by 1st Div. Cyclists to 139 Bde AAA Command of corps front passes to GOC 6 Div at 0930 on 6 Oct at which time 46 Div command will be 137 Bde in ASCENSION VALLEY 138 Bde W. of CANAL 46 MG Bn about CANAL RE RAMC in present billets AAA DHQ SE pf VENDELLES AAA 139 Inf: Bde will come under orders of GOC 6 Div AAA 2 Life Guards 5 Cav.Bde IX Corps Cyclists will be transferred to 6 Div AAA 46 DA remains in line

App 21

From 46 Div.
Place
Time 1520

The above may be forwarded as now corrected.

Censor.

(Z) (sgd) GF.Jerram, Lt-Col.

Signature of Addressor or person authorised to telegraph in his name.

* This line should be erased if not required.

750,000. W 2186—M509. H. W. & V., Ld. 6/16.

"A" Form

Army Form C. 2121
(In pads of 100.)

MESSAGES AND SIGNALS.

No. of Message..........

...Code..............m. | Words | Charge. | This message is on a/c of: | Recd. at......m.

...Service Instructions

Sent At ....m. To .... By ....

War Diary ....Service.

(Signature of "Franking Officer")

Date.............. From .... By..............

TO — 9 Corps

Sender's Number.	Day of Month.	In reply to Number.	AAA
G125	5		

Location	0600	6th	aaa
VANA	G29 d 0 2	aaa	WUFA
H 26 d	37	WUQU	G 21 c 2050
WUWO	H 25 a 23		

App "V"

From 46 Div

Place

Time 1930

The above may be forwarded as now corrected.

(Z) (Sd) M Baron Liddon Capt

Censor. Signature of Addressor or person authorised to telegraph in his name

* This line should be erased if not required.

Order No. 1625. Wt. W3253/ P 511. 27/2 H. & K., Ltd. (E. 2634).

War Diary

App 24

Secret.

Copy No. 17

Operation "D".
46th Division Instructions No. 1.

Ref: Maps 62.B. 1/40,000.

46th Division G.115/10. 7/10/18.

1. It is not yet definitely ascertained whether the 1st or 46th Divisions will be the first to move forward after the advance of the 6th Division.

2. In the event of the 46th Division leading, the following will be the dispositions of the Division at Zero Hour :-

DHQ Advanced Report Centre	- MAGNY LA FOSSE.
DHQ Rear.	VENDELLES (R 8 b).
137th Inf: Bde.	E. Bank of CANAL. Squares G 35, 29, 23. HQ.- BELLENGLISE TUNNEL.
138th : :	Area about H 14, 15, 16, 20, 21 22, keeping clear of guns. HQ.- MAGNY LA FOSSE.
139th Inf: Bde and 1/1st Monmouth Regt.	In the Line, SEQUEHART Sector.

3. Should the operations of the 6th Division prove successful, it is probable that the 139th Inf: Bde and 1/1st Monmouth Regt will return to the 46th Division, in which event they will concentrate about LEVERGIES.

4. Exact locations of Brigade and Battalion HQ at Zero will be wired to DHQ as early as possible.

5. From Zero hour, all units of the Division will be in readiness to move with or without transport. Animals will be harnessed, but not hooked in.

6. To take up the above dispositions, the 138th Inf: Bde will move to the MAGNY LA FOSSE Area on 'Y' day.

7. The most probable operations for which the division may be used are :-

   (a) To exploit success to the EAST.
   (b) To assist in holding the SOUTHERN Flank of the 6th Division attack.

8. ACKNOWLEDGE.

[signature]

Lieut-Colonel,
General Staff, 46th Division..

Issued at 1030

Copy No. 1 to CRA.
2 CRE.
3 Signals.
4 137th Inf: Bde.
5 138th : :
6 139th : :
7 1st Monmouths.
8 46th Bn, MGC.
9 AA & QMG.
10 ADMS.

Copy No. 11/12 to IX Corps.
13 6th Division.
14 GSO I.
15/16 File.
17/18 War Diary.

Secret.

ACCOUNT OF THE PART TAKEN BY THE 46TH DIVISION IN THE BATTLE OF RAMICOURT, ON THE 3RD OCTOBER, 1918.-

1. At 4.30 pm on the 2nd October, orders were received at a Corps Conference that the 46th Division was to attack and capture the line SEQUEHART (exclusive) - MONTBREHAIN, joining with the 2nd Australian Division, NORTH-WEST of the latter place. At the same time, 32nd Division was to attack and capture SEQUEHART.

The area of attack consisted of the BEAUREVOIR-FONSOMME Line, the last defensive position of the enemy in this neighbourhood, and the villages of RAMICOURT and MONTBREHAIN; whilst on our RIGHT Flank was MANNEQUIN HILL, running in a N.E. direction from SEQUEHART. Little was known about the area to be attacked or about the position of our own troops. For the latter reason, a forming up line was arranged sufficiently far back to ensure that there would be no enemy opposition to our troops forming up for the attack. The 32nd Division, which was holding the line, was asked to withdraw all their troops behind this line.

At 5.5 am, 3rd October, the Division attacked with 137th Inf: Bde: on the RIGHT, 139th Inf Bde on the LEFT, and 138th Infantry Brigade to whom was attached the 1/1st Bn, Monmouthshire Regt (Pioneers) in Divisional Reserve.

3 Brigades of Artillery had to be moved up during the night to positions which it was impossible previously to reconnoitre, but in spite of this fact, the barrage opened well to time, and though slightly more short shooting was reported than usual, it was otherwise every thing that could be desired.

Considerable opposition was encountered in the BEAUREVOIR-FONSOMME LINE, where the enemy fought to the last, some five hundreds being killed in the Left Brigade Sector alone.

On our RIGHT, the 32nd Division quickly occupied SEQUEHART, but the troops attacking on our LEFT were unable to break through the very strong defences opposed to them.

The 137th Infantry Brigade was able to report that it had captured all its objectives up to time. The 139th Infantry Brigade, pushing forward to RAMICOURT found its LEFT Flank exposed: two Companies were promptly detailed to move through WIANCOURT and form here a defensive flank. After the capture of RAMICOURT, the defence rapidly weakened, and this Brigade captured over one thousand prisoners in MONTBREHAIN alone. In both RAMICOURT and MONTBREHAIN, French civilians were found and some seventy of them brought back to our lines. In the latter Village, a battery of field guns was also captured.

Two companies of Tanks operating with this attack did excellent work, especially in clearing the outskirts of RAMICOURT. Immediately SOUTH of MONTBREHAIN, one of these Tanks attacked a machine gun nest consisting of sixteen guns and killed the whole of the crews before it was in its turn disabled.

By 1030 a severe defeat had been inflicted on the enemy and the whole of the objectives of the 46th Division obtained.

The 5th Cavalry Brigade was thereupon directed to move forward and keep in close touch with 46th Division to exploit their success. Unfortunately, this Brigade was a considerable distance to the rear and by the time they arrived in the forward area, the opportunity for using them had passed.

By 1500 the Division with both flanks exposed and having suffered very severe casualties, was attacked from an EASTERLY direction. At this angle our line was overlooked by the high ground round DOON and MANNEQUIN HILLS, on which the enemy quickly established himself, in spite of heavy and continued Artillery fire from our guns, and by the point blank fire of field guns and machine guns, soon made a gap in our defence immediately SOUTH of MONTBREHAIN.

Our troops in this neighbourhood, were slowly pressed back SOUTH WEST of the Village, and a heavy attack commencing shortly afterwards from the NORTH of the Village, our troops were withdrawn to a General Line E. of WIANCOURT - RAMICOURT and the Spur in I 15. In the meantime, 138th Infantry Brigade had been moved forward to occupy the BEAUREVOIR-FONSOMME Line and , were placed at the disposal of the Brigades in the line. later in the day the Australians on our LEFT were enabled to advance, occupying WIANCOURT and gaining touch with our LEFT NORTH-EAST of that place.

During the afternoon, the enemy developed a very strong counter-attack against our RIGHT Brigade and succeeded in forcing us off the slopes of MANNEQUIN HILL.

5th Cavalry Brigade and the IX Corps Cyclists, some 150 strong, were ordered to occupy the BEAUREVOIR-FONSOMME Line and were placed under the orders of the GOC, 137th Infantry Brigade.

A counter attack partially restored the situation, and the NORTH-WESTERN Slopes were again occupied by us. We were, however, unable to retain the summit of the HILL which was continuously swept by machine gun fire.

During the night 3rd/4th, 139th Infantry Brigade was relieved by the 138th Infantry Brigade plus 1st Monmouthshire Regt, and the former was withdrawn into divisional reserve. During the whole of the 4th October, the Division retained this line under continuous pressure from the enemy.

On the night 4th/5th October, 2nd Australian Division took over the LEFT Brigade Sector and 3rd Brigade, 1st Division, was placed at the disposal of the GOC, 46th Division, and was used to relieve the 137th Infantry Brigade in the RIGHT Sector.

This completed the action so far as troops of the 46th Division were concerned.

The fighting in this action was of the heaviest nature, and our casualties, especially in officers, were heavy, including the loss of five battalion commanders, and one hundred other officers.

The captures amounted to some 2,000 prisoners and a battery of guns.

Between the 29th of September and the 6th of October the 46th Division has fought two general engagements and, with the exception of a small piece of open country to the SOUTH of JONCOURT, has captured a fortified area between its own front line, WEST of the CANAL, and RAMICOURT, on a front of never less than 4,000 yards.

During these operations, inspite of the fact that both its flanks were continuously in the air, it has captured and maintained all objectives with the exception of the Village of MONTBREHAIN, taking six thousand prisoners, over seventy guns, and machine guns too numerous to count, at a loss to the Division of some two thousand, five hundred.

A List of Casualties for the period 29th September to 7th October, is attached.

--- *** ---

before they were able to put up any organised resistance. The centre (5th South Staffordshire Regt) and the LEFT (6th North Staffordshire Regt) found a considerable depth of water in the CANAL. The officers swimming over first with were soon joined by the leading lines of their men, and, assisted by bridges, rafts and boats, the whole force was soon across and dealing with the enemy in the strongly held trenches on the EASTERN Bank. At RIQUEVAL, the bridge was found to be intact. The Royal Engineers with some of the storming troops bayonetted the enemy pioneers who were about to light the fuzes, and withdrew the charges. The saving of this bridge, due entirely to the rapidity and gallantry of the advance was of inestimable value, and by it, and the pontoon bridges which were later made by the 46th and 32nd Divisional Engineers and Pioneers, the whole of these two Divisions with their artillery, were later enabled to pass over.

The Infantry rapidly clearing the trenches up to the BLUE Objective, advanced on the BROWN LINE which they reached in scheduled time, capturing on their way a battery of four guns, the gun teams of which were all either killed or captured together with horses. Owing to the density of the fog, little use could be made of the Divisional Observers' Section. The Divisional Mounted Troop, consisting of men from the DAC and Field Ambulances were, however, sent forward to reconnoitre, and by questioning prisoners and wounded men, were able to send back most valuable information, showing that our infantry had successfully crossed the CANAL. On this information, orders were issued for 139th and 138th Infantry Brigades* to push straight across the Canal up to the barrage and move directly on the objectives assigned to them.

The leading battalion of these two brigades had already pushed forward after the 137th Infantry Brigade and crossed the CANAL close on their heels. The two brigades reached the BROWN LINE in excellent time, where they were joined by the two Companies of Tanks, and in spite of the dense fog, the whole were enabled to move forward towards their objective as the barrage lifted.

After passing the YELLOW Objective, the fog, having cleared considerably, much inconvenience was caused to the RIGHT Battalion by the enemy occupying the high ground SOUTH of the CANAL. Machine guns from this direction swept our RIGHT Flank continuously and enemy field guns firing at point blank range quickly put out of action all six tanks allotted to 139th Infantry Brigade. This battery was in its turn put out of action by a party of 139th Infantry Brigade, who, with great gallantry crossed the CANAL and shot or bayonetted the gunners. Little infantry trouble was experienced from SOUTH of the CANAL; several feeble attempts to counter attack on this flank were made, and one mounted German officer made three gallant attempts to rally his men; on the third attempt, however, both he and his horse were killed, whereupon the enemy immediately retired.

On our LEFT, 138th Infantry Brigade were successfully carrying forward their advance, and at 12.30 pm, we advanced from the YELLOW Line on to MAGNY LA FOSSE. At this time it was definitely ascertained that the troops on our left, who, until now, had been thought to occupy the high ground about NAUROY, had been hung up on their first objective: both flanks of the 46th Division were therefore in the air, and steps were taken to form a left defensive flank and to hold the bridgeheads along the CANAL on the right flank. The advance from the YELLOW Line was slightly delayed by this operation, and the barrage was some distance ahead of the advancing infantry. In spite of this, our infantry advanced and soon caught up the barrage, most ably assisted on our LEFT by the Tanks attached to the 138th Infantry Brigade.

By three pm, the whole of our objectives had been taken, and the 32nd Division, pressing forward, passed through our lines, to the RED LINE. During the later stages of our advance, a number of guns were encountered, giving opportunities for many acts of gallantry on the part of both officers and men. One battery was seen to be limbering up EAST of our final defensive barrage, and an attempt was made to pass through our barrage and prevent the withdrawal of these guns. Horses and drivers were shot down, and immediately our barrage began to thin, this battery was captured. Several bayonet charges against the enemy's artillery were made, the crews being killed and the guns captured. The German artillery men fought with the greatest valour and continued to fire their guns at point blank range up to the last.

During the following night, the Division was continuously in action owing to both flanks being open to the enemy. On the morning of the 30th, the 1st Division, on our RIGHT eased the situation by the capture of THORIGNY and TALANA HILL, whilst on the LEFT, the 2nd Australian Division, pushing forward, joined up with our LEFT Flank during the day.

7. Work of the Artillery. The preparatory work of the Heavy Artillery cannot be too highly praised, and, it was owing in a great measure to their excellent shooting that the storming of the CANAL with its concrete defences was made possible. The Field Artillery, in spite of the fact that the majority of the guns were in silent positions up to Zero Hour, and unable to register, put down one of the finest barrages that the troops have ever advanced under. During the action, the majority of the Field Artillery was moved forward to new positions already selected. These movements were so expeditiously carried out as to make little appreciable difference in the intensity of the barrage.

8. The work of the Royal Engineers, Machine Gunners, Pioneers and RAMC, was beyond all praise. The first named, besides saving the RIQUEVAL Bridge, were able to assist the infantry in many ways outside their ordinary scope, and incidents of individual gallantry in attacking machine gun nests, etc, were of common occurrence.

9. Infantry. As for the infantry, in addition to the magnificent behaviour of every officer and man, the leadership shown by regimental officers and NCO's was of a very high nature. The faultless leading of their men across some 5,000 yards of enemy territory in a thick fog, during which some 4,200 prisoners and seventy guns were taken, is worthy of the highest traditions of the Service. Their success, and the lightness of their casualties, some eight hundred in all, is due to this power of leadership and to the fact that not the slightest hesitation was shown throughout the whole engagement.

All ranks were determined to push through to the final objective regardless of the flanks, and right well they carried it out, not only on this occasion but subsequently on the 3rd October.

--- *** ---

Report on Operations of 3/10/18.

1. Sections proceeded from MAGNY LA FOSSE independently to JONCOURT, leaving at 3-0 a.m. each section with its two fighting limbers.

Limbers were unloaded in JONCOURT and returned to lines.

No 4 Section reported to 8th Bn S.F.

No 3 Section reported to 5th Bn.S.F.

Nos 1 & 2 Sections reported to 6th Bn.S.F.

No 4 Section was to follow close behind left flank of 8th Bn and No 3 behind Right flank of 5th Bn. Nos 1 & 2 sections closely supporting the reserve Bn watching for Gaps or strong points.

At Zero I went forward with 4 (four) runners to reconnoitre ground and routes for pack mules and limbers. At 7.0 a.m. the 8th Bn were taking WIANCOURT and there was a gap on the left. No 4 section took up a position on high ground B.28.c., I then sent for pack animals already assembled in railway cutting H.15.a. with a message to a mounted orderly in cutting to send for S.A.A. limbers to come up to SWISS COTTAGE. The attack was now held up in SUNKEN Road H.5.b. two enemy field guns on sky line B.30.a. causing casualties at point blank range. I then proceeded to RAMICOURT where I found No 1 section and put it in action in road H.5.d. where it covered exits from MONTBREHAIN. I then entered MONTBREHAIN and met the Headquarters of the 6th Battn. who were about to retire and they asked for guns to be placedn in Quarry H.12.b. to cover gap on Right flank. This I ordered to be done. No 2 section had meanwhile pressed through MONTBREHAIN and came into action against two trench mortars silencing them. As Infantry withdrew before enemy assembling No 2 Section fell back to SUNKEN Road H.5.d. where they fired 3,000 rounds at advancing enemy. I then reported my situation to Major Wade in Railway cutting. Here I met two men of No 3 Section who reported Lieut.Park killed and seven men wounded.

This section had engaged and silenced enemy M.Gs. at very short range 50^{x}. It then under the senior remaining N.C.O. took up its position on HILL H.12.c., I met them here at 3.0 p.m. The enemy were advancing down from high ground I.8 and also through MONTBREHAIN.

We engaged enemy and forced him to retire. Own troops in SUNKEN Road H.12.c. and d. now gave way isolating six guns of 'C' Company in H.12.c. who were forced to retire. The enemy brought up two field guns in I.8. and enfiladed our line at road H.12.c., H.18.d.

The Infantry Commander then requested me to assist in securing his Right flank, to do this one platoon plus two M.Gs. were moved round to SUNKEN Road H.17.b. Here it was found that our immediate right was secure, 'C' Company's guns being in action H.17.d. Meanwhile our troops in H.18.d. continued to retire. The pioneer battalion and a squadron of cavalry arrived at this moment to re-inforce and enemy advance was checked. No 3 section guns had targets from 700^{x} to 1500^{x}, putting out two enemy M.Gs. attempting to come into action and caused casualties to enemy infantry.

At 5.30 p.m. the enemy put down a heavy barrage in rear of SUNKEN Road H.5.d. This lasted 1½ hours.

Conclusions. Pack animals proved most useful, filled belts arriving for Nos 4 & 3 sections at a critical moment. Our losses of 35 all ranks made the keeping up of supplies very difficult.

All firing was direct - 10,000 rounds expended with observed fire. Mounted Orderlies proved most useful. My first 8 pack mules came under heavy artillery fire at 7.30 a.m. owing to the Corporal in charge not making proper use of cover and 4 (four) were wounded delaying the supply.

No 4 section had pushed on with the Infantry and established themselves in the SUNKEN Road and Railway cutting H.5.b.

At the end of the day there were 14 (fourteen) guns still in action with an ample supply of filled belts and water.

(Sd) H.S.Windeler, Major,
O.C.'A' Company
46th Battn.M.G.Corps.

To H.Q. PIGE.

Reference 62.b.N.W.
Report on operations on October 3rd.

'C' Company arrived at WHISTLE COPSE at PT.25 and laid out lines and prepared for barrage. Our target was the Hill in H.17.b. and H.18.a. Sixteen guns fired from zero to zero plus 30na total of 51,000 rounds. Several shrapnel shells burst over the teams during the firing of the barrage and 2/Lieut.Johnson was wounded.

At 07.30 sections with limbers moved forward independently across country to H.17.b. 5.2.

While limbers were being unpacked I made a reconnaissance along the railway to H.18.a.55.60 from where I saw a party of the enemy, about a platoon strong, in action facing North at about H.18.a.6.9, I withdrew to bring up two guns but by the time they arrived a party of our infantry had worked up from about H.18.a.7.7 taking the Boche in rear and killing or capturing the garrison. I then disposed two sections along the railway ready for action while section officers made reconnaissance.

Our Infantry has passed over the crest of MANNEQUIN HILL but there was considerable fighting at close quarters as the result of which our infantry were pushed back to the blue line (SUNKEN Road from I.19.a.10.00 to I.13.b.70.30).

(Continued).

Report on Operations. 'B' Company.

'B' Company, after firing barrage moved forward 12 (twelve) guns for the consolidation of the FONSOME line. One section moved to about H.17.d.90.20 and established touch with 'D' Company on the right and 'C' Company on the left.

Early in the afternoon the infantry in front withdrew and took up position on the FONSOMME line so the section officer placed his guns on the road in front of PRESELLES and opened direct fire.

A second section moved to positions in FONSOMME line, two guns were placed at H.16.b.50.70 to cover Valley and two guns in SUNKEN Road H.4.d.30.00 to guard left flank. At 3.0 p.m. small parties of enemy were seen moving in H.6.a., H.6.b. and B.30.c. on whom fire was opened, 250 rounds per gun being fired. No further movements were seen.

A third section moved forward to a position on forward slope overlooking RAMICOURT. About 1430 our troops were seen retiring on RAMICOURT. As the withdrawal continued small parties of both friend and foe were so mixed that fire was impossible. Simultaneously extreme enemy activity beyond crest on the right indicated commencement of a counter-attack. Fire of all arms was heard and the section officer withdrew two guns from the task of covering RAMICOURT and placed them in shell holes facing East. A little firing was done at enemy moving North of RAMICOURT. The officer then approached a company of 5th Lincolns who had orders to hold FONSOMME line in H.16.b. at all costs. The Company Commander was offered the support of the 4 (four) Vickers guns which he gladly accepted, and dispositions were made accordingly.

The fourth section was kept in reserve at H.15.d.70.30 and mounted guns to fire at low flying hostile aeroplanes. One of these was destroyed by shell fire.

'C' Company (continued)

Owing to the close nature of the fighting it was impossible to fire any support with M.G. fire.

The situation to the NORTH and NORTH EAST was obscure. The enemy was holding the crest of MANNEQUIN HILL and was very active with machine guns. One tank at I.13.d.1.3 appeared to be unable to get forward on account of an Anti-tank gun just beyond the ridge which fired at practically point blank range. As the result of officers reconnaissance I decided to push forward three sections; one to MANNEQUIN HILL and two to about H.18.b.7.3. No 2 section moving to MANNEQUIN HILL came under artillery fire and much M.G. fire but pushing on withbgallantry and determination reached a defensive flank put out by the infantry from about I.13.c.75.05 to I.13.c.75.45.

In the afternoon this section was engaged heavily with artillery fire. All four guns were put out of action. The section officer Lieut.Smart was killed,and Sgt.Abbott with 7 O.Rs, The survivors of the teams, moved back and reported for duty to the O.C.No 4 section.

Nos 1 & 3 sections got into position at H.18.b.7.3. At 13.30 the infantry withdrew over the spur in I.13.a. I saw the Company Commander concerned who stated he had to withdraw because both his flanks were in the air and he was running out of S.A.A.

He was then endeavouring to get in touch with the troops on MANNEQUIN HILL and he intended to hold a line from about I.13.d.0.3 along grid to I.13.b.0.6, thence in the direction of H.12.d.7.8.

Under the circumstances I instructed the section officers to keep in close touch with this party of infantry and conform to their movements. Soon after 14.00 parties of the enemy moved behind the spur in I.13.a. towards the railway in H.12.d. and threatened our left flank. The infantry had to withdraw from the line taken up and Lieut.Hoff ordered his section Sgt to withdraw his guns to the high ground in order to give covering fire. He then rallied and organised a party of the infantry and led them forward in a counter-attack. Our guns gave covering fire during this operation - firing 9,000 rounds, and inflicted casualties on the enemy, including the officer who was conducting the operation. A tank also moved forward to assist but was put out of action, the crew being killed or wounded. The enemy eventually withdrew namely, I think, as the result of our M.G. fire. The situation from this point onwards appears to be rather obscure. Our infantry continued to hold the sunken road from H.24.d.7.0 to I.13.c.3.7 but withdrew from their positions in H.18.b. and I.13.a. to the Hill in H.18.a. and H.17.b. and d.

My remaining 12 (twelve) guns took up positions as follows :-

1 section at H.16.c.20.20 to fire East covering MANNEQUIN HILL and the valley between.

1 section at H.18.a.30.70 to fire NORTH and NORTH EAST.

1 section along trench H.17.d.60.70 - H.17.d.90.20 firing North East into the valley. These positions were maintained until the Company was relieved.

Casualties in the Company during the operation were as follows :-

Lieut.Smart, Missing believed killed.
Lieut.Hoff wounded.
2/Lieut.Johnson wounded.
2/Lieut.Prins wounded.
13 O.Rs. killed.
21 O.Rs. wounded.
1 O.R. wounded (at duty)
2 O.Rs. missing.

Reports on officers, N.C.Os. and men recommended for conspicuous gallantry and devotion to duty are forwarded herewith.

(Sd) W.T.Boughey, Major,
O.C.'C'Company
46th Battn.M.G.Corps.

6/10/18.

Report on Operations. 'D' Company.

After firing the preliminary barrage 'D' Company which was detailed for the defence of the right flank, moved forward and took up dispositions as follows :-

1 section in H.29.a. firing towards SEQUEHART.
1 section in H.23.a. & d. from East and South East.
1 section near TULIP COPSE H.24.a. firing South and
1 section in H.24.b. firing East and South.

There is no special incidents to bring out here.

The total number of rounds fired in the barrage by 'B', 'C', and 'D' Companies was approximately 170,000.

4.10.18

S E C R E T.

No. G. 4.

Headquarters,

46th Division.

Herewith Report on the Operations carried out by my Brigade on the morning of 3rd inst.

1. FORMING UP. This was carried out in an orderly manner, the two front line Battalions forming up on Compass bearing and pivoting from the Cross Sunken Roads at H.15.b.8.3.
The light during the forming up period made it possible to move or less locate ones position though the march up to the forming up line was carried out under very dark conditions.
The Support Battalion formed up 200 yards in front of the Road running from JONCOURT to SEQUEHART. All Battalions were in position by 5.15 am.

2. THE ATTACK (Advance to RED LINE)

Direction was well maintained as far as line running N.W. & S.E. through H.11.Central, where the 2 leading Battalions appeared to lose direction slightly passing through the N. & S. outskirts of RAMICOURT. In view of this, O.C. 6th Battalion, Sherwood Foresters pushed his Reserve Company and Battalion H.Qrs through the Village and mopped it up; later Support Companies of the leading Battalion also assisted in the mopping up.
The advance met with strong resistance from the enemy who had many Machine Guns on the BEAUREVOIR FONSOMME Line; he also had Machine Gun Sections dug in rifle ~~posts~~ pits immediately in rear of this line. These troops proved tough fighters and practically the whole garrison with the exception of a few prisoners were killed. It is estimated that at least 150 to 200 of the enemy were killed in this Area.
In RAMICOURT itself some fighting took place though not of such a stiff character, about 400 of the enemy were rounded up in RAMICOURT. N. of this Village in the Sunken Roads the proof of heavy fighting remains.
The Left Company of the 8th Battalion, Sherwood Foresters moved through WIANCOURT taking a few prisoners, shortly after crossing the FONSOMME LINE, Lt-Col. B.W.VANN M.C. was killed and Lt-Col. A.HACKING M.C. wounded. The latter however remained with his Battalion until the situation appeared clear and his men had passed E. of RAMICOURT. Major SHEDDON M.C. took Command of the 6th Battalion, Sherwood Foresters and Capt. LITTLEBOY M.C. Command of the 5th Battalion, Sherwood Foresters pending the arrival of Captain PRATT M.C. from the Battle Details.
The hedge in Sunken Road H.11.d. proved a temporary obstacle and was strongly held by the enemy.
On passing through RAMICOURT troops were engaged by heavy hostile M.G. fire from high ground in B.30.A. & B. To avoid casualties therefore Sunken Roads and hedges had to be resorted to.
The RED LINE was captured up to time, in fact troops had to wait for the barrage to lift throughout the advance. Our barrage was thick though there was more short shooting than usual.
On arrival at the RED LINE and finding that there was no trace of the AUSTRALIANS on the Left, a defensive flank was formed by 8th Battn. Sherwood Foresters along the line of Sunken

(Road

Road running W. to E. through H.5.b. H.6.a. & b. with Posts pushed up Railway cutting towards H.30.d.Central.

Our casualties to the RED LINE were fairly heavy, the majority being caused crossing the BEAUREVOIR FONSOMME line most of remainder were caused from machine guns on high ground in B.30.A. & B.

3. ATTACK (From RED LINE to BLUE LINE)

The 6th Battalion, Sherwood Foresters moved forward on protective barrage lifting off the RED LINE.

In the Village of MONTBREHAIN the enemy fought well at the start, especially in the area about the Cemetery. This latter place was after several small organised attacks, rushed and cleared of the enemy though it was not possible to occupy it on account of Machine Gun fire coming from high ground in C.25.A. & B. where the enemy was in great strength. From this latter point we completely commanded the Cemetery. Enemy was in strong numbers in the Village and considerable sniping and M.G. fire was encountered, especially from direction of C.25.D. Several Officer casualties were inflicted on us during this Village fighting. Shortly after our entry, two houses in the main Street of Village, near the Church were blown up.

The 5th & 8th Battns. Sherwood Foresters pushed forward Companies into the Village to assist in the mopping up whereupon the enemy fancying himself outnumbered surrendered more freely.

Altogether it is estimated that 1000 prisoners were taken from the Village of MONTBREHAIN.

The BLUE LINE with the exception of high ground in C.25.c. was captured up to scheduled time. Several attempts were made to capture this high ground but the open state of the Country at this point and the strength of the enemy made it impossible.

On the capture of the BLUE LINE the forward troops were as far as possible reorganised and allotted defensive positions. At the same time platoons made attempts to push out in front to the BLUE DOTTED LINE, but as soon as any movement was made in this direction by our men, heavy M.G. fire was directed against them from DOON COPSE, elements of trenches in C.26.D. & 27.C. also from trees in I.2.B.0.6. Field guns also opened with direct sight from direction of DOON COPSE & MILL in C.27.c.5.9. A Battery of 5.9s in BRANCOURT was also very troublesome.

In the Village itself there were a number of inhabitants and several shops which had recently been in use. Some inhabitants rushed out to give our men hot coffee as they passed.

A Battery of field guns was captured at about I.1.B.7.6. the crews were either killed or taken prisoners.

The remnants of 1 Company were placed to form a defensive flank facing S.E. in Orchards in I.1.d.; remnants of another Company held the high ground from H.6.d.7.3. to Railway at H.12.b.5.8. These dispositions were made as touch with the Staffords on the Right had not been established. A Field Ambulance or Dressing Station was found at about I.1.B.1.4. the Doctor being taken prisoner.

The Village Commandants house is at junction of Road I.1.B.2.3. Our Troops in the Village naturally became pretty mixed up, re-organisation was however soon proceeded with and defensive positions allotted.

The Village of MONTBREHAIN was completely mopped up by 11.30 am.

4. FLANKS.

Our Left Flank was throughout very insecure. The foremost post of the Australians being in Sunken Road at about B.28.D.9.4.; from here their Line appeared to run back to the BEAUREVOIR FONSOMME LINE in H.3.B. Our Right flank was

(also

also apparently very insecure and though we were right up to the inter-Brigade boundary at I.1.D.7.2. no trace of the Staffords could be found. Parties were pushed out to try and gain touch but no results were obtained. At one time troops presumed to be Staffords were seen on MANNEQUIN HILL. Thus it would appear that both our flanks were unprotected though this was of course not known for certain until some time afterwards.

6. ACTION OF TANKS.

The Tanks formed up close behind our Infantry prior to Zero. At the start they appeared to get slightly behind but caught up on our Troops reaching RAMICOURT. One Tank reached H.11.D.4.2., another H.5.d.3.2. and a third H.5.b.1.1. The one at H.5.d.3.2. did some very good work, the remainder of the Tanks were knocked out W. of RAMICOURT. Had a Tank been successful in getting through it would have been invaluable to deal with enemy M.Gs in C.25.Central. There is no doubt however that the enemy morale was affected by the sight of Tanks.

7. COUNTER ATTACK.

Enemy Scouts were seen about 12.30 pm, moving through CHAMPIGNONS COPSE. These were apparently followed by other troops in Artillery formation. From several accounts received it appears that they finally formed up in waves about Sunken Road running N. & S. through T.7.B. & D. Our Troops however in S.E. corner of MONTBREHAIN were unable to deal with this owing to lie of ground and trees. This Counter Attack forming up was observed from house at H.6.d.7.4. but from accounts since received it would appear that the enemy counter-attack had started by the time the news had reached our Artillery. The enemy advanced due W. in waves and reached Road running due S. from NEVILLE'S CROSS. Later he filtered into Sunken Road running S.W. from NEVILLE'S CROSS as far down as H.12.d.7.7. In this position he came under heavy Lewis Gun and Machine Gun fire from our troops E. of RAMICOURT. He therefore worked into Quarries and again finding himself under heavy fire filtered into S.W. corner of MONTBREHAIN where he was lost from view.

In view of this situation and the fact that a report was received that the enemy was massing for a counter attack N. of MONTBREHAIN it was decided to withdraw our troops at once from the Village and it was only owing to greatenergy on the partof Officers and N.C.Os that the withdrawal from this bottle neck was successfully carried out. The line taken up by our Troops, assisted by Companies of the 4th Leicester Regiment ran from H.18.A.3.9. along Sunken Road to H.12.c.9.2. thence to Railway at H.6.c.9.0. and along Railway to B.29.d.9.4. Battalions were again rather disorganised and mixing up of Units was unavoidable.

Reserves were kept in Sunken Road N.& S. of RAMICOURT. The enemy soon reoccupied MONTBREHAIN and placed M.Gs on the W. edge but any further attempts to advance by him were stopped by our troops.

One Section of M.Gs during the enemy counter attack situated about H.5.d.3.5. did excellent work with overhead fire against the enemy in vicinity of Quarries.

The Village of RAMICOURT was too heavily shelled to be occupied troops were therefore disposed outside the Village. The Line handed over to 138th Infantry Brigade during night 3/4th October, was as above with the exception that troops in Railway line N. of H.6.a.0.5. were withdrawn to Road running from H.6.a.0.5. to Brigade Boundary at H.5.a.7.9. This was by request of G.O.C. 138th Infantry Brigade (who was taking over) in view of the Australians on our Left at that time being still in B.28.d.

(On relief

On relief our Troops were withdrawn to Sunken Roads in H.15.B. & D. and H.16.A. & C. It is believed however that a small number are still in the line mixed up with Leicesters & Monmouths. This was unavoidable owing to the darkness of the night.

8. **GENERAL.**

The action of all Officers and men throughout the action was magnificent and all Troops fought admirably.

It is estimated that between 1400 and 1500 prisoners were taken by this Brigade in addition it is thought that at least some 300 odd were killed.

In addition about 35 Officers were captured.

Our casualties were approximately :-

20 Officers and about

650 O.Rs.

John Harington Brig - General.

4th October 1918. Commanding, 139th Infantry Brigade.

SECRET

Headquarters,
46th Division.

137th Bde: C/495.

Ref: map 62.B. N.W.
1/20,000.

I have the honour to submit the following report on the operations of the Brigade under my command for the days 2nd, 3rd and 4th October, 1918, vide 137th Infantry Brigade Order No. 226 and Instruction.

1. On the night of the 2nd/3rd October, orders were received that the Brigade would attack and capture a line from H 30 b 60.40 to I 1 d 80.20.

The Brigade was disposed with all three Battalions in the line as under :-

<u>Right Battalion</u> - 1/6th South Staffs Rgt. (Lieut: Col: C.Lister, MC. Northants Regt).

<u>Centre Battalion</u> - 1/5th South Staffs Rgt. (Lieut: Col: A.White, East Surrey Rgt.).

<u>Left Battalion.</u> - 1/6th North Staffs Rgt. (Lieut: Col: T.R.Evans, Royal Welsh Fusiliers).

Dispositions were as under :-

<u>Right Battalion</u> - 2 Companies formed up on a taped line. 2 Companies in support.

<u>Centre Battalion</u> - Support Battalion - 500 yards behind the front line.

<u>Left Battalion.</u> - 2 Companies formed up on a taped line. 2 Companies in support.

II. <u>EVENTS</u>. Battalions moved up to starting point and were in position on the taped line at 04.30 hours - the 1/6th South Staffs Rgt., when formed up and waiting for the barrage, lost 1 Officer and 6 men from an explosion of a shell.

The night 2nd/3rd was dark and favourable for moving troops during the early hours, and towards dawn a heavy fog prevailed which lifted shortly after.

Companies were formed up on their respective points 200 yards behind the barrage line.

III.(a) <u>THE ATTACK</u>. Right Battalion, 1/6th South Staffs Rgt., with one Section Light Trench Mortar Battery, attacked on a two-Company frontage, and two Companies in support. No opposition was encountered until high ground about H 23 d. was reached, when considerable opposition was encountered but was overcome, the enemy retiring down the valley and suffered heavy casualties by Lewis Gun fire.

After passing Sunken Road in H 24 a. and c., several concrete machine gun emplacements were encountered, which harassed the advance, and they were only silenced by the teams being charged and bayonetted.

The final objective in H 30 b. and H 24 d., I 19 a. and I 13 d., was reached at 08.10 hours, and posts were pushed forward towards the ridge of MANNEQUIN HILL. Great difficulty was experienced on the Right flank as the enemy held the high ground in H 30 d., owing to the troops on the left having to withdraw and the enemy opposition on the Right of the Battalion who, unable to hold the top of MANNEQUIN HILL, withdrew and consolidated on the final objective (the Sunken Road).

III.(b) CENTRE BATTALION - 1/5th South Staffs Rgt.

The Battalion was in support and moved up 600 yards behind the attacking Battalions in two lines of Companies at 200 yards interval and 200 yards between Companies, and divided in two lines of Platoons at 100 yards interval and 50 yards distance.

The Battalion moved forward at Zero hour. The enemy barrage fell in the valley along the Southern slopes of LEHACOURT VALLEY and to avoid it the Battalion assembled on the higher ground thereby avoiding further shells. The Battalion suffered 4 casualties until CHAPAINIES WOOD was reached, when the front line (1/6th North Staffs Rgt.) had to be reinforced - one platoon being sent to mop up the WOOD in the meantime. The front Battalion had moved to the Right which left a gap of 1,000 yards between the 1/6th North Staffs Rgt. and the 139th Infantry Brigade; in this gap there were enemy elements which were dealt with immediately by "C" Company, who attacked and carried the FONSOMME LINE, taking prisoners and machine guns. With the side-slipping of the 1/6th North Staffs Rgt. one platoon was pushed out throughH 18. in a North-East direction to try and maintain touch with the 139th Infantry Brigade. This platoon suffered heavily through machine gun fire fromMANNEQUIN HILL. Owing to the uncertainty of SEQUEHART, the 1/6th South Staffs Rgt. dropped Companies to this flank as they pushed forward, which attracted the whole Brigade to the Right, leaving the gap on the Left. This forced the Support Battalion into the gap leaving nothing for emergency, until the arrival of the 5th Leicesters.

III.(c) LEFT BATTALION - 1/6th North Staffs Rgt.

The attack was carried out with two Companies in the First wave, and two Companies in the Second wave, with 139th Infantry Brigade on the left (Sherwood Foresters).

At 06.05 hours the Battalion moved forward under a heavy barrage of artillery. At CHATAGNIERS WOOD the Right and Left, and Advance and Support Companies were ordered to move round the South side of the Wood, the Left Front and Support Companies to the North of the Wood. During this movement a tank fired into the Wood clearing out the enemy.

At FONSOMME LINE some stiff fighting took place. The left flank was held up by machine gun fire at H 18 a 20.50 which was also holding up the Left Battalion. The line then passed on to NUVILLE CROSS where two field guns were in action with open sights firing point blank at our advanced line.; a party of Lewis Gunners worked round to a flank and put the enemy gunners out of action. This serious obstacle again resulted in losing touch with the 139th Infantry Brigade. The party then pressed on towards DOONS MILL at I 8 a 60.30 - total strength being 20 of the 1/6th North Staffs Rgt. and 12 of the Sherwood Foresters; it was considered advisable to consolidate, and endeavoured to regain touch with our Right Company and the Left flank, but they were too far in advance of both, and the enemy seen advancing in large numbers to the Left and Right, it was then considered necessary to retire to NUVILLE CROSS and road running South of this, but were unable, after two hours, to hold out owing to heavy enfilade machine gun fire from MANNEQUIN HILL which necessitated retiring to a line H 12 d 05.15 - H 18 b 10.05 - H 18 d 20.35, which line was held and handed over on the night of 4th/5th October.

The Officer Commanding this Battalion was killed in action on the afternoon of the 3rd October. Major Dowding,

Second-in-Command of the 1/5th South Staffs Regt. was ordered to take command.

III.(d) 137th Light Trench Mortar Battery. (Lieut: H.Gregory). Two guns of the Battery reportedto the Right Battalion, and two guns to the Left Battalion. The Right guns opened fire in H 29 a. on the enemy retiring up the slope to SEQUEHART, These guns were kept on the Right to cover the Battalion's right flank. The enemy prepared a counter-attack and the guns were withdrawn to H 30 b 20.60, this position being better able to support the Infantry. At 16.00 hours the guns were removed to H 29 a 50.40 to cover the roads from SEQUEHART to LEVERGIES, thereby strengthening the flank.

The guns with the Left Battalion opened fire on the enemy at H 17 c 95.00, and a machine gun at H 23 b 50.40. When the Left flank was threatened, the two guns were placed at H 20 a 10.90 and H 24 a 15.85 and remained in this position as mobile guns.

III.(e) One Company, 46th Battalion, Machine Gun Corps - was attached to this Brigade for this operation during the period under review.

IV. ARTILLERY. The barrage put down by our artillery was excellent.

The enemy barrage fell in the Valley along the southern slopes of the BEHAUCOURT Ridge, and along the Valley gas shells were used extensively.

V. COMMUNICATIONS. Owing to the fog, no visual signalling was possible during the early morning. Incessant cutting of lines made communication impossible with Battalions. Runners proved the best means of communication.

VI. GENERAL REMARKS. Close following of the barrage lifts saved many casualties, and enabled the Infantry to surprise garrisons of enemy positions.

What was most satisfactory during these operations, as well as the Battle of 28th/29th September, 1918, was the fighting spirit of all ranks - 25% of the men actually used their bayonets.

All objectives were gained up to time, with a minimum of casualties, but advantage could not be taken of this and the Brigade fell back, which caused many casualties.

The Brigade was relieved by the 3rd Infantry Brigade on the night of the 3rd/4th October, 1918.

The enemy fought very stubbornly, and his artillery fire very accurate. His aircraft too, was excellent, and caused a great deal of trouble, receiving no attention from our own aeroplanes, on evening of Oct. 3rd

John V. Campbell

21-10-18.

Brigadier General.
Commanding 137th Infantry Brigade.

Secret.

ACCOUNT OF THE PART TAKEN
BY THE 46TH DIVISION IN THE BATTLE OF
BELLENGLISE ON THE 29TH SEPTEMBER, 1918.

****

46th Division G.114/24. 7th October, 1918.

1. General Idea of the Operations. The General Idea of these operations was the breaking of the main HINDENBURG LINE NORTH of ST QUENTIN. The Special Role of the 46th Division being to storm the ST QUENTIN CANAL between BELLENGLISE and RIQUEVAL, and take the villages of BELLENGLISE, LEHAUCOURT and MAGNY LA FOSSE.

On the RIGHT of the Division, the 1st Division was to exploit any success gained, by working to the EAST, SOUTH of the CANAL, and occupying the high ground about THORIGNY, should the enemy retire from these positions.

On our LEFT, the American Corps were to storm the BELLICOURT defences and then, turning SOUTH, were to join the 46th Division in the neighbourhood of ETRICOURT.

The 32nd Division and 2nd Australian Division were to move through the 46th Division and 30th American Division respectively, after the capture of their final objectives, and seize the general line LE TRONQUOY - LEVERGIES and to the NORTH.

2. General Description of the Ground on the 46th Division Front.

The defences in front of the 46th Division were of a very formidable nature, consisting of strong lines WEST of the CANAL, the CANAL itself; with the main HINDENBURG LINE, a strong supporting line and four strongly defended Villages to the EAST of it. The CANAL may be divided into two parts, the SOUTHERN half running practically along the ground level contained little water; but, on the other hand, the defences were far stronger than in the NORTHERN part. The NORTHERN half, where the water was from seven to ten feet deep, ran through a deep cutting with almost perpendicular sides, thirty to fifty feet high. The lower ten feet of the CANAL throughout formed a perpendicular obstacle, faced with brick; and both inner and outer banks were strongly wired.

In BELLENGLISE, were the entrances to the famous tunnel which ran from the direction of MAGNY LA FOSSE into this Village, and was known to be capable of holding some 2/3,000 men. The whole area was known to be exceptionally strong in concrete machine gun defences and was believed by the enemy to be impregnable.

3. Preliminary Arrangements.: The first order for the attack was 46th Division Order 326, issued on the 25th September, and prior to the attack many preliminary arrangements had to be made. The main difficulty lay in crossing the CANAL and for this purpose some 3,000 lifebelts were obtained and issued to the storming troops. On the day prior to the attack, these lifebelts together with light portable rafts, ladders, collapsible boats and heaving lines, were tested on the banks of the SOMME, and it was found that the ordinary lifebelt would easily support a man in fighting order, provided that the weight he was carrying was kept low on his body.

A preliminary operation with the object of ensuring that there would be little opposition WEST of the CANAL was undertaken by the 138th Infantry Brigade on the 27th September against the trenches in G 28. These trenches were occupied under a barrage, but on the 28th September, severe fighting ensued here, and it was decided that on Y/Z night, our troops should be withdrawn and formed up WEST, and well clear of any possible enemy opposition.

4. <u>General dispositions of the 46th Division.</u> The area to be occupied by the 46th Division was divided into two main objectives - the BROWN Objective and the GREEN Objectives. These were further sub-divided,- a BLUE Objective included the CANAL and the defences immediately EAST of it, whilst the YELLOW and DOTTED BLUE objectives were inserted between the BROWN and the GREEN on the main tactical features, in order to allow of Inter-Brigade "Leap-frog".

To the 137th Infantry Brigade (Brigadier-General J.V.CAMPBELL, VC, CMG, DSO) Coldstream Guards was entrusted the storming of the CANAL, the Village of BELLENGLISE and the capture of the BROWN Objective. On this, an halt was made for three hours, in order to allow of the complete mopping up of th area and give time for the 139th Infantry Brigade (Brigadier-General J.HARINGTON, DSO) on the RIGHT, and 138th Infantry Brigade (Brigadier-General F.G.M. ROWLEY, CMG, DSO) on the LEFT, to pass through to capture the final objective.

To the storming infantry were allotted a few sections of Engineers, whilst the remainder of the Royal Engineers and 1/1st Monmouthshire Regt (Pioneers) followed close in rear with the necessary bridging material.

The artillery allotted to the Division consisted of one Brigade, RHA, and eight Brigades of Field Artillery, whilst a very powerful concentration of Heavy Artillery was arranged by the IX Corps, to deal with the enemy defences and engage his batteries.

Two additional maching gun battalions, that of the 2nd Life Guards and 100th Machine Gun Battalion, were also allotted to the Division, and took part in the initial barrage.

Two Companies Mark V Tanks, were to cross over the BELLICOURT Tunnel immediately the Americans had captured their first objective, and moving SOUTH were to join the Division prior to its advance from the BROWN LINE. One Company was allotted to each of the 139th and 138th Infantry Brigades.

5. <u>Forming Up.</u> Forming up was successfully carried out on the night 28th/29th September. 137th Infantry Brigade formed up on a three battalion front, whilst 139th and 138th Infantry Brigades formed up some distance in rear on a one battalion front, with orders that their leading battalion should occupy the trench system on our "jumping off" line, as soon as the 137th Infantry Brigade had left. These battalions detailed one company each to follow the 137th Infantry Brigade in order to mop up the area WEST of the CANAL, and the Battalion Commanders were instructed to keep in close touch with the situation, and to so handle their battalions, as to ensure that the 137th Infantry Brigade, having crossed the CANAL, should not be out-fought in the trench system beyond it. The remainder of the 139th and 138th Infantry Brigades were instructed not to move forward pending orders from Divisional Headquarters.

Zero Hour was fixed for 5.50 am.

6. <u>The attack.</u> The attack was launched at Zero in a thick mist which rapidly increased to a dense fog as the smoke which had been placed in the barrage and on the flanks began to make itself felt. Under cover of this fog the 137th Infantry Brigade, having stormed the first line trenches and killed most of the garrison, who put up a tough resistance, reached the CANAL well up to time. At the same time, the 1st Division formed a defensive RIGHT flank from our original trenches along the Spur towards BELLENGLISE. The RIGHT Battalion, (6th Bn, South Staffordshire Regt) found little water in the CANAL, and only in few places were they forced to swim. The enemy here at first put up considerable resistance, but, after a number of our men had crossed, surrendered freely, and the battalion was able to proceed to the BLUE Line and occupy the tunnel entrances in BELLENGLISE where some hundreds of prisoners were taken

Secret.

ACCOUNT OF THE PART TAKEN BY THE 46TH DIVISION IN THE BATTLE OF BELLENGLISE ON THE 29TH SEPTEMBER, 1918.

****

46th Division G.114/24. 7th October, 1918.

1. **General Idea of the Operations.** The General Idea of these Operations was the breaking of the main HINDENBURG LINE NORTH of ST. QUENTIN. The Special Role of the 46th Division being to storm the ST. QUENTIN CANAL between BELLENGLISE and RIQUEVAL, and take the villages of BELLENGLISE, LEHAUCOURT and MAGNY LA FOSSE.

On the RIGHT of the Division, the 1st Division was to exploit any success gained, by working to the EAST, SOUTH of the CANAL, and occupying the high ground about THORIGNY, should the enemy retire from those positions.

On our LEFT, the American Corps were to storm the BELLICOURT defences, and then, turning SOUTH, were to join the 46th Division in the neighbourhood of ETRICOURT.

The 32nd Division and 2nd Australian Division were to move through the 46th Division and 30th American Division respectively, after the capture of their final objectives, and seize the general line LE TRONQUOY - LEVERGIES and to the NORTH.

2. **General Description of the Ground on the 46th Division Front.**

The defences in front of the 46th Division were of a very formidable nature, consisting of strong lines WEST of the CANAL, the CANAL itself; with the main HINDENBURG LINE, a strong supporting line and four strongly defended villages to the EAST of it. The CANAL may be divided into two parts, the SOUTHERN half running practically along the ground level contained little water; but, on the other hand, the defences were far stronger than in the NORTHERN part. The NORTHERN part, where the water was from seven to ten feet deep, ran through a deep cutting with almost perpendicular sides, thirty to fifty feet high. The lower ten feet of the CANAL throughout formed a perpendicular obstacle, faced with brick; and both inner and outer banks were strongly wired.

In BELLENGLISE, were the entrances to the famous tunnel which ran from the direction of MAGNY LA FOSSE into this village, and was known to be capable of holding some 2/3,000 men. The whole area was known to be exceptionally strong in concrete machine gun defences and was believed by the enemy to be impregnable

3. **Preliminary Arrangements.** The first order for the attack was 46th Division Order 53[illegible], issued on the 25th September, and prior to the attack many preliminary arrangements had to be made. The main difficulty lay in crossing the CANAL and for this purpose some 3,000 lifebelts were obtained and issued to the storming troops. On the day prior to the attack, these lifebelts together with light portable rafts, ladders, collapsible boats and heaving lines, were tested on the banks of the SOMME, and it was found that the ordinary lifebelt would easily support a man in fighting order, provided that the weight he was carrying was kept low on the body.

A preliminary operation with the object of ensuring that there would be little opposition WEST of the CANAL was undertaken by the 138th Infantry Brigade on the 27th September against the trenches in G.20. These trenches were occupied under a barrage, but on the 28th September, severe fighting ensued here, and it was decided that on Y/Z night, our troops should be withdrawn and formed up WEST, and well clear of any possible enemy opposition.

4. General dispositions of the 46th Division. The area to be occupied by the 46th Division was divided into two main objectives - the BROWN Objective and the GREEN Objective. These were further sub-divided, - a BLUE Objective including the CANAL and the defences immediately EAST of it, whilst the YELLOW and DOTTED BLUE Objectives were inserted between the BROWN and the GREEN on the main tactical features, in order to allow of Inter-Brigade "Leap-frog".

To the 137th Infantry Brigade (Brigadier General J.V.CAMPBELL, VC, CMG, DSO., Coldstream Guards) was entrusted the storming of the CANAL, the village of BELLENGLISE and the capture of the BROWN Objective. On this line a halt was made for three hours, in order to allow of the complete mopping up of the area and give time for the 139th Infantry Brigade (Brigadier General J.HARINGTON, DSO) on the RIGHT, and the 138th Infantry Brigade (Brigadier General F.G.M.ROWLEY, CMG, DSO) on the LEFT, to pass through to capture the final objective.

To the storming infantry were allotted a few sections of Engineers, whilst the remainder of the Royal Engineers and the 1/1st Monmouthshire Regiment (Pioneers) followed close in the rear with the necessary bridging material.

The Artillery allotted to the Division consisted of one Brigade, RHA, and eight Brigades of Field Artillery, whilst a very powerful concentration of Heavy Artillery was arranged by the IX Corps, to deal with the enemy defences and engage his batteries.

Two additional machine gun battalions, that of the 2nd Life Guards and the 100th Machine Gun Battalion, were also allotted to the Division, and took part in the initial barrage.

Two Companies Mark V Tanks were to cross over the BELLICOURT Tunnel immediately the Americans had captured their first objective, and moving SOUTH were to join the Division prior to its advance from the BROWN LINE. One Company was allotted to each of the 139th and 138th Infantry Brigades.

5. Forming up. Forming up was successfully carried out on the night 28th /29th September. The 137th Infantry Brigade formed up on a three battalion front, whilst the 139th and 138th Infantry Brigades formed up some distance in rear on a one battalion front, with orders that their leading battalion should occupy the trench system on our "jumping off" line, as soon as the 137th Infantry Brigade had left. These battalions detailed one company each to follow the 137th Infantry Brigade in order to mop up the area WEST of the CANAL, and the Battalion Commanders were instructed to keep in close touch with the situation and to handle their battalions as to ensure that the 137th Infantry Brigade, having crossed the CANAL, should not be outfought in the trench system beyond it. The remainder of the 139th and 138th Infantry Brigades were instructed not to move forward pending orders from Divisional Headquarters.

Zero hour was fixed for 5.50 a.m.

6. The attack. The attack was launched at Zero in a thick mist which rapidly increased to a dense fog as the smoke which had been placed in the barrage and on the flanks began to make itself felt. Under cover of this fog the 137th Infantry Brigade, having stormed the first line trenches and killed most of the garrison, who put up a tough resistance, reached the CANAL well up to time. At the same time, the 1st Division formed a defensive RIGHT Flank from our original trenches along the Spur towards BELLENGLISE. The

/RIGHT.......

operation, and the barrage was some distance ahead of the advancing Infantry. In spite of this, our Infantry advanced and soon caught up the barrage, most ably assisted on our LEFT by the Tanks attached to the 138th Infantry Brigade.

By three p.m. the whole of our objectives had been taken, and the 32nd Division, pressing forward, passed through our lines to occupy the RED LINE. During the later stages of our advance, a number of guns were encountered, giving opportunities for many acts of gallantry on the part of both officers and men. One battery was seen to be limbering up EAST of our final defensive barrage, and an attempt was made to pass through our barrage, and prevent the withdrawal of these guns. Horses and drivers were shot down, and immediately our barrage began to thin, this battery was captured. Several bayonet charges against the enemy's artillery were made, the crews being killed and the guns captured. The German artillerymen fought with the greatest valour and continued to fire their guns at point blank range up to the last.

During the following night, the Division was continually in action owing to both flanks being open to the enemy. On the morning of the 30th, the 1st Division on our RIGHT eased the situation by the capture of THORIGNY and TALANA HILL, whilst on the LEFT, the 2nd Australian Division, pushing forward, joined up with our left flank during the day.

7. <u>Work of the Artillery.</u> The preparatory work of the Heavy Artillery cannot be too highly praised, and, it was owing in a great measure to their excellent shooting that the storming of the CANAL with its concrete defences was made possible. The Field Artillery, in spite of the fact that the majority of the guns were in silent positions up to Zero hour, and unable to register, put down one of the finest barrages that the troops have ever advanced under. During the action, the majority of the Field Artillery was moved forward to new positions already selected. These movements were so expeditiously carried out as to make little appreciable difference in the intensity of the barrage.

8. The work of the Royal Engineers, Machine Gunners, Pioneers, and RAMC, was beyond all praise. The first named, besides saving the RIQUEVAL Bridge, were able to assist the Infantry in many ways outside their ordinary scope, and incidents of individual gallantry in attacking machine gun nests, etc, were of common occurrence.

9. <u>Infantry.</u> As for the infantry, in addition to the magnificent behaviour of every officer and man, the leadership shewn by regimental officers and N.C.Os. was of a very high nature. The faultless leading of their men across some 5,000 yards of enemy territority in a thick fog, during which some 4,200 prisoners and seventy guns were taken, is worthy of the highest traditions of the Service. Their success and the lightness of their casualties, some eight hundred in all, is due to this power of leadership and to the fact that not the slightest hesitation was shewn throughout the whole engagement.

All ranks were determined to push through to the final objective regardless of the flanks, and right well they carried it out, not only on this occasion but subsequently on the 3rd October.

--- 283 ---

RIGHT Battalion, (6th Bn, South Staffordshire Regiment) found little water in the CANAL, and only in few places were they forced to swim. The enemy here at first put up considerable resistance, but, after a number of our men had crossed, surrendered freely, and the Battalion was able to proceed to the BLUE LINE and occupy the Tunnel entrances in BELLENGLISE, where some hundreds of prisoners were taken before they were able to put up any organized resistance. The CENTRE (5th Bn, South Staffordshire Regiment) and the LEFT (6th Bn, North Staffordshire Regiment) found a considerable depth of water in the CANAL. The officers swimming over first with ropes were soon joined by the leading lines of their men, and, assisted by broken bridges, rafts, and boats, the whole force was soon across and dealing with the enemy in the strongly held trenches on the EASTERN Bank. At RIQUEVAL, the bridge was found to be intact. The Royal Engineers with some of the storming troops bayonetted the enemy pioneers who were about to light the fuzes, and withdrew the charges. The saving of this bridge, due entirely to the gallantry and rapidity of the advance, was of inestimable value, and by it, and by the pontoon bridges which were later made by the 46th and 32nd Divisional Engineers and Pioneers, the whole of these two Divisions with their Artillery, were later enable to pass over.

The Infantry rapidly cleared the trenches up to the BLUE Objective, advanced on the BROWN LINE which they reached in scheduled time, capturing on their way a battery of four guns, the gun teams of which were all either killed or captured together with their horses. Owing to the density of the fog, little use could be made of the Divisional Observers' Section. The Divisional Mounted Troop, consisting of men from the DAC and Field Ambulances were, however, sent forward to reconnoitre, and by questioning prisoners and wounded men, were able to send back most valuable information, showing that our Infantry had successfully crossed the CANAL. On this information, orders were issued for 139th and 138th Infantry Brigades to push straight across the CANAL up to the barrage and move directly on the objectives assigned to them.

The leading battalion of these two Brigades had already pushed forward after the 137th Infantry Brigade and crossed the CANAL close on their heels. The two Brigades reached the BROWN LINE in excellent time, where they were joined by the two Companies of Tanks, and in spite of the dense fog, the whole were enabled to move forward towards their objective as the barrage lifted.

After passing the YELLOW Objective, the fog, having cleared considerably, much inconvenience was caused to the RIGHT Battalion by the enemy occupying the high ground SOUTH of the CANAL. Machine guns from this direction swept our RIGHT Flank continuously and enemy field guns firing at point blank range quickly put out of action all six Tanks allotted to 139th Infantry Brigade. This battery was in its turn put out of action by a party of 139th Infantry Brigade, who, with great gallantry crossed the CANAL and shot or bayonetted the gunners. Little Infantry trouble was experienced from SOUTH of the CANAL; several feeble attempts to counter attack on this flank were made, and one mounted German officer made three gallant attempts to rally his men; on the third attempt, however, both he and his horse were killed, whereupon, the enemy immediately retired.

On our LEFT, 138th Infantry Brigade were successfully carrying forward their advance, and at 12.50 pm, we advanced from the YELLOW LINE on to MAGNY LA FOSSE. At this time it was definitely ascertained that the troops on our left, who, until now, had been thought to occupy the high ground about NAUROY, had been hung up on their first objective: both flanks of the 46th Division were therefore in the air, and steps were taken to form a left defensive flank and to hold the bridgeheads along the CANAL on the right flank. The advance from the YELLOW LINE was slightly delayed by this

/operation........

14 10 18

At a Conference held at Divisional H.Q. on the 14th October, instructions were received that the Brigade would be required to attack in conjunction with the French on the Right, and the 6th Division on the Left, from the BOHAIN-VAUX ANDIGNY Road in a south easterly direction to ANDIGNY LES FERMES.

The attack took place at 05.20 on the 17th Instant and during the night of the 16th/17th the Battalions moved from FRESNOY-LE-GRAND to their assembly positions.

During this time the enemy shelled the assembly area with H.E. and gas shells.

The Brigade attack was to be carried out through the line of British trenches running through E.7.,E.1.b.& d. and W.25.b.& d., Trenches at that time being held by units of the 6th Division. These were withdrawn at ZERO minus 1 hour.

The Brigade had attached to them a Company of Machine Guns and 3 Tanks were allotted to the Division.

At ZERO minus 1 hour the Brigade was formed up as follows :-

4th LEICESTERSHIRE REGT& on the Right from E.1.a.2.8. to W.25. central, with the 139th Infantry Brigade on the Right.

5th LINCOLNSHIRE REGT. from W.25.central to W.26.a.2.8. in touch with the 6th Division on the Left.

5th LEICESTERSHIRE REGT. were in Reserve in V.30.b.

Each of the front line Battalions had a section of M.G's, and the 5th LINCOLNSHIRE REGT. had a section of T.M's attached to them.

The objective of the attack was from E.9.c.6.4. to E.11.a.2.8. with instructions to push out and establish platoon posts some 200 yds in front of this line.

Brigade Headquarters were established at D.11.central.

The attack took place ina dense fog,which made the difficulties of keeping direction and communication very great.

At 07.00 the O.C., 4th LEICESTERSHIRE REGT. reported that he had under his command elements of CAMERONS,BLACK WATCH, N.LANCS,SHERWOODS, and 5th LINCOLNSHIRES in the area E.1.b.

At 06.54 it was reported that we had reached the REGNICOURT-ANDIGNY LES FERMES Road, and that several enemy M.G's had not been properly mopped up and were still firing from the Old German Front Line in E.2.a.& b. There was also considerable M.G. fire from BELLE-VUE and LES GOBELETS. All this opposition was, however, eventually overcome, and at 11.30 it was reported that ANDIGNY LES FERMES was in our hands. Previous to this at 10.15 two companies of the Reserve Battalion (5th LEICESTERSHIRE REGT,) had received instructions to move forward via the high ground in W.26.b., W.27.c., and E.3.b., and mop up BELLE-VUE and LES GOBELETS. This move was, however, cancelled as the opposition from this ridge had been overcome by the 6th Division, and the two Companies of the 5th LEICESTERSHIRE REGT. were ordered to concentrate in the Old German Front Line and placed under the command of the O.C., 5th LINCOLNSHIRE REGT. with instructions that he could use them for exploiting the success down the ANDIGNY LES FERMES- MENNEVRET Road, and if possible get in touch with the French at LA NATION in E.17.b.

At 16.40 the dispositions of the Brigade were as follows :-

5th LINCOLNSHIRE REGT. - 3 Companies round E & S of ANDIGNY LES FERMES. 1 Company in E.4.c.8.0. H.Qtrs. E.2.b.4.7.

4th LEICESTERSHIRE REGT& - 1 Company at E.9.c.3.3., 1 Company E.9.a.2.3., 1 Company at E.9.a.7.5. with H.Qtrs at E.2.cen.

5th LEICESTERSHIRE REGT. with H.Qtrs and 1½ Companies at V.30.a., 1 Company Old German Front Line about E.2.b., 1 Company patrolling the ANDIGNY LES FERMES-MENNEVRET Road, 2 platoons with 5th LINCOLNSHIRE REGT.

Machine Gun Company had 8 guns disposed in front of the Objective, 1 Section in E.9.b. and 1 Section in E.8.a. covering LES GOBELETS FARM.

At 17.50 hrs orders were issued that the 5th LEICESTERSHIRE REGT. would take over the Front Line from the 4th LEICESTERSHIRE REGT. and 5th LINCOLNSHIRE REGT.

* 1 Company E.9.c.5.7 with post at E.9.c.7.2.

1900

At 19.00 the Company of the 5th LEICESTERSHIRE REGT. which had been sent down the ANDIGNY LES FERMES- MENNEVRET Road reported that they had met with M.G. fire from about E.11. central ; they were instructed to keep trying and if possible get in touch with the French, who were working up through MENNEVRET.

The dispositions of the Brigade, after the 5th LEICESTERSHIRE REGT. had taken over the Front Line, were as follows :-

5th LEICESTERSHIRE REGT. on the line from E.9.c.5.3. to E.11.a.2.8. held by 3 Companies, 1 Company patrolling down the ANDIGNY LES FERMES-MENNEVRET Road. Headquarters at E.2.central.

5th LINCOLNSHIRE REGT. in Sunken Road in E.2. with Headquarters in E.2.b.4.7.

4th LEICESTERSHIRE REGT. in Old German Front Line with Headquarters at VALLEE HASSARD, D.6.b.6.6.

At 00.40 on the 18th October instructions were received that the Brigade would have to take over a Battalion front of the 1st Division, who had passed through the 6th Division, and were now on our Left Flank. Two sections of M.G's were given to the Brigade for the purpose of thid relieve. The 5th LEICESTERSHIRE REGT. were ordered to move one Company fromt the Right Flank to take over this Battalion Front - Relieve to be completed by 06.00 hrs. M.G's were disposed in E.5.c.

During the night our patrols on the ANDIGNY LES FERMES-MENNEVRET Road reached LA NATION Cross-roads, but were unable to remain there on account of the enemy's bombing parties, and it was not until 05.30 on the 18th that definite touch was established with the French at this point. The two Companies defending ANDIGNY LES FERMES and area in E.5.c. were told to link up with the French and establish a line through E.11.c., E.11.a., and E.5.c. The Company from E.9.c. was moved up to the East of ANDIGNY LES FERMES.

At 10.20 on the 18th October instructions were received that the Brigade would be relieved by the 137th Infantry Brigade during the course of the morning. This was eventually completed by 14.15 hrs, anf the Brigade marched back to FRESNOY LE GRAND.

War Diary

App 48

SECRET. Copy No. 17

46th DIVISION ORDER No. 333.

Ref: Map "A", 1/40,000. 15th October, 1918.

1. The 46th Division will attack, as part of a major operation, the BLUE Line shown on Map "A". This Map also shows -

(a)	Jumping Off Line.	GREEN.
(b)	Divisional Boundaries.	BROWN.
(c)	Inter-Brigade Boundary.	YELLOW.

The RED Line is that held by our troops at present.

2. Detail. The 139th Inf: Bde will attack on the RIGHT.
The 138th : : : : : : LEFT.
The 137th : : : hold its present line.

The 6th Division is making a simultaneous attack on our LEFT, and it is expected that the French will attack SOUTH of the FORET D'ANDIGNY on our RIGHT.
The 1st Division is following the 6th Division and exploiting success to the EASTWARD.

3. BARRAGE. The attack will be carried out under a switching barrage which will rest on the opening line for three minutes and then move forward at the rate of 100 yards in three minutes. On reaching the general line of the FORET D'ANDIGNY, the barrage will rest thirty minutes and then cease.

4. CONSOLIDATION. The Infantry will consolidate with their advanced posts well to SOUTH of the Road.

5. TANKS. One Section of three Tanks has been allotted to the Division; these will assemble at a point to be selected by the Section Commander and will move forward with the Supporting Infantry to the Strong Point about E 1 d; they will move along the line of trenches to E 13 b 7.0, when one will continue along the trench to D 19 b 9.5; the other two moving EAST to assist in the mopping up of REGNICOURT and ANDIGNY-LES-FERMES.
On reaching ANDIGNY, one Tank will mop up the trench from E 10 c 6.9 to E 10 c 9.3, should this trench exist.
On completing these missions, the Tanks will withdraw under cover to an assembly position N. of the BOHAIN - ANDIGNY Road.

6. MACHINE GUNS. The following M.G's will take part under command of the O.C, 46th Bn, MGC.-

2 Coys, 2/Life Guards.
1 Coy, 6th MG. Bn in position about D 18 b.
46th Bn, MGC, less one Coy.

One Coy, 46th Bn, MGC, will be at the disposal of the GOC 137th Inf: Bde for holding the RIGHT Pivot of the attack.
The OC, 46th Bn, MGC, will detail at least sixteen guns to follow the infantry closely with a view to taking up positions on or close to the final objective, where they can bring direct fire across the front of the Infantry.

P.T.O.

7. CAVALRY. One troop, Royal Scots Greys, has been placed at the disposal of the 46th Division, and will be used for reconnaissance purposes. The remainder of the Squadron now with the Division will return to their Regiment on the afternoon of Y Day.

8. AEROPLANES. Will call for flares at 0 plus One Hour Thirty Minutes.

9. R.E. The CRE will place sufficient R.E at the disposal of the G.O's.C, 138th and 139th Inf: Bdes to assist in the formation of Strong Points about -

E 13 b 6.0.
REGNICOURT.
E 9 c 9.4.
ANDIGNY-LES-FERMES.

10. ARTILLERY. Six Brigades of RHA and RFA will be at the disposal of the CRA, 46th Division. The general principle of the barrage will be -

(a) A thick 18-pdr barrage with one round of smoke per lift.
(b) A 4.5" How: barrage beyond the 18-pdrs.

The 4.5" Hows: will fire in the Barrage until such time as the Infantry begin to reach the crest on the line of the BOHAIN - ANDIGNY Road, when they will lift on to the N. edge of the FORET D'ANDIGNY and fire smoke shell.

11. PRELIMINARY BOMBARDMENT. Preliminary artillery work will consist of .

(a) Wire cutting throughout the whole area of attack and bombardment of German front line.
(b) Destruction of ANDIGNY-LES-FERMES and the trenches immediately WEST of it, if such exist.
(c) Harassing fire throughout the night, and keeping the wire open in co-operation with the Infantry holding the Line.

12. DIVISIONAL OBSERVERS. O.C, Divisional Observers, will select positions for his observers and wireless and will report these to Divisional Headquarters.

13. ACTION OF 137th INF: BDE. The GOC, 137th Inf: Bde will be responsible for holding the RIGHT Pivot of the attack and will have at his disposal one Battalion of Infantry, one MG Coy and one L.T.M Battery.

Remaining two battalions of this Brigade will be in Divisional Reserve and will be located -

One Battalion along the SEBONCOURT - BOHAIN Road.
One Battalion in the SOUTHERN part of BOHAIN.

The Infantry holding the Line will be thinned out as much as possible and all troops will be withdrawn one Hour before Zero to positions WEST of a SAFETY Line which will be marked on the Artillery Barrage Map.

14. ACTION OF UNITS OF THE 6th DIVISION. The MG Coy, of the 6th Divn, in position about D 18 b, will come under the orders of the OC, 46th Bn, MGC, from Zero - One Hour. The GOC, 6th Division, has been requested to withdraw all his troops, at present holding the Line, WEST of the SAFETY Line by Zero - One Hour.

15. SPECIAL ARRANGEMENTS. Dummy Tanks and Dummy Figures will be provided by Corps and will be drawn by the CRE. These will be placed in position during Y/Z night, so as to be apparent at dawn, and simulate an attack on the BOIS DE RIQUERVAL from a WESTERLY direction.

A Special Rolling Barrage will come down at Zero on a line at safety distances from our Advanced Posts and will move through the BOIS DE RIQUERVAL in an EASTERLY direction at the rate of 100 yards in four minutes. On reaching the open space E 26 a - E 20 c and a, the barrage will rest until the main barrage replaces it, or, in the case of the SOUTHERN Portion, until the main barrage ceases.

16. FORMING UP. The Line will not be taken over from the 6th Divn. The 138th and 139th Inf: Bdes, arranging their starting points and times so as not to clash, will be in position by Zero - One Hour.

The Reserve Battalion of the 139th Inf: Bde will take up an assembly position about D 18 a, avoiding the Valley in D 18 b 12 d.

Brigades will report when in position to Divisional H.Q.

17. SIGNALS. Sites for visual Stations should be reconnoitred as soon as possible, by all Arms.

18. TOOLS. A large proportion of entrenching tools will be carried by the Infantry and MG personnel.

19. HEADQUARTERS. Divisional Headquarters will remain in its present location.

138th and 139th Inf: Bde H.Q will be together at a position to be notified.

One Artillery Liaison Officer (Brigade Commander) will be at Infantry Brigade H.Q.

20. Z Day. Z Day and Zero Hour will be notified separately.

21. ACKNOWLEDGE.

NOTE. In view of the number of civilians in the area, it is more than ever important that these operations should be kept SECRET.

[signature]

Lieut-Colonel,
General Staff, 46th Division.

Issued at 1050

Copy No.			Copy No.	
1 to	CRA.	x	16/17 to	War Diary.
2	CRE.	x	18/19	IX Corps.
3	Signals.		20	6th Division.
4	137th Inf: Bde.	x	21	1st : %
5	138th : :	x	22	126th French Division. %
6	139th : :	x	23	French Liaison Offr %
7	1/Monmouths.	%	24	IX Corps HA.
8	46th Bn, MGC.	x	25	IX Corps CBSO. %
9	AA & QMG.	x	26	9th Sqdn, RAF.
10	ADMS.	%	27	2/Life Guards.
11	DAPM.	%	28	Sqdn, Royal Scots Greys.
12	Div: Observers.		29/30.	16 Tank Bn.
13	GSO I.	x		
14/15	File.			

x Map already issued. % No map.

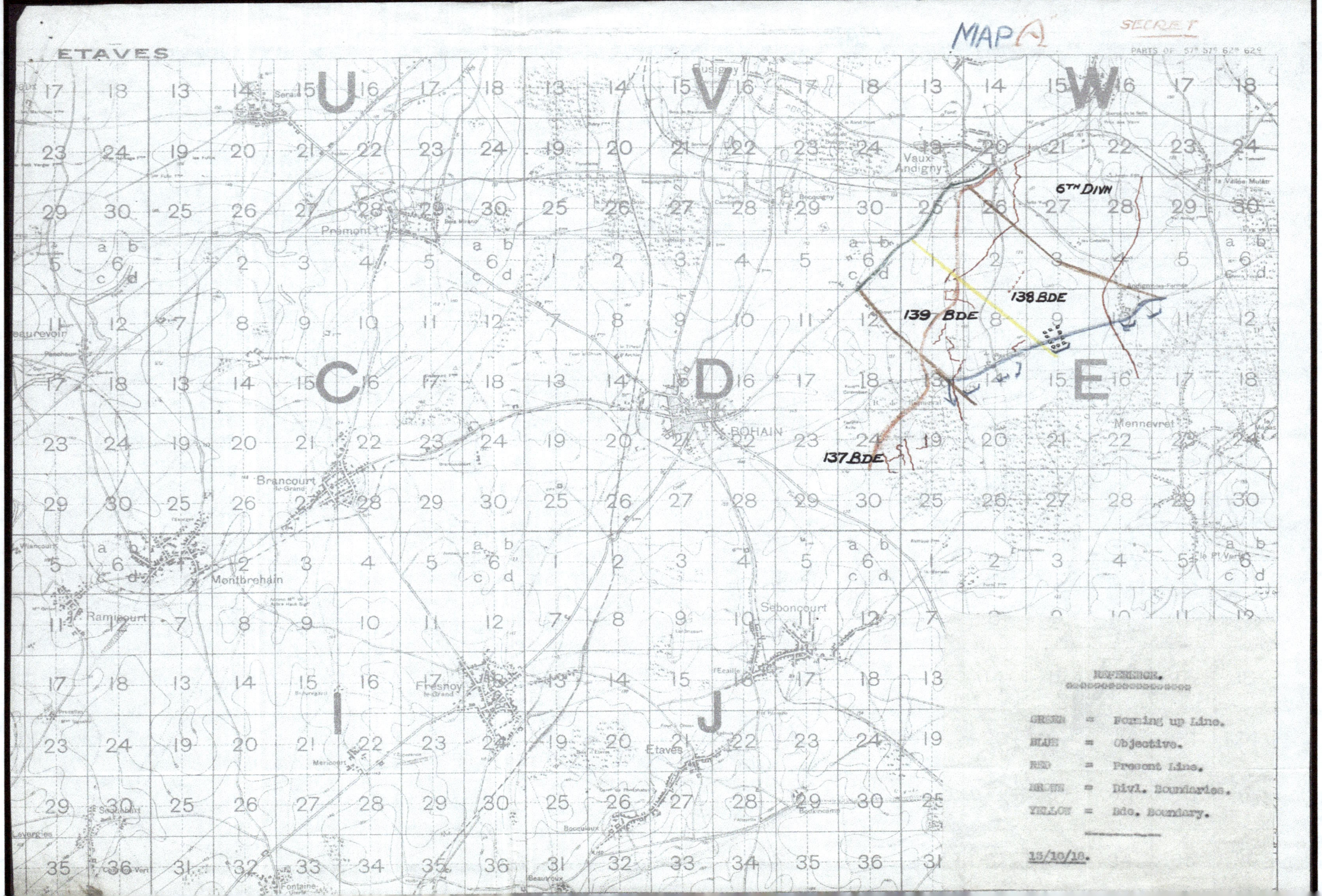

MAP A

SECRET

ETAVES

PARTS OF 57B 57C 62B 62C

6TH DIVN

138 BDE

139 BDE

137 BDE

Vaux Andigny

Premont

Serain

Bohain

Brancourt le Grand

Montbrehain

Ramicourt

Fresnoy le Grand

Seboncourt

Etaves

Mennevret

REFERENCE.

GREEN = Forming up Line.
BLUE = Objective.
RED = Present Line.
BROWN = Divl. Boundaries.
YELLOW = Bde. Boundary.

15/10/18.

REPORT ON THE EVACUATION OF THE WOUNDED, DURING THE ATTACKS CARRIED OUT BY THE 46TH DIVISION, ON THE 29TH SEPTEMBER, 3RD OCTOBER, and 17TH OCTOBER, 1918.

****

1. Attack 29th September on SCHELDT CANAL, BELLENGLISE.

At the beginning of the operation, the evacuation was carried out as laid down in R.A.M.C. Operation Order No.148, attached.

Sixteen R.A.M.C. Bearers were attached to each Battalion of the 137th Infantry Brigade, and eight to each Battalion of the 138th and 139th Infantry Brigades.

An A.D.S. was established on the left at R.5.a.80.30. This was taken over by the A.D.M.S., 32nd Division on "Y" day; and the evacuation of wounded from there to M.D.S. was carried out by him.

On the night of the 28th September, an A.D.S. was established North of VADENCOURT at R.11.a.90.70., and a Bearer Relief Post near BERTHAUCOURT at M.2.d.60.80.

From the A.D.S. the patients were taken by Divisional motor ambulance cars to the Corps Main Dressing station at POEUILLY, and thence to C.C.S. by M.A.C. cars.

The earlier casualties were evacuated through the A.D.S. at R.5.a.80.30., but as the advance proceeded, the line of evacuation was almost entirely by the VADENCOURT-BELLENGLISE Road.

A Bearer Post was pushed forward to G.33.a.8.2., 1500 yards East of BELLENGLISE, and Relay Posts along the BELLENGLISE Road as far as ST. HELENE.

To begin with, the motor ambulance cars were loaded up at R.11.a.90.70.; but early in the forenoon they were running up to ST. HELENE Cross Roads, and soon afterwards to the West side of the Canal.

An officer went into BELLENGLISE about 11.0 a.m. on the 29th Sept., to see if it was possible to establish an A.D.S. there, but reported that it was still subjected to considerable shell fire; so an A.D.S. was established at M.2.d.60.80. until the following morning, when it was opened at G.34.d.75.80.

Walking Wounded.

The walking wounded were collected at the Walking Wounded Collecting Post, VADENCOURT. They were dressed and fed there, and then sent direct to C.C.S. by motor lorries and busses which, on the evening of the 29th September, were able to get to a point about 200 yards West of the Canal.

The attack on the 29th September was the first time that the R.A.M.C. of the Division carried out evacuation of wounded from a quickly advancing front and a retreating enemy. On all previous occasions the A.D.S. and R.A.P's. had remained stationary.

To begin with, on account of the thick mist there was great difficulty in getting in touch with the various posts.

A number of bearers attached to the Infantry Battalions got lost; and no information whatever was received from the front. When the mist cleared away, and the Bearer Officer had got in touch with the different relay posts, the evacuation was carried out without difficulty, except for the congestion of the roads which delayed the return of the motor ambulance cars.

Over 1000 wounded were cleared before 6.0 p.m.

2. Attack on RAMICOURT, 3rd October, 1918.

No orders were received as regards the impending attack till midnight of the 2nd October, and no orders could be given till 1.0 a.m. to the Field Ambulances which were now situated at a considerable distance from rear Divisional Headquarters.

The attack was due to begin at 6.0 a.m.

An Advanced Dressing Station and Walking Wounded Collecting Post were established at MAGNY-LA-FOSSE.

Eight bearers were attached to each Battalion.

/Major H.D.LANE

Major H.D.LANE was detailed to act as Bearer Officer for the Left Sector. Fifty Bearers and two motor ambulance cars were assigned to him; and he was instructed to establish Car Posts as far as possible along the JONCOURT Road.

Captain A.U.MILLAR, with fifty bearers and four motor ambulance cars was detailed to evacuate cases in a similar manner along the LEVERGIES Road. As the road from LEVERGIES to A.D.S. at MAGNY was hopelessly blocked by a derelict Tank, he was instructed to clear wounded straight to IX Corps Main Dressing Station VADENCOURT, without passing through A.D.S.

Three Horsed Ambulances were detailed to work as far as possible up the Valley between the JONCOURT and Levergies Roads to meet any stretcher squads using that route, and to convey wounded to A.D.S.

On the Left Sector Major LANE established a Car Post, in the first place, at Railway Crossing JONCOURT, H.15.a.4.9., but very soon advanced it to SWISS COTTAGE, H.10.b.2.9., which was in close proximity to all the R.A.P's. of that Sector. Major LANE was wounded early in the day but continued to carry out his duties for 36 hours till relieved.
He collected a number of civilians from JONCOURT, fed them, and kept them in the cellars at SWISS COTTAGE, till they could be evacuated by motor ambulance cars on the following day.

On the Right Sector, Captain MILLAR established a Car Post at Railway Crossing LEVERGIES, H.33.b.7.9. near the R.A.P's. in his Sector.

Walking wounded were directed to the W.W.C.P. in MAGNY-LA-FOSSE, and after being fed and dressed were evacuated by lorries to C.C.S..

Evacuation proceeded smoothly and fairly rapidly; the only serious difficulty being that of getting ambulances through the densely congested mass of traffic on the roads. Many hours were taken by each car performing the double journey. At one time in the A.D.S. there were about 100 wounded awaiting removal.

On several occasions the A.D.S. was subjected to severe shell fire; but luckily none of the patients were injured.
In the early morning of the 4th October, after all the patients had been evacuated, a high explosive shell containing gas burst at the door of the A.D.S. Three R.A.M.C. Officers and 20 other ranks were gassed.
One of the Officers, Major S.S.B.HARRISON, continued to perform his duties and visited all his posts before he would allow himself to be evacuated. He died in the C.C.S. on the 10th October.

The M.T. drivers did splendid work. Those going to SWISS COTTAGE had to drive through an area severely shelled, both with Gas and High Explosive Shells. Many continued at work continuously for 24 hours. Two were wounded and five were evacuated suffering from Gas Poisoning.

Over 800 wounded were evacuated before 6.0 p.m.

3. <u>Attack at ANDIGNY WOOD, 17th October, 1918.</u>

Attack commenced at 5.20 a.m.

The evacuation of wounded was carried out as laid down in Operation Order No.151 attached.

An A.D.S. and W.W.C.P. were established at the HOSPICE, BOHAIN, D.22.a.6.2., and Bearer Relay Posts as laid down in Operation Order No.151.

The great majority of the wounded were evacuated along the BOHAIN-VAUX ANDIGNY Road. Motor ambulance cars were sent along this road as soon as the mist cleared; and by 9.0 a.m. nearly 300 cases had been admitted. The cars were pushed along the road to the most advanced R.A.P. Cases were brought into the A.D.S. much quicker than they could be cleared from there to the Corps Main Dressing Station.

NATURE OF WOUNDS.

A large proportion of the casualties in the attacks of the 29th September, and 17th October, was due to rifle or Machine Gun fire, and was much less severe in character than those received during the attack of the 3rd October.

The morale of the wounded men was excellent. Many of them asked if they could not be patched up and returned to their Battalions.

During the attacks nearly 3000 wounded were evacuated by the Field Ambulances of the Division. Included among these were 200 Germans, and about 100 French.

****

The casualties among the R.A.M.C. were -

2 Officers killed - 5 wounded.

5 Other Ranks killed - 55 wounded.

Five Motor Ambulances were put out of action by shell fire.

T. Kay.
Colonel.
A.D.M.S., 46th Division..

21/10/18.

War Diary

app 49.

Secret.

To all recipients of 46th DIVISION ORDER No. 333.

46th Division G.115/77. 15th October, 1918.

Reference para. 4, 46th Division Order No. 333. The 138th Inf: Bde will be prepared, on receipt of orders, to join hands with the French along the MENNEVRET - ANDIGNY Road.
Men will be warned that the Forest has been gassed and must be prepared to adjust their gas masks on moving through it.

Reference paras. 13 and 14. The WESTERN edge of the Barrage danger zone is a line D 12 a 0.7 - E 13 d 0.5.

Reference para. 15. The Flanking Barrage is shown on a Map issued to those concerned by 46th Div'l Art'y. (Issued herewith to 126th French Division).

Reference para. 19. The Location of Infantry Brigade H.Q will be D 11 b 5.0.

Reference para. 9. The remainder of the R.E and the 1/1st Bn, Monmouthshire Regt (Pioneers) will be held in readiness to repair the NOHAIN - ANDIGNY Road when ordered by Divisional H.Q.

Reference para. 16. The Forming UP Line will be taped under arrangements to be made by the CRE. The following will meet the CRE's representative at 1715 on Y Day at V 6 c 5.0 for the purpose of laying out this line -

GSO II, 46th Division.
A Staff Officer from each of the 138th and 139th Inf: Bdes.

[signature]

Lieut-Colonel,
General Staff, 46th Division...

War Diary

App 50

Secret.

To all Recipients of 46th DIVISION ORDER No. 333.

46th Division G.115/89. 16th October, 1918.

1. CHINESE ATTACK. The Chinese attack on the BOIS DE RIQUERVAL will be carried out under the orders of the GOC, 137th Inf: Bde, who will direct the CRE as to positions of Dummy Tanks and Figures.

At Zero Hour as much attention as possible will be directed to this flank, and the M.G. Coy allotted to the Brigade will put down a barrage to correspond with the Artillery Barrage.

No fire will be placed SOUTH of the SOUTHERN Boundary of the Artillery Barrage.

2. DIVISIONAL MOUNTED TROOPS. Divisional Mounted Troops will be disposed as follows :-

Troop of Royal Scots Greys in Divisional Reserve at FRESNOY.

Platoon of Cyclist Bn (Less 1 NCO and 3 men) in Div'l Reserve at 137th Inf: Bde H.Q., BOHAIN, to be used under orders from DHQ only.

1 NCO and 3 men at Bde HQ, D 11 b 5.0 for use of OC, Divisional Observers; to be used as directed by him.

Rations for all men of this Platoon will continue to be issued by 137th Inf: Bde.

Divisional Mounted Detachment. 1 NCO and 4 men with O.C, Signal Coy.

Two men with Brigade HQ, D 11 b 5.0, at disposal of Brigades.

Two men with DAPM.

3. TRAFFIC. From Zero Hour onwards, the BOHAIN - VAUX ANDIGNY Road will be used by the 46th Division as little as possible.

During the earlier stages of the battle, it will be necessary to use this route for evacuation of wounded, prisoners, etc.

These will in no case use the road, but will be directed along the tracks on either side.

As soon as the situation permits, the REGNICOURT - ANDIGNY Road will be taken into use and all possible traffic will be diverted on to this route and the cross country tracks S.W. of it.

4. ACKNOWLEDGE.

[signature]

Lieut-Colonel,
General Staff, 46th Division.

Issued at 1120

"A" Form
MESSAGES AND SIGNALS.

Army Form C. 2121 (In pads of 100.)

No. of Message............

Prefix.......Code.......m. | Words | Charge. | This message is on a/c of: War Service. | Recd. at....m.

Office of Origin and Service Instructions

Op. Priority
137 CRA.
126 Fr.Div.
6 Div. 9 Corps.

Sent At ......m. To ...... By ......

Diary (Signature of "Franking Officer")

Date ...... From ...... By ......

TO
9 Corps HA.
137 Bde. 126 Fr.Div. CRA. 6 Div. IX Corps.
MG Bn. 138 139 Bdes. Signals. CRE.
IX Corps HA. GOC. GSO I. File. War Diary.

Sender's Number.	Day of Month.	In reply to Number.	AAA
G.290.	12		

The French are making a general attack today first objective of 126 French Division is the line HENNECHIES FM inclusive - E 26 central - E 26 b 0.9 AAA Their barrage opens on the enemy trenches K 1 d b and a where it rests for three minutes to allow infantry to close on it and then advances at rate of 100 metres in three mins AAA Exploitation objective the MENNEVRET Line E 28 and 22 AAA 137 Bde will at the same time attack and capture the line E 20 d 2.0 - E 20 central and trenches from E 20 a 0.4 to 13 b 6.1 making as a first objective the trench system E 25 c 4.7 - 19 a 8.2 The attack will be made under a creeping barrage all details of which will be arranged between GOC 137 Bde and CRA AAA

From
Place
Time

The above may be forwarded as now corrected. (Z)

Censor. Signature of Addressor or person authorised to telegraph in his name

* This line should be erased if not required.

Order No. 1625 Wt. W3253/ P 511 27/2 H. & K.. Ltd. (E. 2634)

Army Form C. 2121
(In pads of 100.)

"A" Form
MESSAGES AND SIGNALS.

No. of Message..........

Prefix..............Code..............m.	Words	Charge.	This message is on a/c of:	Recd. at......m.
Office of Origin and Service Instructions	Sent		.............................Service.	Date..............
	At ....m.			From ....
	To			
	By		(Signature of "Franking Officer")	By................

TO (2)

Sender's Number.	Day of Month.	In reply to Number.	AAA

CRA will arrange for 6" hows to shell ahead of creeping barrage and bombard REGNICOURT and will arrange with Corps HA for any additional Heavy Hows and Guns to be included in barrage and harass enemy approaches AAA 137 Bde will detail a liaison post under an officer to advance with LEFT of French attack AAA GOC 137 will be prepared to throw back a flank from his final objective along the SE edge of the BOIS DE RIQUERVAL AAA Zero hour is noon AAA Watches will be synchronised by OC Signals at once and with 137 Bde MG Bn CRA and G when obtained from French

From 46 Div.
Place
Time 1020

The above may be forwarded as now corrected. (Z)

Censor. Signature of Addressor or person authorised to telegraph in his name

(Sgd) CF. Jerram, Lt.Col.
General Staff.

* This line should be erased if not required.

Order No. 1625 Wt. W3253/ P 511 27/2 H. & K., Ltd. (E. 2634)

"A" Form.

Army Form C. 2121.
(In pads of 100.)

MESSAGES AND SIGNALS.

No. of Message...........

Prefix ...... Code ...... m.	Words.	Charge.	This message is on a/c of:	Recd. at ...... m.
Office of Origin and Service Instructions.	Sent		War Diary Service.	Date
Priority to 137, 138, 139 Bdes CRA & M.G. Bn All ...	At ...... m.			From
	To			
	By		(Signature of "Franking Officer.")	By

TO			
137 Bde	CRA	6 Bn	
138	46 M G Bn	126 French Div	
139	9 Corps		

* Sender's Number.	Day of Month.	In reply to Number.	AAA
G 299	12		

137	Bde	will	consolidate
in	depth	on	original
line	aaa	2	M G
Coys	will	be	~~placed~~
under	orders	of	137
Bde some	guns	being	pushed
well	forward	and	groups
being	placed	so	as
to	cover	all	exits
from	wood	aaa	same
artillery	programme	as	for
last	night	with	variations
aaa	CRA	to	arrange
with	G O C	137	for
safety	limits	aaa	M G C
to	consult	with	G O C
137 as	to	M G	barrage for

From			
Place			
Time			

The above may be forwarded as now corrected. (Z)

Censor. Signature of Addressor or person authorised to telegraph in his name.

* This line should be erased if not required.

(3796.) Wt. W 492/M1647. 650,000 Pads. 5/17. H. W. & V., Ld. (E. 1187.)

"A" Form.

Army Form C. 2121.
(In pads of 100.)

MESSAGES AND SIGNALS.

No. of Message..............

Prefix.......... Code.......... m.	Words.	Charge.	This message is on a/c of:	Recd. at .... m.
Office of Origin and Service Instructions.	Sent		.... Service.	Date..............
	At.............. m.			From..............
	To..............			
	By..............		(Signature of "Franking Officer.")	By..............

TO

Sender's Number.	Day of Month.	In reply to Number.	AAA
*			

Remaining	M G	Coys	one
SEBONCOURT -	BOHAIN	Rd	one
in	reserve	aaa	Devl
line	of	resistance	SEBONCOURT-
BOHAIN	Road	aaa	Outpost
line	of	resistance	the
present	line	aaa	138
Bde	responsible	for	line
of	resistance	aaa	139
Coordinate	attack	as [illegible] Bde [illegible] G 27	aaa
addressed	137	138	139
Bdes	46	M G Bn	and
CRA	aaa	repeated	9
Corps	6	Div	and
126	French	Div	

From 46th Division

Place

Time 1800

The above may be forwarded as now corrected. (Z) R H Thomas Capt

Censor. Signature of Addressor or person authorised to telegraph in his name.

* This line should be erased if not required.

(3796.) Wt. W 492/M1647. 650,000 Pads. 5/17. H. W. & V., Ld. (E. 1187.)

War Diary

66

App XX

NOTES BY THE DIVISIONAL COMMANDER ON TRAINING DURING A SHORT REST AFTER ACTIVE OPERATIONS.

46th Division G.5/21. 20/10/18.

The 46th Division has now been withdrawn for a short time, after a period of hard and successful fighting.

The Division took over the line on the 21st September: since that date, three general actions have been fought, in all of which the Division was allotted a role of supreme importance.

In spite of every difficulty, by the determination and good leading of officers, non-commissioned officers and private soldiers, the objective has always been reached, regardless of success or failure on the flanks.

In addition many minor actions have been fought, all of which were of considerable importance, and in all of which the Troops displayed great gallantry.

The successes of the Division have led to decisive results, and a shortening of the War.

Since the 21st September, over 7,000 prisoners and over 70 guns, besides hundreds of machine guns, have been captured by the Division, and large numbers of the enemy killed and wounded.

No less than 16 different German Divisions have been severely mauled.

It is a record second to none in the Allied Armies.

The Soldiers of the North Midlands have made a name for themselves which is famous throughout the World. The Men have confidence in themselves and in their leaders.

Leaders of all ranks, officers and non-commissioned officers, must see to it that they are mentally and physically fit to lead the magnificent troops it is their honour and privilege to command in action.

P.T.O.

1. Organization. Battalions must be thoroughly organized on the principles laid down.

2. Ceremonial Drill. Most valuable. Short and good. Men absolutely under control and under the strictest discipline whilst drilling.

Brigade Ceremonials and March Past should be carried out at least once, the senior Colonel taking command of the parade.

3. Physical Fitness. The best men are of little value unless they are physically and mentally fit to carry out any duty that may be required of them.

Physical and Mental Training will include Physical Drill, Marching, Bayonet Fighting, Games, Football and Recreation of all kinds, Cinemas, etc.

4. Training of Leaders. The leadership displayed by both Officers and N.C.O's has hitherto been excellent, but many casualties have occurred and, if the high fighting standard is to be maintained, every opportunity must be taken to train young officers, N.C.O's and privates in leadership. Such training should include :-

(a) The expression "Noblesse oblige" as applied to the British Regimental Officer; i.e.- his men first in all things, himself last.
Interest in their comfort, food, games and minor troubles and difficulties, and a cheerful countenance.

(b) The leading of Companies and Platoons in attack on M.G Nests: the value of outflanking movements; covering fire; fire combined with moves to a flank.

(c) The leading of Fighting and Reconnoitring Patrols.

(d) The use of the Compass; invaluable during our recent fighting.

(e) Outposts.

(f) Map Reading: 1/40,000 and 1/100,000 Maps.

(g) The value of digging in <u>at once</u> on positions on which it is desired to make a halt.

(h) Writing messages and sending verbal reports, using map references.

(j) The fighting formation (open worms).

(k) Interior economy.- Sanitation.- Fresh air in billets, open windows, etc.

5. <u>Training of Drafts</u>. Drafts at present come straight through the Reinforcement Camp and do not therefore receive that valuable final polish to which we had become accustomed. As soon as battalions are made up to strength it is hoped that further drafts arriving may be retained at the Reinforcement Camp as heretofore.

In the meantime, officers and men arriving should be made to realise the Honour of being drafted to a Battalion in the 46th Division.

Earliest opportunity should be taken of speaking to them of the work of their battalion in the recent fighting, of gallant deeds done by their new comrades (some of these might well be read out on parade on the day after joining).

The value of determination and the will to "get there" somehow, should be rubbed in, with examples.

6. <u>Guards</u>. The importance of good guard mounting cannot be over estimated. A good guard reflects a smart, keen battalion which takes a pride in itself.

A good ceremonial never fails to interest men and a Guard Mounting or Retreat with Band or Drums will attract men to go and watch it, with pride if done well, and determination to do better if not done so well as in a neighbouring Battalion.

(The Demonstration Platoon is available, and can be allotted to Brigades. It is now at Divisional H.Q.)

7. <u>Transport</u>. What has been said about guards applies equally to Transport.

P.T.O.

Good Guards and good Transport never fail to catch the eye and increase 'Pride in the Regiment' the Brigade and the Division.

8. Reports. In the present open warfare it is of even greater importance than ever to know as soon as possible where everybody is, in order that assistance from behind may be given to the forward troops, and advantage taken of a favourable situation by the Higher Command.

All information is of importance.

Higher Commanders must not rely on getting information back, but get it by personal observation or by means of Staff and attached officers. Horses are invaluable as a means of getting information quickly. They should be brought up to some safe place close to Headquarters whence they can easily be brought forward as the battle progresses.

Ideas of dug-out warfare must be eradicated.

9. Recreation. Opportunity should be taken to get those who most need it, away for a few days on Paris leave.

Concerts should be organized and short lectures given on the general situation.

10. It is the intention that Machine Guns and Field Guns should be allotted to Battalions in future, when the occasion demands. This should be considered.

11. The Divisional Commander is confident that all ranks will work hard, and play hard, so that when the Division is called upon once more, it will prove itself invincible as always.

Lieut-Colonel,
General Staff, 46th Division.

Issued to :- CRA. (15). CRE. (4). Each Inf: Bde (5). 1st Monmouths. (1). 46th Bn, MGC. (5). ADMS. (4). AA & QMG. Divisional Reception Camp. (1).

War Diary

App 51

SECRET.

46th Division No. G.115/97. 16th October, 1918.

****

Protective Barrage.

The protective barrage covering the first objective will remain only for 10 minutes and then lift to the S.O.S. Line, where it will rest for 20 minutes.

The Chinese attack barrage and all Machine Gun barrages concerned will conform with this.

for Lieut-Colonel,
General Staff, 46th Division.

Issued to all recipients of
46th Division Order No. 335.

(Copy). War Diary G.3.

App 67

To 138th Inf: Bde.

Ref: your B.M. 43 dated 19th inst.

On the 17th instant, when my leading Companies were moving forward to their objectives, they were held up by heavy flanking fire from BELLEVUE RIDGE and the village of ANDIGNY-LES-FERMES.

They were in a very insecure position until the 1st Bn, LOYAL NORTH LANCS REGT pushed forward and in the face of great opposition cleared the ridge and secured the left edge of the village.

I understand they had severe casualties in so doing and I should like to express my thanks for the great assistance they rendered my Battalion.

(sgd) H.G. Wilson,
Lt-Col:
Comm'g 1/5th Lincoln Regt.

19/10/18.

(2)

138th Inf:Bde 106/G.

46th Division.

I should be glad if you would send my thanks to the Brigade concerned, as 1st L.N.L Regt undoubtedly contributed to our success.

(sgd) F.H. Edwards, Lt-Col:
Comm'g 138th Inf: Bde.....

19/10/18.

(3)

G.O.C, 1st Division.

In forwarding the attached letter from the O.C, 1/5 Lincolns, I would like to add in the name of the 46th Division, my appreciation of the conduct of the 1/LOYAL NORTH LANCS.

Without their help my left would have suffered heavily, and the success of the whole operation might have been jeopardized.

I would deem it a favour, if you would convey my thanks to the Commanding Officer.

(sgd) Gerald Boyd, M.G.,
Commanding 46th Division...

20/10/1918.

War Diary

68

App

Secret.

Amendment No. 1 to 46th Division Order No. 334.

Following amendments are issued with reference to Movement Table to accompany 46th Division Order No. 334.-

Serials No. 3 & 4. Remarks Column. For '1400' read '1300' - and add 'to keep roads in BOHAIN clear on arrival.'

No. 5 & 6. Date of move will be 1st November and not as stated 31st October. BOHAIN to be clear by 1200

No. 7. Remarks Col: For '1530' read '1430'.

No. 8. : : For '1600' read '1500'.

No. 9. Date : For '31st Oct:' read '1st Nov:'

No. 10. Remarks : For '1630' read '1530'.

P. Hayman

for Lieut-Colonel,
General Staff, 46th Division.

Issued at 1400, 30th October, 1918.
To all recipients of 46th Division Order No. 334.

War Diary

Secret. Copy No. 28

46th DIVISION ORDER No. 334.

Ref: Maps,- Sheets
57.B and 62.B, 1/40,000.

29th October, 1918.

1. The Division (less Artillery) will move to the BOHAIN Area in accordance with the attached Movement Table.

2. O.C, Divisional Train and A.D.M.S will arrange with corresponding officers of the 32nd Division as to details of accommodation to be taken over, etc, reporting arrangements made to this office.

3. Divisional Headquarters will close at FRESNOY at 1500 on 31st October and will re-open at the same hour at BOHAIN,- RUE de CHATEAU.

4. ACKNOWLEDGE.

P. Hayman
for. Lieut-Colonel,
General Staff, 46th Division.

Issued at 2000

Copy No. 1 GOC.
2 GSO I.
3 Q.
4 137th Inf: Bde.
5 138th : :
6 139th : :
7 CRA.
8 CRE.
9 OC, Div: Sig: Co.
10 46 Bn, MGC.
11 1/1st Monmouth R.
12/13 O.C, Div'l Train.
14 ADMS.

Copy No. 15 Camp Comm't.
16 DAPM.
17 DADOS.
18 DADVS.
19 DGO.
20 Div: Reception Camp.
21 T.M, FRESNOY.
22 T.M, BOHAIN.
23/24 IX Corps.
25 6th Division.
26 32nd :
27/28 War Diary.
29 File.

VEMENT TABLE TO ACCOMPANY 46th DIVISION ORDER No. 334.

Serial Number.	Date.	Formation.	From.	To.	To take over accommodation now occupied by.-	Remarks.
1.	Octr. 30th.	139th Inf:Bde.	FRESNOY.	BOHAIN.	14th Inf:Bde.	Not to enter BOHAIN before 1500
2.	30th.	1 Coy 46 MGBn.	FRESNOY.	BOHAIN.	1 Coy 32 MG Bn.	To march under orders GOC, 139 Inf:Bde.
3.	31st.	(HQ 137 Inf:Bde (1/6 S.Staffs R	MONTBREHAIN.	BOHAIN.	97th Inf:Bde.	Not to enter BOHAIN before 1400 and to be clear by 1530.
4.	31st.	1/5 S.Staffs R 1/6 N.Staffs R	FRESNOY.	BOHAIN.	97th Inf:Bde.	do. do.
5.	31st.	HQ 138 Inf:Bde 1 Bn 138 Bde.	FRESNOY.	BUSIGNY.	16th Inf:Bde.	Via BOHAIN. Not to enter BOHAIN before 1000 and to be clear of town by 1200
6.	31st.	2 Bns 138 Bde.	FRESNOY.	BECQUIGNY.	16th Inf:Bde.	do. do.
7.	31st.	HQ 46 MG Bn. 46 MG Bn (less 1 Coy).	FRESNOY.	BOHAIN.	32nd MG Bn.	Not to enter BOHAIN before 1530
8.	31st.	HQ & 2 Fd. Coys, RE.	FRESNOY.	BOHAIN.	32nd Div: RE.	No to enter BOHAIN before 1600
9.	31st.	1 Fd.Coy RE.	FRESNOY.	BUSIGNY.	6th Div: RE.	To march under orders GOC, 138 Inf:Bde.
10.	31st.	1/1st Monmouth Regt. (Pioneers).	FRESNOY.	BOHAIN.	16th Bn Highland Light Infantry, (Pioneers).	Not to enter BOHAIN before 1630
11.	31st.	HQ, Div: RA.	FRESNOY.	BOHAIN.	HQ recently occupied by 137th Inf:Bde.	
12.	31st.	46th Div: HQ.	FRESNOY.	BOHAIN.	HQ, 32nd Division.	

War Diary App No. 69.

Secret. Copy No. 22

46th DIVISION ORDER No. 335.
Operation "F".

Ref: Map - Sheets 57.A & 57.B, 1/40,000 and Map "A" to be issued. 30th October, 1918.

1. The IX Corps, at an early date, is attacking the SAMBRE-OISE CANAL in conjunction with the XV French Corps on the RIGHT and the XIII British Corps on the LEFT.

2. Map "A", showing the boundaries and objectives, will be issued shortly. (Not issued to those marked x).

3. The 1st Division is attacking on the RIGHT.
The 32nd Division on the LEFT.

4. The 46th Division will be in Reserve and will be prepared to relieve the 1st Division after its capture of the final objective and exploit success to the EASTWARD.

5. Three Companies of the 46th Bn, M.G Corps, will take part in the initial barrage supporting the 1st Division attack; O.C, 46th M.G Bn will get in touch with O.C, 1st M.G Bn and arrange details.
On completion of this Barrage, these three companies will be required to assemble at once with a view to moving forward with the 46th Division.
Ammunition from Limbers will not be used in the initial barrage.

6. All Units will reconnoitre routes from Billets to the line of the MAZINGHIEN - BAZUEL Road, on which the head of the Division will rest at Zero, and thence to the CANAL between S 9 c 1.4 and M 19 b 6.8.

7. Further details will be issued under the heading of Instructions to those concerned.

8. ACKNOWLEDGE.

[signature]
Lieut-Colonel,
General Staff, 46th Division...

Distribution over.-

Issued at 1430.

Copy No. 1 137 Inf:Bde.
2 138 : :
3 139 : :
4 CRA.
5 CRE.
6 OC, Signals.
7 OC, 46 Bn, MGC.
8 1/1st Bn Monmouth R.
9 ADMS.
10 Q.
11 GOC.
12 GSO I.
13/14 IX Corps. (x)
15 1 Division. (x)
16 32 Division. (x)
17 IX Corps HA. (x)
18 9 Sqdn RAF. (x)
19 OC, Div'l Observers.
20/21 File.
22/23 War Diary.
24 French Division. (*)
25 Squadron, Cavalry. (*)
26 Tank Corps. (*)

(*) not yet issued.

War Diary   Apps 70

Secret.   Copy No. 23

OPERATION "F".
46th Division Instructions No. 1.

46th Division G.117/7.   31st October, 18.

1. Dispositions of 46th Division at Zero. Headquarters and Dispositions of Infantry Brigades are shown on Map "B".

(a) Infantry Brigades. Brigade Commanders will ensure that their Commands are in position at Zero.
Brigade H.Q are being selected by the Divisional Staff and exact position will be notified to-morrow.
Note.- The 1st Division will be clear of these areas by midnight Y/Z Day.

(b) R.E and Pioneers. The R.E and Pioneer Battalion will be disposed, under orders to be given by the C.R.E, in such positions as will ensure that they can proceed to the work allotted to them with the least possible delay.
The C.R.E will inform Divisional Headquarters as to these dispositions.

(c) R.A. Will be in the line under the orders of the G.O.C, 1st Division.

(d) M.G Battalion. Will be disposed; three Companies under orders of 1st Division, one Company with 138th Infantry Brigade, tactically under command of O.C, 46th M.G Battalion.

(e) Field Ambulances. Will be disposed by the A.D.M.S in such positions that they will be able to relieve those of the 1st Division on that Division gaining their RED Line; and further be prepared to support an attack by the 46th Division beyond this Line.

Dispositions to be notified to Divisional Headquarters by the A.D.M.S.

(f) Troop of Cavalry.) With Advanced Divisional H.Q.
Platoon of Cyclists.)

(g) Divisional Troop. With O.C, Signal Company.

2. Subsequent Moves. (a) 138th Inf: Bde will be prepared, on receipt of orders, to move to the line of the road X 11 b - R 30, with a view to :-

(i) Supporting the 1st Division, if required to do so.
(ii) Relieving the RIGHT Brigade of the 1st Division.

(b) 139th Inf: Bde will be prepared to move so as to bring its head on the cross roads R 28 d, with a view to relieving the LEFT Brigade of the 1st Division.

(c) 137th Inf: Bde will be prepared to move to the LA LOUVIERE Area E. of the R 33, 34 Grid, to be in Divisional Reserve after the relief of the 1st Division.

3. H.Q after relief of 1st Division. Should the 1st Division be relieved approximately on the RED Line, Adv. Divisional H.Q will be at L'ARBRE DE GUIZE (W 6 b).
Brigades in the Line at BOIS DE L'ABBAYE (M 32 c).
Reserve Brigade at LA LOUVIERE (R 35 c).

P.T.O.

4. Reconnaissance. So far as is possible at present, reconnaissance of the above areas will be undertaken, commencing to-morrow.

5. Intelligence. An Intelligence Map showing present Canal crossings broken and unbroken, Dispositions of Enemy and known M.G Nests, etc, will be issued to-morrow to CRA, CRE, Inf: Bdes and M.G Battalion.

6. R.E and Bridges. The R.E arrangements will be notified later. The C.R.E will prepare a Map showing the exact positions and capabilities of bridges to be built by the 1st, 32nd and 46th Divisions. Copies of this Map will be issued later.

7. Machine Gun Battalion. On completion of their Barrage, the three Companies.M.G Battalion will be disposed, one with 139th Inf: Bde, under tactical command of O.C, 46th M.G Bn; two in Divisional Reserve about MAZINGHIEN.

8. Map "A". Is issued herewith to those recipients marked in Divisional Order No. 335.

9. ACKNOWLEDGE.

Lieut-Colonel,
General Staff, 46th Division..

Issued at 2230

Copy No. 1 137 Inf: Bde.
2 138 : :
3 139 : :
4 CRA.
5 CRE.
6 OC, Signals.
7 OC, 46 Bn, MGC.
8 1/1st Bn, Monmouth R.
9 ADMS.
10 Q.
11 GOC.
12 GSO I.
13
14 IX Corps.
15 1 Division.
16 32 :

Copy No. 19 OC, Div: Observers.
20/21 File.
22/23 War Diary.
24 Fr. Division.
25 Troop 20th Hussars.
26 Platoon Cyclists.

War Diary

App 23

Secret.

Copy No. 17

46th Division Order No. 331.

6th Oct 18

1. The IX Corps is attacking in the early morning of a date which will be communicated separately.
Objectives and boundaries are shown on the attached Map "A". (No Map "A" to those marked *).

2. The XV French Corps will be on the RIGHT: the American Corps on the LEFT.

3. The attack on the IX Corps front is being carried out by the 6th Division with the 46th Division and 3rd Inf: Bde in Corps Reserve.

4. Further instructions as to locations on "Z" Day, etc, will be issued.

5. The operation will be known as "Operation "D"."

6. ACKNOWLEDGE.

Lieut-Colonel,
General Staff, 46th Division....

Issued at 2000

Copy No. 1 to CRA.
2 CRE.
3 Signals.*
4 137th Inf: Bde.
5 138th : :
6 139th : :
7 46th Bn, MGC. %
8 1st Monmouths.%
9 AA & QMG.*
10 ADMS.*
11/12 IX Corps.*
13 6th Division.*
14 GSO I.
15/16 File.
17/18 War Diary.
19 3rd Inf: Bde.

% Map follows.

Report on Operations on October 17th, 1918.

1. The role of the machine guns was as follows :-
One Company was allotted to each of 137th, 138th & 139th Infantry Brigades and one remained in reserve.
Two Companies of the 2nd Life Guards Machine Gun Battalion and one Company of the 6th Battalion Machine Gun Corps were allotted to the 46th Division, for Barrage Purposes.

2. The company attached to the 137th Infantry Brigade had a dual role
(1) To defend by direct fire, if necessary, the original Divisional area West of RIQUERVAL WOOD.
(2) To barrage the Wood in E.25.a., b & c, and in E.19 from ZERO till ZERO + 123.
Four guns were placed at each of following positions :-

J 6 c 62.82	J 5 a 82.95
J 4 b 90.20	D 28 d 70.50

This company expended 82,000 rounds in the latter task, two sections having to fire for ¾ of an hour in box respirators on account of Green Cross Gas Shells which fell about J 6 b & d.
At 07.45 the Officer Commanding the Section at J 6 c 62.82 reported that the enemy was shelling the wood in E 25 c & d.
This information was forwarded to the 137th Infantry Brigade and patrols were sent into the Wood.
One patrol returned at about 09.30 having penetrated to the clearing in E 20 c & 26 a.
At 14.00 the 137th Infantry Brigade ordered two sections forward to support a battalion of infantry in E 14 & 20.
One section was sent to about E 26 a 40.80 and another to about E 13 d 90.20.
The remaining two sections were disposed for direct fire on to Western edge of the BOIS DE RIQUERVAL, one section at J 6 b 2.4 and one at D 29 c 1.8.

3. The Machine Gun Barrage lasted from Zero till Zero + 123 minutes. It progressed by bounds in front of the advancing infantry and was carried out in accordance with the Fire Organization Orders issued with 46th Battalion Machine Gun Corps Order No 71 of 16/10/18, slight alterations being made in the lifts to conform with alterations in the "artillery barrage".
Four hundred and sixty six thousand rounds were expended.

4. The Company operating with the 139th Infantry Brigade had tasks as follows :-
No 1 section was to assemble in rear of left company 8th Battalion Sherwood Foresters and to follow to objective E 9 c 3.2.
No 2 section was to assemble in rear of 'B' Company, 5th Battalion Sherwood Foresters and was to follow them through E 7 d, E 8 c and REGNICOURT consolidating on objective ORCHARD E 14 a.
No 3 section lined up in rear of 'C' Company 5th Battalion Sherwood Foresters and was to assist in consolidation of wood E 14 c.
No 4 section assembled in rear of 'D' Company 8th Battalion Sherwood Foresters and was to occupy embankment E 13 b.
Sections advanced at ZERO + 9 minutes.
No 1 Section proceeded towards high ground E 7 b. At 05.50 the officer & N.C.O. were wounded by close range Machine Gun Fire and the section halted 100^{x} in rear. Two gun teams then moved to high ground D 6 d. where they joined No 4 section. The remaining sub-section was placed by Major Rigby of 'B' Company in trench E 7 b 7.7.

No 2 Section.

At 07.00 approximately three guns were at E 13 a 9.5 and were moved by the Company Commander and placed with the infantry along embankment E 13 b 30.15.
The infantry were forced to withdraw at 08.00, one gun team went with them. Reinforcements almost immediately reoccupied the embankment and the section officer moved the two guns to high ground E.13.b.7.7.

<u>No 3 Section.</u>

In the mist the section lost touch with the infantry but moved forward and posted two guns in embankment E 13 b 7.6 and two guns in trench in front.

At 11.30 the section again advanced and dug in on spur E 14 c 6.6.

<u>No 4 Section</u>, proceeded up valley E 1 c, E 7 a & d where they were fired on by enemy Machine Guns in the clearing. Section came into action and were about to engage enemy when an infantry officer arrived, stating that his own troops were mopping up the clearing.

Troops of the 1st Division then came up from the rear, firing on the section and finally charging them. The Section Officer showed them where they were and they then moved off through E 7 b.

Owing to the wood not being mopped up the section withdrew under fire to D 6 d, being joined there by two gun teams of No 2 Section, previously mentioned, and by two of No 1 Section.

Four strong teams were organized and the remaining guns etc were sent to Company Headquarters at D 6 c 00.25.

At 10.00 the section pushed forward on to high ground E 9 c on the forward slope, but was forced back on to the reverse slope by artillery and Machine Gun fire.

At 19.00 reinforcements arrived and two gun teams with guns were sent up to Nos 1 & 2 Sections, 16 (sixteen) guns being in action at 20.00.

5. The Company operating with the 138th Infantry Brigade had orders to push two sections forward with the infantry battalions and to get two guns into each of the posts to be established at :-

E 10 b 3.5.
E 10 d 1.9.
E 9 c 9.3.
E 9 c 7.2.

Two sections were to watch the left flank and ANDIGNY-LES-FERMES in case of attack not succeeding, or in case of counter attack.

The Company formed up on the East side of the road from W 25 c 2.0 to W 25 b 2.5.

Teams were small and each section took two pack mules carrying belt boxes.

Teams and mules were in place by 00.45.

The guns moved forward at Zero as closely as possible in support of the infantry.

At 15.00 their disposition was as follows :-

2 guns E 10 b 3.5.
2 : E 10 d 1.9.
2 : E 9 c 9.3.
2 : E 9 c 7.2.
4 : E 9 a 8.5.
4 : E 8 a 7.8.

The guns remained in these positions till withdrawn on evening of 18th.

6. Eight guns of the reserve company advanced close behind the barrage with orders to support the advance of the infantry by direct overhead covering fire from the high ground in E 7 b. on to ANDIGNY-LES-FERMES. When they advanced to this position they found that it was strongly held by the enemy who greeted them with machine gun fire. The sections withdrew and waited till the trenches had been mopped up. It was then too late to afford covering fire so the sections took up defensive positions to deal with any counter attack.

7. Owing to the mist no favourable targets were seen but had the enemy counter attacked heavily at any time he would have found our machine guns in great strength and amply supplied with ammunition.

8. Our casualties in this operation were :-

Officers 3
O.Rs. 32.

[signature] Major,

Commanding 46th Battn.M.G.Corps.

21/10/18.

(1)

attack of 46th Division on REGNICOURT-ANDIGNY-LES-FERMES

Oct. 17th 1918

On October 13th instructions were received that the IX Corps would on October 17th take part in a operation with the XV French Corps attacking on the Right and the 2nd American Corps on the Left.

The distribution of the IX Corps for this operation was the 46th Division attacking on the Right of the Corps front, the 6th Division on the Left followed by the 1st Division which was to exploit eastwards any success gained by the 6th Division. The XV French Corps was to attack the FOREST of ANDIGNY from the South.

On October 16th the distribution of the Division was as follows:-

Divisional Headquarters	...	FRESNOY-LE-GRAND.
138th Infantry Brigade	...	do.
139th : :	...	
137th : :		holding a line E.13.a.5.8. - E.13.a.8.0. - E.13.c.1.0. - D.24.b.5.0.

The objectives of attack allotted to the Division were the road from ~~E.11.a.5.8~~. E.13.b.5.0. to E.11.a.5.8. including the villages of REGNICOURT and ANDIGNY-LES-FERMES.

The following additional troops were at the disposal of the G.O.C., 46th Division, for the purposes of this attack :-

One Troop Royal Scots Greys.

Four Brigades R.H.A. and R.F.A.

One Section Tanks.

Two Companies Life Guards Machine Gun Battalion.

One Company 6th Machine Gun Battalion.

The dispositions of the Division for this operation were as follows :-

137th Infantry Brigade was instructed to maintain line at present held by them.

139th Infantry Brigade to attack on the Right.

138th Infantry Brigade to attack on the Left.

/the dividing.......

the dividing line between 139th and 138th Brigades being E.1.a.3.8. - E.1.central - E.8.b.5.0 - E.9.c.8.0.

The forming-up line for the attack was about one hundred yards South-east of the BOHAIN - VAUX ANDIGNY ROAD, which line lay within 6th Divisional area. It was arranged that the present line held should not be taken over from the 6th Division but that our Infantry should be in position on the line of deployment by Zero minus one hour, at which hour all troops of the 6th Division were to be West of the Safety Line.

It will be noticed that the attack was not a frontal one on to the enemy position, but was to be delivered from the flank and to start from the area of the neighbouring Division. This method of advance, although it proved more successful than - judging from the strength of the enemy wire &c. - any form of frontal attack could possibly have been, necessitated special arrangements as regards the barrage. Owing to the positions occupied by guns of the 6th and American Divisions, it was not possible to locate the artillery at the disposal of the 46th Division in such a position that they could bring down a normal frontal barrage, but from the positions held by them West and North-west of BOHAIN, such barrage had to be of an oblique nature. It is instructive to note that the fact of the barrage being oblique to a certain extent caused the Infantry, accustomed as they were to following a frontal barrage, to lose direction during their advance.

The actual instructions given as regards Artillery support were for a thick 18-pounder barrage with one round of 'smoke' per lift, and a 4.5 How. barrage beyond the 18-pounders. The 4.5 Hows. were instructed to fire in the barrage until the Infantry began to reach the crest on the line of the BOHAIN - VAUX ANDIGNY ROAD when they were to lift on to the Northern edge of the FOREST of ANDIGNY and fire smoke shell. The barrage was to rest on the

/opening............

opening line for three minutes and then move forward at the rate of one hundred yards in three minutes. On reaching the general line of the FOREST of ANDIGNY, it was to rest for thirty minutes and then cease.

Artillery work prior to Zero consisted of wire-cutting, steady bombardment of the German front line, the destruction of ANDIGNY-LES-FERMES and such trenches immediately West of that place as should exist. Arrangements were also made for harrassing fire and the keeping open of gaps in conjunction with the Infantry then holding the line.

The task allotted to the three Tanks working with the Division was as follows :- They were to move forward with the supporting Infantry to the strong point about E.1.d., then along the line of trenches to E.13.b.7.0 when one tank was to continue along the trench to D.19.b.9.5., the others to move east to assist in the mopping-up of REGNICOURT and ANDIGNY-LES-FERMES. Having completed these tasks the tanks were to withdraw under cover North of the BOHAIN - ANDIGNY ROAD.

As regards Machine Guns, one Company was placed at the disposal of the 137th Infantry Brigade for holding the right pivot of the attack and one Company to closely follow the attacking Infantry with a view to taking up position close to the final objective from where they should be able to bring direct fire across the front of the Infantry.

Special parties of R.E. were placed at the disposal of the 138th and 139th Infantry Brigades to assist in the forming of strong points at E.13.b.6.0., REGNICOURT, E.9.c.9.4., and ANDIGNY-LES-FERMES. The remainder of the Field Coys. and the 1/1st Monmouthshire Regiment were held in readiness to repair the BOHAIN-ANDIGNY ROAD as soon as orders to do so were received from Divisional Headquarters.

Headquarters during this action were located as follows :-

Divisional Headquarters	...	FRESNOY-LE-GRAND
137th Inf. Brigade.	...	BOHAIN.
138th and 139th Inf. Bdes.	...	D.11.b.5.0.

As has already been stated, the role of the 137th Brigade was to maintain its existing line holding the right pivot of attack. This was arranged for by one Battalion, one Machine Gun Company and a Trench Mortar Battery being in the line, the remaining two Battalions in Divisional Reserve one along the SEBONCOURT-BOHAIN ROAD, the other in BOHAIN.

In order to deceive the enemy as to the direction of the real attack which was to be delivered from the flank, arrangements were made for a "Chinese" attack by the 137th Brigade on the following lines. Dummy tanks and dummy figures were to be used to simulate an attack on the BOIS DE RIQUERVAL from a westerly direction and there was a special rolling barrage, in which the Machine Gun Company allotted to the Brigade joined, to come down at Zero on a line at safety distance from the advanced posts and move through the BOIS DE RIQUERVAL in a easterly direction at the rate of 100 yards in 4 minutes. It may be stated at once that the enemy was apparently deceived by the above preparations, because at ten minutes after Zero he put down a heavy barrage on the outpost line of this Brigade.

Zero hour for the 17th was fixed for 0520 and the attack was launched in a thick mist which, as will be seen later on, caused certain units to lose direction and led to some enemy Machine Gun nests being overlooked by the leading troops during their advance.

To give a more detailed account of this action it will be necessary to deal with the part played by each Brigade separately.

The 139th Infantry Brigade attacking on the Right of the Division, advanced on a one Battalion front, its units being distributed as follows :-

The 8th Battalion, Sherwood Foresters, formed up on a tape line approximately 100 yards South of the BOHAIN-VAUX

/ANDIGNY ROAD.........

ANDIGNY ROAD with the 2 Supporting Companies of the 5th Battalion, Sherwood Foresters, in rear.

The 5th Battalion, Sherwood Foresters, less 2 Companies, were dug in under bank of wood in D.12.d.

The 6th Battalion, Sherwood Foresters, were in Brigade Reserve in D.11.a. & b.

All troops were in position by Zero minus 1½ hours.

The attacking troops moved forward under the barrage, but, owing to the dense fog, it was impossible to judge lifts. This, combined with the oblique nature of the barrage already referred to, resulted in the loss of direction by certain companies.

The 8th Bn, Sherwood Foresters, attacked on a three company frontage with one company in close support.

In rear of this one company of the 5th Bn, Sherwood Foresters followed the centre company of the leading battalion and another company of the 5th Bn, Sherwood Foresters, followed the Right company of leading battalion.

The Left Company of the leading Battalion advanced and about 0740 captured the high ground in E 7 b., after meeting with enemy opposition. Several machine gun nests were overcome, though owing to the fog a few were not located and were mopped up later.

This company then lost direction and instead of advancing South-east to the objective moved practically due East, and on the fog lifting found itself in the vicinity of E 9 b., i.e. just West of ANDIGNY-les-FIRMES. In the meantime, the extreme Right leading company had pushed forward and reached a position near the railway track in E 13 b.

The centre company was then held up by heavy machine gun fire from the direction of a clearing in E 7 d. The net result of this state of affairs on the fog lifting was that the Right company suffered heavy casualties from hostile machine guns situated in the above mentioned clearing.

On seeing this the Battalion Commander at once pushed his

/reserve..........

Reserve Company, to which was added Sections of leading Companies who had lost their way, via the high ground in E 7 b., which was already captured, towards the clearing in E 7 d. At the same time, the extreme Left Company realising that they had lost direction moved down towards high ground East of REGNICOURT from a North-easterly direction.

The outcome of this manouvre ~~resulted in~~ was that the enemy in the clearing realising that they were out-manouvred, ~~whereupon~~ after further slight resistance,they surrendered.

140 of the enemy and 27 machine guns were actually collected from this small area.

The enemy then took up a line approximately along the main REGNICOURT-BOHAIN Road in E 13 b., where he had strongly wired and entrenched positions.

The Officer Commanding 5th Bn. Sherwood Foresters on hearing that our troops on this flank had been compelled to withdraw slightly owing to being outnumbered, pushed forward on authority from Brigade, the remaining two companies which he had in hand in the Valley in D 12 d.

After stiff fighting and a further flanking movement from the direction of REGNICOURT the enemy ~~were~~ was dislodged from his position; this resulting in the capture of the ~~third objective~~ BLUE line by us throughout.

The capture of the Brigade objective was complete by 1015.

This objective was at once consolidated and attempts made to push forward platoon posts in front. These efforts were however met by direct fire over open sights by an enemy field gun about E 21 a.

This was later compelled to withdraw, by the action of one of our guns whereupon posts well South of the road were established.

At 1110 the enemy were reported by 8th Bn. Sherwood Foresters to be massing for counter-attack in E 15 c. Guns of the whole group were immediately turned on and at 1145 it was reported that

/the counter-attack

the counter-attack had been broken up by our Lewis Gun and Artillery fire. In fact, only one of the enemy succeeded in reaching our positions alive.

The consolidation being completed, the troops of the Brigade were then thinned out and re-organised in depth, 2 Battalions being in line, the 5th Battalion, Sherwood Foresters, on the Right, the 8th Battalion, Sherwood Foresters, on the Left, and the Reserve Companies on the general line of the BOHAIN - ANDIGNY ROAD.

Patrols were sent out to get in touch with the French at about E.22.a.0.0. They were eventually located holding ~~the~~ a post about 100 yards South of Foresters ~~Hut~~ House. When this position had been located the outpost line was formed running North and South from E.15.a. and c., touch being obtained with the 138th Infantry Brigade at E.3.c.7.0. At 1730 instructions were issued to the 139th Infantry Brigade not to move further East and they were informed that the 137th Infantry Brigade would keep touch with the French and move Eastwards with them through the Wood as far as the line MINNEVRET - ANDIGNY ROAD.

To turn to the action of the 138th Infantry Brigade, while forming up, the enemy shelled their assembly area with H.E. and gas shells without, however, causing many casualties and at Zero minus one hour the Brigade was formed up as follows :-

The <u>4th Leicestershire Regt</u>. on the Right from E 1 a 2.8 to W 25 central in touch with 139th Infantry Brigade.

The <u>5th Lincolnshire Regt</u>. from W 25 central to W 26 a 2.8 in touch with the 6th Division on the Left.

The <u>5th Leicestershire Regt</u>. were in reserve in V 30 b.

Each of the front line battalions had a section of machine guns and the 5th Lincolnshire Regt. had a section of T.Ms. attached to them.

The attack took place in a dense fog which made the difficulties of keeping direction and communication very great.

At 0654 it was reported that the Brigade had reached the REGNICOURT-ANDIGNY-les-FERMES Road but that several machine guns had not been properly mopped up and were still firing from the old German front line in E 2 a. and b. This is to be accounted for by the thick fog and to show the difficulties caused thereby it may be stated that at 0700, the O.C., 4th Leicestershire Regt. reported that he had then under his command elements of the Cameron Highlanders, Black Watch, Loyal North Lancashire Regt., Sherwood Foresters and 5th Lincolnshire Regt., all in the area E 1 b. The machine gun nests passed over in the first advance were eventually dealt with by supporting troops.

The Brigade having reported that they were suffering from M.G. fire from BELLE VUE and LES GOBELETS, were at 0930, instructed from Divisional Headquarters to take the necessary steps to work round that position and two companies of the Reserve Battalion, 5th Leicestershire Regt., were detailed to do so. This movement, however, proved unnecessary, as, in the meantime, the 1st Bn.

/Loyal.......

Loyal North Lancashire Regt. had in the face of great opposition, cleared that position. The same battalion later on rendered great service to the 138th Infantry Brigade in clearing the Left edge of ANDIGNY-les-FERMES village. At 1130, the Brigade held the village of ANDIGNY-les-FERMES. Instructions were issued from Divisional Headquarters that immediately ANDIGNY was occupied the Brigade were to push strong fighting patrols South-east towards MENNEVRET with a view to assisting the French and to capture the guns in that village. An officer's liaison post was to be established on the cross-roads at E 17 c 1.5. Throughout the day and night efforts were made to obtain touch with the French but up to 1900 on the 17th, the company of 5th Leicesters patrolling for this purpose had been held up by machine gun fire from E 11 central. Later on a junction was effected at LA NATION Cross-roads but the company were unable to remain there on account of the enemy bombing parties, and it was not until 0530 on the 18th that definite touch was established at this point.

At 1640, the dispositions of the 138th Infantry Brigade were:-

<u>5th Lincolnshire Regt</u>. - 3 companies round E. and S. of ANDIGNY-les-FERMES. 1 company in E 4 c 8.0. Headquarters E 2 b 4.7.

<u>4th Leicestershire Regt</u>. - 1 company at E 9 c 3.3. 1 company E 9 a 2.3. One company at E 9 a 7.5 with Headquarters at E 2 central.

<u>5th Leicestershire Regt</u>. - Headquarters and 1½ companies at V 30 a. 1 company old German front line about E 2 b. 1 company patrolling the ANDIGNY-les-FERMES - MENNEVRET Road, 2 platoons with 5th Lincolnshire Regt.

The machine gun company had 8 guns disposed in front of the objective, 1 section in E 9 b. and 1 section in E 8 a., covering LES GOBELETS FARM.

On instructions being received from Divisional Headquarters

/that a..........

that a fresh battalion was to be placed in line, relieving the attacking battalions who were to reorganise in close support, at 1750 orders were issued that the 5th Leicester Regt. would take over the front line from the 4th Leicestershire Rs and the 5th Lincolnshire Regiments. After this order had been carried out, the dispositions were as follows:-

5th Leicestershire Regt. - on the line from E 9 c 5.3 to E 11 a 2.8 held by three companies, one company patrolling down the ANDIGNY-les-FERMES - MENNEVRET ROAD, Headquarters at E 2 cent.

5th Lincolnshire Regt. - in sunken road in E 2 with Headquarters in E 2 b.4.7.

4th Leicestershire Regt. - in old German front line with Headquarters at VALLEE HASSARD, D 6 b 6.6.

At 2321, orders were issued to the Brigade to take over from the 1st Division the line from ANDIGNY to E 5 a 9.2, which line was to be taken over by daybreak on the 18th. Owing to the suitability of this ground for machine gun defence instructions were given from Divisional Headquarters that the line should be held by not more than one infantry company and two groups of machine guns about E 5 c., eight additional machine guns from the Reserve Company being given to the Brigade for this purpose. The 5th Leicestershire Regt. were ordered to move one company to take over the above front and the relief was completed by 0600 on the 18th.

Touch having been gained with the French at 0530 at LA NATION Cross-roads, the two companies defending ANDIGNY-les-FERMES and the area E 5 c. were told to link up with the French and establish a line from E 11 c., E 11 a. and E 5 c. The company from E 9 c. was now moved up to the East of ANDIGNY-les-FERMES.

In the meanwhile during the early stages of the attacks by the 138th and 139th Infantry Brigades, the 137th Infantry Brigade was holding the Right pivot of attack having, as has already been recounted, apparently succeeded in deceiving the enemy as to the real direction of attack.

At 0930 Orders were issued from Divisional Headquarters that this Brigade should push patrols through RIQUERVAL WOOD and clear up the situation. Acting on these instructions, they were able to report at 1045 that they had established a post at E.13.d.7.0. and that they were in touch with the 139th Infantry Brigade on their Left and were pushing patrols Southwards to get in touch with their Right Company. At 1135 Divisional Headquarters issued instructions to the Brigade that as soon as they were established on the eastern edge of the BOIS DE RIQUERVAL they were to bring up their Support Battalion and push strong fighting patrols into the FOREST of ANDIGNY with objective the spur E.15.c., then pushing S.E. towards Foresters House in E.22.c.3.1. to join with the French who were being harassed from the eastern edge of the wood about E.2.a and c.

At 1200 the French reported that they held FORESTERS HOUSE and that the enemy were retiring N.E. This information was passed on to 137th Infantry Brigade who had already been told to get in touch with the French at that place, and in addition the 138th and 139th Infantry Brigades were instructed to push forward fighting patrols to try and cut off the enemy.

By 1330, the 137th Infantry Brigade were able to report that RIQUERVAL WOOD was clear, that a post was established at E 26 a., and that patrols were being pushed forward towards E 21 c. to obtain touch with the French. At 1530 their line ran along the Western edge of HENNECHIES WOOD, through E 20 c., and E 26 a., and patrols were advancing E.N.E. and S.E. The Headquarters of the leading Battalion were established at E 26 a 5.8 and three companies of the supporting Battalion had

been.......

been moved up in close support as also one battery R.H.A.

The 139th Infantry Brigade, having reported at 1700 that they were in touch with the French about E 222 a 0.0, was instructed not to move further East, and the 137th Infantry Brigade were told to keep in touch with the French Division and move Eastwards with them through the wood as far as the line MENNEVRET - ANDIGNY, on which line the Brigade was to establish itself.

In the meantime, 138th Infantry Brigade was endeavouring to establish liaison with the French by patrolling down the ANDIGNY - MENNEVRET ROAD. The general situation of the Division at about 1930 on the evening of the 17th October was as follows :-
137th Infantry Brigade had established an outpost line in touch with the French at E 28 a 2.8 and joining on to the 139th Infantry Brigade at E 21 b 5.7, The 139th Infantry Brigade outposts ~~line~~ ran North to E 9 c 5.0 where they met the 138th Infantry Brigade which Brigade held the line to ANDIGNY inclusive. Orders were issued to all Brigades to hold their present line with battalions disposed in depth and the 138th Infantry Brigade was instructed to keep on seeking ~~to obtain~~ liaison with the French as previously ordered. S.O.S. arrangements to cover up the above line had to be made so as to keep the barrage West and North of the edge of the wood from E 16 c 2.0, E 10 d 0.3, E 16 b 7.0, to the cross-roads at E 11 c 7.2. This restriction was necessary as the French proposed to continue pushing forward through the wood. It was not the wish of the French Division that we should advance beyond the general line E 22 c 2.8, to E 21 b 5.7, but when they reached a line of the MENNEVRET - ANDIGNY ROAD the 138th Infantry Brigade were to join up with them at the LA NATION Cross-roads as previously arranged.

At the end of this days hard fighting the Division had secured all objectives allotted to the attacking Brigade and in addition 137th Infantry Brigade cleared the BOIS DE RIQUERVAL and established itself well through the Forest of ANDIGNY.

To add to the difficulties attending ~~ing to~~ and on any attack, our advancing infantry had to contend during the earlier stages with the confusion and loss of direction resulting from a thick fog. Throughout the whole action our troops were met by heavy machine gun fire and, as an example of the number of these weapons employed by the enemy, it may be stated that in one instance, nine machine guns were found in a length of trench not one hundred yards long.

The captures on this day amounted to about 15 officers, 500 other ranks, 2 field guns, several trench mortars and over 100 machine guns. Prisoners taken were identified from 17 different Regiments of 6 different divisions

ACTION ON THE 18th OCTOBER, 1918.

At dawn on the 18th as already related in the account of the part played by the 138th Infantry Brigade, that Brigade took over the front held by the 1st Brigade from ANDIGNY to E 5 a 7.3. Later in the day the 137th Infantry Brigade as ordered over night took over the whole of the Divisional front and, as the French had by then (0830) taken MENNEVRET, the line then ran E 17 b 2.5, E 11 c 0.8, E 5 c 7.3, E 5 a 7.3. The relieved Brigades withdrew to the following areas:- 139th Infantry Brigade to about D 12 and 18, E 7 and 13, and the 138th Infantry Brigade to about E 1, 2, and 3.

The role of the 137th Infantry Brigade on the 18th was to keep touch with the 126th French Division on the Right and the 1st Division on the Left. For this purpose, 1 troop Scot's Greys and 1 Platoon Cyclists were placed at the disposal of the Brigadier and instructions were issued that these mobile troops would be supported as necessary by infantry and forward artillery.

The advance continued during the day and at 1830 instructions were given that the battalions of the 137th Infantry Brigade at BOHAIN and REGNICOURT could return to their billets at FRESNOY-le-GRAND. The battalion still in line was to be withdrawn to BOHAIN or some place selected by the Brigadier as soon as the French and the 1st Division had joined hands.

About 2130, information having been received that this junction had been effected at WASSIGNY, the remaining battalion and mobile troops were withdrawn, the mission of the 46th Division being then terminated.

E 21 a.

41. This was later compelled to withdraw, whereupon posts well SOUTH of the road were established.

At 1110 hours, the enemy were reported by the 1/8th Bn, Sherwood Foresters, to be massing for counter attack in E 15 c. Guns of the whole RIGHT Group were immediately turned on and at 1145 hours, it was reported that the counter attack had been broken up by our L.G and artillery fire.

In fact, only one of the enemy succeeding in reaching our position alive.

~~42.~~ A patrol was sent out to get in touch with the French, who were found to be holding a position approximately a hundred yards SOUTH of FORESTERS HOUSE.

42 In the meantime, the LEFT Brigade having consolidated the final objective, pushed forward one company to patrol the ANDIGNY-LES-FERMES - MENNEVRET Road, endeavouring to gain touch with the French, but were held up by M.G fire from about E 11 central.

During the whole attack, our troops met with heavy M.G fire, and as an example of the number used by the enemy, it may be stated that nine M.Gs were afterwards found in a length of trench not one hundred yards long.

43. On the 18th Octr, the 137th Inf: Bde took over the line E 17 b 2.5 - E 11 c 0.8 - E 5 c 7.3 - E 5 a 7.3,- from the 138th Inf: Bde, and the 139th Inf: Bde, and was ordered to keep touch with the 1st Division on the LEFT and the 126th French Division on the RIGHT. At 2125, the 1st Division and 126th French Division, having joined hands at WASSIGNY, the mission of the 46th Division ceased, and orders were sent to the 137th Inf: Bde to withdraw and concentrate in the BOHAIN Area, where the 138th and 139th Inf: Bdes were.

44. The fighting during the 17th and 18th Octr. was very stiff and the captures during these two days amounted to about fifteen officers, five hundred other ranks, two field guns, one hundred machine guns, and several T.M's.

45. From Octr. 19th to Novr. 2nd, the Division was out at rest.

46. On the 3rd Novr. the Division, acting on orders from the IXth Corps, moved from rest to places of assembly for operations against the SAMBRE - OISE CANAL, in conjunction with the XVth French Corps on the RIGHT and the XIIITH British Corps on the LEFT.

47. On 3rd Novr. the dispositions were DHQ MOLAIN; 138th Inf: Bde MOLAIN Area; 137th Inf: Bde VAUX ANDIGNY Area; 139th Inf: Bde ESCAUFORT Area.

On the morning of the 4th Novr. 138th Inf: Bde moved with head on NORTH and SOUTH road through X 5 d and sent one battalion across the Canal to Area about S 2 b under orders of the 2nd Inf: Bde.

48. On the night 4th/5th Novr. the Division having been ordered to pass through the LEFT of the 1st Division and RIGHT of the 32nd Division and to continue the pursuit, relieved the 1st Inf: Bde by the 138th Inf: Bde, the 137th Inf: Bde being at BOIS DE L'ABBAYE and LA LOUVIERE and the 139th Inf: Bde at CATILLON.

49. The following Divisional Troops were now at the disposal of the GOC, 46th Division.- 1Squadron Greys, 1 Squadron 20th Hussars and one M.G Section, 1 Bde R.G.A, 2 Bdes R.F.A 1 Section (3) Tanks and one platoon IXth Corps Cyclists.

Two Bdes R.F.A were moved across the Canal that night, one Bde being attached to each of the 137th and 139th Inf: Bdes, the remainder of the artillery being under orders of the CRA, 46th Division.

Half a Field Company R.E was attached to each of the above Inf: Bdes. One M.G Company was allotted to each Inf: Bde, the remaining Company being kept in Divisional Reserve.

Some Mounted Troops and Cyclists were allotted to Inf: Bdes.

Two Tanks were sent to 137th Inf: Bde and one to the 139th Inf: Bde.

50. The 138th Inf: Bde was instructed to endeavour to locate enemy during the night by active patrolling and the following orders were issued for action on the 5th.- Mounted Troops to be in position by 0500 and move forward at dawn, covering the whole divisional front and to probe the enemy's defences. If the enemy were met in force, the mounted troops were instructed to withdraw to CATILLON and the 137th and 139th Inf: Bdes were ordered to pass through the 138th and 14th Inf: Bdes respectively at 0800 covered by the Mounted Troops. Should, however, Cavalry have met the enemy in force and been withdrawn, the advance of these Brigades was to be made under cover of artillery barrage; the objectives allotted to the above brigades being -

(a) The road O 26 - N 11.

(b) The line P 20 - O 18 - I 36.

Headquarters for 5th Novr. at 0800 being DHQ MOLAIN, with Advanced Report Centre at L'ARBRE DE GUISE; three Inf: Bdes at BOIS DE L'ABBE.

51. During the early hours of 5th Novr. the 138th Inf: Bde pushed forward to a line GD.TAILLON FME - ZOBEAU, no opposition being met with and during the advance captured four 77 mm, three 10.5 cm guns and four machine guns.

By the evening of the 5th, the 137th Inf: Bde had established a line BARZY - PRISCHES being in touch with the French at BARZY.

Only slight opposition was met with by the 139th Inf: Bde from enemy rearguards and by nightfall an outpost line was established on the Grid Line between N 10 and 11 and N 16 and 17.

52. The advance was resumed on the 6th Novr. the objectives for that day being 137th Inf: Bde the High Ground due SOUTH of CARTIGNIES; the 139th Inf: Bde CARTIGNIES and the bridgehead in O 6.c,5.d and High Ground due NORTH to divisional boundary; whilst the 138th Inf: Bde were instructed to march on the CATILLON-PRISCHES.

At 0730 on the 6th, the advance was resumed each Inf: Bde sending forward one Battalion as Advance Guards.

Only slight resistance was met with by the 137th Inf: Bde, who by the end of the day had gained the whole of their objective.

On the front of the 139th Inf: Bde the enemy held the High Ground NORTH and EAST of PRISCHES in some strength. The attack on this front was therefore carried out under a barrage of 18-pdrs and 4.5" howitzers, which barrage crept forward for one thousand yards; the result being the abandonment by the enemy of these positions.

From now onwards very little resistance was met with and by dusk the objectives allotted to this Brigade had been attained.

53. On the evening of the 6th, the 138th Inf: Bde relieved the 137th and 139th Inf: Bdes and were instructed to push forward on the 7th towards AVESNES, the relieved Inf: Bdes withdrawing to the area WEST of CARTIGNIES to PRISCHES.

54. The 138th Inf: Bde with a Squadron of 20th Hussars and a section of Corps Cyclists, continued the advance towards a line along High Ground Q 13 a - Q 17 d - Q 8 a - Q 7 c - K 33 - K 27 d.

Owing to heavy rain during the previous two or three days the PETIT HELPE was in flood and all bridges had been destroyed by the enemy. The 1/5th Bn, Lincolnshire Regt. however, by collecting carts, etc, and running them into the stream, succeeded in crossing. Later, the detachment of R.Es with the Brigade, constructed a pontoon bridge across and the whole of the Brigade was over by 0900.

Considerable resistance was encountered in the close country S.W of AVESNES and along the AVESNES - ETROEUNGT Road.

The 1/5th Bn, Leicestershire Regt gained the portion of the road in P 19 a, capturing a four gun battery and sixteen prisoners. The French on the RIGHT, were counter attacked and compelled to retire; our RIGHT flank being thus exposed our men withdrew slightly and were compelled to abandon three of the guns.

55. On the evening of the 7th, the situation was as follows - the 138th Inf: Bde held the line - P 17 c and a - P 5 c - P 5 d and a - R 34 c and a, being in touch with the 32nd Division at R 28 c. To protect the RIGHT Flank which was not in touch with the French, a defensive flank was formed by two companies in P 17 c. The 137th Inf: Bde was in the area between P 20 central - O 1 central and the 139th Inf: Bde WEST of the 137th Inf: Bde and EAST of RIVIERETTE River.

56. On the 8th Novr. the 138th Inf: Bde was given orders to advance towards the final objective given them for the 7th and to establish an outpost line EAST of it along the ZOREES - SEMERIES Road. Cavalry and Cyclist patrols sent out at dawn reported enemy holding approximately same positions as before, chief points of resistance being :-

QUART-de-ROUTE (P 24 a) cross roads P 12 a, Houses P 35 c. Owing to the enemy's strong resistance, artillery concentrations were put down at 0830 and 1100 and 60-pdrs co-operated, engaging the High Ground in Q 7. The Armoured Car attached to the 138th Inf: Bde was sent up to assist the 1/5th Bn, Lincolnshire Regt. in the attack, but 'ditched' behind our lines and did not recover in time to take part in the operations.

After several hours of heavy fighting, the enemy's resistance completely broke down and at 1350 our troops advanced without opposition and reached their final objective (Line Q 7 d 0.0 - K 28 central) at 1800. Patrols were at once pushed out and the outpost objective established before dawn on the 9th.

57. On the evening of the 8th, DHQ was established at PRISCHES, the 137th Inf: Bde being in CARTIGNIES and the 139th Inf: Bde at PRISCHES.

58. On 9th Novr. the 138th Inf: Bde was ordered to halt on a general line SAINS DU NORD (Q 11 - Sheet 57 A, 1/40,000) - SEMERIES inclusive; 137th Inf: Bde to close up behind with a view to passing through the 138th Inf: Bde on the pursuit EASTWARDS, and the 139th Inf: Bde had orders to move as soon as possible to BOULOGNE and CARTIGNIES.

59. The dispositions on the night of the 9th/10th Novr. were 138th Inf: Bde outpost line, 137th Inf: Bde in billets SAINS -Du-Nord - SEMERIES(exclusive)- P 16 central - J 34 central, and the 139th Inf: Bde BOULOGNE - CARTIGNIES Area.

60. On 10th Novr. all the Cavalry, and the IXTH Corps Cyclists attached to this Division were transferred to Major-General BETHELL'S FORCE, which force had orders to maintain touch with the retiring enemy, and the 138th Inf: Bde was accordingly ordered to stand fast on the Outpost Line held by them.

SECRET

Headquarters,
46th Division.

137th Bde: C/496.

21 10 18

Ref: map 62.B. N.E.
1/20,000. Ed: 3.A.

I have the honour to submit the following report on the operations of the 137th Infantry Brigade from the 8th October to 18th October, 1918 :-

1/5th South Staffs Rgt.	Lieut: Col: White.
1/6th South Staffs Rgt.	Lieut: Col: Lister, MC.
1/6th North Staffs Rgt.	Lieut: Col: Dowding, DSO. MC.

1. On the night 7th/8th October, 1918, the 137th Infantry Brigade was ordered to be in readiness to support attack to be carried out by the 138th Infantry Brigade at 07.50 hours on the 8th October. The Brigade moved one Battalion to the West side of ST. QUENTIN Canal, and two Battalions to the East side of the Canal, to be in support of the 138th Infantry Brigade, whose progress was not being held up. On the 9th October, the 137th Infantry Brigade moved off at 05.00 hours in further support of the 138th Infantry Brigade. The Brigade was disposed as follows :-

1/6th North Staffs Regt. in advance to MANNEQUIN HILL, with the two other Battalions in rear of this position.

As the advance of the 138th Infantry Brigade progressed the enemy evacuated FRESNOY-le-GRAND, and the 137th Infantry Brigade moved up to MERICOURT area with Brigade Headquarters at SEQUEHART.

II. 10th October. Progress of the advancing Brigade was more difficult, as the enemy offered more resistence. The Brigade moved forward to FRESNOY-le-GRAND area with Brigade Headquarters at BEAUREGARD.

III. 11th October. At 05.30 hours, the Brigade moved forward to relieve the 138th Infantry Brigade who had one Battalion in the line, one in Support, and one Battalion in Reserve. The two Battalions (Support and Reserve) were relieved by the 1/6th North Staffs Rgt. and 1/6th South Staffs Rgt. respectively, but great difficulty was experienced in relieving the 1/5th Leicestershire Rgt., who were in RIQUERVAL WOOD, and could neither advance nor get away to hand over. The 1/5th South Staffs Rgt. obtained communication by Lucas Lamp with the 1/5th Leicestershire Rgt. and informed them of their intention to relieve them. The Battalion advanced at 09.30 hours with two Companies in the line, one in Support and one in Reserve - the Right Company to advance to South-West edge of Wood in D 30 b. and E 25 c.; the Left Company to move to FONTAINE de COLUMBIER and relieve what Companies of the 1/5th Leicestershire Rgt. he might find. One Company in Support, towards centre E 19 c. and occupy trenches. One Company in Reserve about D 29 b.

At 10.30 hours the Right Company was in touch with the enemy on the South West side of the Wood, and held up by machine gun fire, and the Supporting Company was under machine gun fire from RETHEUIL FARM. The Left Company was in position E 19 central to E 13 a 3.5, in touch with the 6th Division.

At 14.25 hours, the Battalion was ordered to attack the trench system in E 19 c. with the aid of a Tank which had to work South and help the Right flank, clear the South West edge of the Wood, and get the Commanding Officer of the 1/5th Leicestershire Rgt. out. This attack was to be at 16.00 hours, but the Tank broke down and could not move. The Battery of R.H.A. bombarded the trenches in E 19 c. and another attack was organised, but as the Company was assembling, the enemy brought down a barrage on them, with the result that the attack failed with several casualties.

At the same time, the Right Company made another attempt to relieve the 1/5th Leicestershire Rgt., but machine gun and artillery fire broke this attack, and also drove the 1/5th Leicestershire Rgt. out, when they were immediately relieved.

The line then ran along high ground as follows :- J 6 a. - D 30 a. - D 24 b. and d. - D 30 a. - D 13 central - across road to D 13 d 2.3. On this line the Battalion consolidated.

IV. 12th October. The Brigade was ordered to attack the Wood in conjunction with the French - Zero hour being 12 noon. The disposition was as follows :-

1/5th South Staffs Rgt.	In the line.
1/6th South Staffs Rgt.	In Support.
1/6th North Staffs Rgt.	In Reserve.

The French barrage came down 5 minutes before ours. The Battalion was held up almost immediately by machine gun fire from the Right flank, and was much disorganised before it reached the Wood. The Battalion pushed on in spite of harassing fire, one Company (Centre) gaining the trenches E 19 central, and the Right Company penetrated to the edge of Wood in D 30 d. and b. Two Companies of the 1/6th South Staffs Rgt. were sent up to help the attack. The Right Company penetrated about 150 yards inside the edge of the Wood in D 30 d. and b. Here the enemy brought down a heavy barrage of machine gun, trench mortar and artillery, and counter - attacked along front E 25 c. to E 19 central causing considerable casualties, and the Battalion was driven out. The French attacked but were unable to dislodge the enemy from RETHEUIL FARM.

At 17.00 hours the 1/6th North Staffs Rgt. relieved the 1/5th South Staffs Rgt. and held the line as before :- J 6 a. - D 30 a. - D 24 b. and d. - D 30 a. - D 13 central - across road to D 13 d 2.3.

V. 13th October. Quiet night 12th/13th October. The 1/6th North Staffs Rgt. in the line, 1/6th South Staffs Rgt. in Support, and the 1/5th South Staffs Rgt. in Reserve.

VI. 14th October. Quiet night 13th/14th October. The 1/6th South Staffs Rgt. relieved the 1/6th North Staffs Rgt. in the line, 1/5th South Staffs Rgt. moved into Support and the 1/6th North Staffs Rgt. into Reserve.

VII. 15th October. Patrols pushed out. Enemy machine guns and snipers active. The 1/5th South Staffs Rgt. relieved the 1/6th South Staffs Rgt. in the Line, the 1/6th North Staffs Rgt. moved into Support, and the 1/6th South Staffs Rgt. into Reserve.

VIII. 16th October. The 1/6th North Staffs Rgt. relieved the 1/5th South Staffs Rgt. in the Line, the 1/5th South Staffs Rgt. moved into Support, and the 1/6th South Staffs Rgt. into Reserve.

IX. 17th October. In preparation for a general attack, the Battalion in the Line withdrew from RIQUERVAL FARM to a line of safety from our barrage.

Dummy figures and Tanks were put up to simulate an attack.

At Zero hour (05.20 hours) our barrage came down followed 10 minutes later by the enemy barrage, which fell in E 13., D 24., D 23 b. and d., and E 18 d., which continued for one hour and 20 minutes. Gas shells were used.

At 07.30 hours, the Battalion moved back to old line, and strong fighting patrols were sent out as far as a line E 19 b. and d. - E 20 c., and E 26 a. and c., and tried to get touch with the French on the Right at RETHEUIL FARM. The line was taken and touch gained with the French at E 26 c. This Battalion pushed on to clear HENNECHIES WOOD, which was done at 14.30 hours and touch gained with French at E 28 a 30.80, and the 1/8th Sherwood Foresters at E 15 c 70.00.

During the clearing of the HENNECHIES WOOD, 20 prisoners, 4 Trench Mortars, 2 Field Guns and a few machine guns were captured.

X. 18th October. The Brigade relieved the 138th Infantry Brigade in the Line as follows :-

1/6th South Staffs Rgt.	Line E 19 b 2.5 - E 11 c 0.8 - E 5 c 7.3 - E 5 a 7.3.
1/5th South Staffs Rgt.	In close support to the 1/6th South Staffs Rgt. about REGNICOURT.
1/6th North Staffs Rgt.	In Reserve.

The Brigade had two Platoons of the Corps Cyclist Battalion, and one troop of Cavalry (Scots Greys) attached.

The Brigade had to maintain touch with the 1st Division on the Left, and the French on the Right.

At 11.30 hours, the attack of the 1st Division and the French Division commenced. The two Cyclist Platoons supported by the 1/6th South Staffs Rgt. were immediately pushed out to fill the gap between the attacking Divisions until they linked up on the line WASSIGNY - BLOCUS d'en BAS - BLOCUS d'en HAUT. Touch was gained with the 1st Division at E 6 d., and with the French Division at cross roads in F 7 d.

At 22.45 hours, the two Divisions had joined hands on the line WASSIGNY - BLOCUS d'en BAS, when the Brigade withdrew to billets in the following areas :-

1/6th North Staffs Rgt.	FRESNOY-le-GRAND.
1/5th South Staffs Rgt.	-ditto-
1/6th South Staffs Rgt.	BOHAIN.

XI. 137th LIGHT TRENCH MORTAR BATTERY. (Lieut: H.Gregory).

Three guns of the Battery were with the Front Battalion during the period under review.

XII. 46th BATTALION, MACHINE GUN CORPS.

One Company was in close support to the Battalion in the line during the period under review.

XIII. ARTILLERY. As observation in the Wood was absolutely impossible, the artillery was not used to any great extent.

XIV. COMMUNICATION. Visual signalling was possible during this period. Although lines were laid to each Battalion, communication by wire was delayed owing to incessant cutting of lines. Runners proved the most reliable means of communication.

XV. GENERAL REMARKS. The Brigade having been in preparation for battle since the 12th September, 1918, and after having fought three big battles, the strain of 8 days continuously in the line commenced to tell on all ranks.

John W. Campbell

Brigadier General.

21-10-18. Commanding 137th Infantry Brigade.

21 10 18

REPORT ON OPERATIONS ON MERICOURT, FRESNOY-le-GRAND, RIQUERVAL WOOD, REGNICOURT & ANDIGNY-les-FERMES.

Reference Map :- ETAVES (Parts of 57.B., 57.C., 62.B., 62.C.) 1/40,000.

On the 7th October the Brigade was disposed on the West of the ST QUENTIN CANAL in the Old German Front Line with instructions to be ready to move at very short notice.

At 22.30. orders were received that the Brigade had to be prepared to move in co-operation with an attack by the 6th Division should it prove successful. Instructions to carry out the above move were received at 23.00. on the 7th instant and the Brigade with M.G. Company and T. M. Battery was ordered to move at 05.00. on the 8th to area about H.14. to 16. and 20. to 22., transport to follow Brigade and assemble on the East side of the CANAL. Brigade Headquarters were to move to MAGNY-la-FOSSE. There was a considerable amount of rain during the night which made it difficult for transport to move across country. Crossing the Canal Bridge the Brigade was shelled slightly.

At 07.20. Battalions reported themselves in position as follows :-

5th LINCOLNSHIRE REGT along Railway in H.16. and 22.
4th LEICESTERSHIRE REGT in H.15. and 21.
5th LEICESTERSHIRE REGT in H.14. and 20.
Brigade Headquarters at MAGNY-la-FOSSE.

During the morning the 5th LEICESTERSHIRE REGT were moved to the ~~right~~ South of the 4th LEICESTERSHIRE REGT in H.21.d.

The attack of the 6th Division on the high ground round MANNEQUIN HILL and DOON HILL was successful and they eventually reached a line running approximately N. & S. through I. central exclusive of MERICOURT.

In the evening of the 8th the Division issued instructions that the Brigade would relieve the 16th Infantry Brigade in the line from the junction of the French about I.27. to as far North as the grid line I.9. central with instructions to be prepared to push forward and capture MERICOURT and FRESNOY-le-GRAND, in conjunction with 6th Division who had received orders to attack and capture JONNECOURT FARM in I.6. central.

During the night of the 8th/9th the Brigade Commander verbally gave instructions to all Battalion Commanders in regard to the relief of the 16th. Infantry Brigade, and this was completed by 07.00. on the 9th instant under very difficult circumstances, as the Battalion Commanders had very little idea where their front line was, whilst the enemy were continually shelling the area with gas shells and H.E. ~~the area~~.

At that hour the dispositions of the Brigade were as follows :-

5th LEICESTERSHIRE REGT on the Right from about I.27.d. in touch with French.
5th LINCOLNSHIRE REGT in the Centre.
4th LEICESTERSHIRE REGT on the Left in touch with the 6th Division at I.9. central.
Brigade Headquarters in the neighbourhood of PREOELLES FARM.

The attack of the 6th Division took place at 05.20. on the morning of the 9th instant.

At 07.20. 3 Companies of the 5th LEICESTERSHIRE REGT pushed forward and occupied MERICOURT.

At 08.26. the 4th LEICESTERSHIRE REGT had pushed on and occupied GORDON COPSE and SUNKEN ROAD in I.10.c. and had pushed patrols out in the direction of FRESNOY-le-GRAND. It was then obvious that the enemy was retiring and instructions were sent out to this effect and that the advance must be pushed on with all expedition.

At 08.45. received word that ~~our~~ the Battalions had entered FRESNOY-le-GRAND and were pushing on through the village to the Railway.

At 11.00. Brigade Headquarters were moved to MERICOURT, and it was ascertained that the battalions had passed right through the village of FRESNOY-le-GRAND and were being met by M.G. fire from the Railway in the neighbourhood of the station. At this time FRESNOY-le-GRAND was being heavily bombarded by the enemy and they were intermittently putting down a barrage on the N.E. side of the village.

At 18.00. the 5th LEICESTERSHIRE REGT reported that the enemy's M.G. opposition had been overcome and that the whole of the Brigade objective had been gained. The 5th LINCOLNSHIRE REGT were then ordered to take over the whole of the Brigade front in touch with the French on the right in about J.13.d. and in touch with the 6th Division on the left on the FRESNOY-BOHAIN Road about J.2.a.

During the afternoon of the 9th instant, a troop of cavalry (SCOTS GREYS) reported for attachment. These were to be used for patrol work.

At 18.00. dispositions of the Brigade were as follows :-

5th LINCOLNSHIRE REGT on Railway from J.13.d. to J.2.a.
4th LEICESTERSHIRE REGT in FRESNOY Village.
5th LEICESTERSHIRE REGT on high ground in MERICOURT and BEAUREGARD.

Brigade Headquarters were established in BEAUREGARD FARM.

At 23.25. patrols of the 5th LINCOLNSHIRE REGT were being pushed out to ~~establish~~ SECURE the SEBONCOURT-BOHAIN Road and gain touch with the 6th Division on the left and the French on the right.

Early on the morning of the 10th the cavalry had pushed forward patrols, gained the SEBONCOURT-BOHAIN Road and reached the Farm in J.5.a. and had returned via BOHAIN Village.

At 09.15. THE 5th LINCS reported that they were on the SEBONCOURT-BOHAIN Road and the 4th LEICESTERSHIRE REGT were instructed to pass through and make good the AISONVILLE-BOHAIN Road.

At 12.00. the 4th LEICESTERSHIRE REGT established position on the AISONVILLE-BOHAIN Road in D.30. and D.22. and had pushed out patrols to get in touch with enemy in BOIS de RIQUERVAL. They reported that they had come in contact with enemy who were holding the edge of the wood with M.G's.

At 16.00. patrols of the Corps Cyclists, who had been attached to the Brigade reconnoitred the BOHAIN-REGNICOURT Road and reported that they had come in touch with the enemy at REGNICOURT.

At 18.00. the 5th LEICESTERSHIRE REGT were instructed to relieve the 4th LEICESTERSHIRE REGT in the forward positions and to establish a line on the edge of the BOIS de RIQUERVAL from about D.30.d. to D.23.d. and to push up 2 Companies along the REGNICOURT-BOHAIN Road and get in touch with the 6th Division who reported that they had gained E.13. central. They were also instructed to get in touch with the French at RETHEUIL FARM with an Officer's patrol.

At 19.50. on the 10th dispositions of the Brigade were as follows :-

5th LEICESTERSHIRE REGT - 2 Companies in BOIS de RIQUERVAL on grid line running through E.13. to 19. central, 1 Company in D.24.a. and 1 Company in D.30.b.
4th LEICESTERSHIRE REGT. - 4 Companies on AISONVILLE-BOHAIN Road.
5th LINCOLNSHIRE REGT. - on SEBONCOURT-BOHAIN Road.
Machine Gun Company attached were disposed on high ground in J.4. and D.28.
Cavalry Troop in LANDRICOURT WOOD in J.9.c.
Brigade Headquarters on Railway embankment in J.2.c.

/3.

5th LEICESTERSHIRE REGT had heavy fighting in the BOIS de RIQUERVAL and at dusk had to withdraw the Company in D.24.c. and D.30.b. to the AISONVILLE-BOHAIN Road.

At 21.32. instructions were received that during the night the Brigade would be relieved by the 137th. Infantry Brigade.

The 5th SOUTH STAFFORDSHIRE REGT had been placed at the disposal of the B.G.C. 138th. Infantry Brigade and at 21.32. they were instructed to relieve the 5th LEICESTERSHIRE REGT in the Front Line, relief to be completed by 07.00. At the same time they were told that before relief the 5th LEICESTERSHIRE REGT would establish a line through E.20.d. to REGNICOURT. Relief of the 2 Left Companies of the 5th LEICESTERSHIRE REGT was carried out but the Headquarters and the 2 Right Companies of the 5th LEICESTERSHIRE REGT were not able to be relieved owing to daylight and they were consequently forced to remain in their positions until dusk.

During the day they had very heavy fighting and captured the house on the edge of the BOIS de RIQUERVAL in E.25.c. The Headquarters of the Battalion only had reached the wood, the 2 Companies not being able to get as far. The Headquarters thus found themselves isolated with the enemy on both sides of them. During the early hours of the morning, reinforced by about 9 or 10 Frenchmen with 2 mitrailleuses, they attacked the house in E.25.c. and captured it but in hand-to-hand fighting were later driven out and eventually were compelled to withdraw on to the AISONVILLE-BOHAIN Road.

The relief by the 137th. Infantry Brigade was not completed by 07.00. but the B.G.C. of the 137th. Infantry Brigade expressed himself satisfied and took over command of the front from 09.00.

The Brigade, less Headquarters and 2 Companies of the 5th LEICESTERSHIRE REGT, concentrated in FRESNOY-le-GRAND. The Headquarters and 2 Companies of the 5th LEICESTERSHIRE REGT joining at night.

These operations were most successful; the methods of open warfare that the Brigade had been practised in were found to have been well assimilated by both Officers and men. Casualties were few, and these mostly occurred on the last day when the Battalions were trying to make the BOIS de RIQUERVAL.

Communications are the greatest difficulty that Battalions appear to have to contend with: Messages from front line Companies taking at least 3 and 4 hours to come back to Brigade Headquarters. Visual was not sufficiently practised, Companies relying too much on Runners, who are as a rule very slow.

On October 12th, 13th, 14th, 15th, and 16th the Brigade remained in FRESNOY-le-GRAND.

On the 14th instant received instructions at a Conference held at Divisional Headquarters that the Brigade would be required to attack in conjunction with the French on the Right and the 6th Division on the Left from the BOHAIN-VAUX ANDIGNY Road in a south easterly direction to ANDIGNY-les-FERMES.

The attack took place at 05.20. on the 17th instant and during the night of the 16th/17th the Battalions moved from FRESNOY-le-GRAND to their assembly positions.

During this time the enemy shelled the assembly area with H.E. and gas shells.

The Brigade attack was to be carried out through the line of British trenches running through E.7., E.1.b. & d. and W.25.b. & d. trenches at that time being held by units of the 6th Division. These were withdrawn at ZERO minus 1 hour.

The Brigade had attached to them a company of Machine Guns, and 3 Tanks were allotted to the Division.

At ZERO minus 1 hour the Brigade was formed up as follows :-

/4.

4th LEICESTERSHIRE REGT on the right from E.1.a.2.8. to W.25. central with the 139th. Infantry Brigade on the Right.

5th LINCOLNSHIRE REGT from W.25. central to W.26.a.2.8. in touch with the 6th Division, on the Left.

5th LEICESTERSHIRE REGT were in Reserve in V.30.b.

Each of the front line battalions had a section of M.G's and the 5th LINCOLNSHIRE REGT had a section of T.M's attached to them.

The objective of the attack was from E.9.c.6.4. to E.11.a.2.8. with instructions to push out and establish platoon posts some 200 yards in front of this line.

Brigade Headquarters were established at D.11. central.

The attack took place in a dense fog which made the difficulties of keeping direction and communication very great.

At 07.00. the O.C. 4th LEICESTERSHIRE REGT reported he had under his command elements of CAMERONS, BLACK WATCH, N. LANCS, SHERWOODS, and 5th LINCOLNSHIRES in the area E.1.b.

At 06.54. it was reported that we had reached the REGNICOURT -ANDIGNY-les-FERMES Road and that several enemy M.G's had not been properly mopped up and were still firing from the Old German Front Line in E.2.a. & b. There was also considerable M.G. fire from BELLE-VUE and les GOBELETS. All this opposition was however eventually overcome and at 11.30. it was reported that ANDIGNY-les-FERMES was in our hands. Previous to this at 10.15. 2 Companies of the Reserve Battalion (5th LEICESTERSHIRE REGT) had received instructions to move forward via the high ground in W.26.b., W.27.c. and E.3.b. and mop up BELLE-VUE and les GOBELETS. This move was however cancelled as the opposition from this ridge had been overcome by the 6th Division, and the 2 Companies of the 5th LEICESTERSHIRE REGT were ordered to concentrate in the Old German Front Line and placed under the command of the O.C. 5th LINCOLNSHIRE REGT with instructions that he could use them for exploiting the success down the ANDIGNY-les-FERMES-MENNEVRET Road and if possible get in touch with the French at LA NATION in E.17.b.

At 16.40. the dispositions of the Brigade were as follows :-

5th LINCOLNSHIRE REGT - 3 Companies round E. & S. of ANDIGNY-les-FERMES. 1 Company in E.4.c.8.0. Headquarters E.2.b.4.7.

4th LEICESTERSHIRE REGT - 1 Company at E.9.c.3.3., 1 Company E.9.c.5.7. with post at E.9.c.7.2., 1 Company E.9.a.2.3., 1 Company at E.9.a.7.5. with Headquarters at E.2. central.

5th LEICESTERSHIRE REGT with Headquarters and 1½ Coys at V.30.a., 1 Company Old German Front Line about E.2.b., 1 Company patrolling the ANDIGNY-les-FERMES-MENNEVRET Road, 2 Platoons with 5th LINCOLNSHIRE REGT.

Machine Gun Company had 8 guns disposed in front of the objective, 1 section in E.9.b. and 1 section in E.8.a. covering les GOBELETS FARM.

At 17.50. orders were issued that the 5th LEICESTERSHIRE REGT would take over the FRONT LINE from the 4th LEICESTERSHIRE REGT and 5th LINCOLNSHIRE REGT.

At 19.00. the Company of the 5th LEICESTERSHIRE REGT which had been sent down the ANDIGNY-les-FERMES-MENNEVRET Road reported that they had met with M.G. fire from about E.11. central; They were instructed to keep trying and if possible get in touch with the French who were working up through MENNEVRET.

The dispositions of the Brigade after the 5th LEICESTERSHIRE REGT had taken over the front line were as follows :-

5th LEICESTERSHIRE REGT on the FRONT LINE from E.9.c.5.3. to E.11.a.2.8. held by 3 Companies, 1 Company patrolling down the ANDIGNY-les-FERMES-MENNEVRET Road. Headquarters at E.2. central.

5th LINCOLNSHIRE REGT in Sunken Road in E.2. with Headquarters in E.2.b.4.7.

4th LEICESTERSHIRE REGT in Old German Front Line with Headquarters at VALLEE HASSARD, D.6.b.6.6.

At 00.40. on the 18th instructions were received that the Brigade would have to take over a battalion front of the 1st Division, who had passed through the 6th Division and were now on our left flank. 2 sections of M.G's were given to the Brigade for the purpose of this relief.

The 5th LEICESTERSHIRE REGT were ordered to move 1 Company from the right flank to take over this battalion front - relief to be completed by 06.00. M.G's were disposed in E.5.c.

During the night our patrols on the ANDIGNY-les-FERMES - MENNEVRET Road ~~had~~ reached LA NATION Cross Roads but ~~had been~~ WERE unable to remain there on account of the enemy's bombing parties and it was not until 05.30. on the 18th that definite touch was established with the French at this point. The 2 Companies defending ANDIGNY-les-FERMES and area in E.5.c. were told to link up with the French and establish a line through E.11.c., E.11.a. and E.5.c. The Company from E.9.c. was moved up to the East of ANDIGNY-les-FERMES.

At 10.20. on the 18th instructions were received that the Brigade would be relieved by the 137th. Infantry Brigade during the course of the morning. This was eventually completed by 14.15. and the Brigade marched back to FRESNOY-le-GRAND.

F. G. Edwards.

Lieut Colonel,

Commanding 138th. Infantry Brigade.

21st October 1918.

31.10.18

SECRET

Headquarters,
46th: Division.

At 5 p.m. on October 2nd: orders were received that the 46th: Division would make an attack at Daybreak the following day in conjunction with the Australian Corps on the Left, and 32nd: Division on the Right.

The Field Artillery to cover the advance of the 32nd and 46th: Divisions, consisting of 8 Brigadesof R.F. . and 1 Brigade of R.H.A. was placed under the Command of the C.R.A. 46th: Division.

Five of these Brigades - 16th: Army Brigade R.H.A., 14th: Army Brigade R.F.A., 23rd: Army Brigade R.F.A., 161st: Brigade R.F.A. and 168th: Brigade R.F.A. were already in action on the front of the attack - the remaining 4 Brigades - 5th: Army Brigade R.F.A., 230th: and 231st: Brigades R.F.A., and 232nd: Army Brigade R.F.A. were in positions in reserve some distance West of the ST QUENTIN Canal. It was decided that the 5 Brigades already in action should cover the whole front of the attack, and that the Brigades which had to move forward should be given zones superimposed over the other Brigades.

With this object in view verbal instructions were immediately sent out to the Officers Commanding 230th:, 231st: and 5th: Army Brigades R.F.A. to make an immediate reconnaissance of possible Battery Positions within about 2.000 yards of the Front Line, and to make the necessary arrangements to get their Batteries into action, with ammunition dumped and communications established during the night, so as to be able to open fire in the initial barrage, or as soon after as possible.

The 232nd: Army Brigade R.F.A. was considerably further away, and was not in telephonic communication with Divisional Artillery Headquarters. Orders were therefore sent to the Brigade Commanders to make any reconnaissance which he considered necessary of the Bridges over the Canal and routesto the forward area, and to have his Brigade East of the Canal by 6 a.m., with reconnoitring parties well in front, and to come into action in the vicinity of the FONSOMME - BEAUREVOIR Line, S.E. of JONCOURT, as soon as possible after the Infantry had advanced.

Owing to the lateness of the hour, and the very limited time available, it was impossible to issue an elaborate barrage map. A map however, was attached to each copy of the Operation Orders which were issued, showing the exact zone to be covered by each Brigade in the Barrage and giving the various lines on which the barrage halted for long periods.

The Brigades which were moving up from rear positions were given instructions that if they were not able to open fire on the initial barrage line they must take up their zone in the Barrage at whatever point it had reached when they were ready to open fire, but in order to give a safety margin, 18 Pdrs: were to place their fire 200 yards in advance of the Barrage Line,

continued.

and 4.5" Hows:

and 4.5" Hows: 400 yards in advance of the Barrage Line.

To explain the great difficulties to be contended with by the Artillery in this operation, it should be noted that the Brigade and Battery Commanders received their verbal instructions little more than 1 hour before dark, so that most of the reconnaissance work was actually done in the dark, which as far as the Brigades not already in action were concerned, included the selection of Battery Positions, Brigade and Group Headquarters, and the establishing of communications. In addition to this, it was found necessary to move the Division and Divisional Artillery Headquarters, during the night, to LA BARACQUE a distance of about 5 Miles. There was also the difficulty of sending the orders and maps to Brigades, which were on the move. Owing however, to the magnificient work of Brigade and Battery Staffs, and of the Signal department, all Brigades, with the exception of the 232nd: Army Brigade R.F.A., which was moving, were in position and ready to open fire, and Communications were established with all Units, at least an hour before ZERO (6.5 a.m.).

The Infantry report that the Barrage though a bit uneven, and with some short rounds, was extremely good and very effective.

The Barrage was arranged in depth - 4.5" Hows: firing 106 Fuze, 200 yards in front of the 18 Pdr:, and 6" Hows: crept forward in front of the 4.5" Hows:. On the Protective Barrage Line being reached various targets were detailed for the 4.5" Hows:.

The Heavy Artillery in addition to firing in advance of the Creeping Barrage with 6" Hows:, Bombarded the Villages of SEQUEHART, RAMICOURT and MONTBREHAIN with Heavy Hows:, and engaged the various approaches and commanding features in the area with 60 Pdrs: and 6" Hows:.

The Field Artillery for this operation was grouped as follows :-

LEFT GROUP Lieutenant Colonel J.H.W. TAPP. R.F.A.	RIGHT GROUP (H.Qrs: 32nd: D.A. - Lieut-Colonel CARRINGTON)
230th: Brigade R.F.A.	161st: Brigade R.F.A.
231st: Brigade R.F.A.	168th: Brigade R.F.A.
232nd: Army Brigade R.F.A.	5th: Army Brigade R.F.A.
14th: Army Brigade R.F.A.	23rd: Army Brigade R.F.A.
	16th: Army Brigade R.H.A.

The operation as far as the 46th: Division was concerned was quite successful, but early in the day the Australians on the Left got held up. The 32nd: Division was also counter attacked and driven out of SEQUEHART, (which they retook later in the day,) thus leaving both flanks of the 46th: Division in the air.

At 9.45 a.m. it was reported that our Infantry were in MONTBREHAIN, and orders were sent to both Groups to move forward 2 Batteries into the area West of RAMICOURT.

One 18 Pdr: and One 4.5" How: Battery of LEFT Group, and one 18 Pdr: and one 13 Pdr: Battery of RIGHT Group went forward.

continued.

CONTINUED (3)

At about this time a German Battery was reported firing from BEAUREGARD, and another from the vicinity of DOON HILL. These were engaged by 6" Hows:.

Several reports were received of the enemy massing at various points, and these were immediately engaged by Heavy and Field Artillery. At about 4 p.m. it was reported that we had been driven out of MONTBREHAIN. At about 6.30 p.m. information was received that a gap had been made in the line held by our Right Infantry Brigade, South of RAMICOURT, and that the enemy were breaking through. In order to close the Gap a very heavy Barrage was immediately put down by both groups of Field Artillery and by the Heavy Artillery, until the situation had been cleared up.

--:--:--

The 46th. Division on October 17th: attacked REGNICOURT and ANDIGNY les FERMES in conjunction with the 6th: Division on the Left and the French on the Right.

The Field Artillery supporting this operation was composed of the following Brigades grouped as under :-

RIGHT GROUP.
Commanded by Lieutenant Colonel N.G.M. JERVIS. R.F.A.

5th: Army Brigade R.H.A. 16th: Army Brigade R.F.A. 231st: Brigade R.F.A.	) Affiliated to) 139th: Infantry) Brigade.

LEFT GROUP.
Commanded by Lieutenant Colonel J.H.W. TAPP. R.F.A.

23rd: Army Brigade R.F.A. 230th: Brigade R.F.A.	) Affiliated to) 138th: Infantry Brigade.

16th: Army Brigade R.H.A. Commanded by Major A.W. VAN STRAUBENZEE. D.S.O. M.C. supporting the 137th: Infantry Brigade.

Owing to the very restricted area available for Battery positions, it was impossible to arrange for a frontal fire barrage.

The Batteries were therefore, placed as near as possible in direct enfilade of the line of attack, and a creeping barrage of enfilade fire was arranged. The 18 Pdr: Barrage was put down on 2 parallel lines 100 yards apart, each line leap frogging over the one in front of it every alternate lift. The idea of this was to have a barrage in depth and give Batteries more time between each switch.

A Creeping Barrage of 4.5" Hows: firing 106 fuze was put down 200 yards in advance of the forward line of the 18 Pdr: Barrage. Both 18 Pdrs. and 4.5" Hows: fired a small percentage of Smoke Shell.

The Infantry report that the Barrage appeared to be accurate and effective, but owing to the men being accustomed to hearing the shells coming over their heads they were inclined to lose direction. This difficulty was considerably increased by a very thick ground mist which was intensified by the smoke of the

Barrage drifting back with the South wind.

On the Protective Barrage Line being reached, a Section of 18 Pdrs: of the 231st: Brigade R.F.A. from the Right Group, and of the 230th, Brigade R.F.A. from the Left Group, were sent forward to closely support the Infantry. These Sections apparently did very good work silencing Machine Guns, but great difficulty was experienced owing to the mist, in obtaining observation, and as our Infantry had got very much mixed up, it was difficult for the Artillery Officers to find out exactly what points were held by us, and what by the enemy.

Earlyin the day the 14th, Army Brigade R.F.A. were ordered to move forward to positions South East of REGNICOURT. Owing to this Brigade having their Wagon Lines at some distance from their Battery Positions considerable delay was caused, and all the Batteries were not in action intheir new positions till nearly 4 o'clock.

During this attack the 16th, Army Brigade R.H.A. had supported the 137th, Infantry Brigade in a dummy attack on MICQUERVAL WOOD from the West. This was most successful and drew a heavy barrage on to that front.

At about 3 p.m. the 230th, Brigade R.F.A. and one Battery of the 16th, Army Brigade R.H.A. were ordered to move forward in close support and occupied positions between GUYOT FARM and REGNICOURT.

[signature]

Brigadier General.
C.R.A. 46th, Division.

Headquarters R.A.
30/10/18

War Diary

App 25

Secret.

Copy No. 17

Operation "D".

46th Division Instructions No. 2.

46th Division G.115/14. 7th October, 1918.

1. The 46th Division will be the leading Division of the Reserves of the IX Corps.

2. With reference to Instructions No. 1, para. 2. The 137th and 138th Infantry Brigades will hold themselves in immediate readiness to move to these positions from Zero Hour; but will not move pending instructions from DHQ.
Para. 6 of the above Instructions is cancelled.

S. Hay Muir
for.
Lieut-Colonel,
General Staff, 46th Division..

Issued at 1530
To all recipients of Instructions No. 1 (Copies as before).

War Diary

App 26

SECRET.

Copy No. 17

Operation "D".

46th Division Instructions No. 3.

46th Division G.115/16. 7th October, 1918.

1. 46th Divisional Report Centre will open at 0515, 8th October; Divisional Headquarters remaining in its present location.

2. Each Infantry Brigade will send a mounted officer or NCO to the Report Centre by this hour.

3. The 138th Infantry Brigade will move forward at 0500 to its position of assembly WEST of FRESELLES.

4. The transport of the 138th and 137th Infantry Brigades will move to the EAST Bank of the CANAL commencing at 0500.- 138th Infantry Brigade transport clearing the Bridges first.
All Bridges, except the main BELLENGLISE Bridges may be used.

[signature]

Lieut-Colonel,
General Staff, 46th Division....

Issued at 2000

Copies to all recipients of Instructions No. 1 (Copies as before).

Secret.

Reference 46th DIVISION ORDER No. 329.
dated 1st October, 1918.

137th Bde Group. To "Remainder RFA" add "less DAC".
Add "A" Coy, Div'l Train."

138th Bde Group. Add "DAC"
"B", "C", "D" Coys, Div'l Train."

Lieut-Colonel,
General Staff, 46th Division.

Issued at 2000, 1st October, 1918,
To all recipients of 46th Division Order No. 329.

"A" Form.

Army Form C. 2121.
(In pads of 100.)

MESSAGES AND SIGNALS.

No. of Message............

Prefix.........Code..........m. | Words. | Charge.

Office of Origin and Service Instructions.

Priority.

Sent
At.............m.
To..............
By..............

This message is on a/c of:
War Service.
Diary
(Signature of "Franking Officer.")

Recd. at.......m.
Date..........
From..........
By............

TO 137 Bde
Q.

Sender's Number.	Day of Month.	In reply to Number.	
* G.465	18		AAA

Bns of 137 at BOHAIN and REGNICOURT may
return to billets at FRESNOY forthwith AAA
Bns in line will be withdrawn to BOHAIN
or such other place as GOC 137 may select
when 1 Div and French join AAA Information
on this later

From 46 Div
Place
Time 1830

The above may be forwarded as now corrected.

Censor.

(Z) (sd) C.F.Jerram Lt-Col.

Signature of Addressor or person authorised to telegraph in his name.

*This line, except **AAA**, should be erased if not required.

Wt. W 3253/P511. 500,000 Pads. 1/18. B. & S. Ltd. (E2389.)

"A" Form.

Army Form C. 2121.
(In pads of 100.)

MESSAGES AND SIGNALS.

No. of Message............

Prefix .... Code .... m. | Words. | Charge.

Office of Origin and Service Instructions.

Priority

137

Sent
At............m.
To............
By............

This message is on a/c of: War Service.

Diary

(Signature of "Franking Officer.")

Recd. at ...... m.
Date............
From............
By............

TO			
137		Q	
1 Div.		CRA	
126 French Div			

Sender's Number.	Day of Month.	In reply to Number.	AAA
* G.465	18		

The 1st Div and 126 French Div are now in touch at WASSIGNY and the mission of 46 Div ceases AAA All troops of and attached to 137 Bde less artillery will withdraw to billets forthwith AAA Orders for Artillery have been issued by CRA AAA Addsd 137 rptd those concerned

From 46 Div

Place 2125

Time

The above may be forwarded as now corrected.

(Z)

Censor.

(sd) C.F.JERRAM Lt-Col. G.S.

Signature of Addressor or person authorised to telegraph in his name.

*This line, except AAA, should be erased if not required.

Wt. W 3253/P511. 500,000 Pads. 1/18. B. & S. Ltd. (E2389.)

On His Majesty's Service.

War Diaries

Secret & Confidential

DAG

3rd Echelon

Base

17/2

HQ G.S 46 Div

Vol 45

November 18

Army Form C. 2118.

Instructions regarding War Diaries and Intelligence Summaries are contained in F. S. Regs., Part II. and the Staff Manual respectively. Title pages will be prepared in manuscript.

WAR DIARY
or
INTELLIGENCE SUMMARY.
(Erase heading not required.)

Place	Date	Hour	Summary of Events and Information	Remarks and references to Appendices
			Month of November 1918.	
			Division in Rest with Headquarters at BOHAIN.	

(A7092). Wt. W12839/M1293. 750,000. 1/17. D. D. & L., Ltd. Forms/C.2118/24.

Instructions regarding War Diaries and Intelligence Summaries are contained in F. S. Regs., Part II. and the Staff Manual respectively. Title pages will be prepared in manuscript.

WAR DIARY
or
INTELLIGENCE SUMMARY.
(*Erase heading not required.*)

Army Form C. 2118.

Place	Date	Hour	Summary of Events and Information	Remarks and references to Appendices
BOHAIN	NOV. 1		Division resting Headquarters at BOHAIN	
	2		DIVISION resting Headquarters at BOHAIN	
	3		Division moving to places of assembly (vide 46 Div. Instruction No 2) order No 335 Appendix No 1 Division Headquarters at BOHAIN	App 1
			46 Division Instructions No. 3	App 2.
MOLAIN	4		Division Headquarters MOLAIN with three Brigade HQs at L'Arbre de GUISE.	App 3
			46 Div. Instruction No 5 (App 3) Relieving of 1st Division. The 138 Bde. to move at once with head on N-S Road through X5 D Order G 633 App 4	app 4.
			138 Bde will move one Bn across Canal to S 26 and come under Orders of 2nd Inf Bde 139 will move to S2.d8.7. Order 636. (app 5)	App 5
			138 Bde will relieve left Bde 1st Div Bde HQs at Bois de L'ABBAYE Order 645 (App 6.) 137 Bde HQ at Bois de L'ABBAYE.	app 6
L'Arbre de GUISE	5		Line for night: BARZY - PRISCHES. 137 Bde to get in touch with French about Barzy 139 Bde with 32 Div about N5 C00. Squadron 20th Huss. placed under 137 Bde each less one troop - advance under orders of 139 Bde Greys under 137 Bde. to continue tomorrow Cav. to cross line at dawn Prisches to be taken tonight. Objectives for tomorrow vide (Order 693 App 7)	app 7
			Divisional Headquarters ~~at~~ ~~[illegible]~~ L'ARBRE de GUISE	

(A7092). Wt. W12839/M1293. 750,000. 1/17. D. D. & L., Ltd. Forms/C.2118/14.

Instructions regarding War Diaries and Intelligence Summaries are contained in F. S. Regs., Part II. and the Staff Manual respectively. Title pages will be prepared in manuscript.

WAR DIARY
or
INTELLIGENCE SUMMARY.
(*Erase heading not required.*)

Army Form C. 2118.

Place	Date	Hour	Summary of Events and Information	Remarks and references to Appendices
1918 NOV	6		Divisional Headquarters to CATILLION	
CATILLION			46 Div has orders to push forward to AVESNES 137 Bde and 139 Bde in the line after objectives have been taken 138 will push through with this object. 2 armoured cars 2 troops Cavalry 1 Batt 6" How 2-60 pdrs and all field guns will be attached to 138 for this move (Order GA 1)(App 8)	App 8.
			When objectives allotted 137 & 139 Bdes have be reached 138 Bde will in accordance verbal instruction already issued will push forward to AVESNES. Mtd troops Armoured cars supported by one Bn Infantry Coy 138 Bde will take over line to night held by 137 and 139 Bdes. H.Q. main body 138 Bde CARTIGNIES 137 & 139 on relief will withdraw to W. of CARTIGNIES to PRISCHES and 139 Bde North of 137 Bde HQs of both Bdes PRISCHES (Order G723 app 9)	app 9
			138 Bde having relieved 137 and 139 Bdes will push on tomorrow towards AVESNES Sqd Grays at disposal of 138 Bde (Order G728 app 10)	app 10
			Objectives (Ref G728) for tomorrow of 138 Bde High ground Q13 a Q9 d Q8 a Q2 c K33 K27 d. (Order G733 App 11) 138 Bde will have at their disposal tomorrow troop of Scots Greys & one troop 20 Hussars (Order G735 app 12)	app 11 app 12

(A7092). Wt. W12839/M1293. 750,000. 1/17. D. D. & L., Ltd. Forms/C.2118/14.

Army Form C. 2118.

WAR DIARY
or
INTELLIGENCE SUMMARY.
(Erase heading not required.)

Instructions regarding War Diaries and Intelligence Summaries are contained in F. S. Regs., Part II. and the Staff Manual respectively. Title pages will be prepared in manuscript.

Place	Date	Hour	Summary of Events and Information	Remarks and references to Appendices
PRISCHES N17 Sheet 57A (1:40000)			G850 orders Cavalry to hold line Eastwards of railway R10a to LIESSIES inclusive whilst 138th Bde continue to hold infantry outpost line as laid down in previous appendix. Infantry will not be moving forward tomorrow.	App 17
			G839 Dispositions: D.H.Q. remain at PRISCHES for the present with Advanced Report Centre at P3a CARTIGNIES.	App 18
	10th		At midday all Cavalry and IX Corps Cyclists attached to the Division became detached and constitute part of BETHELLS FORCE – a force, composed of various arms of the service, fitted to maintain touch with the retiring enemy. This force renders a further advance by IX Corps unnecessary and 138th Bde are ordered under 46th Div. Order no. 337 to maintain the outpost line already held by them. Owing to the constant	App 19

(A7092). Wt. W12839/M1293. 750,000. 1/17. D. D. & L., Ltd. Forms/C.2118/14.

Instructions regarding War Diaries and Intelligence Summaries are contained in F. S. Regs., Part II. and the Staff Manual respectively. Title pages will be prepared in manuscript.

WAR DIARY
or
INTELLIGENCE SUMMARY.
(Erase heading not required.)

Army Form C. 2118.

Place	Date Nov	Hour	Summary of Events and Information	Remarks and references to Appendices
CATILLON	7		Orders for tomorrow 138 Bde continue its objective if not taken - consolidate outpost position Cavalry in advance 3rd 20 Hussars to relieve Scot Greys now with 138 Bde (Order 764 app 13)	App 13
			Dispositions by to night will be 138 Bde group on line E of CARTIGNIES 137 between lines P30 Cent I35 Central O28 Central O1 Central B HQs CARTIGNIES (Order 753 app 14)	app 14
PRISCHES	8		Divisional HQ at PRISCHES Brigades as follows 139 PRISCHES 137 CARTIGNIES 138 Bde in the line H.Q. CARTIGNIES.	
			Orders for November 9th including relief of 138th Bde by 137th Bde. 138th given orders to complete capture of todays objective	App 15
			Caaa.	
	9th		G829 Cancels the relief of 138th Bde by 137th Bde. 138th Bde are ordered to halt on general line SAINS DU NORD (Q11 Sheet 57A 1:40000) - SEMERIES. inclusive. 137th Bde to close up behind with a view to passing through 138th Bde on the march	app 16

(A7092). Wt. W12839/M1293. 750,000. 1/17. D. D. & L., Ltd. Forms/C.2118/14.

Instructions regarding War Diaries and Intelligence Summaries are contained in F. S. Regs., Part II. and the Staff Manual respectively. Title pages will be prepared in manuscript.

WAR DIARY
or
INTELLIGENCE SUMMARY.
(Erase heading not required.)

Army Form C. 2118.

Place	Date	Hour	Summary of Events and Information	Remarks and references to Appendices
PRISCHES			destruction of railways in the back area by fuse delay action mines and the enemy's thorough system of destroying all bridges and blowing up most of the cross roads on his line of retreat the feeding of our advanced troops has become a serious problem. It is the difficulty of supply that is hampering our advance. The enemy's defensive policy is of a nature that shows clearly that he has no intention of attempting an organised resistance – yet at any rate. He is attempting to hold us off by means of M.G. posts placed in carefully selected positions for a sufficient length of time to allow his main body to retire in order. He is carrying out a vast and well managed rear guard action. His artillery fire is negligible except for short bursts of fire which are generally directed against the main roads	

(A7092). Wt. W12839/M1293. 750,000. 1/17. D. D. & L., Ltd. Forms/C.2118/14.

Army Form C. 2118.

WAR DIARY
or
INTELLIGENCE SUMMARY.

(Erase heading not required.)

Instructions regarding War Diaries and Intelligence Summaries are contained in F. S. Regs., Part II. and the Staff Manual respectively. Title pages will be prepared in manuscript.

Place	Date	Hour	Summary of Events and Information	Remarks and references to Appendices
PRISCHES	10 (Contd.)		46th Div. Order No. 338 refers to the entrance of the 1st Australian Division into the line and resultant relief. AAA	App 20
	11		At 11 am hostilities ceased on the whole western front – the German Delegates & German Government having agreed to the terms of an armistice dictated by Marshal FOCH. 138th Bde outpost line continues to be held. Disposition of Brigades is as shewn in App 21. DHQ closed at PRISCHES at 12 midday and opened at the same time at SAINS du NORD (Q11). Orders re cessation of hostilities sent out under G893 AAA	App 21 App 22
SAINS du NORD (Q11 Sheet 57A 1:40000)	12		Dispositions remain unchanged: outpost line still held by 138th Bde. Orders were received from IX Corps that the Division is to move commencing to	

(A7092). Wt. W12839/M1293. 750,000. 1/17. D. D. & L., Ltd. Forms/C.2118/14.

Words "inclusive to 137th Inf. Bde should, I think read "inclusive to 139th Inf: Bde." See Map "A" & also orders of 1/6 Sherwood Foresters 139th Bde

[illegible]
4/5/38

WAR DIARY
or
INTELLIGENCE SUMMARY.
(Erase heading not required.)

Army Form C. 2118.

Instructions regarding War Diaries and Intelligence Summaries are contained in F. S. Regs., Part II. and the Staff Manual respectively. Title pages will be prepared in manuscript.

Place	Date	Hour	Summary of Events and Information	Remarks and references to Appendices
SAINS DU NORD	12 (Contd)		AVESNES and take over billets from 32nd Div. who will come into their present Divisional area. On 14th inst the 46th Div. will move to the area LANDRECIES, BOUSSIES, ROBERTSART and ultimately further East. Divisional Orders issued on these lines to Formations under 46th Div Order No 339 [initials]	App 23
	13		137th & 138th Bde Groups moved to AVESNES preparatory to the whole Division moving to the LANDRECIES area out of IX Corps to XIII Corps. GOC saw 137th & 138th Bdes march into AVESNES. Remainder of Division did not move. 46th Div. Order No 340 issues orders and march tables for the move on 14th inst. [initials]	App 24
	14		Whole Division less Artillery moved into area LANDRECIES, PREUX, BOUSILES, ROBERTSART. Location of units is shewn in App 25. Div. Artillery remained	

(A7092). Wt. W12839/M1293. 750,000. 1/17. D. D. & L., Ltd. Forms/C.2118/14.

Instructions regarding War Diaries and Intelligence Summaries are contained in F. S. Regs., Part II. and the Staff Manual respectively. Title pages will be prepared in manuscript.

WAR DIARY
or
INTELLIGENCE SUMMARY.
(Erase heading not required.)

Army Form C. 2118.

Place	Date	Hour	Summary of Events and Information	Remarks and references to Appendices
LANDRECIES	14 (Contd)		in SAINS DU NORD area. DHQ closed at SAINS DU NORD at 0800 hours and opened at LANDRECIES on arrival at about 1200 hours. CRAA	
	15		Divisional Artillery moved up to new area, the C.R.A. establishing his H.Q. at LANDRECIES. The remainder of the Division got themselves fitted up in their billets, refitted and generally spent a quiet day. CRAA	
	16		Company training, bathing and refitting generally were carried out. CRAA	
	17		Divisional Church Parade took place at 1030 hours just E of LANDRECIES at which all arms and branches were represented. The parade mustered about 2650 in all. After the ceremony the G.O.C. presented	

(A7092). Wt. W12839/M1293. 750,000. 1/17. D. D. & L., Ltd. Forms/C.2118/14.

Instructions regarding War Diaries and Intelligence Summaries are contained in F. S. Regs., Part II. and the Staff Manual respectively. Title pages will be prepared in manuscript.

WAR DIARY
or
INTELLIGENCE SUMMARY.
(Erase heading not required.)

Army Form C. 2118.

Place	Date	Hour	Summary of Events and Information	Remarks and references to Appendices
LANDRECIES			medals which had been awarded as immediate rewards to Officers and OR's of the Division for the fighting since and including the Battle of BELLENGLISE on Sept 29th. After this function the Division marched past the GOC through LANDRECIES Square. No other work or training was carried out today.	
	18		46th Div. G 17/45 followed by G 17/46 which contained an amendment were sent out to all formations: dealing with the general policy of work on which the Division is to be employed. In short this policy is to clear a part of the country E. of the devastated area – the devastated country itself being cleared by German prisoners of war. In the words of the Corps Commander the duty of the Division in conjunction with other Division	App 25A App 26

(A7092). Wt. W12839/M1293. 750,000. 1/17. D. D. & L., Ltd. Forms/C.2118/14.

Army Form C. 2118.

WAR DIARY
or
INTELLIGENCE SUMMARY.
(Erase heading not required.)

Instructions regarding War Diaries and Intelligence Summaries are contained in F. S. Regs., Part II. and the Staff Manual respectively. Title pages will be prepared in manuscript.

Place	Date	Hour	Summary of Events and Information	Remarks and references to Appendices
LANDRECIES	18 (Contd.)		and Corps is "to remove as far as possible all trace of the ravages of war and hand over to the inhabitants in the shortest possible time the tract of country for which the "Division" is responsible". Attached to G17/45 (referred to above) is a map shewing the area allotted to 46th Div. for Clearing and Salving work. this area is further divided into Brigade areas for which Brigades are variously responsible.	
			The G.O.C. went on leave to Paris and Brig-Gen. M.L. HORNBY C.M.G., D.S.O (Commanding 137th Inf. Bde.) temporarily took over Command of the Division.	
			Carr	
	19		Work of Salving Commenced as ordered in App 25. Training also Carried out as ordered in same appendix	

(A7092). Wt. W12839/M1293. 750,000. 1/17. D. D. & L., Ltd. Forms/C.2118/14.

Army Form C. 2118.

WAR DIARY
or
INTELLIGENCE SUMMARY
(Erase heading not required.)

Instructions regarding War Diaries and Intelligence Summaries are contained in F. S. Regs., Part II. and the Staff Manual respectively. Title Pages will be prepared in manuscript.

Place	Date	Hour	Summary of Events and Information	Remarks and references to Appendices
LANDRECIES	20		Salving operations and training proceeded CARR	
	21		Salving operations and training carried out as before. GOC returned from Paris and resumed command of Division CARR	
	22		Salving and clearing work as before. The area is rapidly being cleared – ammunition in boxes salved, dud shells blown up by R.E., trenches filled in etc. CARR	
	23 to 29		Salving operations continued as described above. CARR	
	30		Divisional Race meeting held W. of LANDRECIES. CARR	

2449 Wt. W14957/M90 750,000 1/16 J.B.C. & A. Forms/C.2118/12.

War Diary   App No 1

Secret.   Copy No. 22

OPERATION "F".
46th Division Instructions No. 2.

46th Division G.117/22.   1st November, 1918.

1. Preliminary Moves.   (a)   Reference 46th Division Instructions No. 1, para. 1 (a), Brigades need not be in position until 0800 on Z Day.

(b)   The following preliminary moves will take place on Y Day.-

138th Inf: Bde and affiliated M.G Coy to the Area :-

MOLAIN, all unoccupied accommodation, less that reserved for Divisional H.Q., and Squares W 16, 17, 10, 11, 12, 5.

137th Inf: Bde to the Area :-

VAUX ANDIGNY, all unoccupied accommodation and squares W 14, 15, 21 (less Villages).

139th Inf: Bde to the Area :-

ESCAUFORT (billets for about 200 are vacant), and squares W 1, 2, 3, 7, 8, 9 (less Villages).

Heads of Brigades will not enter VAUX-ANDIGNY or cross the VAUX-ANDIGNY - ESCAUFORT Road before 1730.
Tents and shelters may be drawn from 46th Division "Q".

(c)   Brigade Headquarters may remain in present locations, if desired, until Z day.

(d)   The 138th Inf: Bde will be EAST of the WASSIGNY - S.SOUPLET Railway by 0700 on Z day.

2. ACKNOWLEDGE.

W. Burns Lindow Capt for Lieut-Colonel,
General Staff, 46th Division.

Issued at 0700, 2/11/18.

Copy No. 1 137th Inf:Bde.
2 138th : :
3 139th : :
4 CRA.
5 CRE.
6 Signals.
7 46 Bn, MGC.
8 1st Monmouths.
9 ADMS.
10 Q
11 GOC.
12 GSO I.

Copy No. 13/14 IX Corps.
15 1 Division.
16 32 :
17 O.C, Div'l Observers.
18 Troop, 20th Hussars.
19 Platoon, Cyclists.
20/21 File.
22/23 War Diary.

War Diary App No 2.

Secret. Copy No. 22

OPERATION "F".
46th Division Instructions No. 3.

46th Division G.117/32. 2nd November, 1918.

1. Signal Communications. (a) The main Signal Route for the 46th Division will be -

BOHAIN - MOLAIN - L'ARBRE de GUIZE - MAZINGHIEN - REJET - LA LOUVIERE - BOIS DE L'ABBAYE - S 4 central - M 36 a - LE SART- PRISCHES - CARTIGNIES.

Through Motor Cycle D.R's crossing the CANAL will make a detour through S 9 c.

(b) Divisional and Brigade Headquarters will be established, throughout the advance, as close to this line as possible.

(c) The usual aeroplane signals will be used: other light signals being as heretofore.-

S.O.S.- Red - Red - REd.
Success. White - White - White.

2. Traffic. The main Traffic Route for advance on Z plus 1 day will be the MAZINGHIEN - S 9 c - FESMY - LE SART-PRISCHES - CARTIGNY Road.

On Z day bridges will be available as shown on Map "C" (issued herewith).

Bridges in the 32nd Division area are also shown; these will not be used by 46th Division unless it is required to support the 32nd Division.

The three Pontoon Bridges to be constructed by the 46th Division are reserved on Z Day for EAST bound Infantry Traffic of the 46th Division only.

The C.R.E will arrange to have direction boards and lamps placed, showing the tracks to these bridges; and, as soon as the situation permits, tracks from them on the EASTERN side to the main Traffic Route.

As soon as these bridges are capable of taking wheeled traffic, they will be so labelled.

The D.A.P.M, 46th Division, will arrange to control the Traffic over these three bridges and their approaches, in accordance with these orders.

[signature]

Lieut-Colonel,
General Staff, 46th Division..

Issued at 1400

As in Div: Order No. 335.
Copies 1 - 16.
19 - 23.
25.

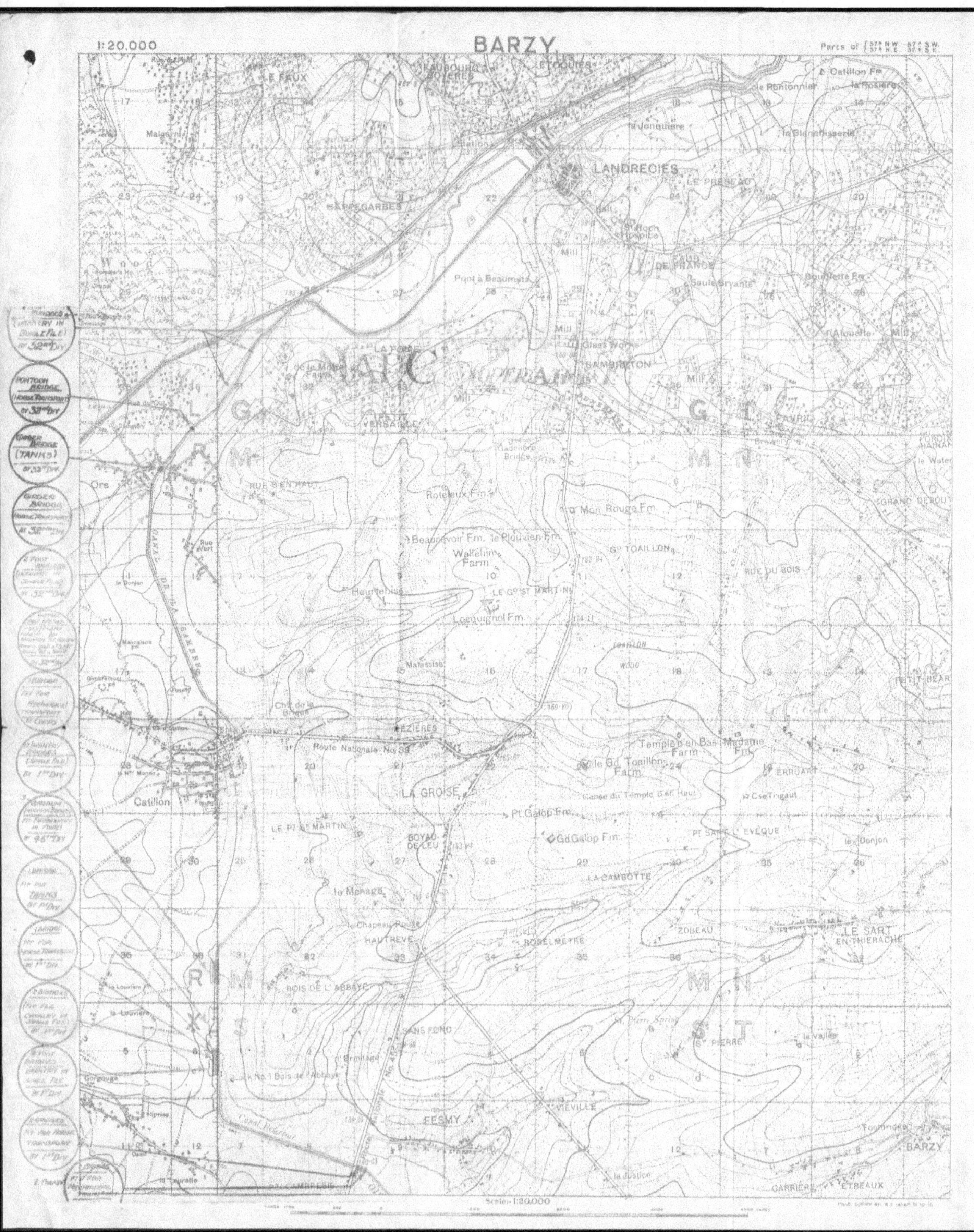

1:20,000
BARZY
LANDRECIES
LE PRESEAU
la Jonquière
la Blanchisserie
Catillon Fm
la Rosière
HAPPEGARBES
Pont à Beaumetz
DE FRANCE
Saule Bryante
Bouillette Fm
Alouette
Glass Works
SAMBRETON
PETIT VERSAILLE
Ors
RUE D'EN HAUT
Roteleux Fm
Mon Rouge Fm
Beaurevoir Fm
Wattelin Farm
Gd TOAILLON
RUE DU BOIS
LE Gd ST MARTIN
Lorquignol Fm
Malassise
TOAILLON WOOD
GRAND DEROUT
PETIT BEAR
Catillon
Route Nationale No 39
LA GROISE
Templeu en Bas Farm
le Gd Toaillon Farm
Pt Galop Fm
Gd Galop Fm
LE Pt St MARTIN
BOYAU DE LEU
Pt SART L'EVEQUE
les Donjon
LA CAMBOTTE
le Menage
le Chapeau Rouge
HAUTREVE
BOREL METRE
ZOBEAU
LE SART EN THIERACHE
BOIS DE L'ABBAYE
la Louvière
SANS FOND
St PIERRE
la vallée
Gorgouge
No. 1 Bois de l'Abbaye
VIEVILLE
FESMY
Canal Réservoir
BARZY
la Justice
ETREAUX
CARRIERE
Scale 1:20,000
PONTOON BRIDGE
GIRDER BRIDGE (TANKS)

War Diary App 3

Secret.

Copy No. 22

OPERATION "F".
46th Division Instructions No. 5.

46th Division G.117/87. 4th November, 1918.

Reference Maps :- 57.A. 57.B. 1/40,000.

Confirming Instructions given at a Conference at 138th Inf:Bde Headquarters at 1630.

1. Information. From Air and other observations, it would appear that the enemy is retiring, and opposition on the IX Corps front has considerably weakened.
The 1st and 32nd Divisions are probably now on their RED objective.
The French have crossed the CANAL and attacked BERGUES at 1600 to-day.

2. Task of 46th Division. The 46th Division has been ordered to pass through the LEFT of the 1st and RIGHT of the 32nd Divisions and continue the pursuit.
The 32nd Division and 66th French Division are conforming.

3. Divisional Troops. The following additional troops are placed at the disposal of the GOC, 46th Division.-
1 Squadron, The Greys.
1 " XXth Hussars and 1 M.G Section.
1 Brigade, RGA.
2 Brigades, RFA.
1 Section of 3 Tanks.
1 Platoon IX Cyclists Bn.

4. Reliefs, etc. The 138th Inf:Bde will relieve the 1st Inf:Bde of the 1st Division in the line to-night with H.Q at BOIS DE L'ABBAYE. 1st Brigade HQ are at LA LOUVIERE.
The Brigade will be covered by the 1st Div'l Artillery with Group HQ at LA LOUVIERE.

5. Disposal of other Units. 137th Inf,Bde will move at once to the area :-
BOIS DE L'ABBAYE *** 1 Bn.
LA LOUVIERE. *** 2 Bns.
HQ at L'ARBRE DE GUIZE.
139th Inf:Bde will move at once to CATILLON with HQ at L'ARBRE DE GUIZE.
2 Brigades of Field Artillery will move across the CANAL to-night and will be attached; one Bde to each of the 137th and 139th Inf:Bdes.
Remainder of the Artillery will be under the orders of the CRA, 46th Division.
The Squadrons of The Greys and XXth Hussars under orders being given by the 1st and 32nd Divisions respectively, will concentrate at L'ARBRE DE GUIZE, reporting to 46th Division Advanced Report Centre.
Half troop of The Greys will be detached (at) to each of the 137th and 139th Inf:Bdes, to whom they will report as soon as possible.
The CRE will attach half a Field Company each to the 137th and 139th Inf:Bdes, retaining under his own Command the other two Companies and the Pioneer Bn for work on forward roads.
The M.G.O will attach a M.G Company to each of the three Inf: Bdes, retaining one in Divisional Reserve.
The Cyclist Platoon will be disposed - one Section to each Inf: Bde and one Section with the Div'l Observers.
The Div'l Mounted Troop is at the disposal of the OC, Signal Co.
The Div'l Observers will move under instructions to be given by the GSO III, so as to be able to watch and report on the advance; they will have with them one Section of the Cyclist Platoon.
The Section Tanks will be concentrated at CATILLON and will work; two with the 137th and one with the 139th Inf:Bdes; Section Commanders to report to Bde HQ for orders.

P.T.O.

6. Dispositions of Troops on the Flanks. 2nd Inf:Bde of the 1st Div: is on our RIGHT with HQ at MAZINGHIEN. The 14th Inf.Bde of the 32nd Div: is on our LEFT with HQ at R 5 c 00. The 97th Inf:Bde is passing through the 96th Inf:Bde on the LEFT of the 14th Inf:Bde at 0800, 5th November.

7. Action of Brigade in the Line. The 138th Inf:Bde will, by active patrolling, endeavour to locate and keep DHQ informed as to the enemy's positions and strength.
The Brigades on the RIGHT and LEFT have been asked to carry out the same policy.
On the 137th Inf:Bde passing through, the 138th Inf:Bde will come into Div'l Reserve and will concentrate so as to be able to move forward along the CATILLON - PRISCHES - CARTIGNIES Road.

8. Action of other Units. The two Cavalry Squadrons, less two troops, and the Cavalry M.G Section, will, under the orders of the Senior Squadron Commander, be in position by 0500 on the 5th November, and will move forward at dawn covering the whole Divisional front and will probe the enemy defences.
The First Bound of the Cavalry will be the Ridge N 35 - N 8.
2nd Bound - The Ridge O 26 - N 11.
3rd Bound - The GREEN Line (P 20 - O 18 - I 33).
Should the enemy be met with in force in front of our Outpost Line, the Cavalry will withdraw to CATILLON and the action outlined under para. 9 will be carried out.

9. Action of 137th and 139th Inf:Bdes. The 137th and 139th Inf.Bdes will move through the 138th and 14th Inf:Bdes respectively at 0800 on the 5th November, covered by the Cavalry.
Should reports have been received that the enemy are in force opposite our Outpost Line prior to this hour, the Cavalry will NOT go out, and an Artillery Barrage will be put down along the whole front under which the Infantry will advance; in the case of the Field Artillery, this Barrage will cease after a few hundred yards.
The CRA will prepare this Barrage to advance at the rate of 100 yards in 5 minutes, but will NOT put it down without orders from DHQ.
The bounds for the Infantry advance will correspond to those of the Cavalry.

10. Boundaries between Brigades. The 137th Inf.Bde is responsible for the protection of its own RIGHT Flank and for getting touch with the French on the Corps RIGHT Boundary as shown on Map "A".
Between 139th and 137th Inf:Bdes, the boundary is :-
The CATILLON - PRISCHES - CARTIGNIES Road inclusive to 137th Inf:Bde.
Between 137th and 97th Inf:Bde of the 32nd Division :-
M 11 b 06.- N 9 a 0.7.- N 5 c 0.2.- I 31 c 0.0.- I 33 central - I 38 central.

11. Roads. The main communication for the 46th Division is the CATILLON - PRISCHES - CARTIGNIES Road.
That of the 137th Inf: Bde -
The CATILLON - PRISCHES - N 18 b - O 3 b - O 5 d Road.
That of the 139th Inf:Bde -
The M 35 - LE SART - PRISCHES - CARTIGNIES Road.

12. Headquarters. At 0800, 5th November,-
DHQ will be at MOLAIN with Advanced Report Centre at L'ARBRE DE GUIZE, now formed.
Three Inf:Bdes at BOIS DE L'ABBAYE.

(3)

On moving forward, Bde HQ will follow the line of the Divisional Route.

13. **ACKNOWLEDGE BY WIRE.**

S. Hartman
for Lieut-Colonel,
General Staff, 46th Division..

Issued at 2210

Copy No. 1 137th Inf:Bde.
2 138th : :
3 139th : :
4 CRA.
5 CRE.
6 OC, Signals.
7 OC, 46th Bn, MGC.
8 1/1st Bn, Monmouth R.
9 ADMS.
10 Q.
11 GOC.
12 GSO I.
13
14 IX Corps.
15 1st Division.
16 32nd :
17 IX Corps HA.
18 9th Sqdn, RAF.
19 OC, Div'l Observers.
20/21 File.
22/23 War Diary.
24 66th French Division.
25 Squadron, The Grays, attchd 46th Div:.
26 : , XXth Hussars, : : :
27 Tank Section, attchd 46th Div:.
28 10th Tank Bn.
29 Platoon, IX Cyclist Bn, attchd 46th Div:.

"A" Form.

MESSAGES AND SIGNALS.

Army Form ... (In pads of 100.)

No. of Message ...... App 4

Prefix ...... Code ...... m. | Words. | Charge.

Office of Origin and Service Instructions.

War Diary

Sent At ...... m. To ...... By ......

This message is on a/c of: ...... *Service.*

(Signature of "Franking Officer.")

Recd. at ...... m. Date ...... From ...... By ......

TO 3 Bdes CRA CRE Q ADMS MG Bn

Sender's Number.	Day of Month.	In reply to Number.	
* G.633	4		AAA

Confirmation telephone conversation AAA
138 Bde to move at once with head on
N. and S. Road through X.5.d. AAA 139 Bde
to have early dinners and be prepared move
noon with head of column LA LOUVIERE AAA
137 Bde to have early dinners AAA Addsd
Bdes CRA CRE 'Q' ADMS MG Bn.

From 46 Div.

Place

Time 1130

The above may be forwarded as now corrected. (Z) sd/ S. Hay, Major, G.S.

Censor. Signature of Addressor or person authorised to telegraph in his name.

*This line, except AAA, should be erased if not required.

Wt. W 3253/P511. 500,000 Pads 1/18. B. & S. Ltd. (E2380.)

MESSAGES AND SIGNALS. No. of Message

Prefix .... Code .... m. | Words. | Charge.

Office of Origin and Service Instructions.

Op. Priority.
138
139

Sent
At .... m.
To ....
By ....

This message is on a/c of: War Service.
Diary
(Signature of "Franking Officer.")

AK/5

Recd. at .... m.
Date ....
From ....
By ....

TO

Sender's Number.	Day of Month.	In reply to Number.	
* G.636.	4		AAA

138 Bde will move one Bn across Canal to area about S 2 b under orders of 2nd Inf: Bde AAA Bn Commander to report to 2nd Bde HQ at X 5 a 2.2 AAA Bn will NOT be used for offence without Corps sanction AAA A Bn HQ of 1 Divn is at L'ERMITAGE S 2 d 8.7 AAA 139 Bde will move to square R 28 and hostile shelling permitting will push forward leading Bn to line of road R 35 a and b AAA Addsd 138 and 139 Bdes.

From 46 Div.
Place
Time 1300

The above may be forwarded as now corrected.
Censor.

(Z) (sgd) CF.J. Lt-Col.
Signature of Addressor or person authorised to telegraph in his name.

*This line, except AAA, should be erased if not required.

Wt. W 3253/P511. 500,000 Pads. 1/18. B. & S. Ltd. (E2389.)

"A" Form.
MESSAGES AND SIGNALS.

Army Form C. 2121.
(In pads of 100.)
No. of Message

Prefix Code m. | Words. | Charge.
Office of Origin and Service Instructions.
War
Deasy
Sent
At m.
To
By
This message is on a/c of: Service.
(Signature of "Franking Officer.")
Recd. at m.
Date
From
By

TO

Sender's Number.	Day of Month.	In reply to Number.	
* G.645	4		AAA

138 Bde will relieve Left Bde 1st Div AAA Relief to commence forthwith AAA Present H.Q. Left Bde LA LOUVIERE AAA H.Q. 138 Bde will be established BOIS DE L'ABBAYE AAA Ack AAA Addsd 138 Bde reptd 1st Div 137 139 Bdes MG Bn Div Sigs. CRE. 'Q' ADMS 9th Corps

From 46 Div.
Place
Time 1540

The above may be forwarded as now corrected.
Censor.
(Sd)/ S. Hay, Major, G.S.
Signature of Addressor or person authorised to telegraph in his name.

* This line, except AAA, should be erased if not required.

Wt. W 3253/P511. 500,000 Pads. 1/18. B. & S. Ltd. (E2389.)

"A" Form.

Army Form C. 2121.
(In pads of 100.)

MESSAGES AND SIGNALS.

No. of Message..........

Prefix........ Code.......... m. | Words. | Charge.

Office of Origin and Service Instructions.

Sent
At .... m.
To ....
By ....

This message is on a/c of: War Diary Service.

(Signature of "Franking Officer.")

Recd. at .... m. Oph
Date 7
From
By

Op. Priority
137. 138. 139.

Priority
9 Corps 51 Fr. Div.

TO 137 138 139 Bdes. 9 Corps. 32nd Div: 51 Fr. Div. CRA. CRE. Signals. Q. ADMS. MGC. Left Div. [illegible] Camp Comdt. GSO1. File (2) War Diary (2). Div: Rear.

Sender's Number.	Day of Month.	In reply to Number.	AAA
G. 693.	5		

Line for the night to be BARZY - PRISCHES Road AAA PRISCHES inclusive AAA Road between N 10 and 11 with patrols pushed well forward AAA 137 to get in touch with French about BARZY AAA 139 with 32nd Div: about N 5 c 0.0 AAA Sqdn 20th Huss. placed under orders of 139 Grays under 137 each less one troop to remain MEZIERES AAA Advance to be continued 0730 to-morrow Cav. to cross line at dawn AAA PRISCHES to be taken to-night if not already done AAA Objectives to-morrow 137 high ground due SOUTH of CARTIGNIES AAA 139 CARTIGNIES and bridgehead in O 6 c 5 d and high ground due NORTH to boundary AAA 138 to march on CATILLON - PRISCHES Road head on cross roads N 19 b 4.6 at 0730 but not to advance beyond this point until ordered by Div: HQ AAA DHQ opens CATILLON 0800 AAA Inf: Bdes to inform all attached troops AAA Added three Bdes

From
Place 46 Div:
Time 1815

The above may be forwarded as now corrected. (Z)

Censor. Signature of Addressor or person authorised to telegraph in his name

(Sgd) C.F. Jerram,
Lt. Col.

*This line, except AAA, should be erased if not required.

Wt. W 3253/P511. 500,000 Pads. 1/18. B. & S. Ltd. (E2389.)

"A" Form.

MESSAGES AND SIGNALS.

Army Form C. 2121.
(In pads of 100.)

No. of Message..........

Prefix .... Code .... m. Office of Origin and Service Instructions.	Words.	Charge.	This message is on a/c of:	Recd. at .... m.
Operations Priority.	Sent At .... m. To .... By		War Diary. Service. (Signature of "Franking Officer.")	Date 8 From .... By ....

TO 137 138 139 Bdes. CRA. MGC. ADMS. Q.

Sender's Number.	Day of Month.	In reply to Number.	AAA
GA 1.	6		

46th Divn has orders to push forward to AVESNES AAA After capture of objective given to 137 and 139 Bdes 138 will be pushed through with this object AAA 138 will keep troops fit as possible with above in view AAA 2 armoured cars 2 fresh troops cavalry 1 Batt 6" How: 2 60 pdr and all field art. will be attached to 138 for this move under instructions to be given later AAA Boundary between 32 Divn J 33 b 6.1 J 30 c 5.3.

From 46 Div.
Place
Time 0745.

The above may be forwarded as now corrected. (Z)
Censor.

(sgd) CF. Jerram, Lt. Col.
Signature of Addressor or person authorised to telegraph in his name.

* This line, except **A A A**, should be erased if not required.

Wt. W 3253/P511. 500,000 Pads. 1/18. B. & S. Ltd. **(E2389.)**

"A" Form.

MESSAGES AND SIGNALS.

Army Form C. 2121.
(In pads of 100.)
No. of Message..........

Prefix........ Code.......... m. | Words. | Charge.

Office of Origin and Service Instructions.

Sent
At.......... m.
To..........
By..........

This message is on a/c of: War Service.
Diary
(Signature of "Franking Officer.")

Recd. at ...... m.
Date ....
From ....
By ....

TO 137 138 139 Bdes. IX Corps. 32 Div. 51 Fr. Div. CRA. CRE. Signals. Q. ADMS. MGC. DAPM. Div. Obs. Camp Commt. GSO I. File (2) War Diary (2).

Sender's Number.	Day of Month.	In reply to Number.	AAA
* G.723.	6		

When objectives allotted 137 and 139 Bdes for today been reached 138 will in accordance verbal instruction already issued push forward towards AVESNES Mtd troops Armoured Cars supported by one Bn Infantry AAA 138 Bde to take over line tonight held by 137 and 139 Bdes AAA HQ and main body 138 Bde CARTIGNIES AAA 137 and 139 Bdes on relief will withdraw to area West of CARTIGNIES to PRISCHES inclusive AAA 139 Bde North 137 Bde South of main road AAA HQ of both Bdes PRISCHES AAA Two Bdes Artillery one Sec. 60-pdrs will be in position cover GREEN Line AAA Sec. 60-pdrs if possible to be in position whence they can shell approaches AVESNES and railway SOUTH that place AAA All troops possible to be got under cover AAA Outposts reduced minimum Arrangements relief 137 139 Bdes by 138 to be made between Brigadiers concerned

From
Place 46 Div.
Time 1555

The above may be forwarded as now corrected. (Z)

Censor. (sgd) S. Hay. Major. GS.
Signature of Addressor or person authorised to telegraph in his name.

* This line, except AAA, should be erased if not required.

Wt. W 3253/P511. 500,000 Pads. 1/18. B. & S. Ltd. (E2389.)

"A" Form.

Army Form C. 2121.
(In pads of 100.)

MESSAGES AND SIGNALS.

No. of Message..........

Prefix......Code......m.	Words.	Charge.	This message is on a/c of:	Recd. at......m.
Office of Origin and Service Instructions.	Sent		War Service.	Date
OP. Priority.	At......m.		Diary	From
137. 139. 138	To		(Signature of "Franking Officer.")	By
C.R.A. M.G.C.	By			

Apb 10

TO 137. 138. 139. Corps. 32 Div. 51 F. Di
CRA. MGC. ADMS. 'Q'. D.O.O. (PRISCHES)
War Diary (2). File. G.S.O. 1. GOC.

Sender's Number.	Day of Month.	In reply to Number.	
* G.728.	6		AAA

138 Bde having relieved 137 and 139 Bdes tonight will push on tomorrow morning towards AVESNES objective as previously ordered AAA Sqdn Grays at disposal of 138 Bde and should be given all possible rest tonight AAA 20 Hussars and all cyclists less those with 138 and D.O.O. come into Div'l: Reserve and should be ordered concentrate PRISCHES by 1000 tomorrow AAA 60 pdrs shoot on exits AVESNES tonight other harassing fire to be arranged by 138 AAA As position on flanks uncertain 137 and 139 responsible for own flank protection by picquetting roads etc AAA D.H.Q. opens PRISCHES 1000 tomorrow

From 46 Div.
Place
Time 1810.

The above may be forwarded as now corrected. (Z)
Censor.

sd/ C.F. Jerram, Lt-Col:
G.S.

Signature of Addressor or person authorised to telegraph in his name.

*This line, except AAA, should be erased if not required.

Wt. W 3253/P511. 500,000 Pads. 1/18. B. & S. Ltd. (E2389.)

"A" Form.

Army Form C. 2121.
(In pads of 100.)

MESSAGES AND SIGNALS.

No. of Message..........

Prefix........Code..........m. | Words. | Charge.

Office of Origin and Service Instructions.

Op. Priority
to 138 Bde.
32 Div.

Sent
At..........m.
To..........
By..........

This message is on a/c of:
War Service
Diary
(Signature of "Franking Officer.")

Recd. at..........m.
Date App 11
From..........
By..........

TO

Sender's Number.	Day of Month.	In reply to Number.	AAA
* G.733	6		

Ref. G.728 AAA Objectives of 138 Bde to-morrow AAA High ground Q 13 a Q 7 d Q 8 a Q 2 c K 33 K 27 d AAA Divisional boundary between 46 and 32 Divs J 31 Central J 32 Central J 33 b 6.1 J 30 c 5.3 K 25 central to K 28 central AAA Divisional Road CARTIGNIES J 32 d P 10 a P 12 a AAA Addsd all concerned reptd Corps 51st French Div. 32nd Div.

From 46 Div.
Place
Time 2025.

The above may be forwarded as now corrected.

(Z) (sgd) S.Hay, Mjr, GS.

Censor. Signature of Addressor or person authorised to telegraph in his name.

*This line, except **A A A**, should be erased if not required.

Wt. W 3253/P511. 500,000 Pads. 1/18. B. & S. Ltd. (E2389.)

Sent

At..........m.

To..........

By..........

Apl 12

..........Service.

(Signature of "Franking Officer.")

Date..........

From..........

By..........

TO War Diary

Appx 12

Sender's Number.	Day of Month.	In reply to Number.
* G.736	6	AAA

Ref. this office G.728 AAA 138 Bde will have at their disposal tomorrow the troop of Scots Greys already attached to them and one troop 20th Hussars AAA Rest of Cavalry will be in Divisional Reserve AAA This cancels distribution of Cavalry ordered by G.728

From
Place 46 Div.
Time 2045

The above may be forwarded as now corrected.

(Z)

Censor.

sd/ G.?.?. Brown Capt.

Signature of Addressor or person authorised to telegraph in his name.

*This line, except AAA, should be erased if not required.

Wt. W 3253/P511. 500,000 Pads. 1/18. B. & S. Ltd. (E2389.)

"A" Form.
Army Form C. 2121.
(In pads of 100.)

MESSAGES AND SIGNALS.

No. of Message.......

Prefix........ Code........ m. | Words. | Charge.

Office of Origin and Service Instructions.

Sent
At........ m.
To........
By........

This message is on a/c of:
.... Service.
(Signature of "Franking Officer.")

War Diary

Recd. at........ m.
Date........
From........
By........

TO
137 138 139 Bdes. CRA CRE ADMS Q
DOC Adv. R. Centre. MGC Pltn Cyclists
9th Corps. 32 Div. 51 Fr: Div. (CATILLON)
G.O.C. G.S.O. 1. FILE. War Diary (2).

Sender's Number.	Day of Month.	In reply to Number.	AAA
G.78[illegible]	7		

Orders for 8th Nov. 138 Bde continues to todays objective if not taken AAA When taken consolidate outpost position AAA Cavalry in advance AAA Sqdn 20 Hussars and Troop GRAYS now with 138 will be relieved on 8th by 2 Troops GREYS now at PRISCHES AAA Sqdn Comdr report to 138 Bde H.Q. with troops by dawn AAA Cyclists with 138 relieved by 2 sections at PRISCHES to report at dawn AAA Cav. and Cyclists on relief to CARTIGNIES AAA Ptn Cyclists at CATILLON to PRISCHES reporting Adv. Div. Report Centre 0900 AAA 137 and 139 detail inlying picquets of 1 Coy per Bn and picquet roads to billets tonight AAA Addsd 137 138 139 CRA and Adv. Report Centre who will inform Cav. and Cyclists at PRISCHES

46 Div.

From 1727
Place
Time

sd/ C.F. Jerram, Lt.Col.

The above may be forwarded as now corrected. (Z)

Censor.

Signature of Addressor or person authorised to telegraph in his name.

*This line, except A A A, should be erased if not required.

Wt. W 3253/P511. 500,000 Pads. 1/18. B. & S. Ltd. (E2388.)

"A" Form. Army Form C. 2121. (In pads of 100.)

MESSAGES AND SIGNALS.

No. of Message..........

Prefix .... Code .... m.	Words.	Charge.	This message is on a/c of:	Recd. at ...... m.
Office of Origin and Service Instructions.	Sent		apl 14	Date ....
Op. Priority 137 138 139. Grays & Hussars at Div. Report Centre.	At .... m. To .... By		War Diary Service. (Signature of "Franking Officer.")	From .... By ....

TO — CRA. CRE. Signals. 137 138 139 Bdes. MGC. Q. ADMS. DAPM. DOO. GSO I. File (2). War Diary (2). 32 Div. 51 Fr. Div. IX Corps. Sqdn 20 Hussars. Sqdn Grays.

Sender's Number.	Day of Month.	In reply to Number.	AAA
* G.753.	7th.		

Dispositions by tonight will be 138 Bde Group in line EAST of CARTIGNIES AAA 137 between lines P 20 central I 35 central and O 28 central O 1 central AAA Bde HQ about CARTIGNIES AAA 139 W. of 137 and EAST of RIVIERETTE River AAA Accommodation to be left in PRISCHES for DHQ AAA MG Coy and F.Amb. with Bde Groups AAA Reserve Coy MG Bn about PRISCHES AAA Remainder 20 Hussars come under orders 138 forthwith present location Adv. Div. Report Centre AAA GRAYS less one troop remain PRISCHES for present AAA Cav. with 138 will keep touch with enemy tonight E. of Inf: objective AAA Probable all Cav. will be so employed and rations should be arranged accordingly Added 137 138 139 ADMS MGC Sqdn 20 Hussars Sqdn Grays reptd those concerned

From 46 Div.

Place

Time 1045.

The above may be forwarded as now corrected. (Z) .... Censor.

(sgd) CF. Jerram. Lt Col.

Signature of Addressor or person authorised to telegraph in his name

*This line, except AAA, should be erased if not required.

Wt. W 3253/P511. 500,000 Pads. 1/18. B. & S. Ltd. (E2385.)

"A" Form.
MESSAGES AND SIGNALS.

Army Form C. 2121.
(In pads of 100.)

Op. Priority.
137. 138. CRA.
Grays.

This message is on a/c of: War Diary Service.

Date 15

TO CRA. CRE. Signals. 137. 138. 139. MGC. Q.
ADMS. DAPM. DCO. CSO I. Files. War Diary. (2).
IX Corps. 32 Div. 51 French Division. AAA

C.802. 8

Orders for 9 Nov AAA 138 Bde to complete capture of objective today AAA 137 Bde to relieve 138 Nov.9 Area Grid line between Sqs. O and P AAA 20 Hussars to withdraw into Divl Res. when 138 no longer require AAA to billot in position allotted by 138 where touch can be gained with them AAA NOT WEST of CARTIGNIES AAA Cyclists with 138 as for Cav. AAA Locations to be sent by 138 to DHQ AAA CRA to arrange transfer of artillery AAA GRAYS and Ptn Cyclist now in Divl Res. under Sqdn Comdr to pass through outposts early morning occupy SAINS AU NORD and picquet roads EAST of it AAA On completion of which to come under orders of 137 Bde AAA On relief 138 to move WEST of 137 and E. of Grid between Sqs. N and O SOUTH of PRISCHES - CARTIGNIES Road AAA Added 137 138 Sqdn GRAYS CRA MGC reptd those concerned

From
Place
Time

46 Div.

1900

[signature] Lt Col. G.S.

* This line, except AAA, should be erased if not required.

Wt. W 3253/P511. 500,000 Pads. 1/18. R. & S. Ltd. (E2389.)

"A" Form.

MESSAGES AND SIGNALS.

Army Form C. 2121. (In pads of 100.)

No. of Message..........

Prefix......Code......m. | Words. | Charge.

Office of Origin and Service Instructions.

Sent At......m. To...... By......

This message is on a/c of: War Diary Service.

(Signature of "Franking Officer.")

Recd. at......m. Date...... From...... By......

Op. Priority

137 138 139

CRE.

TO 137. 138. 139. CRA. CRE. Sigs. MGO. Q. DDO. DAPM. GSO I. File (2). War Diary (2). XX Corps. 32nd Div. 51st Fr. Div.

App 16

Sender's Number.	Day of Month.	In reply to Number.	AAA
G.829.	9.		

Relief of 138 by 137 cancelled AAA 138 to halt on general line SAINS DU NORD - SEMERIES inclusive where will go into billets covered by outposts AAA 137 close up with head about Q 4 c prepared to pass through 138 AAA 139 move as soon as possible to BOULOGNE and CARTIGNIES AAA 138 will order sqdn 20 Hussars to get in touch with Grays and work with them EAST to get in touch with enemy AAA Senior Sqdn Commander to take command AAA Cyclists with 138 to be transferred to 137 AAA CRE to arrange for forward road reconnaissance and repairs AAA Addsd 137 138 139 CRE

From

Place

Time 46 Div.

The above may be forwarded as now corrected. (Z)

Censor.

Signature of Addressor or person authorised to telegraph in his name.

*This line, except AAA, should be erased if not required.

Wt. W 3253/P511. 500,000 Pads. 1/18. B. & S. Ltd. (E2389.)

"A" Form.

MESSAGES AND SIGNALS.

Army Form C. 2121.
(In pads of 100.)
No. of Message..........

Prefix ..... Code ..... m. Office of Origin and Service Instructions.	Words.	Charge.	This message is on a/c of:	Recd. at ..... m.
Op. Priority 20 Hussars & 138 Bde.	Sent At ..... m. To ..... By		War Service. Diary (Signature of "Franking Officer.")	Date ..... From ..... By .....

TO ~~CRA CRE Sigs. 137 138 139 Bdes. MG Bn 20 Hus. 'Q'. ADMS. DAPM. DOO. GSO 1 File. War Diary (2). 9 Corps 32 Div. 66 DIV.~~

Sender's Number.	Day of Month.	In reply to Number.	AAA
* G.850	9		

~~Orders for night AAA Cavalry and Ptn Cyclists under Capt: D'ARCY HALL 20 Hussars to hold line Rly R.10.a. to LIESSIES inclusive with H.Q. at R.2.d.8.1 AAA Orderly to be kept at Div'l: Adv: Report Centre SAINS DU NORD AAA Infantry outpost to be found by 138 Bde EAST of SAINS and SEMERIES AAA Remaindor Infantry remain present locations AAA Infantry will NOT be moving forward tomorrow AAA Orders for Cavalry later~~

From 46 Div.
Place
Time 1700

The above may be forwarded as now corrected. (Z)

Censor. Signature of Addressor or person authorised to telegraph in his name.

G.S.

*This line, except A A A, should be erased if not required.

Wt. W 3253/P511. 500,000 Pads. 1/18. B. & S. Ltd. (E2389.)

"A" Form.

Army Form C. 2121. (In pads of 100.)

MESSAGES AND SIGNALS.

No. of Message..........

Prefix........ Code........ m. | Words. | Charge.

Office of Origin and Service Instructions.

Priority Corps.

Sent At..........m. To.......... By..........

This message is on a/c of: War Diary ....Service.

(Signature of "Franking Officer.")

Recd. at...... m. Date.......... From.......... By..........

App 18

TO

Sender's Number.	Day of Month.	In reply to Number.	AAA
* G.839	9		

Dispositions for night 138 Bde outposts 137 Billets SAINS DU NORD - SEMERIES exclusive to P.16.central J.34.central 139 BOULOGNE CARTIGNIES Area AAA Bdes to report locations of units early as possible AAA DHQ remains PRISCHES with Adv. Report Centre P.3.a. AAA D.O.O. and attached section Cyclists withdraw to D.O.O. Hd.Qrs.

From 46 Div.

Place

Time

The above may be forwarded as now corrected. (Z)sd/ C.F.Jerram, Lt-Col.

Censor. Signature of Addressor or person authorised to telegraph in his name.

*This line, except AAA, should be erased if not required.

Wt. W 3253/P511. 500,000 Pads 1/18. B. & S. Ltd. (E2389.)

SECRET. War Diary

Copy No. 26

App 19

46th DIVISION ORDER NO. 337.

****

Ref:- Maps, Sheets -
VALENCIENNES & NAMUR, 1/100,000.

10th November, 1918.

1. (a) All reports show that the enemy is retreating towards the MEUSE.

(b) No advance by the IX Corps is contemplated until further orders are received.

(c) Touch with the enemy is being maintained by a mobile force consisting of the 5th Cavalry Brigade, Battery, R.F.A., IX Corps Cyclists, No. 17 Armoured Car Bn: and 1 Infantry Brigade, under command of Major-General BETHELL.

(d) IX Corps is holding an outpost line running approximately - 5 cross roads just W. of SAINS-DU-NORD - LA TAQUENNERIE - BOIS DE BEUGNIES, but troops EAST of this line if suitably disposed are not required to be withdrawn.

2. 138th Infantry Brigade will maintain the outpost line at present held E. of SAINS-DU-NORD and SEMERIES.
The line of resistance will be the picquet line.
The exact disposition of outpost companies to be reported to these headquarters.
The main line of resistance will be the high ground in Q.7 to Hill in K.33.
The 137th Infantry Brigade will be prepared to occupy this line if necessary.

3. The fact of the mobile force referred to in 1(c), being in advance of the division will in no way obviate the necessity for taking all proper precautions to guard against surprise.

4. The Mounted Troop and Corps Cyclists today at present attached to the Division will, at 1200, come under orders of Major-General BETHELL, Commanding Mobile Force.

5. The remainder of the Division will be disposed as directed in this Office G.829 of 9th November, 1918.
Any moves therein referred to not yet effected will be carried out forthwith.

6.

6. During the temporary halt every effort will be made to repair bridges and improve roads prior to any further advance.

In the first instance effort will be concentrated on the traffic circuits to SAINS-DU-NORD and on the bridges at BOULOGNE.

7. (a) The Inter-Divisional Boundary between 46th and 32nd Division now runs :-

J.36.central - K.32 central - River junction K.29.b.5.6.

(b) Southern boundary of Corps now runs :-

From R.8.c.0.0 - R.11 central - L.4.c.0.0 - K.31.a.0.0 - L.27.a.0.0.

8. Acknowledge.

P. Hayman

Issued at 1430

Lieut-Colonel,
General Staff, 46th Division..

Copy No. 1 CRA.
2 CRE.
3 Signals.
4 137 Bde.
5 138 :
6 139 :
7 MGC.
8 1 Monmouths.
9 A & Q.
10 ADMS.
11 OC, Observers.
12 GSO I.
13 GOC.
14 51 French Division.
15 32 Division.
16/17 IX Corps.
18/19 File.
20/21 War Diary.

War Diary App 20

Secret. Copy No 25

46th DIVISION ORDER No. 338.

****

Ref: Map, 57.A,
1/40,000.

10th November, 1918.

1. On 12th November, 1918, the 1st Australian Division (less RA) is relieving troops of the 32nd Division on LEFT of Corps front, and at the same time the 32nd Division side slips to the SOUTH relieving troops of the 46th Division.

2. The Boundary between the 46th and 32nd Divisions will then run :-

   Grid Line between L 31 and R 1 to K 32 and Q 2, thence P 5 central - P 3 d 5.0 Road junction O 11 b 0.5 thence along CARTIGNIES - PRISCHES Road to fork in N 21 c thence N 25 a 0.0 - M 30 central - M 25 central.

3. Arrangements for relief on 12th November will be made direct between G.Os.C, 138th and 14th Inf:Bdes (HQ - K 30 b).

4. Completion of relief and subsequent dispositions of Outpost Companies to be reported to this office.

5. ACKNOWLEDGE.

[signature]
for Lieut-Colonel,
General Staff, 46th Division.

Issued at 0700, 11th November, 1918.

Distribution over.-

Copy No. 1 CRA.
2 CRE.
3 Signals.
4 137 Inf:Bde.
5 138t : :
6 139 : :
7 1st Monmouths.
8 46th Bn, MGC.
9 AA & QMG.
10 ADMS.
11 Div'l Train.
12 SSO.
13 DAPM.
14 DADVS.
15 DADOS.
16 GSO I.
17 GOC.
18 32nd Division.
19 51 French Division.
20/21 IX Corps.
22 DOO.
23/24 File.
25/26 War Diary.

Appx 21

Location of Units.- 12th Novr. 1918.

46th Division H.Q.	Q 18 a 2.6.
137th Inf: Bde H.Q.	Q 17 b 4.8.
5th South Staffords.	Q 4 c.
6th : :	Q 9 d.
6th North :	Q 2 central.
138th Inf: Bde H.Q.	Q 12 a central.
5th Lincolns.	Q 12 a 05.20.
4th Leicesters.	R 7 a 1.1.
5th :	Q 11 d 9.8.
139th Inf: Bde H.Q.	O 5 d 4.2.
5th Sherwood For:	P 20 a 30.85.
6th : :	P 19 d 7.9.
8th : :	P 15 c 7.2.
1st Monmouths.	Q 3 a 4.6.
CRA.	Q 11 d 7.2.
230th Brigade, RFA.	Q 12 c 4.6.
231st : :	P 2 c 8.6.
DAC.	I 35 a 8.3.
46th Bn, MGC.	Q 12 a 1.0.
CRE.	Q 12 a.
465th Field Co, RE.	Q 12 d 5.0.
466th : : :	SAINS DU NORD.
468th : : :	ZOREES.

***

Reference Map, 57.A., 1/40,000.

"A" Form.
Army Form C. 2121.
(In pads of 100.)

MESSAGES AND SIGNALS.

No. of Message............

Prefix .... Code .... m. | Words. | Charge.

Office of Origin and Service Instructions.

Sent
At .... m.
To ....
By ....

This message is on a/c of:
War Diary Service.
(Signature of "Franking Officer.")

Recd. at ...... m.
Date ....
From ....
By ....

App 22

TO
ADMS DADVS Camp Cdt.
CRA 137 Mons. Train DADOS G.S.O. I
CRE 138 MG Bn. SSO. DOO File
Sigs 139 Q. DAPM Rec.Camp. War Diary.

Sender's Number. | Day of Month. | In reply to Number. | AAA

G 893. 11th

Hostilities temporarily cease 1100 today when all offensive action will cease AAA Present outpost line to be maintained and no troops of 46th DIVN to pass EAST of it other than Road etc. reconnaissance and working parties AAA No conversation with enemy to be allowed

From
Place
Time 46th DIVN

The above may be forwarded as now corrected.
0705
Censor.

(Z)
Signature of Addressor or person authorised to telegraph in his name.

* This line, except AAA, should be erased if not required.
(Sd.) C.F. JERRAM Lt-

Wt. W 3253/P511. 500,000 Pads. 1/18. B. & S. Ltd. (E2389.)

War Diary App 23

Copy No. 31

Secret.

46th Division Order No. 339.
****

Ref: Map, 57.A,
1/40,000.

12th November, 1918.

1. The 46th Division, less Divisional HQ and 139th Brigade Group, will move to-morrow, 13th November, to AVESNES. At the same time the 32nd Division moves into the SAINS - BOULOGNE Area.
On the following day, 14th November, the Division will move into the area LANDRECIES, BOISSIES, ROBERTSART, via MARBAIX.

2. The moves for the 13th November are shown in Table "A" attached.

3. The 1/1st Bn, Monmouthshire Regt, will join the 137th Brigade Group forthwith.
The Company, 46th Bn, MGC, now in Divisional Reserve, will join the 138th Brigade Group. The Field Company, RE, affiliated to the 139th Brigade will move under orders of the GOC, 138th Brigade, and will join the 139th Brigade Group on arrival in AVESNES.

4. The RA will NOT move on the 13th.

5. 46th Division "Q" will notify Brigades as to Billeting areas on the following lines :-
137th Brigade Group into WESTERN part of AVESNES.
138th " " " EASTERN " " ".
All units will be as far WEST as possible.

6. The DAPM will arrange for the picqueting of all roads entering the routes to be taken, and will refuse passage to all traffic which would interfere with the march of the Division. The Divisional Mounted Troops are available to assist if required (1 officer 10 men).

7. Divisional Headquarters will remain at SAINS until the 14th November.

8. ACKNOWLEDGE.

[signature]

Lieut-Colonel,
General Staff, 46th Division..

Issued at 2000

Copy No. 1 to CRA.
2 CRE.
3 Signals.
4 137th Inf:Bde.
5 138th " "
6 139th " "
7 1st Monmouths.
8 46th Bn, MGC.
9 AA & QMG.
10 Div'l Train.
11 SSO.
13 ADMS.
14 DADVS.
15 DADOS.
16 DAPM.
17 GSO I.
18 GOC.
19 DOC.

Copy No. 20 BGO.
21 Camp Commandant.
22 Div'l Reception Camp.
23 32nd Division.
26 51st French Division.
27/28 IX Corps.
29/30 File.
31/32 War Diary.

Table "A", to accompany 46th Division Order No. 339.

Sorial Number.	Unit.	From.	To.	Route.	Remarks.
1.	137th Bde Group.	SAINS - FOURMA-NOIR Area.	AVESNES.	Q 4 c 0.4 - Q 3 a 4.6 - Q 2 d 1.7 - K 31 b 1.9.	Head to reach K 31 b 1.9 at 1215. To clear FOUR-MANOIR by 1330.
2.	138th Bde Group.	SAINS-DU-NORD.	AVESNES.	SAINS-DU-NORD and thence as for 137th Bde.	To arrive FOURMANOIR at 1345. To cloar Q 11 a 3.0 by 1500. Outposts to be withdrawn 2 hours beforo moving.
3.	139th Bde Group.	BOULOGNE.	Remains.		
4.	D.H.Q.	SAINS.	Remains.		

NOTE.- Troops will march through AVESNES to attention and Bands will play.

War Diary

App 24

SECRET. Copy No. 31

46th DIVISION ORDER No. 340.

****

Ref:- Maps, Sheets 1/40,000.
57.A & 57.B

13th November, 1918.

1. The 46th (North Midland) Division will resume its march to the LANDRECIES Area on the 14th November, 1918, and, on arrival, will join the XIII Corps.

2. March table is attached.

3. The D.A.P.M. will arrange to picquet the Cross Roads at J.21.c.6.4 and H.18.c.9.5, to ensure that the order of march is maintained.

4. Acknowledge.

[signature]
for Lieut-Colonel,
General Staff, 46th Division.

Issued at 1400 hours.

Copy No. 1 to CRA.
2 CRE.
3 Signals.
4 137th Inf: Bde:
5 138th : :
6 139th : :
7 1st Monmouths.
8 46th Bn: M.G.C.
9 A.A. & Q.M.G.
10 Div'l: Train.
11 SSO.
12 ADMS.
13 DADVS.
14 DADOS.
15 DAPM.
16 GSO.I.
17 GOC.
18 DOO.
19 DGO.
21 Camp Commandant.
22 Div'l: Reception Camp.
23 Div'l: Mounted Troop.
24 32nd Division.
25/ 26 IX Corps.
27/ 28 XIII Corps.
29/ 30 File.
31/ 32 War Diary.

P.T.O.

MARCH TABLE.

Unit.	From.	To.	Route.	Remarks.
137th Bde: Group.	AVESNES.	PREUX (A.20 - Sheet 57.A.).	MARBAIX - MAROILLES - LANDRECIES.	To clear Cross Roads J.21.c.6.4 by 0940.
138th Bde: Group.	AVESNES.	BOUSIES (L.4 - Sheet 57.B.).	MARBAIX - MAROILLES - LANDRECIES - FONTAINE.	Head to arrive at J.21.c 6.4 at 0955. To clear this point at 1105.
139th Bde: Group.	BOULOGNE (Fd. Coy. at AVESNES).	LANDRECIES.	P.2.a.9.9 - CARTIGNIES-GD. FAYT - H.22.d.4.8. H.16.d.7.5 - H.16.c.9.5.	Head to debouch on to MAROILLES-LANDRECIES Road at H.16.c.9.5 at 1500, in rear of 138th Bde. To clear this point by 1310.
Royal Artillery.	SAINS Area.	H.Q. LANDRECIES. 2 Bdes: FAUBOURG-SOYERS. (G.15 - Sheet 57.A.) D.A.C. LE PRESSEAU (H.19 - Sheet 57.A.)	AVESNES-MARBAIX, MAROILLES.	Not to arrive at J.21.c. 6.4 until 1130. Not to arrive H.16.c.9.5 until 1620 and will follow 139th Brigade.
Divisional H.Qrs.	SAINS.	LANDRECIES.	AVESNES - MARBAIX MAROILLES.	Close at SAINS 0800 and open at LANDRECIES on arrival.

Note.- All Groups except 137th Brigade Group (which is optional) will make one hour's halt from 1150 to 1300

War Diary

Appx 25

LOCATIONS - 46th DIVISION - 16/11/18.
********* ************* ********

46th Division H.Q.	LANDRECIES.
C.R.A.	do.
230th Brigade RFA.	G 16 c 30.50.
231st : :	G 17 c 7.8.
D.A.C.	G 23 a 2.3.
D.T.M.O.	MEZIERES.
137th Inf: Bde H.Q.	PREUX-AUX-BOIS.
5th South Staffs.	do.
6th : :	do.
6th North Staffs.	do.
138th Inf: Bde H.Q.	BOUSIES.
5th Lincolns.	do.
4th Leicesters.	do.
5th Leicesters.	do.
139th Inf: Bde H.Q.	LANDRECIES.
5th Sherwood For:	do.
6th : :	do.
8th : :	do.
137th T.M Battery.	PREUX-AUX-BOIS.
138th : :	BOUSIES.
139th : :	LANDRECIES.
46th Bn, M.G.C.	BOUSIES.
1st Monmouth Regt.	BOUSIES.
Div'l Train & SSO.	LANDRECIES.
451st Coy, ASC.	G 8 d central.
452nd : :	G 15 a.
453rd : :	G 8 c 8.6.
454th : :	G 15 b 5.3.
A.D.M.S.	LANDRECIES.
1st N.M. Fd. Amb.	do.
2nd : : :	L 4 b 0.8.
3rd : : :	PREUX-AUX-BOIS.
D.A.D.V.S.	LANDRECIES.
1st N.M. M.V.S.	G 29 central.
D.A.D.O.S.	LANDRECIES.
D.A.P.M.	LANDRECIES.
C.R.E.	LANDRECIES.
465th Fd. Co. RE.	do.
466th : : :	PREUX-AUX-BOIS.
468th : : :	ROBERTSART.
D.G.O.	LANDRECIES.
Div'l Mounted Troop.	do.
Div'l Observers.	do.
Div'l Reception Camp.	BOHAIN.
240th Employment Co.	LANDRECIES.
X/46 T.M.B.	MEZIERES.
Y/46 :	M 21 b 7.5.

W Burnett Lindsay Lt Col for

Major-General,
Commanding 46th Division...

16th September, 1918.

War Diary

Appx 25 A

To all recipients of
46th Division G.17/45.
****

46th Division G.17/49. 18th Novr: 1918.
****

Salvage.

In reply to questions which have been raised.-

(a) All wire entanglements will be reeled up and the pickets collected if of iron.

(b) All trenches will be filled in including rifle pits.

(c) Craters will be filled in but not shell holes unless they interfere with traffic.

(d) Timber Dumps will be taken over by the C.R.E. in situ.
Coal Dumps by 46th Division 'Q'.

(e) Light Railways will not at present be taken up. Dumps of rails will be taken over in situ by the C.R.E.

[signature] for Lieut-Colonel,
General Staff, 46th Division.

War Diary
App 25A

CLEARING OF THE BATTLE FIELDS.

****

46th Division G. 17/45. 17th November, 1918.

1. General Policy. The General Policy of the Employment of the British Army for the present is :-

(a) Certain Divisions proceed into GERMANY according to the terms of the Armistice.
(b) Other Divisions remain EAST of the Devastated Area to clear the Forward Battle Fields.
(c) The remainder proceed WEST of this Area to clear the Back Areas.

Enemy Prisoners are occupying and clearing the whole of the Devastated Area.

2. Task of the 46th Division. The 46th (North Midland) Division has been selected to form a part of the Force clearing the Country EAST of the Devastated Area, and will commence by clearing its present billeting area.

Other Areas will be allotted as necessary from time to time, necessitating moving the Division to new Billets.

3. Areas. The Areas to be cleared by Brigade Groups are shown on Map "A" (issued to those marked *).

4. Working Hours and Men to be Employed. (a) Four Hours work in the day, including march, will be carried out, except on Sundays, on which no work will be done.

The remainder of the day will be devoted to Sports, etc.

Should Brigade Commanders desire to give an additional holiday at any time, permission will be obtained from Divisional Headquarters.

(b) Working Parties will be detailed, as usual, in complete units. An average of ¾ of the available men will work daily, the remaining quarter being exercised in drills, etc. Thus, in an Infantry Battalion three Companies would be working and one training.

(c) Working Parties will carry out ¼ hours smartening up drill in working hours.

5. Brigade Groups. 137th Brigade Group. ½ Coy, 466th Fd Co, RE.
137th Inf: Bde.
46th Bn, MGC.
1/3rd (N.M) Fd. Ambce.
2 Coy, Div'l Train

P.T.O.

138th Brigade Group.	230th Bde, RFA. 231st : : D.A.C. ½ Coy, 468th Fd. Coy, RE. 138th Inf: Bde. 1/1st Monmouthshire Regt. 1/2nd (N.M) Fd. Ambce. 3 Coy, Div'l Train.
139th Brigade Group.	½ Coy, 465th Fd Coy, RE. 139th Inf: Bde. 1/1st (N.M) Fd. Ambce. 4 Coy, Div'l Train.

The Remainder of the RE will be employed under the CRE, under instructions to be given by 46th Division "Q", making temporary repairs to Houses in the Divisional Area.

Note.- The whole of the Divisional Artillery is at present placed in the 138th Brigade Group, as in that area is the majority of the known ammunition to be salved. The CRA will make reconnaissances of the Remainder of the Area, and, on the result of these Reconnaissances Units of the Artillery will be transferred to other Groups as may be necessary.

6. Method of Work. (a) Areas must be cleared systematically and thoroughly, so as to avoid waste of time in going over them again.

(b) Separate Dumps will be made for each nature of Stores, as follows.-

(i) Artillery material.
(ii) Engineers' material.
(iii) Food.
(iv) Clothing and equipment, including petrol tins, etc, etc.
(v) S.A.A.

These will be sub-divided according to the nature of the stores: thus, the Artillery Dump might be divided into :-

(i) English Guns.
(ii) Enemy Guns.
(iii) British Ammunition. (Again sub-divided as to Calibre).
(iv) Enemy Ammunition. (do. do.).
(v) T.M. ammunition,.
(vi) Shell Cases.
(vii) Ammunition Boxes.
etc.

(c) Positions of Brigade Dumps will be notified to 46th Division "Q", who will be responsible for clearing.

Dumps will be on a Lorry Road, but, so far as possible, not on a Main Road.

(d) The Artillery with Brigade Groups will be given the task of clearing all artillery material. The responsibility, however, rests with the GOC, Brigade Group. As it is probable that the majority of the work will be Artillery work, Infantry should be attached to Artillery Working Parties to assist.

(e) Grenades and L.T.M. ammunition will be dealt with by special parties including RE.-

Boxed - will be collected at the Artillery Dumps.

Unboxed - will be destroyed in situ by RE.

(f) Unexploded shell, bombs, etc, will be destroyed in situ by the RE, every safety precaution being taken.

(g) The areas will be cleared by Map Squares. A Map will be kept by 46th Division "G", and squares will be coloured RED as they are completed: the necessary information being sent in by Brigades on Tuesdays and Fridays, commencing Friday, 22nd Nov:.

A Square will not be reported until all the "duds" in it have been finally disposed of.

A similar return will be sent by 46th Division "Q" to XIII Corps on Wednesdays and Saturdays, on information to be supplied by 46th Division "G".

(h) The usual rules regarding ammunition dumps will be strictly observed.

The D.A.D.O.S will give any technical advice necessary.

7. Staff Supervision. Whilst in no way interfering in the work and responsibility of the Brigade Group Commanders, the CRA and CRE with their Staffs will generally supervise the work and will be ready to give their expert advice to Brigade Commanders in matters concerning their own departments.

8. Work will commence from receipt of these orders.

Lieut-Colonel,
General Staff, 46th Division.

Distribution over.-

Issued to :-

CRA. *
CRE. *
Signals.
137th Inf: Bde. *
138th : : *
139th : : *
46th Bn, MGC.
1st Monmouths.
"Q". *
46th Div'l Train.
ADMS.
DADVS.
DADOS.
DAPM.
DGO.
SSO.
Div'l Reception Camp.
Camp Commandant.
GSO I. *
GOO. *
File. *
War Diary. (2). *
XIII Corps. (2). *

Appx 6

To all recipients of 46th Division G. 17/45.

46th Division G. 17/46. 19th November, 1918.

Para. 4 (b) is cancelled and the following substituted :-

(b) Working parties will be detailed, as usual, in complete units. An average of two-thirds of the available men will work daily, the remaining third being exercised in drills, etc. Thus, in an Infantry Brigade, two Battalions might be working and one training.

[signature]
for Lieut-Colonel,
General Staff, 46th Division.

On His Majesty's Service.

SECRET

SECRET

SECRET

D. A. G.
G. H. Q.
3rd Echelon,
FRANCE

D.M.S., G.H.Q.,
BRITISH FORCE
IN ITALY.
No. ....
....

46 DIVISION

GEN STAFF

~~1919 JAN~~ — 1919 MAR

1918 DEC

Instructions regarding War Diaries and Intelligence Summaries are contained in F. S. Regs., Part II. and the Staff Manual respectively. Title Pages will be prepared in manuscript.

17/12

WAR DIARY
or
INTELLIGENCE SUMMARY

(Erase heading not required.)

Army Form C. 2118.

HQ G.S. 46 D

Place	Date	Hour	Summary of Events and Information	Remarks and references to Appendices
			Month of December 1918. Divisional Headquarters at LANDRECIES.	VR 46

2449 Wt. W14957/M90 750,000 1/16 J.B.C. & A. Forms/C.2118/12.

Army Form C. 2118.

WAR DIARY
or
INTELLIGENCE SUMMARY

(Erase heading not required.)

Instructions regarding War Diaries and Intelligence Summaries are contained in F. S. Regs., Part II. and the Staff Manual respectively. Title Pages will be prepared in manuscript.

Place	Date	Hour	Summary of Events and Information	Remarks and references to Appendices
LANDRECIES	1		In the afternoon H.M. the King of England came to LANDRECIES and walked through the main street which had previously been lined by groups of men of all arms of the Division. He was given a most enthusiastic reception with which he appeared to be much pleased. He was accompanied by the Prince of Wales and Prince Albert and by the G.O.C. Third Army.	[initials]
	2.		At 11 am the G.O.C. met H.M. the King at BELLENGLISE and showed him the St QUENTIN Canal which had been stormed and the ground which had been taken by 46th Division on Sept. 29th 1918. The King spent about 1½ hours walking round and seeing the localities of especial interest. The G.O.C. Third Army accompanied him.	[initials]

2449 Wt. W14957/M90 750,000 1/16 J.B.C. & A. Forms/C.2118/12.

Army Form C. 2118.

WAR DIARY
or
INTELLIGENCE SUMMARY
(Erase heading not required.)

Instructions regarding War Diaries and Intelligence Summaries are contained in F. S. Regs., Part II. and the Staff Manual respectively. Title Pages will be prepared in manuscript.

Place	Date	Hour	Summary of Events and Information	Remarks and references to Appendices
LANDRECIES	3		Salving work and training carried out as usual. 138th Bde held a Race Meeting.	[illegible]
			A Lecture "Reinstatement Problems" was delivered in the Theatre at Landrecies by Colonel DOWLING	[illegible]
	4th–6th		Salving work and training was continued –	
	7th		The 46th M.G. Batt moved from their present billets at BOUSIES by march route to BOHAIN	App I [illegible]
	8th		His Grace the Duke of Portland inspected the 8th Batt Sherwood Foresters & afterwards presented War Medals won during the recent fighting – Afterwards the party which consisted of The Duke of Portland, Lt Col Foljambe, Lt Col Mellish (formerly commanding 8th Batt Sherwood Foresters) Major Brand The Bishop of Southwell & Chaplain Hales lunched with the G.O.C	[illegible]
	9th		Lt Wamsley R.A.F. delivered a lecture at PREUX to the 137 Bde – entitled "Flying in German East Africa" –	[illegible]

Army Form C. 2118.

Instructions regarding War Diaries and Intelligence Summaries are contained in F. S. Regs., Part II. and the Staff Manual respectively. Title Pages will be prepared in manuscript.

WAR DIARY
or
INTELLIGENCE SUMMARY
(Erase heading not required.)

Place	Date	Hour	Summary of Events and Information	Remarks and references to Appendices
LANDRICIES	9th		Portion of 137 Inf Bde + Section of Field Ambulance commenced their march to the FRESNOY Area as per attached Movement Table. This march was carried out by the other units of this Brigade on 10th 11th + 12th inst.	App I App II
	10th		The G.O.C. said "Goodbye" to 200 miners in the Theatre at LANDRICIES who were returning to ENGLAND to be demobilized.	
	12th		H.Q. 46th Div R.E. moved from LANDRICIES to PREUX. 468 Field Coy + 465 Field Coy R.E. having already moved to PREUX on the 10th + 11th as per attached Time Table	App II
	23rd		Orders were issued for move of D.H.Q to BOHAIN, 138 Inf Bde to LANDRICIES + 139 Inf Bde to PRISCHES (Order No 343) moves to commence on Dec. 30th.	App III
	25th		The G.O.C. visited Xmas Dinners in the 138 + 139 Bdes 230 + 231 R.F.A. ([illegible]) R.E. Divisional H.Q. D.A.C. Vet Section + Field Ambulance	[illegible]

2449 Wt. W14957/M90 750,000 1/16 J.B.C. & A. Forms/C.2118/12.

Instructions regarding War Diaries and Intelligence Summaries are contained in F. S. Regs., Part II. and the Staff Manual respectively. Title Pages will be prepared in manuscript.

WAR DIARY
or
INTELLIGENCE SUMMARY
(Erase heading not required.)

Army Form C. 2118.

Place	Date	Hour	Summary of Events and Information	Remarks and references to Appendices
	26th		G.O.C. visited 137 Inf Bde Xmas dinners & all units in Division not seen on previous day –	
	28th		Divisional Order 343 dated 23rd Dec cancelled –	App IV
			Football matches have been played throughout the month for the preliminary for the Corps Competitions. On the 22nd December a Rugby match was played against the 18 Division at SELVIGNY result 3 Tries to 2 in favour of 40th Division – A Return match was played on the 27th result Three Tries to nil in favour of 18th Division this match played at BOUSIES	[illegible]
			Appendix V shows Education work carried out in Division during past month –	App V
	29th		The G.O.C. went on Leave the Division be placed under the command of Brigadier General M.L. Hornby C.M.G. D.S.O.	

2449 Wt. W14957/M90 750,000 1/16 J.B.C. & A. Forms/C.2118/12.

War Diary App II

SECRET. Copy No. 27

46th DIVISION ORDER No. 342.

****

Ref: Maps, 1/100,000.
Sheets, VALENCIENNES & ST QUENTIN. 7th December, 1918.

1. 137th Infantry Brigade Group (less 466th Field Co, R.E) will move from PREUX to FRESNOY,- and H.Q., 46th Division R.E, with 465th and 468th Field Companies, R.E, will move from present billots to PREUX in accordance with attached Movement Tablo.

2. Further instructions will be issued by "Q" Branch.

3. Completion of moves and location of new Headquartors will be reported to this H.Q by wire.

4. 137th Infantry Brigade and C.R.E to acknowledge.

Major,
General Staff, 46th Division.

Issued at 2000.

Copy No. 1 to CRA.
2 CRE.
3 Signals.
4 137th Inf: Bde.
5 138th : :
6 139th : :
7 1st Monmouths.
8 46th Bn, MGC.
9 AA & QMG.
10/11 Div'l Train.
12 ADMS.
13 DADVS.
14 DADOS.
15 Camp Commandant.
16 Div'l Reception Camp.
17 A.C. BUSIGNY.
18 A.C. FRESNOY-LE-GRAND.
19 A.C. PREUX.
20 A.C. BOUSIES.
21 A.C. LANDRECIES.
22/23 XIII Corps.
24/25 File.
26/27 War Diary.
28/29 GOC. GSO I.
30 DAPM.

P.T.O

MOVEMENT TABLE TO ACCOMPANY 46th DIVISION ORDER No. 342.

Serial Number.	Unit.	Date.	From.	To.	Remarks.
1.	(1/6th S.Staffs.R. (1 Sec.1/3rd Fd.A.	9/12/18.	PREUX.	BUSIGNY.	
2.	do. do.	10/12/18.	BUSIGNY.	FRESNOY.	
3.	468th Fd.Co.RE.	do.	BOUSIES.	PREUX.	Not to enter PREUX before 1000.
4.	(1/5th S.Staffs.R. (137th Bde T.M.B.	do.	PREUX.	BUSIGNY.	
5.	do. do.	11/12/18.	BUSIGNY.	FRESNOY.	
6.	465th Fd.Co.RE.	do.	LANDRECIES.	PREUX.	Not to enter PREUX before 1000.
7.	HQ. 137th Inf:Bde.	do.	PREUX.	BUSIGNY.	
8.	1/8th N.Staffs.R.	do.	do.	do.	
9.	1/3rd Fd.A.(less 1 Sec)	do.	do.	do.	No restrictions as to Roads.-
10.	HQ. 137th Inf:Bde.	12/12/18.	BUSIGNY.	FRESNOY.	
11.	1/8th N.Staffs.R.	do.	do.	do.	
12.	1/3rd Fd.A.(less 1 Sec)	do.	do.	do.	
13.	HQ. 46th Div: RE.	do.	LANDRECIES.	PREUX.	

Further instructions will be issued as to move of 453rd Co, ASC, by OC, 46th Div'l Train.

Att III

SECRET. Copy No. 30

46th DIVISION ORDER NO. 343.

Ref: Maps, 1/100,000.
Sheets, VALENCIENNES & ST. QUENTIN. 23rd December, 1918.

1. The following moves will take place on dates as under :-

Decr: 30th. Divisional Headquarters - LANDRECIES to BOHAIN.

" " 139th Inf: Bde: H.Qrs: and 1 Bn: to PRISCHES.
" " " " " 1 Bn: to CARTIGNIES.
" " " " " 1 Bn: to) LE GD. FAYT.
) LE PT. FAYT.

1919.
Jany: 2nd. 138th Inf: Bde: H.Qrs: & 2 Bns: to BUSIGNY.
" " " " " 1 Bn: to BOHAIN.

" " 1/1st Bn: Monmouth Regt: to WASSIGNY.

G.O.C., 138th Infantry Brigade and O.C., 1/1st Bn: Monmouthshire Regiment to mutually arrange as to hours of starting, etc.

2. There will be no restrictions as to routes for the purpose of the above moves.

3. Orders will be issued later as to the move of the Divisional Artillery.

4. Headquarters Divisional R.E. and Field Companies, R.E., will remain at PREUX.

5. Further instructions will be issued by 'Q' Branch.

6. units concerned to Acknowledge.

J. Hay
Major,
General Staff, 46th Division.

Issued at 14.00 hours.

Copy No. 1 to C.R.A.
2 C.R.E.
3 Signals.
4 137th Inf: Bde:
5 138th " "
6 139th " "
7 1st Monmouths.
8 46th Bn: M.G.C.
9 A.A. & Q.M.G.
10/11 Div'l: Train.
12 A.D.M.S.
13 D.A.D.V.S.
14 D.A.D.O.S.
15 D.A.P.M.
16 Camp Commdt:
17 Div'l: Reception Camp.
17 to A.C. CARTIGNIES.
18 A.C. BOUSIES.
19 PREUX.
20 BOHAIN.
21 PRISCHES.
22 FAYT.
23 BUSIGNY.
24 WASSIGNY.
25 LANDRECIES.
26/27 XIII Corps.
28/29 File.
30/31 War Diary.
32 G.O.C.

"A" Form.
MESSAGES AND SIGNALS.

Army Form C.2121
(in pads of 100).
No. of Message

Prefix .... Code .... m. | Words | Charge
Office of Origin and Service Instructions.
App
Sent IV
At .... m.
To
By

This message is on a/c of:
.... Service.
(Signature of "Franking Officer.")

Recd. at .... m.
Date
From
By

TO War Diary.

Sender's Number.	Day of Month.	In reply to Number.	AAA
* G. 297	28		

Ref.	46th	Divn.	Order	243
of	23rd	Decr.	moves	mentioned
therein	are	temporarily	postponed.	

From 46 Div.
Place
Time

The above may be forwarded as now corrected.
(Z) Sgd/ S Hay, Major

Censor. Signature of Addressor or person authorised to telegraph in his name.

* This line should be erased if not required.

750,000. W 2186—M509. H. W & V., Ld. 6/16.

During the month of December, the Educational Work which had been started in November was continued, and, generally speaking, increased interest was shown and satisfactory progress was made.

The number of Students in General Elementary Subjects was 856, an increase of 236. In Commercial Subjects the number of Students increased from 409 to 647. New Classes were started in Magnetism and Electricity, Electrical Engineering, Hygiene and First Aid, and in various subjects such as Motor Driving, I.C. Engine, Telegraphy, Wireless Telegraphy, Carpentry and Painting.

On the whole, accommodation and heating of rooms were satisfactory, but better provision of Electric Light and Candles is needed; and the supply of Books and Material is far from adequate. An Officer has been sent to England to expend £30 in the purchase of Text Books, etc., and he has been instructed to borrow others if possible, from Educational Authorities at Home.

Lectures have been given in various subjects, including among others the following

Service Gratuities, Settlement for Ex-Service Men, the New Franchise Bill, War Saving Certificates, and Art and Design.

War Diary

LOCATIONS - 46th Division - 2/1/19.

46th Division H.Q.	LANDRECIES.
C.R.A.	do.
230th Bde. R.F.A.	G.16.a.7.7.
231st Bde. R.F.A.	G.17.c.9.5.
D.A.C.	G.23.a.2.6.
D.T.M.O.	G.25.a.2.8.
137th Inf. Bde. H.Q.	FRESNOY-LE-GRAND.
5th South Staffs.	do.
6th " "	do.
6th North "	do.
137th T.M.Battery.	do.
138th Inf. Bde. H.Q.	BOUSIES.
5th Lincolns.	do.
4th Leicesters.	do.
5th "	do.
138th T.M.Battery.	do.
139th Inf. Bde. H.Q.	LANDRECIES.
5th Sherwoods.	do.
6th "	do.
8th "	do.
139th T.M.Battery.	do.
46th Bn. M.G.C.	BOHAIN.
1st Monmouths.	BOUSIES.
Div'l Train & S.S.O.	LANDRECIES.
451st Coy. A.S.C.	G.8.d.central.
452nd " "	L.3.c.5.6.
453rd " "	I.34.d.2.8.
454th " "	G.15.b.5.3.
A.D.M.S.	LANDRECIES.
1st N.M.Fd. Amb.	do.
2nd " " "	L.4.b.0.8.
3rd " " "	FRESNOY-LE-GRAND.
D.A.D.V.S.	LANDRECIES.
1st N.M. M.V.S.	G.29.central.
DA.D.O.S.	LANDRECIES.
DA.P.M.	do.
C.R.E.	PREUX-AUX-BOIS.
465th Field Coy. R.E.	do.
466th " " "	do.
468th " " "	do.
Div'l Reception Camp.	BUSIGNY.
240th Employment Coy.	LANDRECIES.
X/46 T.M.B.	G.28.a.05.90.
Y/46 "	do.

[illegible signature]

Brigadier General,
Commanding, 46th Division.

1/1/19.

War Diary

LOCATIONS - 46th DIVISION - 12/12/18.

46th Division H.Q.	LANDRECIES.
C.R.A.	do.
230th Bde. RFA. H.Q.	G.16.b.3.4.
231st " " "	G.17.c.9.5.
D.A.C.	G.23.a.2.8.
D.T.M.O.	G.23.a.2.8.
137th Inf. Bde. H.Q.	FRESNOY-LE-GRAND.
5th South Staffs.	do.
6th " "	do.
6th North "	do.
137th T.M.Battery.	do.
138th Inf. Bde. H.Q.	BOUSIES.
5th Lincolns.	do.
4th Leicesters.	do.
5th "	do.
138th T.M.Battery.	do.
139th Inf. Bde. H.Q.	LANDRECIES.
5th Sherwoods.	do.
6th "	do.
8th "	do.
139th T.M.Battery.	do.
46th Bn. M.G.C.	BOHAIN.
1st Monmouths.	BOUSIES.
Div'l Train & S.S.O.	LANDRECIES.
451st Coy. ASC.	G.8.d.central.
452nd " "	L.3.c.3.8.
453rd " "	G.8.c.8.6.
454th " "	G.15.b.5.3.
A.D.M.S.	LANDRECIES.
1st N.M. Fd. Amb.	do.
2nd " " "	L.4.b.0.8.
3rd " " "	FRESNOY-LE-GRAND.
D.A.D.V.S.	LANDRECIES.
1st N.M. M.V.S.	G.29.central.
D.A.D.O.S.	LANDRECIES.
D.A.P.M.	do.
C.R.E.	PREUX-AUX-BOIS.
465th Field Coy. R.E.	do.
466th " " "	do.
468th " " "	do.
Div'l Reception Camp.	BOHAIN.
240th Employment Coy.	LANDRECIES.
X/46 T.M.B.	G.28.a.05.90.
Y/46 "	do.

(sd) S.HAY, Major,
General Staff, 46th Division..

11/12/18.

War Diary AML I

SECRET. Copy No. 26

46th DIVISION ORDER No. 341.

****

Ref: Maps, 1/100,000.
Sheets, VALENCIENNES & ST QUENTIN. 5th December, 1918.

1. (a) The 46th Bn, M.G.C, will on 7th December proceed by march route from present area to BOHAIN.
(b) The 1/1st Bn, Monmouthshire Regt will on the same date march to BUSIGNY staying at that place for the night 7th/8th December, and proceed on the following day to FRESNOY-LE-GRAND.

2. Route for above units - CROIX - LE CATEAU - HONNECHY STA. - BUSIGNY.

3. The 46th Bn, M.G.C, will move ahead of the 1/1st Bn, Monmouthshire Regt, and O's.C, these units will mutually arrange as to hours of starting - midday halts, etc.

4. Further instructions will be notified by Q Branch.

5. 46th Bn, MGC and 1/1st Monmouthshire Regt to acknowledge.

L. Hay
Major,
General Staff, 46th Division.

Issued at 2000.

Copy No. 1 CRA.
2 CRE.
3 Signals.
4 137th Bde.
5 138th :
6 139th :
7 1/1st Monmouths.
8 46th Bn, MGC.
9 AA & QMG.
10 Div'l Train.
11 ADMS.
12 DAPM.
13 DADVS.

Copy No. 14 DADOS.
15 Camp Comm't.
16 Div'l Reception Camp.
17 SSO.
18 A.C. BOUSIES.
19 A.C. BUSIGNY.
20 A.C. BOHAIN.
21 A.C. FRESNOY-LE-GRAND.
22/23 XIII Corps.
24/25 File.
26/27 War Diary.
28/29 GOC. GSO I.

Instructions regarding War Diaries and Intelligence Summaries are contained in F. S. Regs., Part II. and the Staff Manual respectively. Title Pages will be prepared in manuscript.

17

WAR DIARY
or
INTELLIGENCE SUMMARY
(Erase heading not required.)

Army Form C. 2118.

HQ GS 46 D

Place	Date	Hour	Summary of Events and Information	Remarks and references to Appendices
			Month of January	
			1919.	
			Divisional Headquarters at LANDRECIES.	

98 47

2449 Wt. W14957/M90 750,000 1/16 J.B.C. & A. Forms/C.2118/12.

Army Form C. 2118.

Instructions regarding War Diaries and Intelligence Summaries are contained in F. S. Regs., Part II. and the Staff Manual respectively. Title Pages will be prepared in manuscript.

WAR DIARY
or
INTELLIGENCE SUMMARY
(Erase heading not required.)

Place	Date	Hour	Summary of Events and Information	Remarks and references to Appendices
LANDRECIES	JAN 1919			
		7th	Divisional Order No 344 issued "D.H.Q. will move to LE CATEAU on Thursday January 9th"	Appx I
		9th	Divisional Order No 345 issued ordering 139 Bde to move to PRISHES Area on 11th inst + one Battalion 138 Bde to LE CATEAU on 12th inst	Appx II
LE CATEAU			Divisional Head Quarters moved to LE CATEAU	
		11th	Amendment to above order. For move of one Battalion to LE CATEAU read POMMEREUIL.	Appx III
		13th	Conference on 'Education' held at Div. Hq. Brig Genl Hornby CMG DSO presided & the Education Officers of formations in the Division were present.	[illegible]
		15th	Lieut J.A. Ball 5/ Leics Regt arrived at Div Hq to take up duties as Education Officer to Army & Corps Troops in the Divisional area.	[illegible]
		16th	Conference of Education Officers of Army & Corps Troops in the Divl area to discuss methods of popularising the Education scheme & of overcoming difficulties in working in the smaller units.	[illegible]

2449 Wt. W14957/M90 750,000 1/16 J.B.C. & A. Forms/C.2118/12.

Instructions regarding War Diaries and Intelligence Summaries are contained in F. S. Regs., Part II. and the Staff Manual respectively. Title Pages will be prepared in manuscript.

WAR DIARY
or
INTELLIGENCE SUMMARY
(Erase heading not required.)

Army Form C. 2118.

Place	Date	Hour	Summary of Events and Information	Remarks and references to Appendices
~~LANDRECIES~~ LE CATEAU	Jan 1919			
	17th		Capt Evan Education Officer demobilised. Capt A.P. Whitehead 1/6 S. Staffs Regt took over the duties.	DY
	21st		Education Officer inspected 139th Inf. Brigade	DY
	22nd		Capt S.E. Moore from Ministry of Labour lectured on Demobilisation & Reconstruction to 138th & 139th Inf Brigades	DY
			Major General Boyd C.B. DSO. DCM returned from leave & took over the duties from Brig Genl. Hornby C.M.G.	DY
	23rd		Capt S.E. Moore lectured to RA & Div Hq	DY
	25th		Capt A.P. Whitehead 1/5 S. Staffs Regt reported to Div Hq to form Divl Advisory Board	DY
	27th		Lt Col J.S. Napier lectured to 137th I.B. on Caucasus Front.	DY
	31st		Training was carried out daily during the month. Education classes also were held daily	

2449 Wt. W14957/M90 750,000 1/16 J.B.C. & A. Forms/C.2118/12.

Instructions regarding War Diaries and Intelligence Summaries are contained in F. S. Regs., Part II. and the Staff Manual respectively. Title Pages will be prepared in manuscript.

WAR DIARY
or
INTELLIGENCE SUMMARY
(Erase heading not required.)

Army Form C. 2118.

Place	Date	Hour	Summary of Events and Information	Remarks and references to Appendices
LE CATEAU	Jan 1919. 31st		During the month Recreational Training was proceeded with. A Divisional Cross Country Run was run on Jan 7th & a XIII Corps Run (4 miles) on Jan 20th at CAUDRY this was won by Corps Troops team, but first man home was Spr Tandy 46 Div Sig Coy. The Corps Boxing Competition in which this Division was represented was completed on 17th & 18th Jan.	DN
			Further progress was made during the month with the Corps Football Competitions but on Jan 26th further matches were postponed owing to the frost.	DN
			On Jan 26th the Division sent both a Rugby & Association team to play the Stade Francais Club of Paris, drawing the former game 3 tries each, & winning the latter by 5 goals to none	DN
			During the month progress was made with the Education Scheme & at this date the students numbered 1590, being 14·2% of the Division	DN
			Demobilisation was proceeded with during the month 1800 officers & other ranks leaving during the month & as 2341 miners & 41 pivotal men were demobilised during December the ration strength of the Division, at this date was 11,176.	DN

2449 Wt. W14957/M90 750,000 1/16 J.B.C. & A. Forms/C.2118/12.

War Diary

App II

SECRET.   Copy No. 21

46th DIVISION ORDER NO. 345.

Reference Map, Sheet,
1/100,000 VALENCIENNES.   9th January, 1919.

1. The 139th Infantry Brigade will move to the PRISHES area on the 11th January, 1919, under arrangements to be made by G.O.C., 139th Infantry Brigade.

2. The 138th Infantry Brigade will move one battalion to LE CATEAU on the 12th January, under arrangements to be made by G.O.C., 138th Infantry Brigade.

3. Bde Concerned to Acknowledge.

W. Burn-Lindow Capt.
for Lieut-Colonel,
General Staff, 46th Division.

Issued at 2000 hours.

Copy No.	to	Copy No.	to
1	C.R.A.	12	A.D.M.S.
2	C.R.E.	13	D.A.D.V.S.
3	Signals.	14	D.A.P.M.
4	137th Bde:	15	Camp Commdt:
5	138th :	16	18th Divn:
6	139th :	17/18	XIII Corps.
7	1st Monmouths.	19/20	File.
8	46th Bn: MGC.	21/22	War Diary.
9	A.A. & Q.M.G.	23	46th Div: Rec: Camp.
10/11	Div'l: Train.	24	D.A.D.O.S.

War Diary

App I

SECRET. Copy No. 21

46th DIVISION ORDER NO. 344.

Reference - Map, Sheet
1/100,000 VALENCIENNES.

7th January, 1919.

46th Divisional Headquarters will move to LE CATEAU on Thursday, 9th January, 1919.

Acknowledge.

[signature] Lieut-Colonel,
General Staff, 46th Division...

Issued at 1400 hours.

Copy No. 1 to C.R.A.
2 C.R.E.
3 Signals.
4 137th Inf: Bde:
5 138th : :
6 139th : :
7 1st Monmouths.
8 46th Bn: M.G.C.
9 A.A. & Q.M.G.
10/11 Div'l: Train.
12 A.D.M.S.
13 D.A.D.V.S.
14 D.A.P.M.
15 Camp Commdt:
16 18th Division.
17/18 XIII Corps.
19/20 File.
21/22 War Diary.
23 46th Div: Recep: Camp.
24 DADOS.

War Diary

App III

SECRET.

Copy No. 21

AMENDMENT TO 46th DIVISION ORDER NO. 345.

11th January 1919.

In para. 3., for LE CATEAU read POMMEREUIL.

W. Newbold Major
for Lieut-Colonel,
General Staff, 46th Division.

Issued to all recipients of Order No.345.

War Diary

LOCATIONS - 46th DIVISION - 9/1/19.

46th Division H.Q.	LE CATEAU.
C.R.A.	LANDRECIES.
230th Bde. RFA.	G.16.a.7.7.
231st : :	G.17.c.9.5.
D.A.C.	G.23.a.2.6.
D.T.M.O.	G.23.a.2.8.
137th Inf. Bde. H.Q.	FRESNOY-LE-GRAND.
5th South Staffs.	do.
6th : :	do.
6th North :	do.
137th T.M.Battery.	do.
138th Inf. Bde. H.Q.	BOUSIES.
5th Lincolns .	do.
4th Leicesters.	do.
5th :	do.
138th T.M.Battery.	do.
139th Inf. Bde. H.Q.	LANDRECIES.
5th Sherwoods.	do.
6th Sherwoods..	do.
8th Sherwoods.	PRISCHES.
139th T.M.Battery.	LANDRECIES.
46th Bn. M.G.C.	BOHAIN.
1st Monmouths.	BOUSIES.
Div'l Train & S.S.O.	LE CATEAU.
451st Coy. A.S.C.	G.8.d.central.
452nd : :	L.3.c.5.6.
453rd : :	I.24.d.2.8.
454th : :	G.15.b.5.3.
A.D.M.S.	LE CATEAU.
1st N.M. Fd. Amb.	LANDRECIES.
2nd : : :	L.4.b.0.8.
3rd : : :	FRESNOY-LE-GRAND.
D.A.D.V.S.	LE CATEAU.
1st N.M. M.V.S.	G.29.central.
D.A.D.O.S.	LE CATEAU.
D.A.P.M.	do.
C.R.E.	PREUX-AUX-BOIS.
465th Field Coy. R.E.	do.
466th : : :	do.
468th : : :	do.
Div'l Reception Camp.	BUSIGNY.
240th Employment Coy.	LE CATEAU.
X/46 T.M.B.	G.28.a.05.90.
Y/46 :	do.

[signature] Capt
for

Brigadier General,
Commanding, 46th Division.

8/1/19.

War Diary

LOCATIONS - 46th DIVISION - 12/1/19.

46th Division H.Q.	LE CATEAU.
C.R.A.	LANDRECIES.
230th Bde. RFA.	G.16.a.7.7.
231st " "	G.17.c.9.5.
D.A.C.	G.23.a.2.6.
D.T.M.O.	G.23.a.2.8.
137th Inf. Bde. H.Q.	FRESNOY-LE-GRAND.
5th South Staffs.	do.
6th " "	do.
6th North "	do.
137th T.M.Battery.	do.
138th Inf. Bde. H.Q.	BOUSIES.
5th Lincolns.	do.
4th Leicesters.	do.
5th "	POMMEREUIL.
138th T.M.Battery.	BOUSIES.
139th Inf. Bde. H.Q.	PRISCHES.
5th Sherwoods.	BEAUREPAIRE.
6th "	CARTIGNIES.
8th "	PRISCHES,
139th T.M.Battery.	do.
46th Bn. M.G.C.	BOHAIN.
1st Monmouths.	BOUSIES.
Div'l Train & S.S.O.	LE CATEAU.
451st Coy. A.S.C.	G.8.d.central.
452nd " "	L.3.c.5.6.
453rd " "	I.24.d.2.8.
454th " "	PRISCHES.
A.D.M.S.	LE CATEAU.
1st N.M. Fd. Amb.	PRISCHES.
2nd " " "	L.4.b.0.8.
3rd " " "	FRESNOY-LE-GRAND.
D.A.D.V.S.	LE CATEAU.
1st N.M. M.V.S.	G.29.central.
D.A.D.O.S.	LE CATEAU.
D.A.P.M.	do.
C.R.E.	PREUX-AUX-BOIS.
465th Field Coy. R.E.	do.
466th " " "	do.
468th " " "	do.
Div'l Reception Camp.	BUSIGNY.
240thbEmployment Coy.	LE CATEAU.
X/46 T.M.B.	G.28.a.05.90.
Y/46 "	do.

[signature]
Brigadier General,
Commanding, 46th Division.

11/1/19.

31

Instructions regarding War Diaries and Intelligence Summaries are contained in F. S. Regs., Part II. and the Staff Manual respectively. Title Pages will be prepared in manuscript.

WAR DIARY
or
INTELLIGENCE SUMMARY
(Erase heading not required.)

Army Form C. 2118.

GS 46 Division
Vol 48

Place	Date	Hour	Summary of Events and Information	Remarks and references to Appendices
			Month of February 1919 Divisional Headquarters at Le Cateau	

2449 Wt. W14957/M90 750,000 1/16 J.B.C. & A. Forms/C.2118/12.

Army Form C. 2118.

WAR DIARY
or
INTELLIGENCE SUMMARY
(Erase heading not required.)

Instructions regarding War Diaries and Intelligence Summaries are contained in F. S. Regs., Part II. and the Staff Manual respectively. Title Pages will be prepared in manuscript.

Place	Date	Hour	Summary of Events and Information	Remarks and references to Appendices
LE CATEAU	FEB 1919			
	3rd		Military Advisory Board formed, as follows Major E.A. Lewis DSO. [illegible] Capt A.T. Whitehead 5/S. Staffs Rgt. Capt M.E. Porter MC 4/Leic Regt & Capt A.P. Whitehead MC 6/S Staffs Rgt. Objects of this Board to afford each assistance & give such advice to Officers & men of similar educational, professional & business qualifications as will enable them to complete the Civil Employment (or Training) Form A.F.Z.15 to the best possible advantage.	[illegible]
	4th		137th Inf Brigade inspected by the Divisional Commander.	[illegible]
			Mr Andrew Sims B.A. (late of Calcutta) lectured on "New India" & "Shaping the New World" to RE at PREUX	
	5th		138th Inf Brigade & 1/1st Monmouth Rgt inspected by the Divisional Commander	[illegible]
			Mr Andrew Sims BA lectured to 137th Inf Brigade	
	6th		139th Inf Brigade inspected by the Divisional Commander	[illegible]

2449 Wt. W14957/M90 750,000 1/16 J.B.C. & A. Forms/C.2118/12.

Instructions regarding War Diaries and Intelligence Summaries are contained in F. S. Regs., Part II. and the Staff Manual respectively. Title Pages will be prepared in manuscript.

WAR DIARY
or
INTELLIGENCE SUMMARY
(Erase heading not required.)

Army Form C. 2118.

Place	Date	Hour	Summary of Events and Information	Remarks and references to Appendices
LE CATEAU	FEB 1919			
	6th		Mr Sims lectured to 138th Inf Brigade & Pte Jones S African Brigade lectured to 139th Inf Bde on "South Africa"	DM
			Three members of the Civil Advisory Board – Mr Cleeg Mellor, Mr Pullen & Mr Buckle arrived & proceeded to BUSIGNY & FRESNOY LE GRAND to interview applicants – 27 cases dealt with.	DM. App I
	7th		RE. inspected by the Divisional Commander	
			Pte Jones lectured to 139th Inf Bde & R.A.	
			Civilian Advisory ~~Committee~~ Board sat at LE CATEAU & interviewed 71 applicants.	DM
			During the period Feb 1st to Feb 7th 4 Officers & 136 Other ranks were demobilised daily	DM
	8th		Pte Jones lectured to R.A & R.E.	
			Civilian Advisory Board left for England	DM

2449 Wt. W14957/M90 750,000 1/16 J.B.C. & A. Forms/C.2118/12.

Army Form C. 2118.

Instructions regarding War Diaries and Intelligence Summaries are contained in F. S. Regs., Part II. and the Staff Manual respectively. Title Pages will be prepared in manuscript.

WAR DIARY
or
INTELLIGENCE SUMMARY
(Erase heading not required.)

Place	Date	Hour	Summary of Events and Information	Remarks and references to Appendices
LE CATEAU	FEB 9th		Pte Jones lectured to R.E. & 138th Inf Brigade	DY
	10th		Examination held at LE CATEAU for students desirous of receiving certificate of Royal Society of Arts	DY
	11th		30 Ride & Drive, & 6 H.D. Horses demobilised & sent to PARIS this with 200 Horses (mixed) sent to England on Jan 27th 62 mules sent to TOURNAI on the same date & 183 (mixed) sent to England on Jan 30th & 31st making a total of 481 Animals demobilised at this date.	DY
	12th		Pte Jones lectured to 137th Inf Brigade	DY
	13th		From Feb 9th to this date 5 Officers & 183 other ranks were demobilised daily	DY
	18th		From Feb 14th to this date 6 Officers & ~~2~~ 224 DY other ranks were demobilised daily	DY

Instructions regarding War Diaries and Intelligence Summaries are contained in F. S. Regs., Part II. and the Staff Manual respectively. Title Pages will be prepared in manuscript.

WAR DIARY
or
INTELLIGENCE SUMMARY

(Erase heading not required.)

Army Form C. 2118.

Place	Date	Hour	Summary of Events and Information	Remarks and references to Appendices
LE CATEAU	FEB		1/1 Monmouths moved to MONTAY	APW
	20th		139th Inf Brigade moved to BETHENCOURT Divisional Artillery moved to QUIEVY ST PYTHON - ST VAAST area	JDI App. 2, 3, 4
	23rd		From Feb 19th to this date 4 Officers & 200 Other ranks were demobilised daily	JDI ~~App. 2 & 3~~ JDI
	24th		138th Inf Brigade moved to SOLESMES	JDI App. 2 & 3
	25th		Major T.C. NEWBOLD D.S.O. leaves Div. H.Q. to command 1/5 Sherwood Foresters	APW
	27th		Lieut. Col. C.F. JERRAM D.S.O. to England.	APW
	28th		R.E. moved to INCHY	APW
			Divisional Machine Gun Battalion moved to INCHY.	APW

2449 Wt. W14957/M90 750,000 1/16 J.B.C. & A. Forms/C.2118/12.

War Diary

App. I.

C.R.E.
157th Infantry Brigade.
158th " "
159th " "
1st Monmouths.

48th Division G.5/58. 27th January, 1919.

Inspections by the Divisional Commander.

The following Programme of inspections will be carried out next week by the Divisional Commander :-

Tuesday, 4th Feby: 157th Inf: Bde: Near FRESNOY.

Wednesday, 5th Feby: 158th Inf: Bde: and 1/1st Monmouthshire Rgt: (Under command of G.O.C., 158th Inf: Bde:) In BOUSIES Area.

Thursday, 6th Feby: 159th Inf: Bde: In PRISCHES Area.

Friday, 7th Feby: Royal Engineers (Less Signal Coy:) Near PREUX.

Infantry Brigades and Field Companies, R.E. will be inspected on the march with available transport.

Companies, etc., will be kept closed up during the march and B.E.F. intervals will NOT be maintained.

Brigade Commanders and the C.R.E. will select their own routes, saluting point and timing, which will be notified to Divisional Headquarters two clear days before the inspection. Saluting point should be about 3 miles from the starting point.

Colours may be carried if desired by Brigade Commanders.

Football teams playing in Corps or Divisional matches on the same day as the inspection need not turn out; otherwise units should be as strong as possible.

[signature] Capt
for Lieut-Colonel,
General Staff, 48th Division...

Copies to :-

G.R.A.
O.C., Signal Co:
48th Bn: M.G.C.
A.A. & Q.M.G.
A.D.M.S.
D.A.D.V.S.
D.A.D.O.S.
D.A.P.M.
Camp Comdt:

War Diary

App. 2

SECRET.

Copy No. 22

46th DIVISION WARNING ORDER NO. 346.

Reference Map, Sheet,
1/100,000 VALENCIENNES.

14th January, 1919.

The Division (less Divisional Headquarters) will be prepared to move to the CAUDRY Area in about 6 days time.
Full details will be given as soon as possible.

[signature]

Lieut-Colonel,
General Staff, 46th Division.

Issued at 1400 hours.

Copy No.	to	Copy No.	to
1	C.R.A.	12	A.D.M.S.
2	C.R.E.	13	D.A.D.V.S.
3	Signals.	14	D.A.P.M.
4	137th Bde:	15	Camp Commdt:
5	138th :	16	D.A.D.O.S.
6	139th :	17	Div: Recep: Camp.
7	1st Monmouths.	18/19	XIII Corps.
8	46th Bn: M.G.C.	20/21	File.
9	A.A. & Q.M.G.	22/23	War Diary.
10/11	Div'l: Train.		

War Diary

App. 3

SECRET. Copy No. 25

46th DIVISION ORDER NO. 340.A.

****

Reference Map, sheet,
1/100,000 VALENCIENNES.

14th January, 1919.

1. The Division will move to the area shown on Map 'A' * according to the attached march table.

2. Administrative arrangements (appointments of Town Majors, Billeting Parties, etc., etc.), are being notified to those concerned by 46th Division 'Q'.

3. Salvage operations will cease for the present, but will be resumed on arrival in the new area.

4. Infantry Brigades and C.R.A. will forward to these Headquarters by the 23rd February, a map showing :-

(a) In RED - Area cleared of salvage and 'duds'.
(b) In RED LINES - area cleared of salvage but NOT of 'duds'.
(c) In PLAIN - area NOT cleared of salvage.

Together with a report showing the position of all salvage dumps, their nature and approximate lorry loads.

It will be understood that (a) and (b) above are cleared only so far as the ground is concerned and that dumps have not been removed.

5. 46th Division Units to acknowledge.

Lieut-Colonel,
General Staff, 46th Division..

* To C.R.A, C.R.E.
and 3 Inf: Bdes: only.
Others may see map at 'G' Office.

Issued at 1400 hours.

Copy No.		Copy No.	
1	to C.R.A.	15	to Camp Commdt:
2	C.R.E.	16	D.A.D.O.S.
3	O.C. Signals.	17	Div: Rec: Camp.
4	137th Inf: Bde:	18	18th Division.
5	138th : :	19	25th :
6	139th : :	20	50th :
7	1st Monmouths.	21/22	XIII Corps.
8	46th Bn: M.G.C.	23/24	File.
9	A.A. & Q.M.G.	25/26	War Diary.
10/11	Div'l: Train.	27	C.S.O.1.
12	A.D.M.S.	28	C.C.O.
13	D.A.D.V.S.		
14	D.A.P.M.		

Note:- Any difficulties in the way of carrying out these orders, such as shortage of animals, will be notified as early as possible 'G' [illegible]

pto

MARCH TABLE to accompany 46th DIVISION ORDER NO. 346.A.

Date.	Unit.	From	To	Route.	Remarks.
1919. Feby: 19th/20th.	139th Bde. Group.	PRISCHES Area.	BETHENCOURT.	Any roads may be used. The roads are being reconnoitred by Divisional Staff and units will be notified as to the best.	Stage at CATILLON-BAZUEL, night of 19th/20th Feby.
19th.	R.E.	PREUX.	QUIEVY.	do.	
19th.	46th Bn: MGC.	BOHAIN.	VIESLY.	do.	Join 139th Bde. Group on arrival.
20th.	1/1st Monmouths.	BOUSIES.	MONTAY.	do.	Leave 138th Bde. Group.
	R.A.	LANDRECIES Area.	SOLESMES - S. PYTHON - S. VAAST.	do.	Date will be notified later.
	137th Bde. Group.	FRESNOY.	INCHY - TROISVILLERS.	do.	Will stage at BUSIGNY in 2 or more reliefs. Dates later.
	138th Bde. Group.	BOUSIES Area.	SOLESMES.	do.	Date later.
	46th Div: Reception Camp.	BUSIGNY.	AUDENCOURT.	do.	Date later.

VALENCIENNES
RA
138
139
137
Montrécourt
Villers en Cauchies
Haussy
Maison Rouge
Maison Blanche
Vertain
Romeries
Neuville
Saulzoir
St. Aubert
Avesnes lez-Aubert
St. Python
St. Vaast
Solesmes
Beaurain
Vendegie au Bois
St. Hilaire les Cambrai
Quievy
Boussières
Briastre
Viesly
Bevillers
Ovillers
Croix
Robersart
Bousies
Fontaine au Bois
Bethencourt
Neuvilly
Amerval
Forest
Caudry
Beaumont
Inchy
Audencourt
Montay
Pommereuil
Bois l'Evêque
Malgarni
Troisvilles
Le Cateau
Ligny-en-Cambrésis
Montigny
Bertry
Bazuel
Caullery
Clary
Maurois
Reumont
Honnechy
St. Benin
Catillon
Bois de Gattigny
St. Souplet
Escaufourt
Mazinghien
Elincourt
Maretz
St. Martin Rivière
Ecaillon
Rejet de Beaulieu
La Louvière
Busigny
Molain
Ribeauville
Serain
Vaux Andigny
La Vallée Mulâtre
Wassigny
Becquigny
Prémont
Bois Mirand
Forêt d'Andigny
Englefontaine
Poix du Nord
Louvignies
Ghissignies
Preux
E
25'
F
30'
G
35'
H
Bohain

War Diary

App 4

SECRET.

Copy No. 25

AMENDMENT TO 46th DIVISION ORDER NO. 346.A.

February,
15th 1919.

The march table issued with 46th Division Order No.346.A dated 14/2/19, will be amended to read as follows, in the case of the undermentioned units :-

R.E. Delete date 19th and substitute "Will be notified later". For QUIEVY read INCHY.

46th Bn: MGC. Delete date 19th and substitute - "Will be notified later". For VIESLY read INCHY.

R.A. Insert date Feby: 20th.
For SOLESMES - S. PYTHON - S. VAAST
read
QUIEVY - S. PYTHON - S. VAAST.
In column of remarks delete "date will be notified later".

137th Bde: Group. Delete INCHY.

[signature]
Lieut-colonel,
General Staff, 46th Division....

Issued to all recipients of
46th Division Order No. 346.A.

LOCATIONS - 46th DIVISION - 21/2/19.

46th Division H.Q.	LE CATEAU.
C.R.A.	QUIEVY.
230th Bde. R.F.A.	do.
231st : :	ST. PYTHON.
D.A.C.	QUIEVY.
137th Inf. Bde. H.Q.	FRESNOY-LE-GRAND.
5th South Staffs.	do.
6th : :	do.
6th North :	do.
137th T.M.Battery.	do.
138th Inf. Bde. H.Q.	BOUSIES.
5th Lincolns.	do.
4th Leicesters.	do.
5th :	POMMEREUIL.
138th T.M.Battery.	BOUSIES.
139th Inf. Bde. H.Q.	BETHENCOURT.
5th Sherwoods.	do.
6th :	do.
8th :	do.
139th T.M.Battery.	do.
46th Bn. M.G.C.	BOHAIN.
1st Monmouths.	MONTAY.
Div'l Train & S.S.O.	LE CATEAU.
451st Coy.R.A.S.C.	G.8.d.central.
452nd : :	L.3.c.5.6.
453rd : :	I.24.d.2.8.
454th : :	BETHENCOURT.
A.D.M.S.	LE CATEAU.
1st N.M. Fd. Amb.	BETHENCOURT.
2nd : : :	L.4.b.0.8.
3rd : : :	FRESNOY-LE-GRAND.
D.A.D.V.S.	LE CATEAU.
1st N.M. M.V.S.	~~G.29.central.~~ LE CATEAU
D.A.D.O.S.	LE CATEAU.
D.A.P.M.	do.
C.R.E.	PREUX-AUX-BOIS.
465th Field Coy. R.E.	do.
466th : : :	do.
468th : : :	do.
Div'l Reception Camp.	BUSIGNY.
240th Employment Coy.	LE CATEAU.

W. Newbold Major for

Major General,
Commanding, 46th Division.

20/2/19.

Instructions regarding War Diaries and Intelligence Summaries are contained in F. S. Regs., Part II. and the Staff Manual respectively. Title Pages will be prepared in manuscript.

WAR DIARY
or
INTELLIGENCE SUMMARY
(Erase heading not required.)

Army Form C. 2118.

Place	Date	Hour	Summary of Events and Information	Remarks and references to Appendices
			Month of March 1919.	
			Divisional Headquarters at	
			LE CATEAU.	

2449 Wt. W14957/M90 750,000 1/16 J.B.C. & A. Forms/C.2118/12.

Army Form C. 2118.

Instructions regarding War Diaries and Intelligence Summaries are contained in F. S. Regs., Part II. and the Staff Manual respectively. Title Pages will be prepared in manuscript.

WAR DIARY
or
INTELLIGENCE SUMMARY

(Erase heading not required.)

Place	Date	Hour	Summary of Events and Information	Remarks and references to Appendices
			Month of March 1919.	
			Divisional Headquarters at LE CATEAU.	

2449 Wt. W14957/M90 750,000 1/16 J.B.C. & A. Forms/C.2118/12.

Army Form C. 2118.

Instructions regarding War Diaries and Intelligence Summaries are contained in F. S. Regs., Part II. and the Staff Manual respectively. Title Pages will be prepared in manuscript.

WAR DIARY
or
INTELLIGENCE SUMMARY
(Erase heading not required.)

Place	Date	Hour	Summary of Events and Information	Remarks and references to Appendices
LE CATEAU	March 1919			
	1st	11 p.m	Summer time begins : clocks advanced one hour.	A.P.W.
	5th		1/1 Monmouths moved to TROISVILLES.	
			1/5 Bn South Staffordshire Regt. (Lt Col A WHITE DSO.) leaves Division for Army of Occupation.	
			137 Inf Brigade moved to TROISVILLE	A.P.W.
	10th		138 Inf Brigade moved to ST HILAIRE	A.P.W.
	15th		F.M. Sir Douglas HAIG Commander-in-chief pays farewell visit to the Division. The Divisional Commander introduced to him Commanders and Staffs of Brigades and Battalions at Div. Headquarters.	A.P.W.
	19th		36 American Generals and Colonels visit battlefield of BELLENGLISE. The Divisional Commander and 12 officers representing 46th Division escort them and describe the part played by their unit in the battle of Sept. 29th.	A.P.W.
	20th		Major-General G F BOYD CB CMG DSO DCM. tours the Division on farewell visit.	A.P.W.

Instructions regarding War Diaries and Intelligence Summaries are contained in F. S. Regs., Part II. and the Staff Manual respectively. Title Pages will be prepared in manuscript.

WAR DIARY
or
INTELLIGENCE SUMMARY
(Erase heading not required.)

Army Form C. 2118.

Place	Date	Hour	Summary of Events and Information	Remarks and references to Appendices
LE CATEAU.	March 1919			
	1st	11 pm	Summer time begins : clocks advanced one hour.	APW
	5th		1/1 Monmouths moved to TROISVILLES.	
			1/5 Bn South Staffordshire Regt. (Lt Col A WHITE DSO) leaves Division for Army of Occupation	
			137 Inf Brigade moved to TROISVILLE	APW
	10		138 Inf Brigade moved to ST HILAIRE	APW
	15th		F.M. Sir Douglas HAIG Commander-in-chief pays farewell visit to the Division. The Divisional Commander introduced to him Commanders and Staffs of Brigades and Battalions at Div Headquarters.	APW
	19th		36 American Generals and Colonels visit battlefield of BELLENGLISE. The Divisional Commander and 12 Officers representing 46th Division escort them and describe the part played by their Unit in the battle of Sept 29th.	APW
	20th		Major-General G F BOYD CB CMG DSO, DCM. tours the Division on farewell visit.	APW

2449 Wt. W14957/M90 750,000 1/16 J.B.C. & A. Forms/C.2118/12.

Instructions regarding War Diaries and Intelligence Summaries are contained in F. S. Regs., Part II. and the Staff Manual respectively. Title Pages will be prepared in manuscript.

WAR DIARY
or
INTELLIGENCE SUMMARY
(Erase heading not required.)

Army Form C. 2118.

Place	Date	Hour	Summary of Events and Information	Remarks and references to Appendices
LE CATEAU	March 1919. 26th		Major-General G.F. BOYD CB CMG, DSO, DCM, leaves Division to command a Brigade in the Midland Division in the Army of the RHINE	APW
			Colonel KAY ADMS leaves Division to assume duties ADMS in RHINE Army	APW

2449 Wt. W14957/M90 750,000 1/16 J.B.C. & A. Forms/C2118/12.

Army Form C. 2118.

Instructions regarding War Diaries and Intelligence Summaries are contained in F. S. Regs., Part II. and the Staff Manual respectively. Title Pages will be prepared in manuscript.

WAR DIARY
or
INTELLIGENCE SUMMARY

(Erase heading not required.)

Place	Date	Hour	Summary of Events and Information	Remarks and references to Appendices
LE CATEAU	March 1919. 25th		Major-General G F BOYD CB, CMG, DSO, DCM, leaves Division to command a Brigade in the Midland Division in the Army of the RHINE	AMW
			Colonel KAY ADMS leaves Division to assume duties ADMS in RHINE Army	AMW

2449 Wt. W14957/M90 750,000 1/16 J.B.C. & A. Forms/C.2118/12.

[illegible] Memorial

[illegible]

1918 Oct

Headquarters,

46th (North Midland) Division.

17th March, 1919.

My dear Duke,

I am anxious that a suitable memorial should be erected on the Battlefield of Bellenglise in memory of the officers and men who gave up their lives for their country in that battle and those of the subsequent days.

I have already had a large oak cross some 15 feet high erected with concrete foundations and a suitable inscription. This will last some years, but is of course not permanent.

I have obtained estimates from a firm in England which was recommended to me, and a drawing of the proposed memorial, which has been approved by the officers of the Division, is enclosed.

The cost of erecting the memorial would be about £550, and I am writing to ask whether you would take up the question of raising the money. Perhaps you might be willing to constitute yourself head of a Committee for raising a fund.

Questions with regard to Memorials at home will I know come up for consideration, but Bellenglise was such a great victory for the soldiers of the North Midlands, that I think it should be commemorated for ever by some memorial on the battlefield.

The Counties concerned are, besides your own, Staffordshire, Leicester and Lincoln, the Infantry consisting of three Battalions of your Sherwood Foresters, three Battalions of Staffords, two Battalions of Leicesters and one Battalion of Lincolns, the Artillery, Engineers, etc., being drawn from men of all these Counties.

I have already approached G.H.Q. out here with reference to obtaining the ground from the French Authorities, and if you think the Midland Counties would guarantee the money, the matter could be put in hand at once.

The memorial will take about 8 months to complete, and no doubt the Government will give special facilities for transport and erection.

I am sending you six copies of this letter in case you might wish to circulate it.

I hope you are quite well.

My Division is now nearly broken up, consisting of little more than Cadres, and I myself am shortly going to join the Rhine Army.

Yrs very sincerely

Gerald F. Boyd

Major General

www.ingramcontent.com/pod-product-compliance
Lightning Source LLC
Chambersburg PA
CBHW080814010526
44111CB00015B/2554
* 9 7 8 1 4 7 4 5 2 1 0 5 5 *